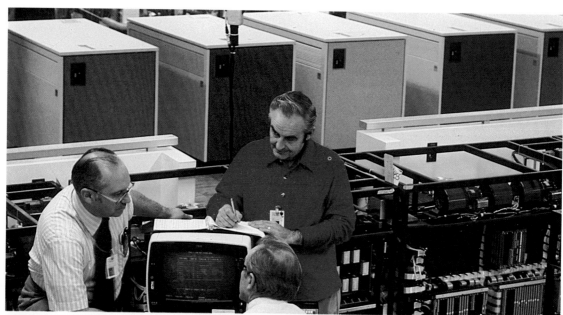

UNDERSTANDING
ECONOMICS

UNDERSTANDING ECONOMICS

Roger LeRoy Miller
Law & Economics Center and
Department of Economics
University of Miami

Robert W. Pulsinelli
Department of Economics
Western Kentucky University

West Publishing Company
Saint Paul   New York   Los Angeles   San Francisco

Library of Congress Cataloging in Publication Data

Miller, Roger LeRoy.
  Understanding Economics.

  Bibliography: p.
  Includes index.
  1. Economics.   I. Pulsinelli, Robert W.   II. Title.
HB171.5.M6438   1983   330   82–21778
ISBN 0–314–69669–5

COPY EDITING   Janet Greenblatt and Gloria Joyce
ILLUSTRATIONS   John Foster
COMPOSITION   Janet Hansen Associates

PHOTO CREDITS
1 © Christopher Morrow/Stock, Boston; 3 Owen Franken/Stock, Boston;
27 © Kent Reno/Jeroboam; 53 Stock, Boston; 77 Mike Mazzaschi/Stock,
Boston; 99 Ellis Herwig/Stock, Boston; 113 © Robert V. Eckert Jr./EKM-
Nepenthe; 129 Rudolph Robinson/Stock, Boston; 143 Peter Simon/Stock,
Boston; 169 Emilio A. Mercado/Jeroboam; 191 courtesy of McDonnell
Douglas; 211 courtesy of U.S. Department of Housing and Urban Develop-
ment; 213 © Phyllis Graber Jensen/Stock, Boston; 233 © Elizabeth Hamlin/
Stock, Boston; 257 Mike Mazzaschi/Stock, Boston; 319 James Holland/Stock,
Boston; Jeff Albertson/Stock, Boston; 357 Emilio A. Mercado/Jeroboam; 375
Ruth Silverman/Stock, Boston; 393 Charles Gatewood/Stock, Boston; 407
Frank Siteman/Stock, Boston.

A student learning guide has been developed to assist you in mastering
concepts presented in this text. The study guide reinforces concepts by presenting them in condensed, concise form. Additional illustrations and examples are also included. The guide is available from your local bookstore
under the title Student Learning Guide to Accompany UNDERSTANDING
ECONOMICS, prepared by Otis Gilley.

CONTENTS IN BRIEF

CONTENTS

Chapter 10

GNP Accounting and National Income Determination 191

● UNIT 3
TAXES, MONEY, AND MACRO POLICY   211

Chapter 11
Taxes   213

Chapter 15

Stagflation, Taxflation, and Supply-Side Economics 297

Chapter 19
Income Differences, Discrimination, and Poverty

PREFACE

Economics, more than any other subject, has consistently dominated the news for the last decade. This increased emphasis on economic issues does not appear to be abating. In other words, economics as a topic of popular discussion is here to stay. While none of us can hope to see the day when such major concerns as unemployment, inflation, interest rates, balance of payments problems, and the like will have disappeared, familiarity with these issues is crucial to an understanding of the world in which we live. Thus today, more than ever before, a college education must include, at minimum, an introduction to the world of economics. In this text, we provide a basic economic foundation that will allow students to analyze the world in which we live.

● MICROECONOMICS VS MACROECONOMICS

The one-term economics course invariably presents a problem of emphasis. Should the major emphasis be on microeconomics? Or should there be more emphasis on macroeconomics? We realize that each instructor has a preference in this regard. We have also observed that those preferences change depending on current topics being discussed in the press.

Consequently, this text provides basic theoretical materials for both microeconomics and macroeconomics. The flow of topics is traditional in the sense that it parallels that of the major two-semester principles text. We have made one exception, however, which we believe makes UNDERSTANDING ECONOMICS a unique text. The last unit in UNDERSTANDING ECONOMICS can assume either a micro orientation or a macro orientation, depending upon the instructor's choice. This unique approach allows for either macroeconomic emphasis or microeconomic emphasis.

In any event, the basic tools to analyze all major economic issues of the day are presented in the following pages. To strengthen the understanding of those tools, we have added a number of pedagogical aids.

● PEDAGOGICAL AIDS WITHIN THE TEXT

For some students, learning economics poses a problem. The concepts themselves are sometimes not readily grasped, and many students have trouble with the vocabulary. To provide help in these areas, each chapter of UNDERSTANDING ECONOMICS contains a number of unique pedagogical aids.

Introductory Questions

At the beginning of each chapter there are two introductory questions for preview purposes. We label these **Chapter Preview**. For the most part, these questions draw on the student's personal experiences, so that he or she can apply economic analysis to those experiences. Since we believe strongly that merely listing questions is a pointless exercise, we have provided short answers to these preview questions at the end of each chapter. The student should be encouraged to jot down brief notes on how he or she would answer each question before reading the chapter. After reading the chapter, the student should review his or her answers and change them if necessary. The student should then read the answers as they appear at the end of the chapter. Comparison between the student's answers and the answers we provide should point out areas of mis-understanding to the student reader, thus providing a means of self-testing.

Glossary Terms

All important economic terms are printed in bold-faced type within the text itself. Definitions for these terms are listed in the chapter margins. Additionally, at the end of the test, there is a complete, alphabetized glossary.

Controversies

Economics abounds with controversial issues. Should we have minimum wages? Are wage and price controls effective in stopping inflation? These and many other issues are constantly brought up in economic discussions. In order to maintain, and indeed heighten, student interest in the subject matter of this text, we have added a controversy at the end of every chapter. Each controversy is divided into two separate sections. The first section presents the argument behind the controversial issue; the second section, called the analysis, presents both sides of the issue. At the end of every controversy, there are two or three discussion questions. These controversies and their accompanying discussion questions allow for classroom participation by the students. In all cases, we have tried to select controversies that utilize the theoretical concepts provided within each chapter. Immediately following the controversy is a section called "What's Ahead". This feature provides the student with a logical transition to the succeeding chapter.

Chapter Summary

Included within each chapter is a brief summary of the key theoretical concepts found within that chapter. This summary is intended as a review of important materials, and also as a self-testing mechanism. When preparing for an exam, the student can read the summary to review points that are unclear and then refer to the text to improve his or her understanding of these points.

Chapter Review

A unique programmed learning system for review is provided at the end of each chapter. The student is asked to complete one or more blanks in a sentence presenting an economic concept or fact. The answers to these fill-in questions are provided in an upside-down format immediately following the review questions. The student should be encouraged to write the answers on a separate sheet of paper after a first reading of the chapter. These answers can then be compared with the answers given in the text. Only for review prior to the final examination should the student write the answers directly on the page of the text.

Our experience over many years of teaching indicates that this programmed learning approach is extremely effective.

Problems

Also included in the chapter ending are two or three problems that the student is asked to work through. These problems may be numerical in nature, or of the essay type. Again, since we do not believe that questions and problems without answers are very useful, we have provided answers to these problems at the end of the text. Because problems get the student directly involved in the theoretical materials within the chapter, they have proven to be a most useful pedagogical aid.

Selected References

Concluding each chapter is a list of selected references. These references have been chosen for one reason only—they provide additional reading material at a level commensurate with the text itself. The student will not find references to scholarly journals and erudite treatises. In other words, we have chosen usable references for the interested student.

Graphic Analysis

A one-term course in economics presents a problem to most instructors: To what extent should graphical analysis be utilized? We do not subscribe to either of the extreme approaches to this problem; that is, a text offering no graphs or one which presents graphical analysis as utilized in a conventional two-semester principles course. Consequently, our use of graphical analysis falls in the middle range—not too few and not too many graphs. Also, in the beginning pages of this text we have provided an explanation of graphical analysis. In order to make the graphs as clear as possible, ample space has been allowed for each of the graphs. Easy-to-read legends accompany each graph.

● A COMPLETE TEACHING PACKAGE

Even though this text is self-contained and represents a complete learning device unto itself, we have also provided traditional supplemental material to make this a complete learning/teaching package.

Student Learning Guide

Dr. Otis Gilley of the University of Texas at Austin has provided a comprehensive, readable, and indeed enjoyable Student Learning Guide. This Student Learning Guide was developed especially for UNDERSTANDING ECONOMICS. It includes the following: learning objectives; brief overview of the chapter; an exercise covering the terminology in the chapter; questions for review; some problems to work; and a question for analysis that allows the student to apply the concepts in the chapter.

Instructor's Manual and Test Bank

The Instructor's Manual and Test Bank have been prepared by Drew E. Mattson of Anoka Ramsey Community College. The manual includes an annotated outline with supplemental lecture notes and a carefully developed bank of multiple choice test questions. Transparency masters are also included in the Instructor's Manual.

● ACKNOWLEDGMENTS

We have been fortunate to obtain the reviewing services of a large number of instructors who are involved in teaching the one-term economics course. These reviewers were kind enough to provide us with numerous comments, suggestions, and criticisms. In most cases, we were able to utilize their criticisms in rewriting the various drafts of the manuscript for this text. The effect of their suggestions will be readily apparent to the reviewers, for the final product was greatly improved through their efforts. The reviewers for this First Edition of UNDERSTANDING ECONOMICS were:

Craig J. Bolton
University of Dallas

Kathleen Brook
New Mexico State University

Daniel Cobb
St. Louis Community College

J. Paul Combs
Appalachian State College
North Carolina

James R. Gibbons
East Michigan State University

John W. Hambleton
California State University,
San Diego

W. L. Johnson
University of Missouri

J. R. Kearl
Brigham Young University

Robert L. Lawson
Ball State University
Indiana

William Luksetich
St. Cloud State University
Minnesota

Michael R. McMahon
University of Kansas

Drew E. Mattson
Anoka Ramsey Community College
Minnesota

Charles E. Pace
Western Illinois University

James A. Phillips
Cypress College
California

Roger F. Riefler
University of Nebraska, Lincoln

Bruce Roberts
Highline Community College
Washington

Guy A. Schick
California State University
Fullerton

George C. Wang
California State University
Dominguez Hills

Daniel P. Williamson
California State University
San Luis Obispo

To these reviewers we extend our sincerest appreciation. We should note that remaining errors in the text are solely the responsibility of the authors. We welcome comments and criticisms from users of this text, for it is only through such participation that we can make further editions of UNDERSTANDING ECONOMICS even more useful for both the instructor and the student reader.

Roger LeRoy Miller
Robert W. Pulsinelli

UNIT 1

Introduction

Contents

1

Scarcity and All That

Chapter Preview
1. Many people argue that college education is so important for our nation that it should be provided free of charge. Can college education ever be truly free?
2. When you look at your income, you know that you can't suddenly have more of everything at any one point in time. But can the United States as a country be different? Can this nation have more spending on defense, or more spending on social programs, or more spending on foreign aid, without sacrifices in other programs?

● KEY TERMS

Absolute advantage

Comparative advantage

Direct relationship

Economics

Economic goods

Free goods

Full employment

Goods

Inverse relationship

Law of increasing relative cost

Linear curve

Opportunity cost

Production possibilities curve

Resources

Scarcity

Specialization

Trade-off

● SCARCITY

In one year the average American consumes 170 pounds of red meat, 352 pounds of dairy products, 120 pounds of sugar and other sweeteners, 11,960 units of energy (kilogram coal equivalent), and much, much more. Yet the average American doesn't feel "rich." Very, very few people can buy *everything* they desire.

In fact, even the wealthiest person in the world faces a constraint —having to choose among several alternatives. It is impossible to achieve every alternative simultaneously. Thus, at the very least, this monied individual faces a *time* constraint. Hours spent working cannot simultaneously be used vacationing. Similarly, one cannot vacation in Monte Carlo and in the Alps at the same time. Nor can one attend a Broadway play and a dinner party simultaneously.

These choices all have agreeable alternatives. Not all choices do, however. Choices made by the average consumer are more likely to involve sacrificing some **goods** to obtain others. For example, when you buy a new television set, you probably won't be going to restaurants for a while. If you go to the movies, you may have to forgo buying a record album or even a lunch. Individually and collectively, consumers face the problem of **scarcity**, the most fundamental of all economic concepts: People simply want more than they can have. And that's why the science of economics exists. If all consumers were able to satisfy their desires for all goods and services, the study of economics wouldn't be necessary. This kind of total satisfaction, however, requires that all goods be free goods.

Free Goods

There are still a few goods in the world that do not require payment. They are called **free goods**, as opposed to **economic goods**. Old economics textbooks called air a free good, but that is really no longer true, because in many cities pollution makes air unfit to

Goods

Those things that human beings desire.

Scarcity

Wants exceed the ability to satisfy those wants; individuals and societies can never be capable of satisfying, or producing enough to satisfy, all their wants at exactly the same time.

Free goods

Any goods or services that are available in quantities larger than are desired at a zero price.

Economic good

Any good or service for which wants exceed the available supply at a zero price.

4

breathe. In many mountain areas, however, clean air is still a free good; once you're there, it's yours at a zero price. Scarcity does not play a part there.

Who is interested in free goods, then? Certainly not most economists. Physicists, hydrologists, biologists, and chemists may be interested in free air and water, but the economist steps in only when the problem of scarcity arises and people become concerned about allocating a scarce resource. We have seen throughout our history that as population and production increase over time, many "free" goods become "economic" goods, such as land for mining, water and air for industrial uses, and water for hydroelectric power. Before the time of Sir Walter Raleigh, native American Indians had unlimited access to tobacco leaves. Later, however, tobacco leaves became (and remain) an economic good.

Resources

The fact is that our world is not one of unlimited free goods. Most goods can exist only if resources are used. **Resources** are inputs or factors used in the production of those goods or services that individuals desire. Typical resources are labor, land, and machines and equipment. By definition, resources are scarce since they produce scarce goods.

● CHOICE

Everyone faces the problem of scarcity. Consequently, all individuals must make *choices*. In fact, some economists define **economics** as the science of choice. Since all individual wants cannot be satisfied, each of us must choose which ones to satisfy. For example, a typical salary increase might pay for either a more expensive apartment *or* a new car, but not both. And a choice must be made between attending a lecture series or studying for an economics test, because both cannot be done simultaneously.

Similarly, a nation may face a choice between producing additional goods and services or directing resources toward cleaner air. The scarce resources devoted to making the air pure cannot also be used to produce goods and services. In short, choice follows scarcity as inevitably as night follows day.

One point should be reemphasized: Scarcity and choice apply to *all* activities. Economists typically speak in terms of goods and services, yet the concepts of scarcity and choice apply equally well to activities of every sort. Individuals seek not only more goods and services, but also more prestige, love, affection, friendship, security, athletic prowess, beauty, health, peace of mind, religion, and

Resources
Scarce inputs necessary for the production of desired goods and services.

Economics
The study, or science, of how individuals in society choose to use scarce resources that have alternative uses.

5

power. All these "goods" are scarce for each individual. For example, time spent obtaining more prestige or power may mean less time spent earning more income to purchase more goods, or less time spent acquiring more friendship.

● OPPORTUNITY COSTS

Since scarcity necessitates choices, individuals must continuously assess the cost (broadly defined) of one good or service in terms of the costs of all *other* goods and services. Even if an individual is unaware of it, this evaluation occurs by necessity whenever choices are made.

The cost of a good or a service is usually viewed in terms of its selling price. For example, the cost of a $1000 videocassette recorder (VCR) is, well, $1000. That's obvious. On the other hand, there is an alternative way of assessing its cost. If you did not buy it, what else could you do with that $1000? You might be able to buy a relatively high-quality stereo, or some new furniture, or even additional semesters of college education. In short, there are numerous ways to spend that $1000. They all represent alternative ways of measuring the cost of that VCR. Of all the possible alternative ways to spend that $1000 (other than on the VCR), the option you prefer above all others is called the **opportunity cost** to you of that VCR. Ultimately, then, the cost of a good or service can be measured in terms of the goods and services that must be sacrificed in order to obtain the particular good or service being considered.

Opportunity Costs Are Different for Everyone

Note that since opportunity cost is defined as the *highest*-valued alternative, each individual will have different opportunity costs for the VCR—or for any other good or service. Your opportunity cost for the VCR may be a stereo, whereas your friend's may be a relatively old used car. Another person may find that the "cost" of the VCR is a trip to the Virgin Islands during Christmas vacation.

Now a question: What is the opportunity cost of your going to listen to your economics professor? That depends. It depends on the highest-valued alternative for you and you alone. That alternative may be an extra hour of sleep. For one of your classmates, it may be an hour on the tennis courts. Why? Because your classmate considers playing tennis the most valuable alternative given up in order to attend a one-hour economics class. Each individual student is likely to assess the opportunity cost of going to class differently, therefore. Whatever the opportunity cost may be for each individual, it does exist. The time spent in class could be spent another way, but it isn't.

Opportunity cost
The *highest-valued alternative* that must be forgone in order to obtain the optional selection.

6

● TRADE-OFFS

People at all times and in all areas of the world face the problem of scarcity. Limits on income, time, and resources affect the satisfaction of individual wants and necessitate choices among a range of goods and services. Remember that "goods" can be tangible items such as cars, boats, food, and houses, but also the abstract values of love, prestige, and companionship.

Since incomes are limited, more of one good means less of another. Economists use the term **trade-off**: Increased consumption of one good means decreased consumption of another.

A simple example will clarify this important economic concept. Suppose that you, on your limited budget, have decided to allocate $40 per month to recreation. For simplicity, assume that only two of your recreational activities require money outlays: movies and record albums. For a clearer view of the trade-offs you must consider, we have constructed a simple table (Table 1–1). Assume that movies cost $2 a showing and that albums cost $10 each. Note that the entire $40 budget is spent for each combination of trade-offs between movie purchases and record purchases. As this table indicates, if you spend the entire $40 on movies, you can go to 20 movies during the month. However, since you have exhausted your limited recreational budget, you cannot purchase any albums. This situation is labeled possibility A in the table. Conversely, you could have allocated all of your recreational budget to record albums. If so, you could have purchased a maximum of 4 albums at $10 each within your $40 monthly recreation budget. This situation is labeled possibility E.

The other possibilities are labeled B, C, and D. Each lettered possibility indicates the *maximum* monthly quantity of one commodity that can be purchased, *given* the quantity of the other purchased. Thus, if you purchase 2 albums during the month, you can see only

TABLE 1–1
The Trade-off between Movies and Record Albums

Assume that you allocate $40 for recreation each month. Each row indicates the maximum number of albums that you can purchase (at $10 each) given a specified number of movies viewed (at $2 each). If you choose row A and 20 movies, no albums can be purchased. On the other hand, if you choose the combination given in row E, with 0 movies, you can purchase a total of 4 albums.

POSSIBILITIES	MOVIES	RECORD ALBUMS
A	20	0
B	15	1
C	10	2
D	5	3
E	0	4

Trade-off

A sacrifice that must be made in order to obtain a good or service. Trade-offs are related to opportunity costs, for scarcity demands that one desired item must be forgone in order to obtain another.

10 movies during that month. Similarly, if you attend five movies in a month, the maximum number of albums you can purchase is three. You should check for yourself that each of the lettered possibilities indicates a total monthly outlay of exactly $40. The main point of this table is that because your recreation budget is *limited*, a *trade-off* exists between albums and movies. There is an important generalization to this concept: Since individuals face limited incomes, an increased expenditure on one commodity forces a decreased expenditure on another commodity. *Because individuals have limited incomes, they face trade-offs for goods and services.*

Inverse Relationships

The information presented in Table 1–1 can also be shown as a graph. Monthly movie trips are plotted on a horizontal number line, and monthly album purchases are plotted on a vertical number line. Graph 1–1 is the result.

The graph demonstrates that the trade-off between albums and movies is such that increased expenditure on one of these goods necessarily means decreased expenditure on the other. In other words, there is an **inverse relationship** between these two goods.

Other types of inverse relationships exist for goods and services. For example, the relationship between an automobile's weight and its miles-per-gallon rating—the distance it travels on a gallon of gas—is inverse. The heavier the automobile, the fewer miles per gallon that auto will average on the road. Conversely, the lighter an auto is, the better (higher) its miles-per-gallon rating will usually be.

An inverse relationship probably exists between a family's income and its purchases of "rice and beans." The higher the family income, the less likely it is to eat rice and beans. It is assumed in these examples that other things are constant, meaning that the only factors that change are those we indicate in the examples; everything else remains the same.

Look at Graph 1–1 again. *Inverse relationships* are always represented graphically by lines that are *downward sloping*. If an increase in the value of one variable causes a decrease in the value of the other, this "plots out" graphically as a downward-sloping line—from left to right. Graph 1–1, which depicts the inverse relationship between purchases of albums and purchases of movies on a fixed recreational budget, is indeed downward sloping—from left to right. Such a line is *negatively* sloped.

Notice that what we have drawn is a straight line. It represents a *constant* trade-off between movies and albums purchased. That means that the opportunity cost of one album is always five trips to the movies (or conversely, the opportunity cost of one movie is one-fifth of an album). Since the opportunity cost is constant, the picture

Inverse relationship
An increase in the value of one variable results in a decrease in the value of the other.

8

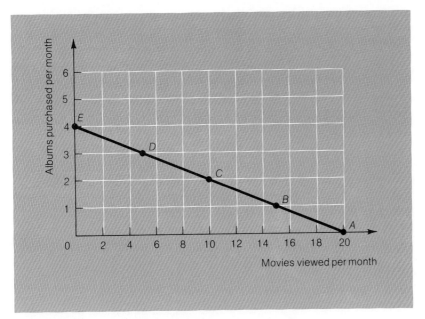

GRAPH 1–1
Graphic Trade-off between Record Albums and Movies

Points A, B, C, D, and E correspond to the possibilities listed in Table 1–1. Note that possibility C indicates, in Table 1–1 *and* Graph 1–1, that if you see 10 movies, you can purchase a maximum of 2 albums. Similarly, if you buy 3 albums, the maximum number of movies you can see is 5. Since a trade-off exists between these two goods, the curve representing this trade-off in the graph will be downward sloping—from left to right. We say this "curve" is linear (a straight line) and negatively sloped, indicating that an inverse relationship exists between possible expenditures on these two goods. Increased expenditures on one necessarily mean decreased expenditures on the other.

that we draw representing this trade-off—a line—will always be straight. The relationship is therefore said to be linear and the "curve" is paradoxically called a **linear curve**.

Direct Relationships

Two variables may be directly related—that is, an increase in the value of one variable results in an increase in the value of another. Such a situation, or relationship, is said to be a **direct relationship**. The relationship between household consumption and household income is normally a direct relationship; the higher the income level, the higher the level of consumption expenditures. Take another example: A direct relationship probably exists between ice cream sales and daily temperature. On days when the temperature is high, more people purchase ice cream. Indeed, the higher the temperature, the more ice cream they buy.

Linear curve

A straight line over the whole range of the relationship between two variables. A relationship in which the trade-off between two variables remains constant will be linear.

Direct relationship

An increase in the value of one variable results in the increase in the value of another.

9

Direct relationships can also be presented graphically. However, the "curve" relating two directly related variables will be *upward sloping*, from left to right. Such a curve is said to be *positively sloped*. In Graph 1–2, two types of direct relationships are depicted—a *linear* direct relationship (a), and a *nonlinear* direct relationship (b).

● GOING FROM CONSUMPTION TO PRODUCTION

So far, we've talked about the trade-offs between consumption possibilities. The same trade-off analysis can be applied to production alternatives. We have choices in how we use our time and our resources in producing goods and services. Consider, for example, the production possibilities that you have with your time. You can use your time to "produce" a higher grade in economics or, let's

GRAPH 1–2

Direct Relationships: Linear and Nonlinear

(a) A direct, linear relationship. As total income rises, total expenditures on goods and services increase. Moreover, the same increase in income will *always* result in the same specific increase in consumption. For example, a $100 increase in income will always lead to a $90 increase in consumption expenditures. So, an increase in income from $1000 to $1100 will result in a consumption increase of $90. Similarly, an income increase from $50,000 to $50,100 will lead to a $90 increase in consumption expenditures.

(b) A direct, nonlinear relationship. The same increase in temperature does not always lead to the same specific increase in ice cream sales. Higher and higher temperatures lead to smaller and smaller increases in ice cream sales. For example, if temperature goes up from 60°F to 70°F, ice cream sales might go up by 2000 gallons per day in a city. But a temperature increase from 90°F to 100°F (the same 10° difference) may lead to an increase in sales of only 1000 gallons of ice cream per day.

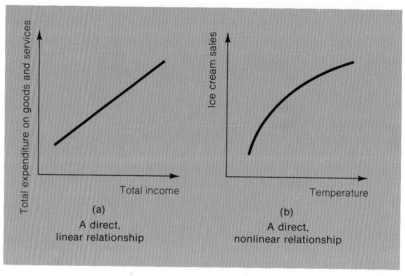

(a)
A direct,
linear relationship

(b)
A direct,
nonlinear relationship

say, a higher grade in English. In other words, given a specified number of hours allocated to studying—that is, to the production of grades in English and in economics—you have a choice to make. You can spend more time attempting to produce a higher grade in English or you can spend more time attempting to produce a higher grade in economics. The result of your production activities is the output we call a letter grade of A, B, C, D, or F.

To make the production trade-off simple, assume that the trade-off is one to one. In order to get one higher letter grade in economics, you must give up, or "pay," one letter grade in English. Consider the five choices that you have in Table 1–2. Here we are assuming that you have allocated 20 study hours to English and economics only. As can be seen in Graph 1–3, the "curve" is linear—a straight line representing a constant trade-off. The straight line goes from A on one axis to A on the other axis. This **production possibilities curve** shows all possible combinations of the maximum amount of any two goods that can be produced from a fixed amount of resources. In this example, your time for studying is limited to 20 hours per week. The two possible outputs are grades in English and grades in economics. If you decide to be at point x in Graph 1–3, then you will spend 10 hours of study time on English and 10 on economics. Your expected grade in each course will be a C. If you want to get a B in economics, you will have to spend 15 hours studying economics, but then you will have only 5 hours left to study English; therefore your grade in that course will drop from a C to a D.

In this extreme hypothetical example, the only way for you to get a high grade in both English and in economics is to study more than 20 hours a week. However, if that were the case you would no longer be operating on the production possibilities curve depicted

TABLE 1–2
Production Possibilities for Grades in English and Economics

Assume that you have a fixed number of hours—20—in which to study both English and economics. If you spend the entire 20 hours studying English, you receive an A in English but fail economics. If you spend the entire 20 hours studying economics, you receive an A in economics but fail English. Your production possibilities trade-off here is linear and, in this case, one to one. To get one higher grade in English, you sacrifice by getting one lower grade in economics, and vice versa.

HOURS SPENT STUDYING		GRADE IN	GRADE IN
ENGLISH	ECONOMICS	ENGLISH	ECONOMICS
20	0	A	F
15	5	B	D
10	10	C	C
5	15	D	B
0	20	F	A

Production possibilities curve

A curve showing the maximum output rates of one good, given specific levels of another.

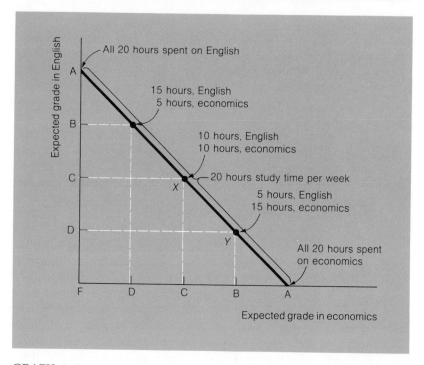

GRAPH 1–3

Production Possibilities Curve for Grades in English and Economics

On the vertical axis, we measure the expected grade in English; on the horizontal axis, the expected grade in economics. We assume that there are only 20 hours that can be spent per week on studying. If all 20 hours are spent on economics, an A is received in economics and an F in English. If 20 hours are spent on English, an A is received in English and an F in economics. There is a one-to-one trade-off. If a student is at point *x*, equal time (10 hours a week) is spent on both courses and equal grades of C will be received. If a higher grade in economics is desired, the student may go to point *y*, thereby receiving a B in economics, but a D in English. At point *y*, 5 hours are spent on English, 15 hours on economics.

by the straight line going from A to A in Graph 1–3. In any event, for any given total amount of resources (here, studying time), your opportunity cost of getting a higher output (a higher grade) in one subject is always the same: A reduction in output (a lower grade) in the other subject. In our simple example, the opportunity cost remains constant. One grade is always sacrificed for another. This analysis can be extended to the production possibilities of the entire country, which we will consider now.

● A NATION'S PRODUCTION POSSIBILITIES CURVE

At any *given* moment, a nation's resources are fixed. Remember, resources are defined as the inputs needed to produce desired goods and services. A nation's resources consist of humans—their labor services—and all the land, equipment, machinery, and so on available for production. If all resources are working at capacity, the nation is at **full employment**. It follows that if all resources are fully employed, increasing the output of one commodity necessarily leads to a reduction in the output of one or more others. In other words, a nation taken as a whole is also faced with trade-offs. We can use a production possibilities curve to represent these trade-offs. Just as with grades in English and grades in economics, the relationship is inverse and is represented by a negatively sloped line.

In keeping with the traditional teaching of economics, we assume that a nation can produce only two types of goods: guns and butter. The category *guns* represents the nation's total output of national defense and internal security. The category *butter* represents the output of all consumer goods. Clearly, given full employment of the nation's resources, a trade-off exists between guns and butter: Producing more guns means less butter will be produced, and vice versa. The nation can use all its resources to produce guns, but then it produces no butter. Alternatively, the nation can use all its resources to produce butter, but then no guns can be produced. In between, it is possible to produce some guns and some butter. Remember that we are considering a situation in which every machine, every worker, and every factory is fully employed, producing some combination of guns and butter. Let's take a closer look at the production possibilities between guns and butter shown in Table 1–3. Consider possibility B. If society wants 28 units of guns (mili-

TABLE 1–3

The Nation's Production Possibilities for Guns and Butter

The production possibilities are labeled A through E. The two extremes are A, the production of 0 butter, which allows for the production of 30 units of guns, and E, the production of 0 guns, which allows for the production of 4 units of butter. Each increase in the production of butter leads to a greater and greater decrease in the production of guns. We show this in the last column as the increasing opportunity cost of butter in terms of guns.

PRODUCTION POSSIBILITIES	GUNS	BUTTER	INCREASING OPPORTUNITY COST OF BUTTER IN TERMS OF GUNS
A	30	0	
			2
B	28	1	
			4
C	24	2	
			6
D	18	3	
			18
E	0	4	

Full employment

The situation occurring when the nation's resources are being fully utilized, or are being worked to capacity.

tary goods), the maximum units of butter (civilian, or consumer, goods) it can produce is 1. Conversely, if society wants 1 unit of butter, the maximum units of guns it can produce is 28. As you might expect, the table indicates an inverse relationship between the production of guns and the production of butter.

Graphing the Production Possibilities Curve

Graph 1–4 converts Table 1–3 to a production possibilities curve. Note that the curve is downward sloping from left to right; the curve is negatively sloped. An inverse relationship exists between the production of guns and the production of butter because, given full employment, increasing production of one of these commodities requires reducing the production of the other. Note that this curve is *not* a straight line as was the production possibilities curve in Graph 1–3. That is to say, it is not linear. Graph 1–4 is nonlinear because the opportunity cost of successive units of butter is not constant; rather, the opportunity cost of butter in terms of guns rises.

GRAPH 1–4
Production Possibilities Curve for Guns and Butter

This curve depicts the nation's production possibilities curve for guns and butter (military and civilian goods). The curve is downward sloping because, given full employment, increases in the output of one of these goods can be accomplished only through a reduction in the output of the other. The opportunity cost for successive units of butter is not constant; it rises. Each successive unit of butter costs the nation more and more in forgone guns. For this reason, the production possibilities curve is nonlinear.

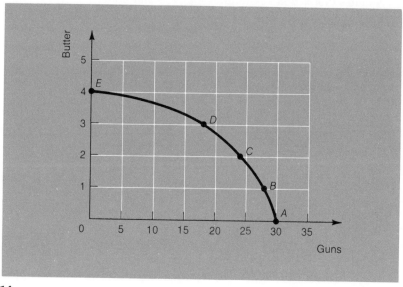

An Increase in Opportunity Costs for Butter

Look again at Table 1–3. A move from possibility A to possibility B demonstrates the opportunity cost of the first unit of butter. With 0 units of butter, the nation could produce 30 units of guns. When the nation produces 1 unit of butter, however, the nation can have only 28 units of guns. The first unit of butter costs society 2 units of guns; the opportunity cost of the first unit of butter is therefore 2 units of guns.

Now suppose that the nation wants another unit of butter. It moves from possibility B to possibility C. With the production of 2 units of butter, the maximum gun output is only 24. The opportunity cost of the second unit of butter is 4 units of guns; a second unit of butter costs society 4 units of guns.

The first unit of butter costs the nation 2 units of guns, but the second unit of butter costs the nation 4 units of guns. The opportunity cost of butter, therefore, has increased, and it continues to increase, as the last column of the table shows. Now we try to answer the question of *why* opportunity costs rise.

Why the Production Possibilities Curve Is Bowed Outward

In Graph 1–3, the trade-off between a grade in English and a grade in economics is one to one. The trade-off ratio is fixed. This is not the case in Graph 1–4. As we saw, the opportunity cost of obtaining more units of butter (civilian goods) rises; each additional unit costs society more in forgone alternatives than a previously produced unit. This is seen even more clearly in Graph 1–5. Each increase in butter is the same, but look at what the nation has to give up in guns when it goes from the next-to-last unit of butter production to the last unit, where the entire economy is producing only butter (civilian goods). The opportunity cost is very large relative to what a one-unit increase in butter costs the society when no butter is being produced at all. Graph 1–5 represents the **law of increasing relative cost**. As society takes more and more resources and applies them to the production of any specific item, the opportunity cost for each additional unit produced increases.

We can reverse our example, letting the opportunity cost of increasing gun output rise as more and more resources are shifted from the output of butter to the output of guns. Suppose we are starting in a world with no guns, that is, no military goods whatsoever. What will happen when military production is increased? At first it is relatively easy for the nation to transfer engineers, mechanics, and technicians from the private sector, where they are producing television sets, cars, and refrigerators, to the military sector, where they can produce guns, tanks, and bombs. Many, if

Law of increasing relative cost

An economic principle stating that the opportunity cost of additional units of a commodity generally increases as society attempts to produce more and more of that commodity.

15

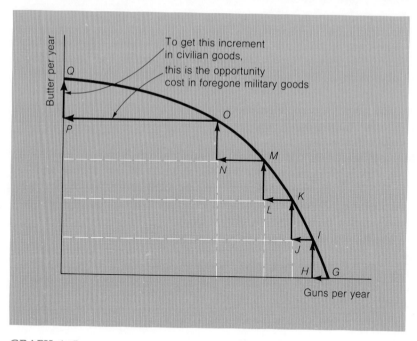

GRAPH 1–5
The Law of Increasing Relative Cost

Consider equal increments in butter production as measured on the vertical axis. Thus, all of the vertical arrows—*H–I, J–K, L–M, N–O,* and *P–Q*—are of equal length. What is the cost to society of obtaining the first such increment in butter (civilian goods)? It is a reduction in guns (military goods) of *G–H.* This cost for additional equal increments in butter rises, however. To get the last increment in butter—*P–Q*—society must give up the entire distance *O–P.* The opportunity cost of each additional increase in butter rises.

not most, of these workers will be doing jobs in the military sector that are quite similar to the jobs they did in the private sector. Thus, their productivity will be approximately the same as it was prior to the move.

Eventually, however, college economics professors, Sunday school teachers, day-care center operators, rock singers, and the like will have to be transferred to factories to make war goods. (This was indeed the case during World War II.) Their talents will be relatively poorly suited to such tasks. For example, 25 economics professors may be needed to get the same increment in output achieved by the engineer hired to build the nation's first tank. Thus, the opportunity cost of an additional unit of war-related goods will be much higher when resources ill-suited to the task are employed. That cost—of using poorly suited resources—will increase as the production of additional military output is attempted. Basically, then, the more specialized the resources are, the more bowed the production possibilities curve will be.

16

● SPECIALIZATION AND COMPARATIVE ADVANTAGE

Specialization

Generally, resources are better suited for some uses than for others; they are specialized. This also applies to the resource called labor, or human beings. Although some individuals prefer to be jacks-of-all-trades, most choose to specialize in one area. Individuals, therefore, become teachers, factory workers, farmers, carpenters, plumbers, secretaries, and the like. Why? Because individuals find they can obtain a higher level of economic satisfaction—usually through obtaining a higher income—by specializing. As it turns out, it is through specialization in production that individuals are able to earn higher incomes. Consider a numerical example of **specialization**.

Table 1–4 shows total output available for two productive workers, Ms. Hanes and Mr. Little, in a small world where they are the only workers. At first, they do not specialize; rather, each works an equal amount of time, 8 hours a day, harvesting turnips and corn. Ms. Hanes chooses to harvest 2 pounds of turnips in 4 hours of work and an additional 2 pounds of corn with the additional

TABLE 1–4

Output before and after Specialization

Here we show the relationship between Ms. Hanes and Mr. Little's daily work effort and the harvesting of turnips and corn. *Before specialization*: When Ms. Hanes works on her own without specializing in either activity, she devotes 4 hours a day to turnip harvesting and 4 hours a day to corn harvesting. For her efforts, she obtains 2 pounds of each. On the other hand, Mr. Little, again not specializing, will harvest in the same two 4-hour periods 3 pounds of turnips and 1 pound of corn. Their total output will be 5 pounds of turnips and 3 pounds of corn.

After specialization: If Ms. Hanes specializes in the harvesting of corn, she can harvest 4 pounds for every 8 hours of daily work effort. Mr. Little, on the other hand, specializing in the harvesting of turnips, will harvest 6 pounds. Their grand total of production will be 6 pounds of turnips and 4 pounds of corn, a pound more of each good than before they specialized.

DAILY WORK EFFORT	OUTPUT		
	MS. HANES	MR. LITTLE	TOTAL
	Before Specialization		
4 hours 4 hours	2 pounds turnips 2 pounds corn	3 pounds turnips 1 pound corn	5 pounds turnips 3 pounds corn
	After Specialization		
8 hours	4 pounds corn	6 pounds turnips	6 pounds turnips 4 pounds corn

Specialization

The condition occurring when resources used in production are concentrated in the production of a limited variety of goods or services.

17

4 hours. Mr. Little chooses to harvest 3 pounds of turnips in his first 4 hours of work but only 1 pound of corn in his second 4 hours. The total amount that the two can harvest without specialization is 5 pounds of turnips and 3 pounds of corn.

Now look at what happens when they specialize. As Table 1–4 shows, after specialization, when Ms. Hanes spends all her day harvesting corn, she can harvest 4 pounds (since she can harvest 2 pounds in 4 hours). Mr. Little, on the other hand, spending all his workday harvesting turnips, produces 6 pounds (since he can produce 3 pounds in just 4 hours). The total output of this two-individual world has now increased to 6 pounds of turnips and 4 pounds of corn. With the same two people using the same amount of resources, the total output of this little economy has increased from 5 pounds of turnips per day to 6, and from 3 pounds of corn per day to 4. Obviously, Ms. Hanes and Mr. Little would be better off (in a material sense) if they each specialized and exchanged. Ms. Hanes would exchange turnips for corn, Mr. Little would do the reverse. (Our discussion, of course, has not dealt with the *disadvantages* of specialization—monotony and drudgery on the job.)

After specialization, each individual would be better off doing what he or she could do *comparatively* better than the other. This leads to the concept of comparative advantage.

Comparative Advantage

Specialization rests on a very important fact: Individuals, communities, and nations are indeed different, at least when it comes to the skills of each in producing goods and services. In our simple two-person example, if each person could do both jobs equally well, specialization would not have been beneficial, since total output could not have been increased. (Go back to Table 1–4 and make Mr. Little equally physically productive in harvesting both turnips and corn, producing, say, 1 pound of each in 4 hours, and then see what happens after specialization.)

In fact, people are not uniformly talented. Even if individuals or nations had the talent to do everything better (for example, by using fewer resources, especially labor hours), they would still want to *specialize in the area of their greatest advantage*, that is, in their **comparative advantage**. A good example involves former President William Howard Taft. Before he became president, he was probably the country's fastest stenographer. At the same time, he might have been the country's best typist, best violin player, and best everything else, but he decided to become president, because that was where his comparative advantage lay. Had he declined the presidency to remain a stenographer, the cost to him of that action would have been tremendous.

Comparative advantage

A situation in which an individual or a nation has the ability to produce a good or service at a lower opportunity cost than another individual or nation can.

18

To take another example, consider the hypothetical dilemma of the president of a large company. Suppose that he or she can type better than any of the typists, file better than any of the file clerks, drive a truck better than any of the truck drivers, and wash windows better than any of the window washers. Such proficiency would give the president an **absolute advantage** in all of these endeavors, since he or she uses fewer labor hours for each task than anyone else in the company. However, his or her *comparative* advantage lies in managing the company, not in doing the aforementioned tasks. How is this comparative advantage determined? The answer is quite easy: The president is *paid* the most for being president, not for being a typist or a file clerk or a truck driver or a window washer for the company. The same is true of the simple two-person economy previously discussed. If someone were paying Ms. Hanes and Mr. Little, Mr. Little would clearly be paid more to specialize in harvesting turnips rather than corn. In fact, he could figure that out all by himself. To get 1 more pound of corn, he would have to give up 3 pounds of turnips. However, for Ms. Hanes to get 1 more pound of turnips, she would have to give up only 1 pound of corn. She therefore has a comparative advantage in harvesting corn, and he therefore has a comparative advantage in harvesting turnips, because in both cases the cost of *not* harvesting the other commodity is lower.

Basically, *one's comparative advantage is found by choosing that activity that has the lowest opportunity cost*. Mr. Little had the lowest opportunity cost in harvesting turnips. He therefore specialized in turnips while Ms. Hanes specialized in corn harvesting.

● EXCHANGE

Gains from specialization implicitly refer to exchange among the individuals concerned. After specialization takes place, the gains from specialization necessarily cannot occur unless one exchanges some of one's output for some of another person's output. Indeed, at the heart of any economy—whether the world economy of industrialized nations or the economy in a prisoner-of-war camp or the economy among the kids on the block—is a system of exchange. People ultimately trade some goods for others. The more sophisticated an economic system, the more frequent, varied, and complicated the exchanges.

People not only exchange goods for goods, but they also exchange labor for money, and money for goods. An exchange takes place when one person rents an apartment or building to another. Even little kids get in the act; they trade comic books and baseball cards.

Absolute advantage

A situation in which an individual or a nation has the ability to produce a good or service at an "absolutely" lower cost, usually (but not necessarily) measured in hours of work required to produce a unit of the good in question.

19

Voluntary and Involuntary Exchanges

When we discuss exchange, or trade, in economics, we are talking about *voluntary* exchange. When economists analyze labor markets, in which labor services are bought and sold, they implicitly assume that laborers sell their services voluntarily, and that employers hire laborers voluntarily.

Economists do not usually consider those cases in which laborers are *forced* to work, or in which employers are required to hire laborers. These are examples of *involuntary* exchange. More dramatic examples of involuntary exchange are slavery and robbery. An individual might be encouraged to surrender his or her money to an armed robber in exchange for his or her life. Certainly this exchange is not voluntary.

When an exchange is voluntary, *both* sides perceive a gain—if they didn't, the exchange would not take place. Moreover, if after the exchange takes place, one partner to the exchange feels that he or she has received no gain (or insufficient gain), then undoubtedly that exchange will not reoccur. It follows that when exchange, or trade, is continually carried out, both sides are benefiting from the transactions.

Of course, in some extreme cases, even voluntary trade may be exploitive; if you have the option of working for only *one* person (or buying from only one company), then such transactions are somewhat less than voluntary. If a person has the option of either working for the sole employer or starving to death, that person may be working "voluntarily" but exploitation is certainly possible. Clearly, however, the greater the number of options available to an employee (or employer, for that matter), the less the possibility of exploitation.

It is important to understand that voluntary exchange almost always leaves *both* parties better off economically. The very essence of trade and commerce is that business can be transacted in such a way that one person's gain need not be another person's loss. Unlike a poker game in which some must lose in order for one to win, trade and commerce normally leave both parties to a transaction (buyers *and* sellers) better off materially.

The Draft Is Cheaper Than a Volunteer Army

THE ARGUMENT

Over the past few years, numerous politicians, as well as concerned citizens and alarmed military leaders, have pushed very strongly for a re-institution of the military draft, otherwise known as conscription. There is much talk about the failure of the volunteer armed forces. More specifically, members of Congress have claimed that a volunteer army is too expensive for the nation. Is there any validity to this argument?

THE ANALYSIS

The fact of the matter is that the cost to the economy is no different whether there is a draft or a volunteer army. The economy suffers an opportunity cost for every person drafted that is totally independent of what draftees are paid by the United States government. The true cost to society of a draftee is what he could be earning as a civilian. When a man is paid $20,000 by an employer, we can usually assume that the employer is obtaining at least that amount in services or the arrangement would have been terminated. If the same man is drafted, the economy is giving up about $20,000 worth of civilian productive services a year to obtain a much smaller amount in military services. *That* amount, and not the $6500 in army pay he might receive, is the true annual cost of his induction.

An Implicit Tax on Draftees

Since a draft army pays (via tax dollars) only a small fraction of the true opportunity cost of draftees, who, then, pays the rest? Obviously, the draftees themselves bear the burden of an implicit tax that roughly equals the difference between their civilian pay and their army pay.[1] But all suffer somewhat, because the output of nonmilitary goods and services is lower and more expensive, since these men are not working at their civilian jobs (unless, of course, all draftees are taken from the ranks of the unemployed).[2]

This hidden-tax aspect of the draft is certainly not new. Benjamin Franklin commented on it over 200 years ago in reviewing a court's opinion concerning the legality of impressment of American merchant seamen. He wrote:

> But if, as I suppose is often the case, the sailor who is pressed and obliged to serve for the defence of this trade at the rate of 25 shillings a month could have 3 pounds 15 shillings in the merchant service, you take from him 50 shillings a month; and if you have 100,000 in

---

[1]To the army pay should be added the benefits of training and education obtained while in the service, plus any consumption value received ("Join the army and see the world").

[2]Some say we benefit because military service "makes men out of boys," good citizens out of bad, and community leaders out of juvenile delinquents. Of course, there may be cheaper ways of obtaining these "goods."

your service, you rob the honest part of society and their poor families of 250,000 pounds per month or three millions a year, and at the same time oblige them to hazard their lives in fighting for the defence of your trade.

Taxpayers Don't Want to Foot the Bill

One of the major complaints about an all-volunteer army is that taxpayers do not want to pay the taxes to have the quantity and quality of armed forces desired by the military. That complaint is totally beside the point. Society pays for the army whether or not the nation's youths are drafted.

DISCUSSION QUESTIONS

1. Who benefits from the draft? Who loses?
2. During the U.S. Civil War, men who were conscripted were allowed to "buy" someone else to go in their stead. What would be the end result of this system today if we were to go back to the draft?

● WHAT'S AHEAD

In the next chapter, you will learn about the forces that determine the terms of exchange engaged in by you and everybody else in this economy. More specifically, you will be looking at supply and demand, the economist's favorite tools. You will find out how the forces of supply and demand usually determine the prices that we must pay for the goods and services that we buy.

● CHAPTER SUMMARY

Because human wants far exceed what is provided to us by nature, scarcity exists at all times for every individual. Even the most wealthy individual faces a time constraint and cannot do more than one thing at a time. Therefore, all of us face the question of choice and, indeed, economics is the study or science of how individuals choose to use scarce resources. Because of scarcity, every activity—whether it be buying a stereo, going to a movie, or seeking more love and companionship—entails an opportunity cost, which is defined as the highest-valued alternative that must be forgone to obtain the option selected. For society as a whole, the opportunity cost of producing more and more of one good usually rises. This is due to the law of increasing relative cost. This law, which results in a bowed production possibilities curve, is usually explained in terms of most resources being better suited for the production of certain goods rather than others.

In a world of scarce resources, individuals must choose among alternative uses of their time and resources. Typically, they will tend to specialize by choosing a limited area of endeavor in which they can maximize their income. They will choose that area where they have a comparative advantage, defined as a situation in which one's ability to produce a good is indicated by the lowest opportunity cost possible. After choosing specialization in a particular area, individuals typically exchange among themselves to maximize the benefits from specialization.

● QUESTIONS FOR REVIEW AND STUDY

1. Choices must always be made because we live in a world of _____.

2. Economics is the science of _____.

3. Opportunity cost is defined as the _____ valued alternative that is forgone, but each of us has a _____ alternative cost because we have different alternatives.

4. A _____ exists whenever choices must be made among alternatives and income is limited.

5. Trade-offs are represented by inverse relationships, which can be shown by a _____ sloping curve on a graph.

6. A _____ relationship is shown by an upward-sloping curve on a graph.

7. For the nation as a whole, the trade-off between, say, military spending and civilian spending is represented by a _____ _____ curve that shows the _____ output of one good, given a specific level of another.

8. As we produce more of one good relative to all others, we use more and more resources less suited to that increased production. The result is that the opportunity cost of successive units _____.

9. The consequence of rising opportunity cost is a production possibilities curve that is _____.

10. Trading among individuals is a form of _____.

11. _____ exchanges that continue over time would seem to indicate that such exchanges are _____ to the parties involved.

12. If you can type faster than anyone in your school, you are said to have a(n) _____ advantage in typing.

13. The concept of comparative advantage involves producing a good or service at a _____ _____ _____ than another.

14. The major benefit of specialization is _____ wealth.

ANSWERS

14. increased
10. exchange 11. Voluntary; beneficial 12. absolute 13. lower opportunity cost
6. direct 7. production possibilities; maximum 8. rises 9. nonlinear
1. scarcity 2. choice 3. highest; different 4. trade-off 5. downward

● ANSWERS TO CHAPTER PREVIEW QUESTIONS

1. Many people argue that college education is so important for our nation that it should be provided free of charge. Can college education ever be truly free?

The individual student can receive a "free" education only in one sense of the word *free*. That sense is zero tuition and fees. Suppose you were given a college education without having to pay any fees whatsoever. You could say you were receiving free education. On the other hand, someone is paying for your education because you are using scarce resources—the use of buildings, professors' time, electricity for lighting, and so on. The opportunity cost of your education is certainly not zero, so in that sense, it is nowhere near being free.

Additionally, by going to college you are giving up the ability to earn income during that time period. Therefore, there is an opportunity cost to your attending classes and studying. You can approximate that opportunity cost by estimating what your after-tax income would be if you were working instead of going to school.

2. When you look at your income, you know that you can't suddenly have more of everything at any one point in time. But can the United States as a country be different? Can this nation have more spending on defense, or more spending on social programs, or more spending on foreign aid, without sacrifices in other programs?

The scarcity constraint affects not just you, but the United States as a country and the United States government also. Indeed, the scarcity constraint affects the entire world. It is impossible for the United States to spend more on military defense and not spend less on other things. The famous trade-off between guns and butter actually exists at every point in time. The same decisions that you have to make about what to do with your limited resources have to be made at the national level. When a politician says, "We can do it," meaning that we can have more of everything, that politician is simply expending hot air—not information. (Of course, we can have more of everything through economic growth. Economic

24

growth represents an increase outward, or a shift outward, in the nation's production possibilities curve.)

● PROBLEMS

1. Estimate as best you can the cost of going to college for one full year. Make sure you specify the costs that you think are important.

2. Consider the following situation:

Daily work effort	Ms. Smith
4 hours	8 videocassettes
4 hours	12 video discs

Daily work effort	Mr. Smith
4 hours	8 videocassettes
4 hours	12 video discs

Total daily output = 16 videocassettes, 24 video discs

Given the above information, answer the following questions:
   a. Who has an absolute advantage in videocassette production?
   b. Who has a comparative advantage in video disc production?
   c. Will Ms. and Mr. Smith specialize?
   d. If they specialize, what will total output equal?

● SELECTED REFERENCES

Crouch, Robert. *Human Behavior: An Economic Approach*. North Scituate, Mass.: Duxbury Press, 1979.

Galbraith, John Kenneth, and Nicole Salinger. *Almost Everyone's Guide to Economics*. Boston: Houghton Mifflin, 1978.

Lekachman, Robert. *Economists at Bay*. New York: McGraw-Hill, 1976.

Pohl, F. "The Midas Plague." *Spectrum: A Science Fiction Anthology*, ed. K. Amis and R. Conquest. New York: Harcourt, Brace, & World, 1962, pp. 13–67.

2

Demand
and
Supply

Chapter Preview
1. You are shopping for a microcomputer. A new one, able to perform twice as many functions as currently available models, has just been introduced. However, it costs substantially more. Should you wait awhile before you buy this particular microcomputer?
2. The price of ordinary table salt has just fallen. How much more will you buy?

● KEY TERMS

Absolute price	Price inelasticity
Complements	Purchasing power
Demand	Quantity demanded
Demand curve	Real income effect
Demand schedule	Relative price
Equilibrium	Shortage
Inferior goods	Substitutes
Law of demand	Substitution effect
Law of diminishing returns	Supply
Law of supply	Supply curve
Normal goods	Supply schedule
Price elastic demand and supply	Surplus
Price elasticity	

Many consumers believe that owners of businesses merely have to raise their prices when they want to increase their profits. However, the profit system isn't that simple. Raising prices usually discourages people from buying more of an item. Lowering prices, on the other hand, can have the opposite effect, and owners of businesses often sell more by reducing prices.

In this chapter, you will see that at various times business decision makers can increase their overall profit by lowering price, because at a lower price buyers purchase more.

● DEMAND AS AN ECONOMIST SEES IT

Most people refer to the "demand" for a product as if they were talking about a specific quantity of that product. They remark that last year there was a demand for 7 million automobiles, or that employers in Anytown, U.S.A., had a demand for only 50,000 laborers.

Economists don't think of demand as a specific quantity. To an economist, **demand** is a relationship between various prices and the **quantity demanded** at each of these prices, other things held constant. In other words, demand refers to a *set* of price-quantity pairs, not the specific quantity demanded at a specific price. When an economist hears of a demand for a particular product, he or she thinks about the range of quantities demanded corresponding to a range of prices for that product.

There are several points that we should explain about the definition of demand that appears in the margin:

1. *Per unit of time* implies that since the quantity of anything demanded in one day is different from the quantity demanded in one

Demand

A relationship showing a set of intentions indicating various quantities that buyers will purchase voluntarily at each of various different prices, per unit of time, all other things held constant.

Quantity demanded

A specific numerical quantity demanded per unit time period, at a specific price.

28

month or one year, it is important to be consistent about time periods when talking about demand.

2. *All other things held constant* means that we are not immediately concerned about any of the other factors in the world that might affect quantity demanded; we are solely concerned about how the quantity demanded is affected by changes in price, and nothing else.

● THE LAW OF DEMAND

Demand, then, is a concept involving quantities demanded at various prices. The distinction between demand and quantity demanded is very important. Demand relates to an entire possible range of price-quantity pairs, whereas quantity demanded is a specific number, such as 1000 bushels of wheat per month, or 400 shirts per week, or 10,000 hot dogs per year. The relationship between the quantity demanded and the price that people must pay for goods and services is given by the **law of demand**. The law of demand can be stated as follows:

At higher prices, a lower quantity will be demanded than at lower prices, all other things being equal.

Or, looked at another way:

At lower prices, a higher quantity will be demanded than at higher prices, all other things being equal.

Recall our discussion of inverse relationships in Chapter 1. The law of demand is an inverse relationship between quantity demanded and price. Economists maintain that individuals respond to price changes. When a price does change, buyers will change the amount they want to purchase in the opposite direction of the price change.

Now, of course, the law of demand doesn't mean that if the price of pizzas goes up by two cents, each *individual* pizza buyer will reduce the quantity of pizza demanded. At the individual level, the law of demand has to be stated a little more loosely. For the individual, the law of demand would be as follows:

At some higher price, the quantity demanded will fall; at some lower price, the quantity demanded will increase.

Law of demand

Price and quantity demanded are *inversely* related. A change in price, other things held constant, leads to an opposite change in the quantity demanded per unit of time.

● WHY WE OBSERVE THE LAW OF DEMAND

There are two main reasons why the quantity demanded of a good is inversely related to its price, other things held constant: the

29

real income effect and the substitution effect. We'll look at each of these in turn.

The Real Income Effect

Suppose you have an income of $100.00 per week and you spend $10.00 per week on hamburgers. The remaining $90.00 is spent on other goods and services. If the price of each hamburger is $1.00, then you can purchase 10 hamburgers per week.

Now, what happens if the price of hamburgers falls to $0.75 each this week? If your income remains at $100.00 and if there's no change in the prices of all the other goods and services that you purchase, what will happen? Clearly, if you continue to purchase the *identical* bundle of goods and services that you purchased last week, you will have income left over. You would still be spending $90.00 a week on other goods and services because their prices have not changed. On the other hand, if you still purchase 10 hamburgers, you will discover that your total expenditure on hamburgers is now only $7.50 ($0.75 per hamburger times 10 hamburgers). Your total expenditure on all goods and services is now only $97.50. Thus, you have an extra $2.50 to spend. That same weekly income of $100.00 now has a greater **purchasing power**. Why? Because the price of hamburgers has fallen, while all other prices have remained constant.

What will you do with the extra $2.50 per week? Normally, you would spend at least part of it. You might even purchase more hamburgers.

Our conclusion is that if the price of hamburgers falls, while money income and the prices of all other goods and services remain the same, you might purchase more hamburgers per week. In short, a reduction in the price of hamburgers leads to an increase in the weekly quantity demanded for hamburgers because *purchasing power rises*. Economists refer to this phenomenon as the **real income effect**. Note that in our example money income remains constant at $100.00 per week, but real income (purchasing power) increases.

Of course, an increase in price, other things held constant, will cause a reduction in real income or purchasing power. As a consequence, an increase in the price of hamburgers, other things constant, will probably lead to a reduction in the quantity demanded of hamburgers.

The Substitution Effect

Let's suppose you still have $100.00 of weekly income. As before, the price of hamburgers falls from $1.00 to $0.75 and you have $2.50 extra to spend. But now the government decides that the extra $2.50 a week would be a good source of tax revenue. If you are taxed ex-

Purchasing power

The ability to consume real goods and services, generally measured by how much you can buy in real things with your money income.

Real income effect

When the price of one commodity falls, other things held constant, people experience an increase in their purchasing power. As a result, they may purchase more of the good whose price has fallen. Conversely, if the price of a good rises, other things held constant, people will feel poorer and they may purchase less of that good.

30

actly $2.50 per week, the increase in your real income will be exactly taxed away. How many hamburgers will you purchase weekly under these circumstances?

Economists would say that even though you no longer experience the effect of an increase in real income, you will still purchase more hamburgers per week, because the price of hamburgers has fallen from $1.00 to $0.75. Why?

It all has to do with comparison and substitution among alternative uses of your limited money income. Suppose that the price of hot dogs is $0.50. When the price of hamburgers was $1.00, hamburgers were twice as expensive as hot dogs. The opportunity cost of one hamburger was two hot dogs. Now that the price of hamburgers has fallen to $0.75, however, hamburgers are only 1.5 times more expensive than hot dogs. The opportunity cost of hamburgers is only one-and-a-half hot dogs. One hamburger now requires a sacrifice of only one-and-a-half hot dogs.

As a result, hamburgers have become *relatively* cheaper with respect to hot dogs, and hot dogs have become relatively more expensive with respect to hamburgers. Note that even though the **absolute price** of hot dogs remains constant, the **relative price** of hot dogs has increased. When the price of hamburgers was $1.00, a hot dog cost you one-half of a hamburger. Since the price of a hamburger has fallen to $0.75, one hot dog now costs you two-thirds of a hamburger. Table 2–1 demonstrates this change in relative price. This phenomenon is known as the **substitution effect**. Like the real income effect, the substitution effect works both ways—increases

TABLE 2–1
Change in Relative Price of Hamburgers and Hot Dogs

Hot dogs remain priced at $0.50 apiece. The price of hamburgers starts out at $1.00 and then falls to $0.75. Here's what happens to absolute and relative prices.

ABSOLUTE PRICE		RELATIVE PRICE
Before Price Change		
Hamburger	$1.00	$\dfrac{\$1.00}{\$0.50}$ = 2 hot dogs
Hot dog	$0.50	$\dfrac{\$0.50}{\$1.00}$ = ½ hamburger
After Price Change		
Hamburger	$0.75	$\dfrac{\$0.75}{\$0.50}$ = 1½ hot dogs
Hot dog	$0.50	$\dfrac{\$0.50}{\$0.75}$ = ⅔ hamburger

Absolute price
The market price given to each of the goods and services available for your purchase.

Relative price
The price of a good expressed in terms of the price of another good.

Substitution effect
A situation in which a reduction in the price of one good, holding all other prices constant, leads to an increase in the quantity demanded for the good whose price has fallen. This occurs because people will substitute the relatively cheaper good for the relatively more expensive good.

and decreases in price. If the price of hamburgers rises, other things held constant, people will substitute more hot dogs for hamburgers and the quantity demanded of hamburgers will fall.

● THE DEMAND SCHEDULE

To demonstrate the law of demand, let's take a hypothetical case: the demand for videocassette recorders (VCRs) in Anytown, U.S.A. Table 2–2 presents a hypothetical **demand schedule**. The table shows that as the price of VCRs gets lower and lower, buyers in Anytown intend to purchase more and more of them. Remember, this is a schedule of intended, or planned, purchases per unit of time at various prices. Obviously, the inhabitants of Anytown could not simultaneously purchase 50 VCRs at $1600 apiece and 80 VCRs at $1000 apiece. In any event, an inverse relationship exists between price and annual quantity demanded, other things held constant. As price gets lower, some individuals who couldn't afford a VCR will now be able to purchase one (the real income effect). Moreover, at lower and lower prices, people are encouraged to substitute the services of a VCR for other forms of entertainment (the substitution effect).

The Demand Curve. The information presented in Table 2–2 can be translated graphically, as is done in Graph 2–1. Combinations A through F are shown as points *A* through *F* on the graph. These points are connected with a straight line. This straight line is a graphic representation of a **demand curve** and is negatively sloped.

● DETERMINANTS OF DEMAND

Demand schedule

A set of pairs of numbers showing possible prices and the quantities demanded at each price. In other words, it shows the rate of planned purchase per time period at different prices of the good.

Demand curve

A graphic representation of a demand schedule that is a negatively sloped line showing the inverse relationship between price and the quantity demanded, other things held constant.

The law of demand explicitly relates the quantity demanded to price. But what about *nonprice* determinants of demand? So far, all other things have been held constant while we looked at the simple relationship between price and quantity demanded. However, other things do change, such as population and income. Changes in these nonprice determinants of demand will move the demand schedule in Graph 2–1 either outward to the right, or inward to the left. Economists certainly don't believe that price is the only factor that determines how much of an item buyers will purchase during a given time period. The number of hamburgers that people in Anytown will purchase every week will depend on nonprice influences also. Briefly, these nonprice influences are as follows:

1. Money income
2. Tastes and preferences

32

TABLE 2–2
A Hypothetical Demand Schedule for VCRs

Here are six price–quantity pairs, combinations A through F. The second column shows the various prices per VCR, and the third column shows the annual quantity demanded, other things held constant.

COMBINATION (1)	PRICE PER VCR (2)	YEARLY QUANTITY DEMANDED (3)
A	$1600	50
B	1400	60
C	1200	70
D	1000	80
E	800	90
F	600	100

GRAPH 2–1
The Demand Curve for VCRs

The inverse relationship between price and quantity demanded, other things held constant, translates into a downward-sloping (from left to right) demand curve.

As price falls, other things held constant, people feel richer and the real income effect encourages them to purchase more VCRs. Moreover, as the price of VCRs falls, other prices held constant, the substitution effect emerges. That is, as VCRs become relatively cheaper, people will substitute them for other types of entertainment which become relatively more expensive.

Conversely, as the price of VCRs rises, the quantity demanded will fall.

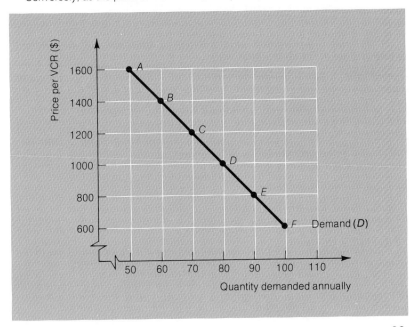

3. Prices of related goods
4. Expectations about future relative prices
5. Population

Money Income

For most goods, increased money income (other things held constant) leads to an increase in demand. The phrase *increase in demand* always refers to a comparison between two *different* demand curves. If the money income levels of people in Anytown fall, we predict that the annual quantity demanded of VCRs will fall even if price does not change. The demand curve for VCRs shown in Graph 2–1 will shift inward to the left. Conversely, if the money income levels of people in Anytown rise, the annual quantity demanded of VCRs will increase. The new demand curve will shift to the right of the curve shown in the graph. Goods for which the demand increases when income increases are called **normal goods**. Most goods are "normal" in this sense. However, there are some goods for which demand decreases as income increases. These are called **inferior goods**. Potatoes might be an example. You may currently purchase large amounts of potatoes and macaroni dinners. As your income increases, however, rather than purchasing even more, you may shift to steaks. (The terms *normal* and *inferior* are merely part of the economist's jargon—no value judgments are associated with them.)

Tastes and Preferences

A change in consumer tastes in favor of a good can shift the demand curve for that good outward to the right. When Frisbees became the rage, the demand curve for them shifted to the right; when the rage died out, the demand curve shifted inward to the left. Fashions depend to a large extent on tastes and preferences. Generally, economists have little to say about the determination of tastes; that is, they aren't concerned about why people buy one brand of a product rather than another.

Prices of Related Goods: Substitutes and Complements

Normal goods

Goods for which demand increases as income increases.

Inferior goods

Goods for which demand decreases as income increases.

Demand schedules are always drawn with the prices of all other commodities held constant. That is, it is assumed that only the price of the good under study changes. For example, when we draw the demand curve for butter, it is assumed that the price of margarine is held constant. When we draw the demand curve for tennis

34

rackets, it is assumed that the price of tennis balls is held constant. When we refer to *related goods*, we are talking about those goods whose demand is interdependent. In other words, if a change in the price of one good shifts the demand for another good, those two goods are related.

There are two types of related goods: **substitutes** and **complements**. Substitutes and complements are distinguished in terms of how the change in price of one commodity affects the demand for its related commodity.

Consider butter and margarine. Generally, butter and margarine are considered substitutes. Let's assume that each originally costs $1.00 per pound. If the price of butter remains the same and the price of margarine falls to $0.50 per pound, people will buy more margarine and less butter. The demand curve for butter will shift inward to the left. If, on the other hand, the price of margarine rises to $2.00 per pound, people will buy more butter and less margarine. The demand curve for butter will shift outward to the right. In other words, an increase in the price of margarine leads to an increase in the demand for butter. Thus, for substitutes, a price change in the substitute will cause a change in the same direction in the demand for the good under study.

With complementary goods, the situation is reversed. Consider tennis rackets and tennis balls. The demand curve for tennis rackets is derived with the price of tennis balls held constant. If the price of tennis balls decreases from $3.00 a can to $2.00 a can, that will encourage more people to take up tennis, and they will now buy more rackets, at any given price, than before. The demand curve for tennis rackets will shift outward to the right. If the price of tennis balls increases from $3.00 a can to $4.00 a can, fewer people will play tennis. The demand curve for tennis rackets will shift inward to the left. A decrease in the price of tennis balls leads to an increase in the demand for rackets. An increase in the price of tennis balls leads to a decrease in the demand for rackets. Tennis rackets and tennis balls are thus said to be complementary goods. The relationship between prices of related goods is shown in Exhibit 2–1.

Expectations about Future Relative Prices

If expectations changed and the people of Anytown believed that the price of VCRs was going to fall next week, they would buy fewer VCRs now at a given price than they would otherwise. They would wait for the lower price. In general, if a rise in the future relative price of a good is expected, then, all other things held constant, people will buy more now. Conversely, the expectation that the future relative price of a good will decrease leads to a decrease in demand today.

Substitutes

Pairs of goods for which an increase in the price of one causes an increase in the demand for the other.

Complements

Pairs of goods for which an increase in the price of one causes a decrease in the demand for the other.

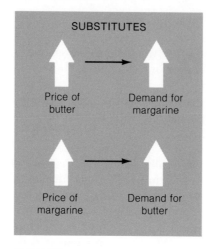
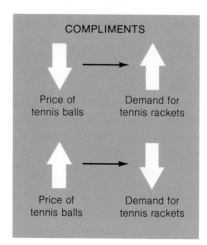

EXHIBIT 2–1
Related Goods

Related goods consist of substitutes and complements. When the price of one good goes up and the demand for the other goes up too, we are dealing with substitutes. When the price of one good goes up and the demand for the other falls, we are dealing with complements.

Population

Usually an increase in the population of an economy (holding per capita income constant) shifts the market demand rightward for most products. This is because an increase in population leads to an increase in the number of buyers in the market. Conversely, a reduction in the population will shift most demand curves leftward because of the reduction in the number of buyers in the market. An example of the impact of a change in the number of consumers in a market is the effect of birth rates on the baby-food industry. As birth rates dropped in the United States, firms dealing in baby food began to diversify. They moved into other fields because of an anticipated shift inward (to the left) in the market demand curve for their product.

● CHANGE IN DEMAND VERSUS CHANGE IN QUANTITY DEMANDED

The distinction between a change in demand and a change in quantity demanded is so important that it is worth reviewing.

A change in quantity demanded is represented graphically as a movement *along a given demand curve*. Nonprice determinants do not change; only price changes. Hence, a change in quantity demanded results exclusively from price changes.

Since the entire demand schedule is represented by a curve on our graph, a change in demand must refer to a change *in the whole curve*. For example, if income increases, we expect an increase in demand. An increase in demand means that the quantity demanded will be greater at each and every price. Graphically, as stated before, an increase in demand means that the entire demand curve will shift outward to the right.

Similarly, if tastes change, causing people to buy less of a commodity than previously, there is a decrease in demand for that commodity. Since quantity demanded will now be less at each and every price, a decrease in demand will be represented by a demand curve to the *left* of the original one. Graph 2–2 shows the difference between a change in quantity demanded and a change in demand.

● SUPPLY AS AN ECONOMIST SEES IT

Supply can be analyzed in much the same manner as demand. The theory of supply is concerned with how *sellers* behave. When

GRAPH 2–2
Change in Quantity Demanded versus Change in Demand

(a) This graph shows a change in quantity demanded. If price P rises from P_B to P_A (other things held constant), quantity demanded, Q, will decrease from Q_B to Q_A. If price falls from P_B to P_C (other things held constant), then quantity demanded will increase from Q_B to Q_C.

(b) This graph demonstrates changes in demand. The shift from demand curve D to D' indicates an increase in demand, resulting from, let's say, an increase in population. The shift from D to D'' reflects a decrease in demand, perhaps resulting from a change in tastes *away* from the commodity in question.

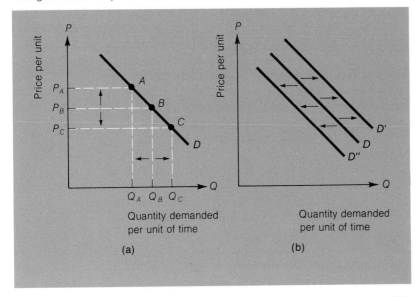

(a)   (b)

Supply
A set of intentions indicating each quantity that sellers will offer voluntarily at each different price per unit of time, all other things held constant.

37

discussing demand, we are concerned with the behavior of *buyers*.

The relationship between various prices and the quantity that sellers intend to offer for sale at each of these prices can be predicted. Again, we are holding constant all the nonprice determinants of the quantity supplied in order to focus our attention on the relationship between price and quantity supplied. Just as we defined demand as a set of intentions, or planned purchase rates, depending on price, we can define supply as a set of intentions that suppliers have—planned rates of quantity supplied at various prices.

● THE LAW OF SUPPLY

Simply stated, the **law of supply** is as follows:

At higher prices, a larger quantity will generally be supplied than at lower prices, all other things held constant.

Or, stated differently,

At lower prices, a smaller quantity will generally be supplied than at higher prices, all other things held constant.

A direct relationship exists between quantity supplied and price. (Recall our discussion of direct relationships in Chapter 1.) Contrast the law of supply—a direct relationship—with the law of demand—an inverse relationship. Basically, producers are willing to produce and sell more of their product at a higher price than at a lower price, other things held constant. The question, of course, is why.

For one thing, if a business is producing several products, it will have an incentive to produce more of that product whose price has increased, and less of those products for which price has not changed. Thus, producers substitute; they allocate more resources to the production of the relatively higher-priced good, and fewer to the relatively lower-priced good. For example, oil refiners have the option of distilling crude oil into either heating oil or gasoline. If the price of gasoline rises, they will convert more of the crude oil into gasoline and less into heating oil. Clearly, the opposite would occur if the price of heating oil rose while the price of gasoline remained constant.

Considering one product in isolation, the higher the price fetched in the marketplace, the more costs a producer could incur and still make a profit. Remember the law of increasing relative cost discussed in Chapter 1? At higher rates of output for a particular product, after some point, it costs more and more to produce an additional unit of that good. Only if the price obtained in the marketplace goes up will the producer be willing to incur this higher cost of production in order to produce more.

Law of supply

There is a direct relationship between price and quantity supplied, all other things held constant.

38

● A SLIGHT DIGRESSION—
THE LAW OF DIMINISHING RETURNS

The discussion of why there is a direct relationship between price and quantity supplied touched on an important aspect of production—the **law of diminishing returns**:

> After some output rate, it will cost more to produce extra units of the good in question.

The concept of diminishing returns applies to many different situations. If you put one seat belt over your lap, a certain amount of additional safety is obtained. If you add another seat belt, more safety is obtained, but the *additional* safety is less than what you gained when the first belt was secured. When you add a third seat belt, the amount of additional safety obtained must be even smaller. In a similar way, Winston Churchill apparently believed that there were diminishing returns to dropping more and more bombs on German steel mills during World War II; later bombs, he thought, merely moved about the wreckage from prior bombs.

The same analysis holds for firms in their use of productive inputs. The returns from hiring more and more workers diminish after some point. Consider a firm that has a certain amount of land, equipment, and buildings. It has now decided to add more workers. In other words, in this example all of the factors of production are held constant except labor, which is considered a variable factor. Beyond some point, the additional product from each additional unit of labor will decrease. *Diminishing returns* merely refers to a situation in which output rises proportionately less than an increase in, say, the number of workers employed.

The law of diminishing returns certainly can be applied to study time. During the first several hours of study, each additional hour may produce increasing amounts of knowledge, as the material you are studying starts to come together and make more sense. After some point, however, you become tired. Each additional hour of study is less productive than the previous hour. Diminishing returns have set in.

● BACK TO SUPPLY—
THE SUPPLY SCHEDULE

Table 2–3 presents a hypothetical **supply schedule** indicating the relationship between various prices of VCRs and the quantities that suppliers will produce voluntarily at each price.

The Supply Curve. Graph 2–3 translates Table 2–3 into graphic form. As you might expect, the direct relationship between price

Law of diminishing returns

As additional units of a variable factor of production are added to fixed factors, after some point the additional output from each additional unit of the variable factor decreases.

Supply schedule

A set of numbers showing various prices and the quantity supplied at each of those prices. It shows the rate of planned production at each price per specified time period.

TABLE 2–3
Hypothetical Supply Schedule for VCRs

This schedule shows the pairs of prices and quantities supplied for VCRs. It represents the hypothetical planned production rates at various prices.

COMBINATION (1)	PRICE PER VCR (2)	YEARLY QUANTITY SUPPLIED (3)
G	$ 600	60
H	800	70
I	1000	80
J	1200	90
K	1400	100
L	1600	110

and quantity supplied is a positively sloped curve. It is called the **supply curve**. Supply curves are normally upward sloping—from left to right.

GRAPH 2–3
Supply Curve for VCRs

This supply curve shows the direct relationship between price and quantity supplied, other things held constant. As price rises, producers will allocate resources from other uses to the production of the good in question. Moreover, as more and more resources less suited to the production of the good in question are used, the *extra* costs of producing successive units rise. As a result, higher and higher prices are required before sellers will voluntarily offer more and more units of output—VCRs in this example.

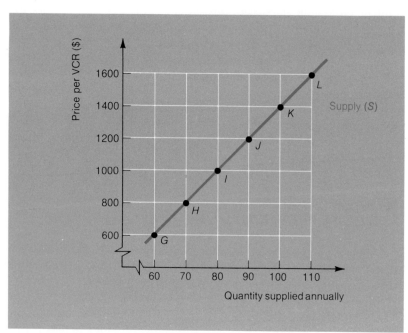

Supply curve

A graphic representation of a supply schedule that is a positively sloped line showing the direct relationship between price and quantity supplied.

40

● DETERMINANTS OF SUPPLY

Just as we analyzed what moves the demand curve, we can analyze what moves the supply curve. That is, we must consider the nonprice determinants of supply. When a supply curve is drawn, all other things are held constant. Some of those other things are as follows:

1. Input cost
2. Technology
3. Taxes and subsidies
4. Number of firms in the industry

● CHANGE IN QUANTITY SUPPLIED VERSUS CHANGE IN SUPPLY

In our analysis of demand, we saw the difference between change in demand and change in quantity demanded. Similarly, for supply, we can distinguish between movement along a given supply curve—a change in quantity supplied—and a shift in a supply curve—a change in supply.

A *change in quantity supplied* results from a change in price, other things held constant. If price rises, the quantity supplied will rise, and will be represented as a movement up a given supply curve. If price falls, the quantity supplied will fall, and will be represented as a movement down a given supply curve.

Since supply refers to the whole curve, a *change in supply* refers to a shift in the whole curve. For example, a decrease in the number of firms in the industry will mean that a smaller quantity of the product will be offered at each and every price. This decrease in supply shows up as a shift of the entire supply curve to the left.

An increase in supply could come about through a change in technology. For example, technological advances might cause a reduction in the cost of producing any output level. As a consequence, quantity supplied will be greater at any price. This will show up as a shift to the right of the entire supply curve. The difference between a change in supply and a change in quantity supplied is shown in Graph 2–4.

● HOW SUPPLY AND DEMAND DETERMINE PRICE

The price of an item will be established as a result of buyer and seller interaction. To illustrate this process, Tables 2–2 and 2–3 are combined into Table 2–4. This new table allows us to see the be-

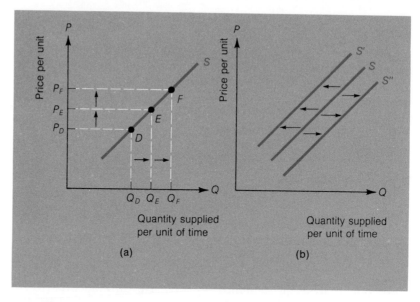

GRAPH 2–4
Change in Quantity Supplied versus Change in Supply

(a) The graph demonstrates the change in quantity supplied resulting from a change in price, other things held constant. As price changes, we move along the supply curve S. As the price increases from P_D to P_F, the quantity supplied increases from Q_D to Q_F. We move from point D to E to F on the supply curve S.

(b) This graph shows changes in supply. A decrease in supply resulting from, for example, a reduction in the number of producers is indicated by a leftward shift from S to S'. A technological improvement reducing cost to everyone is indicated by a rightward shift in the entire supply curve from S to S''.

TABLE 2–4
Putting the Demand and Supply Schedules Together

Here we combine the demand schedule from Table 2–2 with the supply schedule from Table 2–3. Column 1 shows the price; column 2, the annual quantity demanded of VCRs; and column 3, the annual quantity supplied of VCRs. Column 4 shows the difference between the quantity supplied and the quantity demanded at various prices.

PRICE PER VCR (1)	QUANTITY DEMANDED ANNUALLY (2)	QUANTITY SUPPLIED ANNUALLY (3)	QUANTITY SUPPLIED MINUS QUANTITY DEMANDED (4)
$1600	50	110	+60 (Surplus)
1400	60	100	+40 (Surplus)
1200	70	90	+20 (Surplus)
1000	80	80	0 (Equilibrium)
800	90	70	−20 (Shortage)
600	100	60	−40 (Shortage)

havior of both buyers and sellers and what they *intend to do* at different prices for VCRs. In general, when either the group of buyers or the group of sellers is *not* able to realize its intentions, it will have an incentive to change its behavior.

Surplus

Table 2–4 indicates that at a price of $1600 the quantity supplied (110) exceeds the quantity demanded (50). If the quantity supplied exceeds the quantity demanded at a given price, a **surplus** is said to exist at that price.

Let's analyze what is happening here. At the relatively high price of $1600 per VCR, buyers wish to purchase only 50 units per year. Indeed, since sellers wish to sell 110, buyers can easily realize their intentions. Buyers do not have any particular incentive to change their actions.

On the other hand, sellers *cannot* realize their intentions. They are producing 110 VCRs per year, but selling only 50. This means that every year they incur costs of production for 60 VCRs (the surplus), but they don't receive any money for them. Moreover, they must pay the storage costs for building up their VCR inventories.

The Little Matter of Profit.   For the reasons just given, sellers cannot maximize their total profits. In fact, this is a case where they could increase their profits by lowering price and producing less. Sellers competing for sales will cause price to fall. If you examine Table 2–4 again, you will see that as long as price is above $1000 sellers will find it profitable to lower price and reduce output. At any price above $1000, a surplus of VCRs would exist and price would most likely fall. Of course, the higher the price is above $1000, the greater the surplus.

Shortage

Consider a price of $600. At that price sellers find it profitable to produce and sell only 60 VCRs per year. However, buyers intend to purchase 100. This time the sellers are able to realize their intentions, but the buyers cannot.

Those buyers who *really* want VCRs will offer to pay more for them, assuring themselves of the product. As price rises, only those individuals willing to give up more of *other* goods and services will buy VCRs. The opportunity cost of purchasing VCRs rises as the price of VCRs gets higher and higher. In a sense, buyers are competing with each other for scarce VCRs.

Notice that as long as price is below $1000, a **shortage** will exist. At any price below $1000, quantity demanded exceeds quantity

Surplus

A situation that exists when the quantity supplied exceeds the quantity demanded at a specific price. This is also called an *excess quantity supplied*.

Shortage

A situation that exists when at some specific price the quantity demanded exceeds the quantity supplied.

43

supplied; this is what a shortage is all about. Of course, the lower the price is below $1000, the greater the shortage.

Equilibrium

What happens at a price of $1000? At that price, both buyers and sellers are able to realize their intentions. Quantity supplied (80) equals quantity demanded (80), and neither group has an incentive to change its behavior. **Equilibrium** is said to exist. Equilibrium does not mean happiness. Buyers would probably be happier with lower prices, assuming they could get all they wanted at that lower price. Sellers would probably be happier if prices were higher if they could sell all they wanted at the higher price. We call an equilibrium price the market-clearing price.

The determination of price and equilibrium is shown graphically in Graph 2–5, which is simply a combination of Graphs 2–1 and 2–3.

GRAPH 2–5

Supply and Demand Determine Price

This graph points out that the equilibrium price for VCRs will be established at $1000; only at that price will quantity supplied be the same as quantity demanded (80 units in this case).

At any price above $1000, quantity supplied exceeds quantity demanded, resulting in a surplus. Sellers competing for sales will find it profitable to lower price and reduce output.

At any price below $1000, quantity demanded exceeds quantity supplied, resulting in a shortage. Buyers competing for this good will bid its price upward.

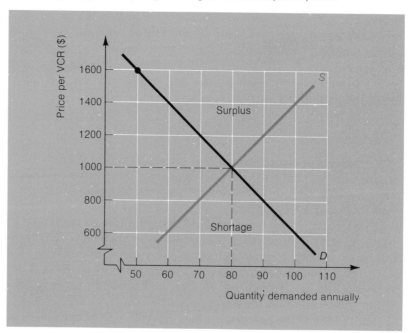

Equilibrium

A condition that exists when there is no tendency to change. Equilibrium occurs at the price at which quantity supplied equals quantity demanded. Here there is a market-clearing price.

44

The Effect on Price of Shifts in Demand and Shifts in Supply

Prices are determined by the intersection of the supply curve and the demand curve. Therefore, whenever one of these curves changes, the equilibrium price also changes. Let's look first at what happens when there is an increase in demand, and then at what happens when there is an increase in supply.

Demand Shifts.   Assume that there is an increase in income. Remember that such an increase will lead to an increase in demand, so that at any particular price the quantity demanded will be greater than it was previously. This is shown in Graph 2-6.

Demand has shifted to the right from D to D' due to the increase in income. This means that the increased demand at the old equilibrium price results in a shortage. The quantity demanded at the higher income is 120, but the quantity supplied is still 80. Buyers of VCRs cannot realize their intentions. The competition among buyers for the available VCRs will cause price to rise. A higher price will

GRAPH 2-6
An Increase in Demand Causes Price to Rise

An increase in income has caused demand for VCRs to increase. This causes a rightward shift in the demand curve, from D to D'. Notice that at the original equilibrium price of $1000, quantity demanded (120) exceeds quantity supplied and a shortage exists. Buyers competing for recorders will bid price upward, and the higher price will encourage sellers to increase the quantity supplied. The end result is that the equilibrium position moves from A to B. At B, price is higher and so is quantity supplied.

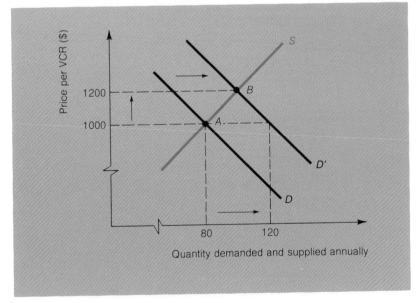

then induce sellers to increase their annual quantity supplied. The equilibrium moves from point *A* to point *B*. At point *B*, the equilibrium price and quantity supplied are higher than they were at point *A*.

Supply Shifts.   Suppose a change in technology occurs such that it is now cheaper to produce every VCR. This means that producers will voluntarily want to produce more at each and every possible price they can obtain in the marketplace. An increase in technology therefore leads to an increase in supply. The supply curve will shift to the right. This is shown in Graph 2–7. Note that the supply curve has shifted rightward from *S* to *S'*. At the old equilibrium price of $1000, a surplus of VCRs now exists. Buyers still want to purchase 80 VCRs a year, but at a price of $1000 sellers want to sell 110 VCRs.

The change in technology has lowered production costs, and sellers, competing for sales, must encourage buyers to purchase more. Sellers can do so by offering a lower price. Price will continue to fall until quantity supplied and quantity demanded are again equated. This will occur at point *E*. At point *E*, at a price of $800 per VCR, the equilibrium quantity is greater compared to what it was at point *C*.

GRAPH 2–7
An Increase in Supply Causes Price to Fall

Here we show the results of a technological breakthrough. Technological changes cause production costs to fall and supply to increase. In order to encourage buyers to buy more, sellers lower price. Note that a technological change normally makes it *profitable* for sellers to lower price and produce more. Equilibrium moves from point *C* to point *E*; at point *E*, price is lower and quantity supplied is higher than at point *C*.

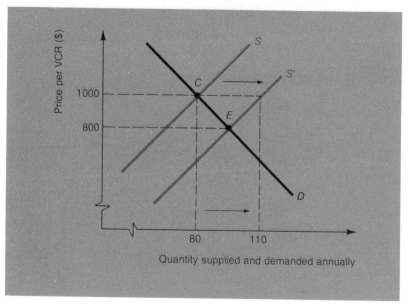

● PRICE RESPONSIVENESS

Just stating the law of demand and the law of supply tells us only one thing: Consumers and producers *respond* to changes in prices. But by how much? That is the subject matter of this section. We want to determine a way to measure the degree to which consumers and producers respond to changes in prices. It's not enough to know that when there is a 10 percent increase in price, the quantity demanded falls and the quantity supplied rises. We want to know how much the quantity demanded rises and how much the quantity supplied falls.

The concept used to measure price responsiveness is **price elasticity**, defined as the measurement of the degree of responsiveness shown by a buyer or a seller to a particular price change.

Price Unresponsiveness

If a given change in price leads to virtually no change in either quantity demanded or quantity supplied, the situation is one of relative **price inelasticity**. Consider an example. If the price of salt goes up by 10 percent, will you change your quantity demanded per year by very much? Probably not. You have a relatively inelastic demand for salt. As another example, suppose that the price of Rembrandt paintings rises dramatically. How many more paintings will be supplied? Virtually none, unless lost paintings are discovered. After all, the total quantity supplied of Rembrandt paintings in existence cannot change. This example demonstrates a very inelastic supply of the product in question.

Strong Responsiveness

On the other end of the spectrum of price elasticities are those called **price elastic demand and supply**. If a 10 percent increase in the price of Coke (all other prices held constant) leads you to reduce your quantity demanded substantially (perhaps because you shift to Pepsi or Seven-Up), then you have a very price elastic demand for Coke. Consider a supply example. If a 1 percent increase in the price of ball-point pens induces suppliers to produce 50 percent more, then supply is definitely price elastic.[1]

Price elasticity

A measurement of the responsiveness of quantity demanded or supplied to a change in price.

Price inelasticity

A relatively weak responsiveness to a price change.

Price elastic demand and supply

Demand and supply exhibiting strong responses to price changes.

---

[1]The arithmetic way to measure price elasticity is to divide the percentage change in quantity by the percentage change in price. A measure of the price elasticity of demand is therefore derived by looking at percentage changes in the quantity demanded; price elasticity of supply is derived by dividing the percentage change in the quantity supplied by the percentage change in price.

47

Price Should Always Be Set at a Market-Clearing Level

THE ARGUMENT

Given supply and demand curves, it can be seen that price will eventually be set at market-clearing (equilibrium) levels. At any other price, a shortage or a surplus will exist, and buyers or sellers will adjust their behavior until market-clearing levels are established. Some individuals, however, have expressed the belief that market-clearing levels are sometimes too high (e.g., gasoline or natural gas), or too low (e.g., unskilled labor), and that a fair price would be more desirable.

THE ANALYSIS

When prices are not allowed to clear markets, shortages or surpluses will result, creating a new set of problems. Whenever a good seems to be "in short supply" and therefore is selling at "too high" a price, mandating a lower price that is "fairer" does not eliminate the problem of scarcity. Some method of rationing every scarce commodity must still be found. Allowing prices to seek their own level—that determined by supply and demand—does have certain advantages. When a good becomes relatively scarcer and its price is allowed to increase, this will lead to an increase in production, as well as voluntary conservation of the scarce commodity. Additionally, a higher price today for a relatively scarce item may lead to a larger number of firms entering the industry in the future, thereby reducing the "problem" somewhat.

Obviously, from a societal point of view, simply letting people "vote with their dollars" causes a problem. Wealthier individuals will be able to buy whatever they want, but poorer individuals will not. If prices go to their market-clearing levels all the time, one is bound to eliminate many individuals with few or no votes (poor people) from the marketplace. This problem is not insignificant, but it really has to do with the way income is distributed among individuals and families in our country. Prices that are set by supply and demand indicate to people the relative scarcity of different goods and services. If the body politic believes that certain low-income individuals are not able to purchase critical items because of the high prices of those items, then this becomes an argument for giving more income to the less-advantaged individuals in question, and not for disallowing prices to clear markets.

Finally, the concept of fairness is indeed a difficult one for an economist to treat. There is no economic definition of fairness, to be sure. Nor is there a set of criteria that will tell the economist which prices are too high and which prices are too low. There are millions, if not billions, of different goods and services that are sold in one year in this country. How does one decide which of those goods and services should be culled for special attention?

DISCUSSION QUESTIONS

1. Can you come up with a definition of fairness?
2. Why do we even have to think about the prices at which goods and services *should* be sold?

● WHAT'S AHEAD

Now that you have learned how demand and supply determine price, in the following chapter we will show what happens when price is not allowed to adjust to changes in demand and/or changes in supply. You will now enter the real world of shortages and surpluses.

● CHAPTER SUMMARY

The relationship between quantity demanded and price is given by the law of demand, which states that at some higher price quantity demanded will fall and at some lower price quantity demanded will rise. Basically, the law of demand exists because, as price changes, both a real income effect and a substitution effect occur. The law of demand, however, is stated holding all nonprice determinants of demand constant. These determinants are income, tastes and preferences, prices of related goods (substitutes and complements), expectations about future relative price, and population. Whenever any of these nonprice determinants changes, the entire demand curve will shift to the right (an increase) or to the left (a decrease).

The law of supply states that, generally, at higher prices greater quantities will be forthcoming than at lower prices. The law of supply is stated holding the nonprice determinants of supply constant, such as input costs, technology, taxes and subsidies, and the number of firms in the industry. A change in price (other things held constant) will cause a movement along the supply curve. Any change in the nonprice determinants just mentioned will cause a shift in the supply curve rightward (an increase) or leftward (a decrease).

When one puts the supply and demand schedules or curves together, the equilibrium price can be found. Equilibrium occurs when quantity supplied equals quantity demanded, and there is no incentive for either buyers or sellers to change their behavior. If demand does not change, but supply increases, a lower equilibrium price will occur. If demand remains the same, but supply decreases, a greater equilibrium price will occur. If supply remains the same, an increase in demand will lead to a higher price; a decrease in demand will lead to a lower price.

Price responsiveness is measured by the price elasticity of either demand or supply. When sellers and buyers are relatively unresponsive to changes in prices, supply and demand are said to be price inelastic. When sellers and buyers are relatively responsive to changes in prices, supply and demand are said to be relatively price elastic.

49

● QUESTIONS FOR REVIEW AND STUDY

1. When the price of a good goes up, the quantity demanded will _____ because of the _____ _____ effect and the _____ effect.

2. The _____ relationship between price and quantity demanded is called the _____ _____.

3. When the price of an item changes, there is a change in _____; when anything else relevant changes, there is a change in _____.

4. Three of the nonprice determinants of demand are _____, _____, and _____.

5. When money income and the price of other goods remain the same, a price reduction in one good will _____ your purchasing power; this is called the _____ income _____.

6. People tend to substitute cheaper goods for more expensive ones. This is called the _____ _____.

7. When population, money income, or wealth increase, this shifts the _____ curve _____.

8. A decrease in demand is shown by a _____ movement of the demand curve.

9. The _____ relationship between quantity supplied and price is called the _____ _____ _____.

10. Some nonprice determinants of supply are _____, _____, and _____.

11. On the supply side of the picture, a price change alters the _____ _____, whereas a nonprice change alters _____.

12. A reduction in input prices will lead to a _____ movement of the supply curve.

13. Surpluses exist because the price is set _____ the _____ price.

14. Shortages exist whenever the price is set _____ the _____ price.

15. If demand doesn't change, but supply increases, the price will _____.

16. If supply doesn't change, but demand increases, the price will _____.

17. Whenever demanders or suppliers are insensitive to price changes, we say that supply and demand are _____.

(For answers see top of facing page)

ANSWERS

● ANSWERS TO CHAPTER PREVIEW QUESTIONS

1. *You are shopping for a microcomputer. A new one, able to perform twice as many functions as currently available models, has just been introduced. However, it costs substantially more. Should you wait awhile before you buy this particular microcomputer?*

Ignoring the problem of technical "bugs" in newly introduced products, there may be a good economic reason for you to wait awhile to purchase the new microcomputer. Most popular items introduced by one manufacturer are quickly more or less copied by other manufacturers. That means that the supply will increase (the supply curve will move outward to the right). Certainly, if the demand remains stable (the demand curve doesn't move), the price of the new microcomputer will fall when new suppliers enter the market. Of course, it is possible that the demand for such a microcomputer will rise. Historically, with such products, the supply has increased *faster* than the demand, and the result has been a *reduction* in price. For example, when pocket calculators were first introduced, they cost $400 or $500, and even more. Today, you can buy a pocket calculator that performs the same functions as the expensive ones, but costs only $10 or $20 — and is one-tenth the size to boot.

2. *The price of ordinary table salt has just fallen. How much more will you buy?*

Chances are that even if the price of table salt falls dramatically, you won't buy too much more. Table salt takes up a very small part of anyone's total budget. Thus, when the price falls, and you continue to purchase the same amount, you still don't have much additional spending power to buy other goods. In other words, the real income effect for table salt will be quite small. Of course, the substitution effect still holds, but there aren't many other items that you use for which salt could be a substitute. On both counts, a price decrease in table salt will not have much effect, although there will certainly be some effect on the economy as a whole. The law of demand still holds here *for all consumers taken together*. It just isn't very strong.

● PROBLEMS

1. For more than a decade, we have had periodic shortages of gasoline and heating oil. Is this because we are running out of crude oil? Or can you offer an alternative explanation using the analysis in this chapter?

2. Construct a demand curve and a supply curve for videocassettes, based on the following data:

Price per videocassette	Quantity demanded per year
$75	3 million
$50	6 million
$35	9 million
$25	12 million
$15	15 million
$10	18 million

Price per videocassette	Quantity supplied per year
$75	18 million
$50	15 million
$35	12 million
$25	9 million
$15	6 million
$10	3 million

What is the equilibrium price? What is the equilibrium quantity at that price?

● SELECTED REFERENCES

Henderson, Hubert. *Supply and Demand*. Chicago: University of Chicago Press, 1958, chap. 2.

Turvey, Ralph. *Demand and Supply*. London: Allen and Unwin, 1971.

Watson, Donald S., and Malcolm Getz. *Price Theory and Its Uses*. 5th ed. Boston: Houghton Mifflin, 1981, chap. 2.

3

The World of Shortages and Surpluses

Chapter Preview

1. There have been times when people were unable to buy as much gasoline as they wanted, and they often had to wait in long lines at the gas pumps. Why has this happened only in some years but not in others?

2. In many cities over the last decade, there have been water crises and restrictions were put on water usage. Are there alternative ways of dealing with such crises?

● KEY TERMS

Embargo   Rent control
Minimum wage rate   Wage and price controls
Price supports

One year there's not enough oil, and the next year there's talk of an oil glut. One year water is in short supply, and the next year there's a shortage of coffee. Other years bring discussions of government gifts of "surplus" cheese. And, in the labor market, there are years when many people can't find jobs—in other words, there seems to be a "surplus" of labor.

In this chapter, shortages and surpluses are analyzed—their causes and cures. You may be surprised to discover that shortages and surpluses are only *indirectly* related to *physical* availability. Usually, shortages and surpluses are the result of pricing policies imposed by the government.

● THE MEANING OF SHORTAGE

Recall from Chapter 2 that a shortage is defined as a situation in which quantity demanded exceeds quantity supplied *at a specific price*. It is important to stress "at a specific price" because the implication is that at some *higher* price, less would be demanded, more would be supplied, and presumably the shortage would disappear.

Indeed, this is precisely what normally happens. During a shortage, buyers who cannot buy as much as they want to buy at the prevailing price compete with each other for the good in short supply. They bid up its price. Those buyers who *are* willing to give up more in other goods and services get the scarce goods; those who are not willing to, do not. At the same time, quantity supplied increases because sellers have an incentive—the higher price they will be paid—to allocate more resources to producing the scarce good in question. Briefly stated, as prices rise, quantity demanded falls and quantity supplied rises until the shortage is eliminated.

Yet there have been fairly long periodic shortages in the United States. Intermittently, supposed shortages of petroleum products have occurred. There have been periodic natural gas shortages in various regions over the past 30 years or so. Why is there a disparity, then, between the predictions of economic theory—that markets eliminate shortages—and the reality we observe—prolonged shortages?

You may have guessed by now that a shortage results when the price of a good is *not allowed to rise*. Look at Graph 3–1. Assume that this graph indicates the supply and demand relationship for

54

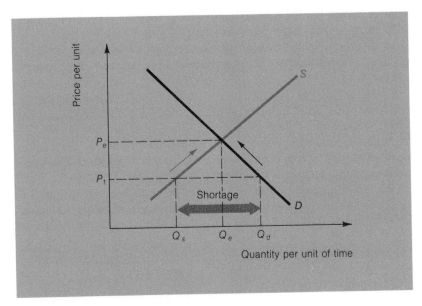

GRAPH 3–1
The Nature of a Prolonged Shortage

In this graph we depict the supply and demand for a particular commodity. The market-clearing price occurs at P_e. Suppose a law is passed forbidding producers to sell this commodity at any price above P_1. At that relatively lower price, buyers will be encouraged to want more (Q_d), but sellers will be encouraged to produce less (Q_s). A shortage will exist.

some commodity. The market-clearing, or equilibrium, price is at P_e. Assume that the government passes a law requiring the price to be at P_1 instead. Look at what happens with this price restriction. At P_1, quantity demanded (Q_d) exceeds quantity supplied (Q_s). A shortage results from this price restriction. Indeed, as long as a price is *fixed* at a limit below P_e, a shortage will exist. The farther the *legally* set price is below P_e, the *greater* the shortage.

● THE MEANING OF SURPLUS

In Chapter 2, a surplus was said to exist when quantity supplied exceeded quantity demanded *at some given price*. As with shortages, we also specified a price when we defined a surplus. Presumably, at some lower price producers would supply less, consumers would demand more, and the surplus would disappear.

Remember that when a surplus exists, sellers are producing a certain quantity per unit of time that they cannot sell completely. They are not maximizing profits. Moreover, inventories will rise,

55

causing inventory costs to rise. For these reasons—to reduce such costs, to sell what is in the warehouses, and to improve profits—suppliers competing for sales will lower prices. Note that suppliers will lower price and reduce the output rate because they will be better off.

As price falls, quantity demanded rises; buyers experience income and substitution effects (see Chapter 2). Thus, when a surplus exists, sellers will lower price and reduce quantity supplied. The lower price, however, will increase quantity demanded. The reductions in output and the increases in quantity demanded will continue until the surplus is eliminated.

If allowed to do so, markets will set market-clearing, or equilibrium, prices. In other words, a price will prevail at which consumers will buy all that is produced and they will want no more at that price.

Prolonged Surpluses

If everything just explained is true, why is it that the United States has experienced prolonged surpluses? In this country, there were large agricultural surpluses during the 1950s and 1960s. Surpluses in certain products have also occurred in the 1970s and 1980s. A surplus will result when the government sets the price *above* the equilibrium price level. Governments throughout the world do this in order to benefit the producers of the good in question. This is what government price-support programs are all about. The only way prolonged surpluses can exist at government-mandated minimum prices is for the government to buy up the surplus good in question.

Consider Graph 3–2. The market-clearing, or equilibrium, price occurs at P_e, but suppose the government sets a policy to support price at P_2. Total annual output will then be provided at Q_s. But buyers will want to purchase only Q_d at the price P_2. The difference between Q_s and Q_d is a surplus. And for the price level to continue at P_2, the government must purchase the surplus. Otherwise, producers will figure out means to rid themselves of excess inventories.

Wage and price controls

A system of government-mandated maximum prices that can be charged for different goods and services, and maximum wages that can be paid to different workers in different jobs.

Embargo

A government-imposed restriction on the shipment of a particular good or goods to specified physical locations.

● THE WORLD OF SHORTAGES: ENERGY

In August 1971, President Nixon felt compelled to fight inflation by imposing **wage and price controls**. In effect, many prices and wages were not allowed to rise—legally, at least.

Then, in 1973, the Arab members of the Organization of Petroleum Exporting Countries (OPEC) placed an **embargo** on oil going to

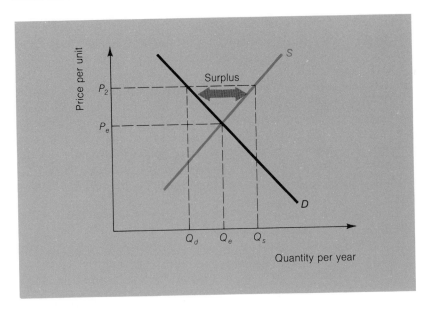

GRAPH 3–2

The Nature of a Surplus

Given supply and demand for a particular commodity, the equilibrium price will be set by the market at P_e. Suppose the government is committed to supporting price P_2 because it wants to aid suppliers in this particular industry. At price P_2 suppliers produce Q_s since that is the most profitable output rate. However, buyers intend to purchase only Q_d. The difference, $Q_s - Q_d$, is the *annual* surplus that the government must purchase in order to maintain price at P_2.

the United States and other nations. In effect, the OPEC members reduced considerably their combined production and sale of crude oil to the world. The original reason was to protest the Western world's policy vis-a-vis Israel and the Arab nations. OPEC discovered that the benefits of restricting its output and sales were higher prices and profits. The lower output produced prices and profits that were so great that OPEC members have continued to restrict output, although with varying degrees of success. In short, two events occurred simultaneously in the United States: The supply of imported oil was sharply reduced, and price–wage controls were kept in effect.

Analyzing the Shortages of Gasoline and Heating Oil

Normally when the supply of a commodity is sharply reduced and demand remains constant, price will rise. Indeed, gasoline and oil prices did rise during 1973–1974 in the rest of the world. On the other hand, in the United States price controls effectively prevented the price of oil and its distillates—gasoline and heating oil—from rising.

Graph 3–3 explains how the 1973–1974 oil shortage in the United States came about. The supply and demand for gasoline before the OPEC oil embargo can be represented by the supply curve S and the demand curve D. The equilibrium, or market-clearing, price for gas was P_e. Since the embargo meant that less oil was available to oil refiners, the decrease in the supply of oil led automatically to a decrease in the supply of gasoline. In Graph 3–3, we show this reduction in supply as a leftward shift in the supply curve from S to S'.

GRAPH 3–3

The 1973–1974 Oil Shortage Explained

The supply curve for gasoline before the OPEC oil embargo is S. Given the demand curve D, the pre-embargo market-clearing price for gasoline was P_e.

The oil embargo led to a decrease in the supply of oil to U.S. markets, which in turn led to a decrease in the supply of gasoline. We show this reduction in the supply of gasoline as a leftward shift in the supply curve from S to S'. Note that quantity supplied is less at every price than previously.

Had no price controls been in existence in the United States at that time, the price of gasoline would have risen from P_e to P_1, and the quantity demanded would have fallen to Q_e as people reduced consumption and, in time, found substitutes for gasoline. The equilibrium position would have moved from A to C, and there would have been no shortage. Since there were wage and price controls at that time, gasoline suppliers were not legally able to sell gasoline for more than P_e. At P_e, quantity demanded was still Q_e and it exceeded the reduced quantity supplied, Q_s (point B). Since quantity demanded exceeded quantity supplied, a shortage resulted at P_e.

This analysis explains why during the early 1970s shortages (and long gas station lines) existed in the United States but not elsewhere in the world, where price was not restricted.

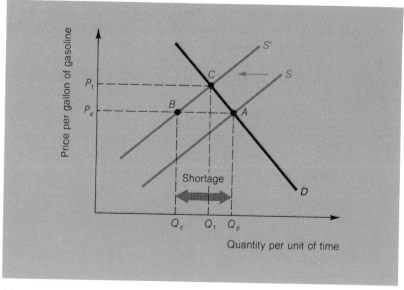

58

Because price-wage controls were in effect at the time, the legal price of gasoline was not allowed to rise above P_e. At P_e, a shortage resulted because quantity demanded was still at Q_e, but what had changed was the quantity supplied, which had fallen to Q_s, well below Q_e.

If the price of gasoline had been allowed to rise at that time, the reduced supply of gasoline would have been allocated only to those buyers willing to give up more in *other* goods and services. Since price remained at P_e, quantity demanded did not fall, and that is why there was a shortage.

Some scheme of allocating the reduced quantity supplied was necessary.

Alternative Rationing Schemes for Gasoline

The United States initially tried a first-come, first-served rationing system when price was kept below its market-clearing level. Long lines at the gas pumps resulted.

Then some gasoline station owners started limiting purchases to $5. The result was still long lines, and people began buying gas at one station and then driving across the street to wait in another long line. In other words, the implicit price of gasoline increased anyway, since it now cost P_e *plus* the value of one's time devoted to waiting in line.

Of course, some gas station owners charged a higher price— illegally, to be sure. Others filled customers' tanks for a "tip." In still other instances, the octane rating of gasoline fell as the gasoline was diluted. Thus, the price actually did rise above P_e. In other nations, however, oil and gasoline prices were allowed to rise (to a greater extent), and shortages and long lines did not appear.

The true cause of the prolonged shortage of gasoline was the fact that gasoline prices were not allowed to rise. This conclusion is supported by the fact that in 1974 the United States experienced shortages for many goods. When price controls were lifted after 1974, most of those shortages disappeared. After 1974, there were only two goods for which spot shortages periodically appeared— oil distillates and natural gas. Is it merely coincidental that these were the only two goods for which controls were not abandoned? We think not.

● THE WORLD OF SHORTAGES: RENT CONTROL

During the inflation-plagued 1970s and 1980s, rapidly rising construction costs and property taxes pushed the price of rental housing even higher. Frustrated citizens struggled to keep the prices of apartments down. For example, in April 1979, residents of Santa Monica, California, voted in Proposition A. That proposition froze rents for 190 days and was supposed to roll them back to the levels of April 1978. Other cities have had a much longer history of legal restriction on rents, or **rent control**. Rent control involves that whole body of law that prohibits landlords—owners of rental housing—from raising rental prices. The results of rent control are quite predictable. A look at its history will show why.

The federal government imposed rent control as a temporary wartime measure in 1943. While the federal program ended after the war, rent control was continued in New York State, and specifically in New York City. The law in the city kept rent for certain categories of apartments at fixed levels, allowing a 15 percent increase when a tenant moved out. Needless to say, an immediate consequence was that landlords tended to encourage departures by such devices as pounding on the pipes and cutting off the heat. Since there were many more people wanting apartments than there were apartments available, a longer-run consequence was the development of a vast array of devices to get around the restrictions. The most obvious was called *key money*, in which a prospective renter was charged a large amount of money simply for the key to the apartment. Or, one could hire the landlord's son to repaint the apartment at a substantial fee. In still other cases, the landlord would discriminate among prospective tenants on the basis of race, religion, pets, children, or whatever. Landlords were able to discriminate because the quantity demanded far exceeded the quantity supplied, and everyone paid the same (rent-controlled) price. Another consequence of rent control was that landlords simply failed to maintain apartments, so that the real costs of upkeep were decreased.

Widespread Evasion and Its Results

All of these policies, of course, suggest that landlords and tenants were simply looking for ways to get around the artificially low price and in fact develop a de facto equilibrium. That is, the real value of deteriorating apartments fell and/or the tenant in fact paid an extra price. Thus, in reality, shifts in the demand and supply curves occurred. Laws were passed in an attempt to force landlords to maintain apartments, but these were widely evaded. Similarly, laws were passed that were designed to prevent subletting for higher prices. These, too, were widely evaded, so much so that a 1960 survey showed that 25 percent of renters were paying more than was legally allowed for the rent-controlled apartments. Note that this did not include bribes or cuts in quality. This was simply a case of people paying rents above the stipulated amount. What can

Rent control

A form of price control in which rents in designated apartments are not permitted to be raised at all, or can be raised only by some specified amount each year.

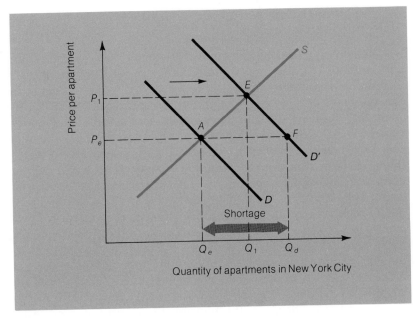

GRAPH 3–4

Rent Control in New York City During and After World War II

S and D represent the supply and demand for apartments before rent control. The equilibrium, or market-clearing, price was at P_e. During the war, and for many years after, population increases and rises in income caused an increase in the demand for apartments. This is shown as a rightward shift in the demand curve from D to D'. Note that the quantity demanded for apartments is now greater at every price.

Had the price been allowed to rise to P_1, no shortage of apartments would have occurred. At very high prices for apartments, individual homeowners would have found more and more "spare" rooms in cellars, attics, and elsewhere in their houses. Single-family houses would have been converted into multifamily dwellings. In the long run, supply itself would have increased, since it would have become more profitable for landlords to build additional apartments in New York City.

However, since the price of apartments was not allowed to rise, a prolonged shortage was induced. Renters wanted to purchase quantity Q_d at price P_e, but the quantity supplied remained at Q_e. After the increase in demand, a shortage of apartments existed at price P_e.

be observed in such a situation is that the market does find its own equilibrium.

In Graph 3–4, the New York City apartment situation is shown. During World War II, an influx of people caused the demand for apartments to rise. After the war, increases in population and income further increased the demand for these apartments. This is shown as a rightward shift in the demand curve, from D to D'. Since at price P_e quantity demanded increased from Q_e to Q_d, but quantity supplied remained at Q_e, a shortage of apartments existed in New York City.

The Consequences for Renter and Landlord

The consequences of rent control are significant for both renter and landlord. Clearly, the landlord suffers in terms of the drop in income, and the renter suffers in terms of the quality reduction in apartments. But that is not the end of the story. In New York City, as of 1975, some 642,000 apartments were rent controlled. An additional 650,000 were covered by another complex form of regulation called *rent stabilization*. During the whole period since World War II, there has been almost no construction of apartments subject to rent control. Moreover, as apartments deteriorated because it was not worthwhile for landlords to maintain them, annual taxes on apartment houses eventually exceeded the income that landlords received and the apartments were simply abandoned. In 1970, 33,000 housing units were abandoned. And as late as 1974, 10,000 had been abandoned. In some parts of the Bronx and on Manhattan's lower East Side, whole rows of abandoned apartment houses stand gutted and stripped by vandals. Thus, the long-run consequences in New York City have been a decay in the housing stock and a decline in the amount of available space for middle- and lower-income tenants (luxury apartments that were exempted from rent control continue to be built). But there are still more serious consequences for the city as a whole: The tax base of New York has been primarily dependent on housing real estate, and with the erosion of this tax base, the fiscal income of New York City has declined.

Other Cities Face Similar Problems

New York City, of course, is not alone in both imposing rent control and suffering the long-run effects. One obvious result of rent control has been the conversion of apartments to condominiums, where each unit is purchased rather than rented. For example, in Washington, D.C., rent controls were instituted in the 1960s. As they became more onerous, the number of condominium conversions increased. In 1976, there were approximately 1000 annually; in 1979, there were approximately 10,000. And, of course, as more and more apartment units are converted to condominiums, the supply of rental apartments declines.

So why is rent control gaining in popularity in such places as California? The answer is not hard to find. Rent control benefits current renters. Current renters, therefore, have an incentive to bring political pressure to bear on legislation limiting their rents. It is the landlords and future renters who will suffer. Current landlords are relatively few, so their political pressure will be less than that of current renters in many situations. Of course, future renters cannot bring political pressure since most of them are not even certain that they will be future renters and thus be adversely affected by a reduced supply in quality rental housing due to rent control.

● THE WORLD OF SHORTAGES: WATER

Concern about water shortages has been increasing rapidly. The water issue may well become one of the most important problems of the 1980s and 1990s.

Back in the 1960s, New York City experienced water shortages virtually every summer. At that time individual water usage was not *metered* in the city. Homeowners paid a fixed annual rate for water regardless of the amount used. Commercial users of water were, however, metered. For almost all other goods, if you want more, you pay more. For water in New York City, if you used more, you paid no extra cost beyond the original flat yearly fee. When faucets leaked—or indeed gushed—there was (and for many people continues to be) little incentive to fix them. Repairs cost money; water did not and in some places still does not. In short, there was an incentive to waste water; the price was set too low.

Problems in the Northeast Today

In the early 1980s, the water shortage again reared its ugly head in the Northeast. In New York City "an official drought emergency" existed in 1981. In New Jersey, approximately 400 towns were placed on restricted-water-use programs. Overall, rainfall in the Northeast since 1979 has been estimated at roughly one-third less than the average annual rate. This problem of reduced available water, and how to allocate it, can presumably be lessened by charging a higher price for water.

A Case Study: Boulder, Colorado

Prior to 1961, the pricing of water in Boulder, Colorado, was similar to the cost in New York City in the 1950s and 1960s—a flat monthly rate was charged no matter how much water was used. An alternative approach is to charge for the amount of water used as measured by meters at each residence. In 1961 in Boulder, the water supply company installed water meters in every home and business it supplied. Each residence was charged $0.35 per 1000 gallons of water used. Under the flat-fee system prior to 1961, consumers increased their water usage and did not concern themselves with the cost. They did think about cost, however, after the metered system was instituted.

Economist Steve Hanke looked at the quantity of water demanded before and after the meters were installed in Boulder.[1] Hanke first developed what he called the "ideal" use of water for each month of the year. He completed his estimates by taking account of the average irrigable area per residence (in other words, the lawn), the average temperature during the month, the average number of daylight hours, and the effective rainfall. The term *ideal* implies nothing from an economic point of view; rather, it indicates the minimum quantity of sprinkling water required to maintain the aesthetic quality of each resident's lawn.

What the Data Show. Table 3–1 shows that homeowners sprinkled their lawns much more under the flat-rate system than under the metered system. Column 1 lists the numbers identifying the different meter routes that were monitored. Column 2 shows how much water was used in the different routes when the flat rate was in effect. Water usage is expressed in terms of actual sprinkling compared to ideal sprinkling. Thus, if 200 gallons per month were considered ideal, but 350 gallons were actually used, the actual

TABLE 3–1

Comparing Water Usage before and after Metering

In this table we show the results of imposing a metering system that charged consumers in Boulder, Colorado, according to the actual quantity of water used. Column 1 lists the arbitrarily assigned meter route numbers; column 2 shows how much water, as a percentage of the ideal quantity of water needed, was used before metering; and column 3 shows how much water, again as a percentage of the ideal quantity of water needed, was used after metering. The ideal quantity was calculated on the basis of number of days of sun, area to be sprinkled, and so forth.

METER ROUTES (1)	ACTUAL WATER USE MEASURED AS A PERCENTAGE OF IDEAL USE	
	FLAT-RATE PERIOD (2)	METERED-RATE PERIOD (3)
16, 18	128	78
37	175	72
53, 54	156	72
70, 71, 72	177	63
73, 75	175	97
74	175	102
76, 78	176	105
79	157	86

Source: Steve Hanke, "Demand for Water under Dynamic Conditions," *Water Resources Research*, vol. 6 (October 1970).

[1]"Demand for Water under Dynamic Conditions," *Water Resources Research*, vol. 6 (October 1970), pp. 1253–1261.

sprinkling to ideal sprinkling comparison would be 350/200, or 175 percent.

Column 3 shows actual sprinkling compared to ideal sprinkling under the system of metered-rate pricing (each user is charged a price commensurate with the actual amount of water used). Notice here that in most routes homeowners used less than the ideal amount of water.

These data allow us to test our demand hypothesis; in effect, it predicts that if people are faced with a higher price for a commodity, they will demand a smaller quantity. We ask this important question: Did residential consumers of water in Boulder return to their old habits?

Graph 3–5 indicates that the answer is definitely no. People continued to respond to the higher price of water by using less of it throughout the 1960s. What does that mean? Simply that given the increased cost per 1000 gallons of water, the residents of Boulder, Colorado, decided to use less water and have browner lawns. That is to say, in the long run, their responsiveness to a change in price was greater than it was immediately after the increase in price due to metering. In the previous chapter, we referred to this as the price

GRAPH 3–5
Actual Water Use

This graph presents the results of the imposition of a metering system for water usage in Boulder, Colorado. After metering was introduced in late 1961, the amount of sprinkling usage dropped dramatically and remained at the lower rate of usage throughout the period studied. Usage rate even dropped consistently from 1962 to 1968.

Source: Steve Hanke, "Demand for Water under Dynamic Conditions," *Water Resources Research*, vol. 6 (October 1970).

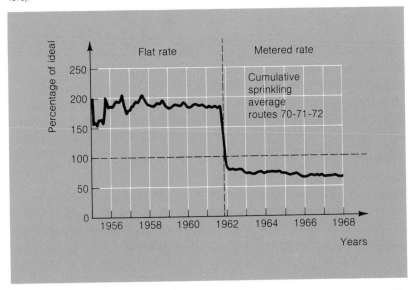

elasticity of demand. Here price elasticity of demand became greater and greater as more time was allowed for adjustment.

● THE WORLD OF SURPLUSES: AGRICULTURE

As indicated at the beginning of this chapter, the United States experienced prolonged surpluses for many agricultural goods during the 1950s and 1960s with some repetition for certain goods, such as cheese, in the 1980s. By now you might have guessed that these surpluses occurred because of government **price supports** for certain commodities above the market-clearing level. If you did guess that, then you are on the right track.

A Little History of the Farmers' Dilemma

Before World War I, there were at least 20 years of continuous agricultural prosperity in the United States. During the war, increased demand for agricultural products added to the "golden age of American farming." Many foreign countries demanded our agricultural products because they were using all of their own productive facilities to fight the war. A sharp depression in 1920 brought the "golden age" to an abrupt halt. Even though the economy picked up in 1921 and we went into the Roaring Twenties, agriculture never did share in the remaining years of prosperity. Europeans reduced their demand for our agricultural exports as they increased their own productive capacities in farming. Also, the United States imposed high taxes on all goods purchased from other countries, thereby restricting the flow of those goods. This restriction on trade caused the amount of farm goods that could be sold to other countries to fall.

Then the Great Depression hit, and American farming was really hurt. Farm prices and farm incomes fell sharply. It was at this time that massive farm programs were put into operation. In 1929, the Federal Farm Board was created and given a budget of $1.5 billion to begin price-stabilization operations for poor farmers. The Farm Board was supposed to use the money to support the price of farm products so that farmers' incomes would not fall so much. Essentially it bought crops to keep their prices from falling. Then, when the Great Depression worsened, a system of price supports was instituted. During the 1940s, 1950s, and 1960s, there were tremendous technological advances on the farm. Farm output increased dramatically and cost per unit fell as a result of improvements in farm machinery, pest control, seed quality, and fertilizers. Though the demand for farm products increased, the supply of farm products increased even more than demand did. The price for agricultural goods would have fallen and many of the smaller, less efficient farmers who were not keeping pace with the technological

Price supports

Minimum prices set by the government for agricultural commodities.

revolution in farming would have been driven off their farms. Price supports were aimed at preventing this.

A Graphic Analysis of Food Surpluses in the United States

The effect of price supports on various farm products during the 1950s, 1960s, and up through the 1970s and 1980s is depicted in Graph 3–6. Wheat is used as the output, but any other agricultural good in the price-support program could be substituted. Note that

GRAPH 3–6
Price Supports and Surpluses for Wheat

The wheat surpluses that existed during the 1950s and 1960s and part of the 1970s and 1980s are depicted in this graph. During that period, technological advances occurred in farming: Seed and farm equipment were improved and so were fertilizers and pest control. The result was an increase in the supply of farm products relative to the demand for them. This is shown as a rightward shift in the supply curve from S to S', with the demand curve, D, unchanged.

Had there been no price supports, price would have fallen to P_1 and buyers would have purchased more wheat. Smaller, less efficient farmers would have been driven off the farms; to protect them, a price-support program was enacted, in which a price floor (P_e) was set. Note that at P_e a prolonged surplus resulted. Quantity supplied increased to Q_s and quantity demanded remained at Q_e. To maintain price at P_e, the government was forced to buy and store the surplus. The money value of this surplus is obtained by multiplying the price-supported price, P_e, times the difference between quantities Q_s and Q_e. This is the surplus that must be purchased annually. The cumulative surplus will increase every year.

For this reason, the government was induced to discourage farmers from producing. The government paid farmers *not* to produce, in hopes of shifting supply back to S from S'.

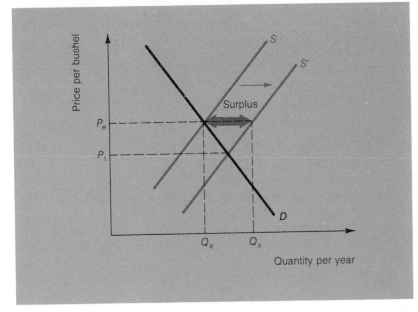

supply increased relative to demand during that period. This is shown by a rightward shift in the supply curve from S to S', given the unaltered demand curve of D.

The original price per bushel of wheat occurred at P_e at the intersection of the original supply and demand curves, S and D, where the equilibrium quantity was Q_e. Technological advances in farming caused an increase in supply from S to S'. With increased supply, the market-clearing, or equilibrium, price would have been established at P_1. The government, however, was committed to supporting price at P_e. A price *floor* was set at P_e. As a result of the technological advances, at a price of P_e, farmers now wanted to produce Q_s and they were capable of producing that increased quantity. Buyers still wanted to purchase only Q_e because price had not fallen. The result was a *prolonged* surplus. (Surplus is calculated annually; with every passing year, the surplus increases and storage costs become greater.)

Increasing surpluses became an embarrassment for the government. It attempted to shift the supply curve back from S' to S by paying farmers *not* to produce. This program, known as Soil Conservation and Crop Restriction, has not been very successful. For example, in 1953, 80 million acres of wheat were cultivated; 1.2 billion bushels grew. In 1960, only 55 million acres of wheat were cultivated, but the output rose from 1.2 billion to 1.4 billion bushels. In other words, a 30 percent reduction in the number of acres cultivated by 1960 was accompanied by an *increase* of 17 percent in output. To be sure, the increase in output would have been even greater had there not been soil banks and acreage restriction programs.

During the early 1970s, worldwide demand for U.S. food increased and the market-clearing price again approached P_e. As a consequence, the surpluses practically disappeared. Times are changing, however. Price supports exist today for most agricultural crops, and the specter of surpluses looms in the future. The extent to which surpluses occur depends on how high the price support is relative to the market-clearing price. There is always a potential for surpluses with this program.

● THE WORLD OF SURPLUSES: MINIMUM WAGE LAWS

Minimum wage rate

The wage rate below which employees in most industries cannot be paid. It is imposed by federal, state, and certain local governments.

Another example of a price support above the market-clearing, or equilibrium, price level is a minimum wage requirement. In effect, the law requires employers to pay a **minimum wage rate**. An employer cannot legally pay lower than the specified minimum wage rate if the job meets the minimum wage rate criteria. More and more jobs are coming under the jurisdiction of the minimum wage rate laws.

68

Graph 3–7 demonstrates that in an unrestricted labor market there will be an equilibrium wage rate, w_e, at which equal quantities of labor are demanded and supplied. What if a legal minimum wage rate were set above the equilibrium wage rate? Who benefits and who loses?

Examining the graph, we see that initially equilibrium exists with the equilibrium wage rate of w_e and the equilibrium quantity of labor demanded and supplied equal to Q_e. A minimum wage, w_m, which is higher than w_e, is imposed. At w_m the quantity demanded for labor is reduced to Q_d, and some workers now become unemployed. Note that the reduction in employment from Q_e to Q_d, or the distance from B to A, is less than the excess quantity of labor supplied at wage rate w_m. This excess quantity supplied is the distance between A and C, or the distance between Q_d and Q_s. The reason the reduction in employment is smaller than the excess supply of labor at the minimum wage is that the latter *also* includes a second component, the additional workers who would like to work

GRAPH 3–7

The Effect of Minimum Wage Rates

The market-clearing wage rate is w_e. The market-clearing quantity of employment is Q_e and is determined by the intersection of supply and demand at point E. A minimum wage equal to w_m is established. The quantity of labor demanded is reduced to Q_d; the reduction of employment from Q_e to Q_d is equal to the distance between B and A. That distance is smaller than the excess quantity of labor supplied at wage rate w_m. The distance between B and C is the increase in the quantity of labor supplied that results from the higher minimum wage rate.

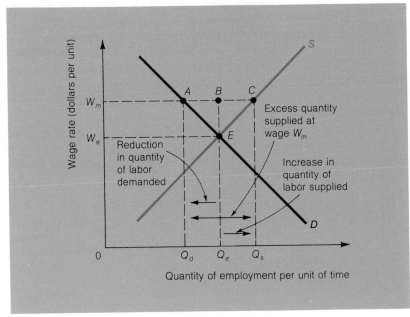

more hours at the new higher minimum wage. Some of these workers may be unemployed, but others may be employed at a lower wage elsewhere in the noncovered sectors of the economy.

In the long run, some of the reduction in labor demanded will result from a reduction in the number of firms, and some will result from changes in the number of workers employed by each firm.[2]

Some Empirical Evidence

Quite a bit of evidence has been gathered to demonstrate the unemployment effects of minimum wages on specific groups, such as teenagers. One study showed, for example, that there was a statistically significant reduction in the ratio of teenage employment to adult employment associated with increased minimum wage level or coverage.[3] The investigator estimated that a 1 percent increase in the effective minimum wage reduces the teenage share of employment by 0.3 percent. Another investigator, Edward Gramlich, confirmed these findings. Teenage workers in the low-wage category clearly lose as a result of an increase in minimum wage rates, because high minimum wage rates substantially reduce full-time employment, forcing teenagers into part-time employment or unemployment. Those teenagers who become unemployed are further disadvantaged because they have a very low probability of qualifying for unemployment compensation. Gramlich found that adult males in the low-wage category break even or benefit slightly from minimum wage rates. Only low-wage adult women appear clearly to gain from the minimum wage, according to his studies. As a group, they received higher wages than they would have received in the absence of the minimum wage.

Other studies have shown that minimum wage legislation weakens the economic status of those at the bottom of the distribution of earnings. The apparent redistribution of income that occurs as a result of the minimum wage appears to be from some have-nots to other have-nots. Additionally, low-wage workers with the greatest number of skills are the very ones who are not put out of work by increases in the minimum wage rate. The group with the greatest degree of poverty—those workers who are least productive—are the most likely to become unemployed due to minimum wage rate increases.

---

[2]Since we are referring to a long-run analysis here, the reduction in labor demanded would be demonstrated by an eventual shift inward to the left of the demand curve, D, in Graph 3–7.

[3]Finis Welch, "Minimum Wage Legislation in the United States," *Economic Inquiry*, vol. 12 (September 1974), 308.

Usury Laws Lower
Interest Rates

THE ARGUMENT

Interest rates have always held a special attention both for the press and for the general population. Many states have legal restrictions, called usury laws, *on the rate of interest that can be charged for consumer credit, home loans, and so on. Do usury laws actually lead to lower interest rates?*

THE ANALYSIS

The history of usury laws is long indeed. The early Babylonians limited the rate of interest. Usury was cautioned against in the Bible. Aristotle considered moneylending to be sterile. In the Roman Republic, interest charges were explicitly forbidden, though they were permitted later, during the period of the Roman Empire.

During the early Middle Ages, religious leaders taught that interest on loans was unjust. Legislation outside the Church responded to its influence and, in general, interest charges and usury were regarded as synonymous.

By the fifteenth century, the situation began to change. Martin Luther, along with other reformers, conceded that creditors could not be explicitly prevented from charging interest. In the eighteenth century, restrictions were relaxed, though most nations had legal maximum usury rates. Most usury laws in the United States were inherited from the British, and remained in force even after they were repealed in Great Britain in 1854.

This persistent opposition to moneylending for interest might, for want of a better explanation, be attributed to an ancient ignorance of economic principles. After all, why should individuals be willing to give up the use of their own money unless they are paid? Modern enlightenment on this topic has not, however, completely changed the picture. The existence of legislation affecting the lending of money makes it clear that a widespread suspicion lingers that the moneylender possesses some unique, shady, and monopolistic influence. Many states have enacted laws setting maximum rates of interest on loans to consumers, and the federal government has legislated the maximum interest rates for various uses of money. What are the consequences?

Suppose a state legislates a maximum interest rate of 12 percent on consumer loans. If this is higher than the generally prevailing interest rate, it has no effect. However, this is an unlikely assumption. Even in the absence of significant inflationary tendencies, the going rate on run-of-the-mill consumer transactions is normally higher than 12 percent. What, then, is the effect of the restriction? At the lower rate, buyers will demand more money than the finance companies are willing to supply at that return. Lenders will react by introducing service charges to cover "handling costs," which formerly had been incorporated in the interest rate. Then they will move to some sort of rationing of the funds available for loans. Understandably they will attempt to eliminate the riskier loans. Since the risk of default on loans is inversely related to the income of the borrower, the refusal of loans to the lowest-income groups will offer the easiest course—the least costly procedure in terms of acquiring information about potential borrowers. The predictable outcome, therefore, is that loans will be made only to the higher-income groups, and the would-be borrower whose income is low will face a closed door.

Restrictions on economic variables always have consequences whereby some persons gain and some persons lose. Economic analysis can help identify both the effects of the restrictions and the groups affected. Restrictions on interest rates lead to curtailment of the supply of loans, with lower-income groups being most adversely affected.

DISCUSSION QUESTIONS

1. If lenders need to reduce costs, what are some of the methods of doing so? (*Hint*: How can bad loans be reduced?)
2. How are usury laws similar to rent controls?

● WHAT'S AHEAD

Supply and demand determine price in what we call markets. Chapter 4 presents a discussion of markets and movements within those markets. In other words, what continuing forces are there that cause prices to change? Furthermore, an analysis of different types of markets is presented, including the well-known competitive market in which no single seller has any control over the price he or she charges for the product. Rather, the competitor simply takes the price as given and produces and sells whatever amount is most profitable at that price.

● CHAPTER SUMMARY

A shortage is defined as a situation in which quantity demanded exceeds quantity supplied at a specific price. Prolonged shortages result when the price of a good is not allowed to rise. Surpluses exist when quantity supplied exceeds quantity demanded at a particular price. Prolonged surpluses result when price is not allowed to fall.

The energy "crisis" that occurred in the 1970s was a direct result of a reduced supply of petroleum coupled with the price controls that were in effect. Price was not allowed to rise to the market-clearing price, so alternative rationing schemes had to be used, such as long lines at gas stations. Rent control is another example of a prolonged shortage (of housing) resulting from price not being allowed to rise. When rent control is effective, it leads to a deterioration in apartments, schemes to charge higher rent despite the control, and so on.

72

Agricultural surpluses occur when price supports are in effect and the government, in essence, buys the excess quantity supplied at the supported price. In order to fight increasing surpluses, the government has at times attempted to restrict the amount of land used for farming. Minimum wage laws also lead to labor surpluses (i.e., unemployment). A minimum wage law requires that firms in covered industries pay no less than a specified minimum wage rate.

● QUESTIONS FOR REVIEW AND STUDY

1. A shortage exists when quantity demanded exceeds quantity supplied at a _____ _____.

2. Without interference, shortages are eliminated by buyers _____ _____ the price.

3. Higher prices cause consumers to _____ and suppliers to _____ _____.

4. A surplus exists when quantity supplied exceeds quantity demanded at a _____ _____.

5. A surplus is eliminated by sellers _____ _____.

6. When prices fall, consumers _____ more and suppliers _____ _____.

7. Prolonged shortages and surpluses can exist only when governments do not _____ _____ ___ _____.

8. Gasoline and heating oil shortages occurred in the 1970s because of a reduction in _____ by OPEC members, coupled with _____ _____.

9. At the price-controlled price, the quantity of gasoline demanded _____ the quantity of gasoline supplied. The result was _____ _____.

10. The implicit price of gasoline rose because of the _____ _____ of time by consumers to get gas.

11. A shift leftward in the demand for housing without a shift leftward in the supply of housing will result in a(n) _____ price of housing.

12. _____ controls reduce the ability of the market to eliminate the housing _____.

13. When people pay the same price for water no matter how much they use, they have a tendency to _____ water from a social point of view.

14. When the government sets a _____ on the price of an agricultural product, _____ usually result.

15. Food surpluses can remain only if the government _____ the surplus.

16. When a minimum wage rate is set above the market-clearing rate, some unskilled workers become _____.

ANSWERS

1. specific price 2. bidding up 3. conserve; increase production 4. specific price 5. reducing prices 6. buy; produce less 7. allow price to change 8. supply; price controls 9. exceeded; long lines 10. increased use 11. increased price 12. Rent; shortage 13. waste 14. floor; surpluses 15. buys 16. unemployed

● ANSWERS TO CHAPTER PREVIEW QUESTIONS

1. There have been times when people were unable to buy as much gasoline as they wanted, and they often had to wait in long lines at the gas pumps. Why has this happened only in some years but not in others?

Although it is true that during certain years in the 1970s, the supply of petroleum was restricted, that is not the reason people had to wait in long lines to get gasoline for their cars. The reason lies in a government-mandated pricing and allocation system that resulted in a legally allowed price set below the market-clearing price. This price generated the shortages people normally associate with a "crisis." If the price of gas had been allowed to rise to clear the market, certain individuals would have been hurt by the rise in price, but it is not at all clear that preventing the price from rising to clear the market is a superior, or preferred, system of rationing a scarce resource. When individuals are presented with incorrect information about the relative scarcity of a product—gasoline in this case—they respond by demanding too much. It turns out to be much easier to get individuals to conserve relatively scarcer resources by allowing prices to rise, rather than by imposing an alternative conservation scheme.

2. In many cities over the last decade, there have been water crises where restrictions were put on water usage. Are there alternative ways of dealing with such crises?

By now, the answer should be automatic. One alternative to avoiding water crises around the country is to charge more for using it. This can be done in a variety of ways. In cities where water is paid for with a flat monthly charge, a metering system can be installed in which each individual water user pays at a specific rate—for example, 1000 gallons of water used. We must point out that much water is owned in common, that is, not really owned by anyone. In order to get people to conserve water, much of this common-property water will have to be owned by someone, even if it is city, state, or federal governments. If government does take over, it will have to act *as if* it were trying to make a profit, by charging higher and higher prices if water is, in fact, becoming relatively more scarce.

● PROBLEMS

1. It is often stated that the United States needs a certain amount of gasoline. That means that we "must" buy the same quantity of gasoline no matter how high the price goes. List some of the ways in which individuals can conserve the amount of gas they use as its relative price rises.

2. Some people maintain that unless farmers are subsidized, many will leave the farms, a small number of farms will take over the industry, and prices will rise correspondingly. In 1974, it was estimated that 2.44 million farms were in existence and that 19 percent of these farms accounted for 78 percent of the value of total farm output.
  a. What is the number of farms accounting for this percentage of output?
  b. In light of this fact, is it likely that farming is *not* a highly competitive industry in the United States?

● SELECTED REFERENCES

Fleisher, B. *Minimum Wage Regulation in Retail Trade*. Washington, D.C.: American Enterprise Institute, 1981.

Hopkins, R. F., ed. *Global Political Economy of Food*. Madison: University of Wisconsin Press, 1978.

Kneese, A. V., and C. L. Schultze. *Pollution, Prices, and Public Policy*. Washington, D.C.: Brookings Institution, 1979.

Nash, H., ed. *Energy Controversy*. Friends of the Earth, 1980.

Simon, Julian L. *The Ultimate Resource*. Princeton, N.J.: Princeton University Press, 1980.

4

Markets and Economic Movement

Chapter Preview
1. When you buy something, do you, as an individual, have any effect on the kinds of goods and services offered for sale?
2. What is the difference between the price of a good sold in a highly competitive market system and the price of that very same good sold in a market where there are only one or two big producers?

● KEY TERMS

Arbitrage	Market economy
Capital	Normal profits
Command economy	Price searcher
Consumer sovereignty	Price taker
Entrepreneurs	Profit
Entrepreneurship	Pure competition
Incentives	Pure monopoly
Labor	Traditional economic system
Land	Transactions costs
Market	

Most of us know of people who are dedicated to improving their financial situation. Acquiring more wealth is something that interests almost everyone. But not everyone has the ability to recognize and, through intellectual skill and a bit of savvy, take advantage of an opportunity to make a **profit**.

Those individuals who have the ability to make a profit can be valuable to society. They and their imitators (after all, you can become rich by copying, too; you can move into an industry that is extremely profitable and "jump on the bandwagon") can cause resources to be allocated in an efficient manner. Profit seekers can also drive down the very high profits that others are making. That is, competition for profits tends to reduce *overall* profits and prices.

● THE MARKETPLACE

You undoubtedly have heard the word **market** used before. To an economist, a market is an arrangement wherein buyers and sellers make voluntary transactions. If you think of markets in this broad sense, you will realize that many markets exist in the United States. Workers and employers interact in the labor market. Consumers and retailers make exchanges in food markets, clothing markets, and appliance markets. Banks and consumers, as well as businesses, make transactions in credit markets. Markets exist for automobiles, antique guns, and books. Indeed, there are thousands of different markets in the United States. Ours is a market-oriented economy.

Markets and Information

One of the major factors involved in a market is the exchange of information about prices, quantities, qualities, and so forth. Different markets have different levels of information and degrees of efficiency with which that information is transmitted. The stock market,

Profit

The income generated by selling something for a higher price than was paid for it. Or, alternatively, the difference between total revenues received and total cost.

Market

An institutional arrangement wherein buyers and sellers voluntarily make exchanges.

78

for example, has information about the prices and quantities of stocks being bought and sold. This information is transmitted almost instantaneously throughout the United States and much of the world. Profit-seeking entrepreneurs are constantly looking for ways to increase profits by improving information networks within markets. That's why every stockbroker can now tell you instantly the last price and quantity traded of any stock listed on a major stock exchange.

Why We Turn to Markets

Individuals turn to markets to conduct economic activities or exchanges because markets reduce **transactions costs**, the costs involved in economic exchange. These costs include the cost of getting information about the qualities of a particular product, its price, its availability, its durability record, its servicing facilities, its degree of safety, and so on. Consider, for example, the transactions costs involved in shopping for a 10-speed bicycle. Among such costs would be phone calls or visits to sellers to learn about product features and prices. There is also the cost of negotiating the sale—that is, the specification and execution of the sales contract, and ultimately the cost of enforcing the contract.

Transactions costs in the most highly organized markets are relatively small. Consider, for example, the New York Stock Exchange. It is quite easy to obtain immediate information on the price of listed stocks, the number bought and sold in the last several hours, the previous day's prices, and so on. Generally, the less organized the market, the higher the transactions costs. No market can completely eliminate transactions costs, but some markets can do a better job of reducing them. Historically, as technological improvements have made it less costly to disseminate information, transactions costs have fallen. Imagine how costly it was years ago, in terms of time and money, for someone in California to find out quickly the price of stocks being sold in New York.

● THREE TYPES OF ECONOMIC SYSTEMS

An economic system is determined by the degree to which markets are controlled. There are three basic economic systems:

1. Traditional economies
2. Command economies
3. Market economies

The distinguishing feature of each economic system is the way in which individuals can organize to mobilize resources to satisfy

Transactions costs

All the costs associated with exchanging, including information costs, such as finding out about the price, quality, service record, and durability of a product, plus the cost of contracting and enforcing that contract.

79

human wants. To some extent all real world economies show traces of each of these three systems. However, a given economy can be classified according to how closely it resembles one of these three.

Traditional Economies

Although the **traditional economic system** has become less important in modern times, it will continue to exist. Under such a system, individuals engage in activities similar to those of their ancestors. Goods that have been produced in the past are still produced, and in much the same way. A person's job or economic status is determined largely by birthright. Change is unwelcome. Major economic questions are decided on the basis of habit, custom, and very often religious beliefs. Consider the Mbuti Pygmies of Africa. These individuals simply eat what is found in their geographical area during their wanderings in search of food. The distribution of food is determined by custom, older members of the tribe getting more to eat than younger members. Sons do what their fathers did, daughters do what their mothers have done. Men hunt, and women gather roots and berries and tend to the children. Numerous important economic activities are decided on the basis of age and sex. Sex roles are more rigidly defined and maintained in traditional economies than in other economies.

Command Economies

A system that involves economywide planning is usually called a **command economy**. A small number of key individuals decide, in broad terms, which goods and services are produced, and in what quantities, and typically the manner in which they are produced. These broad plans are then given to technically skilled managers who attempt to allocate resources so that the goals of the master plan will be attained. There are usually few private ownership rights, and very little individual economic freedom. A small, highly sensitive group makes the key economic decisions for the country.

Examples of command economies, in varying degrees, are the Soviet Union, Albania, Cuba, the People's Republic of China, Hungary, Czechoslovakia, and Yugoslavia. Keep in mind that no economy can be solely of a command nature. There will be individuals other than the central decision makers, who decide a number of economic issues; all economies require the voluntary cooperation of many people.

Market Economies

The economy of the United States is, to a large extent, a **market economy**. Decisions about what is produced, how it is produced,

Traditional economic system

An economic system in which people simply follow in the footsteps of their ancestors and do not attempt to alter the way in which goods are produced, who produces them, and who consumes them.

Command economy

An economic system in which the allocation of resources is determined by a small centralized group of individuals.

Market economy

An economic system in which decisions about what is produced, how it is produced, and how it is distributed are determined by the interaction of the various markets for goods and services.

80

and how it is distributed are determined by the interaction of supply and demand within the various markets for goods, services, labor, and so on. We'll discuss characteristics of market economies in some detail in the next few pages.

Private Property Rights. One of the most important characteristics of a market economy is private ownership of the means of production. Natural resources, machinery and equipment, and labor are all owned privately, not by the state. Laborers are free to work where they choose, producers are free to produce what they wish to produce, and natural resource owners can sell to whomever they choose, if they choose to sell. This is called a system of private property rights.

Self-Interest. Since individuals own the rights to the means of production, they will voluntarily exchange them in pursuit of their own self-interest, by choosing economic activities they perceive to be in their own best interests. Presumably, workers will consider all those jobs for which they are eligible and choose the one that pays the highest wages, other things held constant.

Of course, individuals must make such decisions for themselves. Some people prefer jobs offering prestige or high security but relatively low wages. Others prefer high-paying jobs; they are prepared to take the risk associated with job hazards or insecurity in exchange for those higher wages.

Individuals judge for themselves the effects, whether good or bad, of a given economic change. Sometimes this important point is missed. For example, if Mr. Johnson gets laid off, he may continue to remain idle if his job options are not attractive enough to induce him to work. Similarly, a wealthy person may elect to live in a relatively low-quality, low-rent house rather than a modern apartment with a higher rent. Others may prefer a less expensive car even though they know that it does not provide the same amount of safety as a more expensive one.

The point is that in a market economy individuals are allowed to pursue their own self-interest. Businesses presumably will produce those goods that appear to be the most profitable.

The Price System. A system of prices helps individuals direct the pursuit of their own self-interest. When the price of a resource or product rises relative to others, people will realize that it has become relatively scarce. They will find that the increase in price is a signal to conserve on the use of that resource or product; they will look for substitutes. To repeat, prices are the conveyors of information in the marketplace for both buyers and sellers. For the buyer, the relative price of a good indicates what must be given up to obtain that good. Of course buyers respond differently than sellers. Sellers may see a rise in the relative price of a particular good as an opportunity to increase profits, and eventually such information may result in a larger amount of resources being directed toward production of that good. We also use the term *market system* to describe the system that allocates resources in this manner. Prices convey the information to the individuals in the marketplace. There is no need for a central agency to produce information or to allocate resources. This does not mean that problems won't arise, or that certain economic activities could not be better handled by other than unrestricted market processes. Rather, it means that spontaneous coordination occurs in a decentralized price system; resource allocation ideally requires no outside management.

Consider a student deciding on a major. If he or she learns that wages for computer experts are rising rapidly, but wages for teachers are not even keeping pace with inflation, then the obvious conclusion must follow: Computer experts are relatively scarcer than teachers. Notice the term *relative*. In other words, the demand for computer experts is increasing more rapidly than the supply, whereas the demand for teachers is increasing less rapidly than the supply. In any event, the relative wage gain of these two groups is a price system signal to the student: Major in computer science if you have the interest and ability.

Consumer Sovereignty.   The price system gives signals and information to businesses. If businesses react correctly to these signals, they will reap benefits in the form of higher profits. If they do not so react, they will suffer losses or lower profits.

This suggests that the prime mover in a market is the consumer. By a system of dollar votes, consumers indicate their wishes. Each time a consumer buys something, he or she in effect is "voting" for that commodity at that price. If enough votes are cast to make its production profitable, the commodity will be forthcoming in the marketplace.

When consumers are able to influence the outputs that businesses produce, **consumer sovereignty** is said to exist. Consumers decide, via the price system, what goods are produced in a market economy.

Market economies could be described in more detail than is presented here. The basic point, however, is that a market economy is one in which individuals seeking to benefit themselves voluntarily buy and sell goods, services, and resources without government intervention. All purchases and sales of goods occur within a particular market structure. Market structures relate to the degree of competitiveness within the particular market under study. To that topic we now turn.

Consumer sovereignty
The situation that exists when consumers are able to determine output by their purchasing decisions in the marketplace.

82

● MARKET STRUCTURES

Economists have devised models, or imaginary systems, to help them analyze and predict market behavior. At one extreme is *pure competition*; at the other, *pure monopoly*. In the real world, most goods and services are produced and sold within a market structure that is neither purely competitive nor purely monopolistic. For simplicity, however, in this chapter we'll consider only the extremes.

Pure Competition

Pure competition exists when a large number of buyers and a large number of sellers compete with each other in an industry. Everyone takes price as given. That is, all buyers and sellers are **price takers**. The prevailing price is a market-clearing price, determined by the interaction of all the supplies and all the demands. For example, a wheat farmer is such a small part of the total world supply of wheat that he or she simply takes the going price of wheat as given. A wheat buyer is usually in the same position. Even if a very large purchase is contemplated, that purchase would have no effect on the market price. Both the wheat farmer and the wheat buyer are price takers.

In a purely competitive market, there is *free entry* and *free exit*. That is, any individual seller can enter the market and become a producer. There are no restrictions to entry—legal or otherwise; no licenses or governmental permits are necessary to enter. Existing firms in the industry are *unable* to keep out new competitors. (Note, though, that free entry does not mean *costless* entry; entrants must still pay for the resources they use.)

Similarly, any firm that wishes to leave an industry in a purely competitive market is free to do so. Presumably, firms leave an industry when the profitability of their investment would be higher if their resources were directed elsewhere.

Examples of the purely competitive market include the stock, bond, and futures markets, and many agricultural markets. In the agricultural markets, competition is so intense that sellers don't even recognize it. Competitors are called "neighbors."

Implications of Pure Competition

Profits Are Limited.   One implication of the pure competition market structure is that the selling price will be high enough to permit only **normal profits**. Each firm in a perfectly competitive market is a price taker. All it can do is adjust its rate of output. In a perfectly competitive market, profits that are higher than normal cause economic movement. Suppose, for example, an event brings about a sudden increase in selling price. Profits become higher than normal.

Pure competition

A market structure in which there are many buyers and many sellers, such that no one individual can influence the price.

Price taker

A buyer or seller whose influence in the market is too small to affect price by his or her purchases or sales. Under pure competition, everyone is a price taker by definition.

Normal profits

Profits that are just high enough to encourage a firm to stay in business in a particular industry. When profits are any lower, the firm will leave.

What would happen? Well, since entry is free, new entrants will appear and try to earn those higher profits.

In effect, an influx of new entrants amounts to an increase in supply. An increase in supply, given demand, will cause price and profits in the industry to fall again. Thus, new entrants provide competition and cause higher-than-normal profits to disappear. Under pure competition, higher-than-normal profits can exist only in the short run. In the long run, profits will return to whatever level is normal in the economy.

Profits Will Never Remain "Too Low" for Long.   Just as profits will not remain higher than normal for long, neither will they remain lower than normal. A resource owner must make profits that are at least as high as he or she could make in another comparable endeavor. Otherwise, resources will flow elsewhere. Suppose an event occurs wherein sellers in a purely competitive market find that the selling price is lower and therefore profits are lower. Since exit is free, resources will flow to some other industry or activity. For example, a farmer has a choice of planting corn or soybeans. If, holding other things constant, the price of corn rises dramatically, relative to the price of soybeans, the farmer will switch resources from the production of soybeans to the production of corn. This increase in corn supply will cause the relative price of corn to fall. The reduction in the supply of soybeans will cause their relative price to rise. Try to show this with supply and demand curves.

Pure Competition Results.   Under pure competition, price will be competitively low at all times. In the long run, price will be sufficiently high to ensure only normal profits. Also, purely competitive markets will expand when demand increases, and contract (but not without "pain") when demand decreases. Profits that are higher or lower than normal will provide the signals as to whether consumers want more or less of a particular good.

Pure Monopoly

The opposite of a purely competitive market is **pure monopoly**. As the word *monopoly* suggests, there is only *one* seller in a monopoly market. Entry into and exit from the market are restricted, typically by the government.

If a monopolist wishes to expand production and increase sales, it can do so only by lowering price (since demand curves are downward sloping). A monopolist therefore has the option of selling less at a higher price, or selling more at a lower price. It is widely argued that the monopolist's price will be relatively high and its

Pure monopoly

A market structure in which there is a single seller of a good or service for which there are no close substitutes.

84

output rate relatively low so as not to "spoil the market." If a purely competitive market were suddenly monopolized, output would fall and price would rise. The resulting profit would then be the normal amount earned in a competitive situation. In a monopoly situation, with some government restriction on entry, higher-than-normal profits can be possible even in the long run.

For example, a patent is a restriction on entry into a particular business. If you receive a patent from the government for a product you have invented, you are protected for 17 years. That patent gives you the right to prevent anyone else from producing that product without your permission. Your monopoly derives from your ability to restrict entry into the business legally. In principle, you can have a monopoly in this market for 17 years. During this time you can charge a higher price than you will be able to charge once the patent expires. Why? Because the higher price that gives you higher-than-normal profits cannot attract competitors. By law, they are prevented from copying your product. Of course, if you have a highly successful product and your profits are very high, others will attempt to compete with you by providing substitutes that are not protected by your patent. Also, you will find yourself paying large legal fees in order to protect your very profitable patent.

Implications of Pure Monopoly

Under the pure monopoly market structure, price tends to be higher than under pure competition. Given the inverse relationship between the quantity demanded and price, the higher monopoly price will lead to a lower output produced and sold than under pure competition. Pure monopoly can lead to higher-than-normal profits even in the long run. Don't be fooled into believing that a pure monopolist can ignore price, however. It cannot. Consider telephone services. In the days when American Telephone and Telegraph had a virtual pure monopoly over almost all telephone services in the United States, it still had to worry about the price it charged. Ma Bell did *not* have a monopoly in the communications industry. People serviced by Ma Bell also had the option of communicating by writing letters, sending messages by courier service, traveling in person, sending a telegram, and perhaps even using carrier pigeons. People have always had the option of not using the telephone. It is very difficult to find a pure monopoly in the real world because so many goods and services have substitutes. A pure monopolist is actually a **price searcher** and must take into account the law of demand when it sets price. It will examine the different prices and quantities it can sell in terms of the different costs it will incur for those different quantities. The price-quantity combination that yields the highest profit—the greatest difference between total revenues and total costs—will be chosen.

Price searcher

A firm that must seek the price that benefits it most. The firm has some control over the price it charges.

The Real World

In the real world of market structures, firms usually have *some* control over the price they charge. There are few pure competitors that must take price as given and few pure monopolists that produce a product or service for which there are no substitutes. Even those firms that have been granted monopolistic licenses by the government face competition from firms producing goods that are *possible* substitutes.

● WHY PEOPLE PRODUCE— OUR INCENTIVE STRUCTURE

Incentives

One of the characteristics of the U.S. economy is that people are allowed, within broad limits, to pursue their own economic self-interest. It follows, then, that individuals will respond to **incentives**, as well as to the lack of incentives.

In general, individuals will be productive if it is worthwhile to be productive; they will be unproductive if they believe that their best interests lie in that direction. Much human behavior is purposeful and goal oriented. It is essential to realize that individuals usually respond to economic incentives in a *predictable* way, and that response is the pursuit of self-interest as *they* perceive it.

Incentives and the Four Factors of Production

We have already mentioned resources and the factors of production. These factors can be separated into four categories:

1. Land
2. Labor
3. Capital
4. Entrepreneurship

Each factor is a resource and each responds to incentives.

Incentives

Those things that stimulate, cause, or encourage people's actions.

Land

A factor of production that includes all naturally formed resources that exist without the help of humans. Land includes water, minerals, ores, earth, climate, and so on.

Land. **Land** includes not only the soil, but natural resources in general—large bodies of water, natural seaports, minerals, ores, and so on. Such resources are provided by nature. In a market economy, land is usually owned privately, by individuals or by businesses. Since individuals own land, they are not likely to mistreat it knowingly. In a market economy, the incentives are to use the various forms of land in the most profitable way. Minerals and ores will be sold to the highest bidder; in general, the highest bidder will be that business (or person) able to turn those factors into goods

86

with the highest market value. That is, the most profitable businesses will be those that can *afford* to outbid other potential users for a specific land resource.

In some areas, good farmland may be plowed under so that houses and shopping centers can be built on it. Those who own this land will allow the land to be allocated to nonfarming uses if nonfarmers offer a higher price for it. This fact, of course, is bemoaned by many and has been referred to as urban sprawl, or "the paving of America."

Labor.   Human **labor** resources include the various skills that people acquire or inherit, such as the ability to do mathematics, work with computers, write well, dig ditches, and so on.

Laborers respond to incentives. Other things (many of which are potentially important) held constant, laborers will sell their services to the highest bidders. Also, laborers will be willing to acquire new skills by training or education if they believe sufficiently higher wages will be the result.

In general, laborers will be allocated to those businesses (including self-employment) that are producing the most profitable goods and services. Firms that are more profitable can offer the highest wages and bid laborers away from the less profitable (or unprofitable) businesses.

Capital.   **Capital**, or capital goods, are those goods used in the production of other goods and services. Examples of capital goods are tools, machines, buildings, trucks, and improvements to land. Capital goods command a price. They will be rented out or sold to the highest bidders. In a market economy, individuals are allowed to own capital goods, and they are allowed to keep the income derived from their capital goods.

Entrepreneurship.   **Entrepreneurship**, or entrepreneurial ability, has to do with the risk taken in combining the other three factors of production to form a new business or keep an old one going, or to introduce new products and techniques, all for the profit that can be earned by doing so.

Clearly, entrepreneurship lies at the heart of the market economy. **Entrepreneurs** are those people referred to at the beginning of this chapter—people willing to take a chance for the possibility of profits.

Obviously, entrepreneurs require incentives; without the lure of higher profits (which for many entrepreneurs provide the means for launching still other enterprises), entrepreneurship would diminish greatly.

Labor

The human productive resource that includes not only human beings per se, but their abilities and talents, however obtained.

Capital

All goods made by human beings and used in the production of other goods and services. Examples are tools, equipment, buildings, and improvements to land.

Entrepreneurship

The use of human resources to raise capital, to organize, manage, and assemble other factors of production, and to make basic business policy decisions.

Entrepreneur

A person who is willing to take a risk by investing in production, choosing managers, and making sure that the business succeeds, for the profits that can be earned by the business.

● THE MOVEMENT OF RESOURCES

In a market economy, resources are not allocated randomly. It is not by chance that thousands of workers are employed by a particular corporation, whereas other businesses hire only one or two laborers. When farmland is plowed under to make room for new houses, it is not a chance occurrence. When relatively scarce water is allocated away from farming and toward industry where it is used as a coolant, a definite reason exists. Nor is it mere happenstance that the automobile industry is the largest buyer of steel. In all these cases, resources are moving from many potential uses to one specific use.

In a market economy, there are strong incentives for resources to move from a lower-valued use to a higher-valued one. Consider an example.

Suppose that you own rich farmland and can earn $100,000 per year by producing and selling corn. Then a builder offers you $150,000 per year for the use of your land so that he may build an apartment complex on it. What would you do? Most likely, you would let your land be used for the apartment complex, since that's where the greater incentives are. Because the same land can earn a higher rate of return when it is used for an apartment complex, it follows that the land's highest-valued use is for buildings and not for farming. Here people value the services provided by the apartments more highly than they value the corn grown on the land. If this were not the case, the builder could not afford to bid this land away from farming.

Of course, if farmland truly becomes relatively scarcer, the value of food will rise relative to the value of apartments. Farmers then will be able to outbid builders for farmland.

Consider another example: the profitability of making sailboats. A few years ago, people were afraid that they might not be able to buy gasoline for internal-combustion-powered pleasure boats. This fear (among other things) resulted in a reduction in the demand for such boats. Graph 4–1a shows this drop in demand as a shift inward to the left in the demand curve for powerboats. What happened? The relative price of powerboats fell from the original price of P_e to P_e'.

The prospect of owning a boat that couldn't go anywhere led many people to decide against buying powerboats. People who owned powerboats suddenly wanted to sell them. Boating enthusiasts began to look into sailing, a substitute that required little, if any, gasoline. Thus, the demand curve for sailboats increased. It moved outward to the right, as shown in Graph 4–1b. The relative price of sailboats rose from P_e to P_e''.

Assuming that the cost of inputs for powerboat manufacturing hasn't changed, the lower market-clearing price would imply less

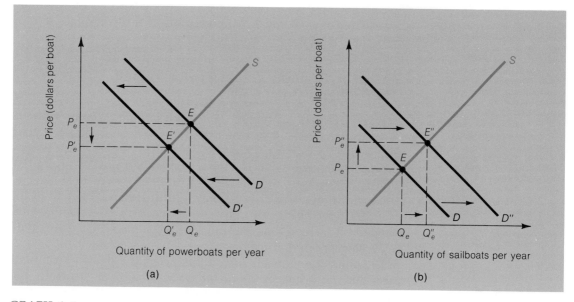

GRAPH 4-1

Shifts in Demand Cause Prices to Change

(a) Supply and demand for powerboats. At the original equilibrium, the market-clearing relative price was P_e. Because of an anticipated gasoline shortage, the demand curve shifted leftward from D to D', and the relative price (and hence profitability) of manufacturing powerboats fell. The new market-clearing price after adjustment became P'_e, with the smaller quantity Q'_e produced.

In panel (b), just the opposite has happened for sailboats. The demand curve has increased from D to D''. The market-clearing price has gone up from P_e to P''_e, with the larger quantity Q''_e produced. The profitability of making sailboats has risen. More resources will flow into the sailboat industry; fewer will be used in the powerboat industry.

profit (or maybe even losses) for manufacturers. On the other hand, again assuming no change in input prices, the higher market-clearing price of sailboats would bring about a higher profit per unit for sailboat producers.

The profitability of powerboat manufacturing clearly fell. The profitability of sailboat manufacturing clearly increased. In time, the increased profitability of sailboat manufacturing caused an increase in the number of new firms coming into the industry. It is very likely that people started making sailboats in their backyards and setting up small sailboat manufacturing companies. Moreover, powerboat manufacturers switched some production facilities for making powerboats to making sailboats. Soon, the output of sailboats increased dramatically and the output of powerboats fell.

What brought about the decision to produce more sailboats and fewer powerboats? It was not a decree by a central political figure. Rather, the incentive to earn higher profits in sailboat manufactur-

89

ing caused resources to flow into that activity. The incentive to minimize losses in powerboat manufacturing caused resources to flow out of that activity.

Moving Resources from Lower-Valued to Higher-Valued Uses

This movement of resources in search of higher profits is simultaneously a movement of resources from lower- to higher-valued uses. When consumers no longer wanted to buy as many powerboats, the demand curve (Graph 4–1a) shifted inward to the left. From a subjective point of view, powerboats were no longer as valuable as they were prior to the shift in demand. Had all of the resources remained in the powerboat industry, they would have generated a lower subjective value to consumers than they could have elsewhere in the economy.

The piling up of unsold inventories acted as a signal to manufacturers that powerboats were no longer as subjectively valuable, and encouraged the manufacturer to switch resources to another product.

When some of these resources were moved from powerboat manufacturing to sailboat manufacturing, they were, by necessity, being put to a use that consumers valued more. How do we know this? Because the demand curve for sailboats shifted outward to the right. With a given supply curve, sailboats brought a higher relative price, indicating that consumers valued marginal (extra) resources in the sailboat industry more than previously.

Consumer Sovereignty Revisited

The movement of resources from lower- to higher-valued uses is dependent on consumer sovereignty. Consumer sovereignty means that the ultimate determiners of the amount of goods produced are consumers, not politicians or businesses. In other words, in a world of consumer sovereignty, consumers are the decision makers. Final production is destined to fulfill their wants and no one else's. In a pure market economy, or price system, each consumer expresses his or her desires (constrained by income) by voting with his or her dollars. When fewer consumers were voting for powerboats, the result was a shift leftward of the demand curve for powerboats. When more consumers were voting for sailboats, the result was a shift rightward of the demand curve for sailboats.

Note that the consumer voting system is not the same as a majority voting system. No firm has to receive 51 percent of the available dollar votes in order to produce a particular product. There are, for example, specialty customized car companies that probably receive on the order of 4/1000ths of 1 percent of the total dollar votes for new cars each year. They continue to exist because that is a sufficient demand to make them profitable. On the other hand, there are many products that are not produced even though they could receive 100 percent of all of the dollar votes by all of a small group of people desiring those goods. Why? Because even with 100 percent of the dollar votes, there would not be enough buyers for a businessperson to make a profit on the product. Suppose someone who liked French cooking wanted to eat out regularly in a high-quality restaurant in town. If that gourmet and, say, 30 others are the only residents of the town, chances are that even if everyone went to the restaurant regularly, there wouldn't be enough business for the restaurant owners to make a normal profit. When you find that a desired good or service is unavailable, your situation may be similar to that of the gourmet.[1]

In sum, in a pure market economy, consumers vote with their dollars, but it is proportional voting, as opposed to majority-rule voting. If you have a spendable income of $100 per week, then you can vote with it in any way you want: $1 for each of 100 different items; or $50 for one item, $30 for another, and $20 for a third. Manufacturers will respond and resources will be allocated proportionally to the way the total population spends its money, or votes with its income.

● ARBITRAGE

Arbitrage is an important concept in economics. It refers to the nearly simultaneous timing of purchases and sales (by the same person or persons) of an equivalent good or service in order to profit from price discrepancies. For example, suppose General Motors stock is selling for $50 a share in New York City and $60 a share in San Francisco. An alert trader could buy in New York and sell in San Francisco and earn almost $10 a share for doing nothing. Clearly, *other* people will get into this game. Arbitrage will see to it that price differentials for equivalent or identical goods will tend to disappear.

Arbitrage is a phenomenon in economics that helps explain resource movements. If one firm is paying $10 an hour for lathe operators, while another firm is paying only $5 an hour for lathe operators with exactly the same skills, there will be a movement of labor from the lower-paying firm to the higher-paying one. The higher-paying firm will observe that it has many applicants and can get

---

[1]There's another difference between political voting and dollar voting. In a market system, you do not have to vote for an entire package at one single time. Rather, you vote for different parts—goods and services—of your total consumption package a little at a time. In a political arena, you usually make your decision once a year, and sometimes only once every four years.

Arbitrage

The simultaneous buying and selling of the same item from different people in order to make a profit.

away with lowering wage rates. The lower-paying firm will find that it is losing laborers and will have to raise its wages. Eventually, firms hiring laborers of *equivalent* skill will pay similar wages. In this case, both firms will probably end up paying between $7 and $8 an hour.

The notion of resources being allocated to eliminate price differentials for equivalent goods or services is a powerful one. It leads to the proposition that wage differences for different individuals having equivalent skills will not be very great. Why not? Suppose Jones is paid $10 an hour for a skill and Smith is paid $3 an hour for that same skill. If Jones and Smith truly have the same skill, entrepreneurs will notice the difference and take advantage of it. Some will entice Smith to leave his current job for a wage rate higher than $3 an hour. Whoever is employing Jones will tell Jones that he cannot be paid $10 an hour because someone else is being paid much less for the same skill. This activity among employers, potential or actual, narrows the spread between individuals' pay for equivalent work. In order to maintain the difference in wage rates for the same skill, entrepreneurs would have to turn down higher-than-normal profits. In other words, if differences in wage rates continued without those differences being reflective of a difference in skill, it would mean that there were few, if any, entrepreneurs willing to take advantage of such wage differentials. This seems unlikely.

● WHEN PROFITS ARE DENIED

What happens when the government decides what a "normal" or allowable profit should be and taxes profits exceeding that level? For one thing, the entrepreneurs behind the firms saddled with the so-called excess profits tax may very well find other countries where their endeavors will be more appreciated and rewarded. At the very least, these entrepreneurs will engage in fewer projects. They will avoid high-risk activities, since the relatively higher risk will no longer be compensated by potentially higher (excessive) profits.

Less risk-taking will certainly make our economy less dynamic. If an excess profits tax were levied on a widespread basis, there would unquestionably be less innovation and fewer technological advances. Look at the U.S.S.R. Risk taking is not rewarded there, and innovation and technological advances, except in a few instances, are rare.

Consumer sovereignty is also likely to suffer. As consumers change their tastes, businesses are likely to respond more slowly since "excessive" profits will be taxed away. Profits may indeed be the price that must be paid for a dynamic, technologically advancing, materially rich society. Those individuals who seek profits have the ability to increase the nation's living standard. They demand wealth in exchange.

92

Production Should Be for People Rather Than for Profit

THE ARGUMENT

Profits are important signals to businesses. They induce entrepreneurs to act in specific ways. Nonetheless, a significant part of the population does not believe that production for profit is appropriate. Is there in fact a difference between producing for people and producing for profit?

THE ANALYSIS

Those who believe that producing for profit will lead to a suboptimal production of important goods and services use as examples education, artificial kidney machines, and safer products. One can argue, however, that if people really want education, artificial kidney machines, and safer products, then it will be profitable for producers to produce them. After all, profits do give signals about what people really want. If there is a demand for more safety, an automobile, or toy, or clothing-manufacturing company could earn higher profits by making safer products and advertising that fact widely. In reality, people often choose cheaper goods over safer ones. It may not always be better to have more safety, regardless of the cost involved. A trade-off exists.

Whatever the argument in favor of producing for people rather than for profit, an operationally meaningful mechanism to allow government policymakers to assess what people want would be necessary. How would policymakers go about deciding the appropriate mix of goods and services, given our resource base? For the most part, we now use the dollar voting system. Should majority rule prevail instead? We already pointed out that the dollar voting system is proportional, whereas a political voting system would probably be majority rule. The array of goods and services offered would drop dramatically with such a system.

Profits are high only when demand is high. Demand is high only when people actually want the good or service in question. Low profits mean that people do not want to pay what is necessary to keep the current level of resources in the industry in question. Nowhere are we stating anything subjectively about the "goodness" or "badness" of people's tastes. Politically, we still may determine that in spite of people's demand for certain goods, such as X-rated movies and hallucinogens, such demand will not be satisfied even though it is profitable for private businesses. Also, the demand for artificial kidney machines and safety may be deemed politically too low. The government, in that case, can, and often does, step in either to provide more of those goods or to mandate minimum levels.

DISCUSSION QUESTIONS

1. In an economic system in which goods are produced for people, what criteria do the producers use to decide what to produce?
2. In an economic system in which goods are produced for profits, what might be the harmful effects of not taking anything else into account?

93

● WHAT'S AHEAD

We described the movement of resources in the market system in this chapter, but we really didn't take into account impediments to such movement. These make up the subject matter of the following chapter, in which we look at market failures, or the inability of the market mechanism to allocate resources to their best uses. We alluded to market failures when we discussed water. In that instance, the fact that not all water is owned certainly presents a problem. We mentioned that some goods may not be in sufficient demand to make it profitable for them to be produced, even though, as a society, we believe that they should be produced.

● CHAPTER SUMMARY

Profit is the guiding force in a market economy, where profit is defined as the difference between total revenues and total costs received for the production of a good or service. In a market economy, profits, or rather relative profits, signal where resources should move—to sectors with higher profits, *away from* sectors with lower profits.

A market economy is one in which there are private property rights, and self-interest reigns. The price system is part of the market system where consumer sovereignty allows individuals to dictate what is produced by buying more of what is desired and less of what is not, thereby affecting relative prices. A market economy can be contrasted to a command economy, in which the movement of resources and the way in which resources are combined are dictated by a central decision-making unit composed of a relatively small number of individuals.

The two extreme market structures are pure competition and pure monopoly. In the former, there are numerous buyers and sellers and each is a price taker, unable to change the price determined by the interaction of market supply and market demand. Pure monopolists, on the other hand, are single sellers of a particular good or service for which no close substitutes exist. The pure monopolist is a price searcher and seeks a price that results in the greatest possible difference between revenues and costs. However, the price searcher does face the law of demand: At higher prices, a lower quantity is demanded.

A comparison of pure competition and pure monopoly shows that, in general, competition leads to a lower price. This lower price also means a higher amount of sales because of the law of demand. With monopoly, output is restricted and a higher price is charged. However, monopolists are not free to charge any price they please. Why? Because of the law of demand.

The four factors of production are land, labor, capital, and entrepreneurial ability, or entrepreneurship. All of them respond to the incentive of a higher rate of return for a given effort. In particular, laborers respond to higher wages by shifting their efforts from one industry to another. So, too, do the owners of capital. Entrepreneurs seek areas where their skills will yield the highest profits. As entrepreneurs move resources from less profitable to more profitable businesses, resources are moved from lower-valued to higher-valued uses.

● QUESTIONS FOR REVIEW AND STUDY

1. Competition for profits tends to _____ profits and prices.

2. Buyers and sellers interact in _____.

3. In a _____ economy, most important economic decisions are made by a highly centralized group.

4. In a traditional economy, a person's job or economic status is largely determined by _____.

5. Two of the most important aspects of a pure market economy are _____ _____ _____ and _____.

6. In a market economy, prices can be viewed as _____.

7. A rising price is a signal to _____.

8. Under a system of consumer sovereignty, consumers _____ with their dollars.

9. The two polar market structures are pure _____ and pure _____.

10. In pure competition, all buyers and sellers are simply _____ _____ because they cannot influence price.

11. Resources are allowed to move in a purely competitive world. That means that there is free _____ and _____.

12. When profits are _____, there will be no change in the number of firms in an industry.

13. When profits are abnormal, we will see _____ or _____.

14. Since a pure monopolist is the entire industry, in order to sell more, it must _____ _____.

15. Even a pure monopolist's product has _____.

16. The four factors of production are _____, _____, _____, and _____.

17. Land includes all _____ resources in general.

18. The incentive luring people to be entrepreneurs is _____.

19. Changes in profits lead to changes in _____ allocation.

20. Within the market economy, the incentive is for resources to move from _____ to _____ valued uses.

21. Price is kept uniform by a process known as _____.

ANSWERS

1. reduce 2. markets 3. command 4. birthright 5. private property rights; self-interest 6. signals 7. conserve 8. vote 9. competition; monopoly 10. price takers 11. entry; exit 12. normal 13. entry; exit 14. lower price 15. substitutes 16. land; labor; capital; entrepreneurship 17. natural 18. profit 19. resource 20. lower-; higher- 21. arbitrage

● ANSWERS TO CHAPTER PREVIEW QUESTIONS

1. When you buy something, do you, as an individual, have any effect on the kinds of goods and services offered for sale?

No, but if you look at your actions in concert with all other consumers' actions, then you form a part of an enormous group of consumers that ultimately affects which goods survive in the marketplace and which goods fail. If you, along with many other consumers, do not like a particular model, brand, or product, you express your dissatisfaction by not purchasing it. Producers of that product, model, or brand will ultimately find such production unprofitable and will reduce the amount of resources that go into producing it. In this way the consumer—you—determines ultimately the mix of goods and services available for purchase. But, of course, this doesn't happen overnight. Also, don't be misled into thinking that, because there are many goods and services that are *not* available even though you want to buy them, you cannot affect production choices. This simply means that you are part of a relatively small number of people. When your individual demands are combined, the total market demand for each good or service is still so small that no producer of that good or service can make a profit. In other words, the production costs are too high relative to the price at which the producer could sell the product and have sufficient sales. Just because you can't buy a good French meal in a town of 30 people doesn't mean, therefore, that the market is not working.

2. What is the difference between the price of a good sold in a highly competitive market system and the price of that very same good sold in a market where there are only one or two big producers?

The good would cost less in a market structure in which there were many competing firms. Competition among those firms would drive prices down relative to the price that would be charged by a pure monopolist, or even that charged by several large firms dominating an industry. Pure competition would also lead to a larger quantity of the good being produced and sold.

● PROBLEMS

1. Some critics believe and have stated that consumer sovereignty is nonexistent in our economy. List the possible reasons that consumer sovereignty might not exist. Also, can you distinguish between consumer sovereignty and consumer choice? (*Hint*: The consumer could be "sovereign" but have few choices.)

2. List the various institutional means through which resources in our economy are used to satisfy human wants. Pick one institution that has changed over the last several hundred years. How has that change altered our economic system?

● SELECTED REFERENCES

Breit, William, and Roger Ransom. *The Academic Scribblers*. New York: CBS Publishing Co., revised edition, 1982.

Galbraith, John Kenneth. *The New Industrial State*. Boston: Houghton Mifflin, 1979.

Heilbroner, Robert L. *The Worldly Philosophers*. 4th ed. New York: Simon & Schuster, 1972, chap. 3.

Klaasen, Adrian, ed. *The Invisible Hand*. Chicago: Henry Regnery, 1965.

5

Market
Failure

Chapter Preview

1. As you enter a city in which the air has been fouled by pollution, you know that pollution is not something anyone desires. But does that mean that the optimal quantity of pollution is zero?

2. What is the difference between the incentives facing you when you pollute the air in your house —let's say by smoking or cooking—and the incentives facing you when you start your automobile and its exhaust gases pollute the air around you?

● KEY TERMS

Common property   Social costs
Externality   Spillover
Market failure   Third parties
Private costs

In Chapter 4, the emphasis was on the market and economic move-ment within markets. A particularly important topic was how the price system within a market economy, coupled with a system of profits, directed resource use. Changing relative rates of profitability lead to resource flows in which resources go from lower-valued uses to higher-valued uses. However, there are circumstances under which this flow of resources will not occur or will not occur suffi-ciently to maximize the available benefits from a given set of re-sources. In other words, there can be situations of **market failure**. One situation in which market failure occurs—pure monopoly—was already mentioned. Remember that under a market structure of pure monopoly, output is restricted compared to what it would be in a competitive situation, and price is higher. Other examples of market failure involve pollution and lack of ownership rights.

● THE POLLUTION OF OUR ENVIRONMENT

Today there seems to be an annoying amount of air, water, noise, olfactory (smell), and visual pollution. At first glance, it seems that the market solution to the problem of allocating scarce resources has gone awry. As pollution increases, so, too, do people's fears that the free working of supply and demand will bring about the ultimate destruction of the world as we know it. The question is why some individuals and business firms have been permitted to harm our environment without paying the consequences.

Private versus Social Costs

Up to this point, discussion has dealt with situations in which the costs of an individual's actions are borne directly by the individual. When a business firm has to pay wages to workers, it knows ex-actly what its labor costs are. When it has to buy materials or build a plant, it knows quite well the cost it will incur. When an individual has to pay for car repairs, or shoe repairs, or for a theater ticket, he or she knows exactly what the cost will be. These costs are called **private costs**. Private costs are borne solely by the individuals who incur them. They are *internal* in the sense that the firm or household must explicitly take account of them.

What about a situation in which a business firm dumps the waste products from its production process into a nearby river? Or in which an individual litters a public park or beach? Clearly, a cost is

Market failure

A situation in which the signals in the marketplace are unable to fully reflect the value of resources, and the actors in the marketplace are unable to direct the flow of these resources to the best possible use.

Private costs

Those costs incurred by individuals when they use scarce resources. For ex-ample, the private cost of running an automobile is equal to the gas, oil, insurance, maintenance, and deprecia-tion costs. Private costs are also called *explicit costs*.

100

involved in these actions. When the business firm pollutes the water, people downstream suffer the consequences. They may not want to drink the polluted water or swim and bathe in it. They may also be unable to catch as many fish as before because of the pollution. In the case of littering, the people who come along after a litterer has cluttered the park or the beach are the ones who bear the costs. In these instances, individuals other than those who commit the actions are the ones who bear the cost. That is, the creator of the cost is not the sole bearer. The costs are not internalized by the individual or firm; they are external. *External* costs, together with *internal*, or private, costs, sum to **social costs**. Pollution problems and, indeed, all problems pertaining to the environment may be viewed as situations where social costs are greater than private costs. Since some economic agents don't pay the full social costs of their actions, but rather only the smaller private costs their actions are socially unacceptable. Situations which create a divergence between social and private costs result in "too much" steel production, automobile driving, and beach littering, to mention only a few of the many examples that exist.

Polluted Air. When automobile drivers step into their cars, they bear only the private costs of driving—gas, maintenance, depreciation, and insurance on their automobiles. However, they create an additional cost—that of air pollution—which they are not forced to take into account when they make the decision to drive. They do not bear this cost *directly*. The social cost of driving includes all of the private costs plus the cost of air pollution, which society bears. Decisions made only on the basis of private costs lead to too much automobile driving or, alternatively, to too little money spent on the reduction of automobile pollution for a given amount of driving.

Consider the example of lights in hotel rooms. Paying guests know that they will not pay any more on any single occasion if they leave lights on in the hotel room. Of course, the more frequently guests leave lights on, the higher the cost of running the hotel will be, and the higher the average room charge will be. But for the individual guest at any one point in time, there is no direct cost involved in being "wasteful" with lights. People will therefore leave lights on more often in hotel rooms than in their own houses and apartments. By analogy, clean air is a scarce resource offered to automobile drivers free of charge. They will use more of it than they would if they had to pay the full social costs.

● EXTERNALITIES

When private costs differ from social costs, a problem of **externalities** arises because individual decision makers are not internal-

Social costs

The full costs that society bears when a resource-using action occurs. For example, the social cost of driving a car is equal to all of the private costs plus any additional costs that society bears, including air pollution and traffic congestion.

Externality

A situation in which a private cost or benefit diverges from a social cost or benefit. The costs or benefits of an action are not fully borne by two parties engaging in an exchange, or by an individual engaging in a scarce resource-using activity.

101

izing *all* the costs. Rather, some of these costs remain external to the decision-making process. Remember that the full cost of using a scarce resource is borne, one way or another, by others living in the society. That is, society must pay the full opportunity cost of any activity that uses scarce resources. The individual decision maker is the firm or the customer, and external costs and benefits will *not* enter into that individual's or firm's decision-making processes.

Consider an example. Suppose you are living in a town that, so far, has clean air. A steel mill moves into your town. It produces steel for which it has paid for the inputs—land, labor, capital, and entrepreneurship. The price it charges for the steel reflects, in this example, only the costs that the steel mill has incurred. In the course of production, however, the mill gets one input—smoke dispersal —free by simply taking it. This is indeed an input because in the making of steel, the furnaces emit smoke. The steel mill doesn't have to pay the cost of cleaning the smoke; rather, the people in the community pay that cost in the form of dirtier clothes, dirtier cars and houses, and perhaps even more respiratory illnesses. The effect is similar to what would happen if the steel mill could take coal or oil free. There has been a *negative* **spillover** effect, or a *negative externality*. Some of the costs associated with the production of the steel have spilled over to **third parties**, that is, parties other than the buyer and the seller of the steel. A negative spillover is called a negative externality because there are costs that you and your neighbors pay—dirtier clothes and cars plus respiratory problems—even though your group is external to the market transaction between the steel mill and the buyers of steel.

This situation is depicted in Graph 5–1. The demand curve for steel is D. The supply curve, as observed by the steel mill in your town, is S. That supply curve includes only those costs that the firm has to pay. The equilibrium, or market-clearing, situation will occur at a quantity of Q_e. If we include the costs of negative externalities in our graph, we find out what the full cost of steel production really is. This is equivalent to saying that the price of some other input into steel production has increased. As we saw earlier, an increase in input prices shifts a supply curve inward to the left. Thus in Graph 5–1, the supply curve shifts from S to S'. The equilibrium (and socially optimal) quantity would fall to Q_e' and the price would rise to P_e'. That price is implicitly being paid, but by two different groups of people. The purchasers of steel and steel products pay only P_e. The difference between P_e' and P_e is being paid by third parties in the form of dirtier clothes, houses, and cars, and increased respiratory illnesses. A steel mill that *voluntarily* installed pollution abatement equipment would be imposing extra costs on itself; the firm would then be placed at a competitive disadvantage. The marketplace would ruthlessly drive it out of business. It follows that too much pollution would emerge in a pure market economy.

Spillover

A situation in which a benefit or cost associated with an economic activity spills over to third parties.

Third parties

Those external to negotiations between buyers and sellers.

102

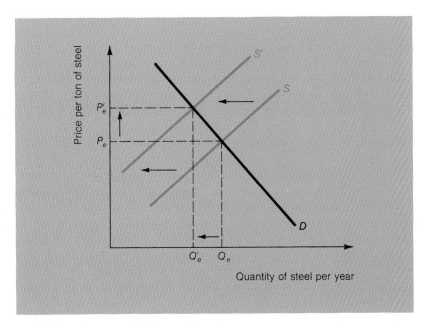

GRAPH 5–1

Negative Externalities—Pollution

Here we show a situation in which the production of steel generates negative externalities. If the steel mill ignores pollution, at equilibrium the quantity will be Q_e, where the demand curve D intersects the supply curve S. If we include the additional cost borne by nearby residents that is caused by the steel mill's production, the supply curve would shift inward to the left to S'. This shows that the society is devoting too many resources to steel production if negative externalities are not taken into account. If consumers were forced to pay a price that reflected the environmental cost of the negative spillover, the quantity demanded would fall to Q_e'; by implication the amount of pollution would fall to the socially optimal rate.

Correcting the Signals
(In Theory, at Least)

We can see here an "easy" method of reducing the amount of pollution and environmental degradation that exists. Somehow the signals in the economy must be changed so that decision makers will take into account *all* the costs of their actions. In the case of automobile pollution, some method might be devised whereby motorists are taxed according to the value of pollutive harm they cause. In the case of a firm, a system might be devised whereby businesses are taxed according to the value of pollutive harm they create. In this manner, they would have an incentive to install pollution-abatement equipment.

Thus, there are two choices open to the polluter who is faced with a higher price for pollution: (1) There can be a change in the production method, thereby reducing pollution, or (2) there can be a reduction in the amount of activity that causes the pollution. In most

103

cases, both techniques will be used. The relative costs and benefits of each will determine for each polluter which will be undertaken and in what quantities.

Essentially, the size of the *economic damages*, rather than the size of the physical amount of pollution, must be ascertained. A polluting electric plant in New York City will cause much more damage than the same plant in an unpopulated area. There are already innumerable demands on the air in New York City, so that the pollution from smokestacks will not naturally be cleansed away. There are millions of people who will breathe that smelly air and thereby incur the costs of sore throats, sickness, emphysema, and even early death. There are many, many buildings that will become dirtier faster because of the pollution, and many cars and clothes that will also become dirtier faster. The list goes on and on, but it should be obvious that a given quantity of pollution will cause more harm in concentrated urban environments than it will in less dense rural environments. If some form of taxation were established to align private costs with social costs and to force people to internalize externalities, a measure of *economic* costs instead of *physical* quantities would have to be devised. But the tax, in any event, should fall on the private sector and modify private-sector economic agents' behavior.[1]

What About Positive Externalities?

Not all externalities are negative. Using a classic example, even people who are not inoculated against communicable diseases can benefit from the inoculations everyone else receives, for then epidemics won't break out. Thus, there are benefits that are external to each individual's decision to be inoculated. We call the existence of such benefits a *positive externality*, or an external benefit. Other examples of external benefits include the pleasure passersby receive from looking at well-kept lawns, and the satisfaction that a neighbor might receive from listening to someone else's high-quality stereo system played loudly. Where the social benefits of an action exceed the private benefits, we would expect that the individual decision makers would provide too little of such an action, from society's point of view. In fact, it is often argued that many endeavors involve large social benefits that are not internalized. It is further argued that government subsidization or provision of such activity is in order. This is often the argument used to justify public education. An educated citizenry, some will argue, votes more wisely and com-

---

[1]Since the economic cost for the same physical quantity of pollution would be different in different locations, according to population density, to the natural topographical setting, and so forth, so-called optimal taxes of pollution would vary from location to location. Nonetheless, a uniform tax might make sense where administrative costs, particularly the cost of ascertaining the actual economic costs, are relatively high.

104

mits less crime, so society should furnish public education priced below its marginal (extra) cost.

To demonstrate positive externalities in graphic form, we will use the example already mentioned concerning inoculations against communicable disease. In Graph 5–2 we show the demand curve, without taking account of any positive externalities, as D and the supply curve as S. The equilibrium price is P_e and the equilibrium quantity is Q_e. If we take into account the positive externalities rendered to individuals not inoculated, the demand curve shifts from D to D'. The new equilibrium (and socially optimal) quantity is Q_e' and the new equilibrium price is P_e'. With no corrective action, this society is not devoting enough resources to inoculations against communicable diseases.

Summary of Externalities

When there are negative spillovers, the market will tend to over-allocate resources to the production of the good in question for it will

GRAPH 5–2

Positive Externalities

Here we show the situation in which inoculations against communicable diseases generate external benefits to individuals who are not inoculated, but benefit because epidemics will not break out. If each individual ignores the external benefit of inoculations, the market-clearing quantity will be Q_e, where D intersects S. If positive externalities are taken into account, however, the demand curve would shift right-ward to D', giving a new equilibrium (and socially optimal) quantity of Q_e'. The price would rise to P_e. This shows that not enough resources are devoted to inoculations against communicable diseases in a pure market economy situation.

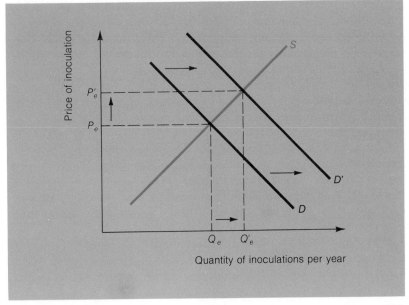

be too inexpensive. In our example, too much steel (and pollution) was being produced. On the other hand, when there are positive spillovers, the market will underallocate resources to the production of that good or service. Both situations are examples of market failure. The price system, or market, fails to present the correct signals to the participants—buyers and producers.

● WHY THERE IS A DIVERGENCE BETWEEN SOCIAL AND PRIVATE COSTS

We've described a number of situations in which there is a divergence between social costs and private costs, but we haven't explained why the divergence occurs. Basically, most problems occur when ownership rights are lacking or ill defined, as in cases involving common property. Externalities do not typically occur in situations where a person's rights to use a resource are well defined and upheld by a legal system.

Common Property

Once again, suppose you live near a smelly steel factory. The air around you—which is something that you have to use—is damaged. You, in turn, are damaged by breathing it. However, you do not necessarily have grounds for stopping the air pollution or for obtaining compensation for the destruction of the air around you. In most cases, you do not have ownership rights; air is a **common property** resource.

Herein lies the crux of the problem: Whenever ownership rights are indefinite or nonexistent, social costs may diverge from private costs. When no one owns a particular resource, people have no incentive (conscience aside) to consider their despoliation of that resource. If one person decides not to pollute the air, there will be no significant effect on the total level of pollution. If one person decides not to pollute the ocean, there will still be approximately the same amount of ocean pollution—provided, of course, that the individual is responsible for only a small part of the total amount of ocean pollution.

Basically, then, pollution exists only when there are no well-defined ownership rights. For example, pollution problems do not exist in people's backyards into which no one else can see. That is their own property, which they choose to keep as clean as they want, given their preferences for cleanliness weighed against the costs of maintaining an attractive backyard.

When ownership rights exist, individuals have legal recourse for any damages sustained through the misuse of their property. When ownership rights are well defined, the use of property—that is, the

Common property

Property owned by everyone and therefore owned by no one (e.g., air and water).

use of resources—will generally involve contracting between the owners of those resources. If you own land, you might contract with a person who wants to use it for raising cows. The contract would most likely be written in the form of a lease agreement.

An Ownership Problem—Water Shortages

In Chapter 3, a discussion of water shortages was presented. Emphasis was placed on the reaction of users of water to higher prices, and the fact that the quantity of water demanded did depend on the price charged. What wasn't discussed is the fact that the nature of water ownership rights makes water shortages, particularly in the western states, somewhat different from other shortages. If everyone owns large bodies of water, then in effect nobody owns them. The result is that the cost to individual water users is practically zero. Unfortunately, the cost to society of water use is positive; that is, water is indeed a scarce good. At a zero price all of us cannot simultaneously use as much water as we want. But individuals tend to disregard the cost to society. Since the private cost to them is nearly zero, they will tend to waste water. The problem is made that much worse when droughts arise. The solution, according to some economists, is to assign ownership rights to all water. No one who owns bodies of water will allow water to be wasted. Water will be priced at above zero values to private users, and these users will conserve its use. Water will be allocated to its most productive use, and the higher price that people pay for its use will encourage them to conserve it.

The solution of allowing private ownership rights to individuals and corporations, who will in turn charge other individuals for their water use, can be made more politically feasible if individuals are allowed to bid for such rights.

Actually, such a system has worked out West in a rough fashion. In earlier days, water rights were given to first users. Later users got what was left. The law recognized this ownership-right system and as different users came to have different relative values to society, a natural result occurred—those with ownership rights were able to sell their rights in water to latecomers.

Other Examples

The ownership problem is not unique to water. Have you ever wondered why there is a "shortage" of bald eagles or whales, but not turkeys or sheep? By all accounts, turkeys and sheep are very stupid, relative to eagles and whales, yet they are surviving species, whereas eagles and whales are not. Why? Because no one owns eagles and whales, but turkeys and sheep are owned—and not wasted.

107

Let's Market the Right to Pollute

THE ARGUMENT

Pollution remains a problem, particularly in major cities. The Environmental Protection Agency (EPA) has for some years attempted to create a marketplace for the buying and selling of rights to pollute. Is this a valid concept? Some argue that it is absurd on its face. Before we explain the plan itself, we must first examine why such a plan is needed. To understand the situation, we have to understand the federal Clean Air Act.

THE ANALYSIS

The federal Clean Air Act was passed in 1963, in an attempt to force a reduction in pollution, particularly in metropolitan areas. Through rules and regulations of the EPA, the Clean Air Act presents localities with specified permitted pollution levels. These so-called National Air Quality Standards must be met in most major metropolitan areas. In many such areas, however, air quality is already poor. Thus, a company that wishes to build a plant there is theoretically barred from doing so because of the detrimental impact on air quality. If adhered to strictly, the guidelines would mean no further industrial growth in many urban areas.

The Offset Policy

The EPA approved an offset policy to circumvent these rules. It requires a company wanting to build a plant to work out a corresponding reduction in pollution at some existing plant. For example, when Volkswagen wanted to build a plant in New Stanton, Pennsylvania, the state of Pennsylvania agreed to reduce pollutants from its highway-paving operations. This reduction offset the Volkswagen plant's additional pollution.

One major problem with the offset policy is the difficulty in finding an offset partner. Each time a firm wants to build a new plant in an already polluted area, it must seek, on an individual basis, an offset partner that agrees to reduce pollution (usually after a payment from the other company). This is where the idea of a bank for the buying and selling of pollution rights comes into play.

Creating the Pollution Rights Bank

Rather than seeking individual offset partners, the EPA has suggested that a bank for pollution rights be formed. It would be a clearinghouse that identifies, records, and stores the credits earned by any company that reduces its pollution to less than the legal limits. Such credits would probably be expressed in terms of the amount of pollutants removed (from some hypothetical level), such as so many pounds of sulfur dioxide per day. A company needing an offset to build a new plant could buy directly from the company that deposited the pollution rights credit. Alternatively, the depositor might use the credit itself later on. The system would probably work best if carried out at the state level, with supervision by the EPA.

The Incentives Involved.   Clearly, there would be economic incentives to reduce pollution levels below those set by law if such a bank existed. Any firm that believed it could cheaply reduce pollutants further would know that at some point another firm would pay it for such reduction in order to build a plant in that area. Presumably, such a marketplace for the right to pollute would encourage further research and development in pollution-reduction techniques. Today, many standards are set on an absolute physical basis, offering companies no additional incentive to reduce pollution below the air quality standard.

DISCUSSION QUESTIONS

1. Does marketing the right to pollute mean that we are allowing too much destruction of our environment?

2. Who implicitly has property rights in the air if a pollution bank is set up and the right to pollute is sold to the highest bidder?

● WHAT'S AHEAD

When market failures do not occur, the price system allocates resources in a unique way. The price system, in effect, answers important questions about how resources should be allocated. That is the subject matter of the next chapter.

● CHAPTER SUMMARY

In a pure price system, market failures can occur because of spillovers, or externalities. When negative spillovers occur, such as with air pollution, an overallocation of resources results. When positive spillovers occur, an underallocation of resources results. Problems of externalities arise when there is a difference between private and social costs. Private costs are those borne by individuals making voluntary exchanges. They are internal to the firm or to the household and are taken account of explicitly. Social costs, on the other hand, include all private costs, plus whatever additional costs society bears, for any activity. These costs may include such things as air and water pollution, for which private individuals do not have to pay. Few individuals or firms voluntarily consider social costs.

Another way of looking at the externality problem is to realize that it involves the lack of definite property rights. This refers to common property resources such as air and water. No one owns them, and therefore no one takes account of the long-run, harmful effects of excessive pollution.

● QUESTIONS FOR REVIEW AND STUDY

1. Most individuals take account of only _____ costs when making their decisions; such costs are internal and are explicitly recognized.

2. Whenever society pays costs that the individual does not recognize, we say that there is a divergence between _____ and _____ costs.

3. Another way of viewing the divergence between private and social costs is to consider such a divergence an _____.

4. When air pollution exists, we say that there is a negative externality, or _____ effect.

5. When there are negative externalities, too _____ resources are being devoted to the production activity.

6. One possible way to correct the economic signals when negative externalities occur is by _____.

7. The benefits that passersby receive when they view a well-cared-for lawn or garden are called _____ externalities.

8. In principle, the existence of positive externalities means that too _____ resources are being devoted to the economic activity.

9. The existence of a divergence between social and private costs often occurs because of a lack of _____ rights. Rather, the property in question is owned in _____.

10. One of the major problems preventing a solution to the water shortage problem throughout the United States is a lack of definite _____ _____ in water.

ANSWERS

1. private 2. social; private 3. externality 4. spillover 5. many 6. taxation 7. positive 8. few 9. property; common 10. ownership rights

● ANSWERS TO CHAPTER PREVIEW QUESTIONS

1. As you enter a city in which the air has been fouled by pollution, you know that pollution is not something anyone desires. But does that mean that the optimal quantity of pollution is zero?

Certainly if the optimal quantity of pollution were zero, we would be spending an unbelievable amount of our resources on preventing all types of pollution. In general, it does not pay for an individual, a company, a government, or society as a whole to undertake any activity past the point where the additional benefits are outweighed by the additional costs. Certainly that would be the case if we tried to eliminate all pollution. Currently, the state of technology is such that early units of pollution abatement are easily achieved at low cost. Attaining higher and higher levels of environmental quality (closer and closer to zero pollution) becomes progressively more difficult as the extra cost rises to prohibitive levels.

On the other side of the coin, the increased benefits of a cleaner and cleaner environment fall. Clearly there is some point at which we should stop trying to reduce pollution, and this is well before the zero level. Recognizing that the "optimal" quantity of pollution is not zero becomes easier when one realizes that scarce resources must be used to reduce pollution. It follows that a trade-off exists between a cleaner environment and the production of other goods and services. In that sense, nature's ability to self-cleanse is a resource that can be analyzed like any other resource, and a cleaner environment must take its place with other societal wants.

2. What is the difference between the incentives facing you when you pollute the air in your house—let's say by smoking or cooking—and the incentives facing you when you start your automobile and its exhaust gases pollute the air around you?

The incentive structure facing you when you, in whatever manner, pollute the air inside your own house is certainly different from that facing you when you start your car and pollute the air outside your house. Within your house, you, in a sense, have property rights in the air. You control, to a large extent, the quality of the air that you breathe. You can install electrostatic air cleaners. You can have air conditioning, you can prevent people from smoking, you can vent your cooking gases to the outside, and so on. You and your family and your guests pay fully for any pollution that anyone in your house causes. Such is not the case for the pollution that your internal-combustion engine causes when you fire it up every morning to go to school or to work. The air outside of your house is common property. Everyone owns it, hence no one owns it. The impact of your pollution-causing exhaust gases is trivial. If you decide not to drive or decide to install additional exhaust-gas purifiers, the total amount of air pollution will change imperceptibly—that is, it will not really change at all. What incentive do you have, therefore, to not pollute the air around you when you are outside of the house? Not very much.

● PROBLEMS

1. Suppose polluters were charged by government agencies for the privilege of polluting.
   a. How should the price be set?
   b. Which firms will treat waste, and which will pay to pollute?
   c. Is it possible that some firms will be forced to close down because they have to pay to pollute? Why might this result be good?

111

d. If producers are charged to pollute, they will pass this cost on to buyers in the form of higher prices. Why might this be "good"?

2. Why has the free market not developed private contractual arrangements to eliminate excess air pollution in major U.S. cities?

● SELECTED REFERENCES

Commoner, Barry. *The Closing Circle: Nature, Man and Technology*. New York: Knopf, 1971.

Kneese, Allen B., and Charles L. Schultze. "Some Technical Background," in *Pollution, Prices, and Public Policy*. Washington, D.C.: Brookings Institution, 1975.

Seneca, Joseph, and Michael R. Taussig. *Environmental Economics*. 2nd ed. Englewood Cliffs, N.J.: Prentice-Hall, 1979.

Thurow, Lester C. *The Zero-Sum Society*. New York: Basic Books, 1980.

6

The Fundamental Questions of an Economic System

Chapter Preview
1. Most economists describe the economic system in the United States as a mixed economy. What does that mean?
2. What prevents producers and sellers from charging you higher prices for the goods and services that you now buy from them?

● KEY TERMS

Capitalism	Mixed system
Economic efficiency	Pure market economy
Free enterprise	Technical efficiency

Until shortly after World War II, the U.S. economy had been considered the wonder of the world. Although that may no longer be the case, it is still an enormously complex economy, producing millions of goods and services in incredible quantities. The U.S. economic system has raised the living standard of the average person in this country to heights unimagined a hundred years ago.

The American economy is capable of producing 10 million automobiles yearly. The labor force of approximately 110 million people can also produce 6 billion bushels of corn, 150 million tons of steel, 2 billion bushels of wheat, and 19,000 trucks, all in a year. In order to fully understand how the American economic system can generate its own annual output of goods and services, the basic questions of production and distribution must first be answered. Individually and collectively, human beings want more than they can have. Resources are scarce, however, forcing everyone to make choices.

This chapter will present a discussion about the three fundamental economic questions that all economies must answer. These common questions are answered differently by the various economic systems. Indeed, the manner in which these questions are answered in a specific economic system helps determine how that particular system is classified. The three questions that every economic system must answer are:

1. What and how much will be produced?
2. How will it be produced?
3. For whom will it be produced?

Each economic system answers these questions in different ways. We'll look at the questions first, and then we'll examine how they're dealt with in a pure market system.

What to Produce and in What Quantities

Since our wants as a nation far exceed the economy's ability to satisfy those wants, choices must be made. When specific amounts of resources are allocated to satisfy specific wants, those same resources in the same amounts cannot be used to satisfy other wants. The labor, coal, iron ore, plastic, and rubber allocated for the production of automobiles cannot simultaneously be used in the production of toys, airplanes, and videocassette recorders. In other words, because of scarcity, the ultimate cost of producing any good is what must be surrendered in other goods and services—the

114

opportunity cost of the good produced. Of course, even after the decision has been made to produce, say, automobiles, another decision must be made: How many automobiles? Thus the *what* question gives rise to the question, "in what quantities?"

No matter how rich a nation is, the first fundamental question must still be answered—what and how much to produce. Only in a situation where scarcity does not exist would this question be irrelevant. In the real world, some mechanism must exist that causes some goods to be produced and others to remain as either inventors' pipe dreams or as individuals' unfulfilled desires.

How to Produce

There are numerous ways to produce a desired item, once the decision has been made to produce it. It is possible to use more labor and less capital, or vice versa. It is possible to use a large amount of unskilled labor, rather than fewer units of skilled labor. Somehow, some way, a decision must be made as to the particular mix of inputs and the way they should be organized.

For example, consider the production of shoes. Shoes can be produced by using more labor relative to land and capital (labor intensity) or a little labor relative to much machinery and equipment (capital intensity). The same is true for the production of food. In the United States, food-production methods are more capital and land intensive than they are in, say, Southeast Asia.

The point is that resources, or inputs, can *substitute* for one another. Capital can substitute for labor, labor for energy or land, fertilizer for labor or land, and so on. Because resources are scarce, a natural incentive exists to use them wisely; that is, to get the most out of them. When this incentive is added to the fact that resources can substitute for one another, the *how* question becomes important.

For Whom to Produce

Since scarcity is a human condition, no one can get everything he or she wants. Since some wants must go unfulfilled, it follows that society must decide how to allocate the goods it does and can produce. The *what* and *how* questions deal with production. The *for whom* question is concerned with the *distribution* of output. Since production will never be sufficient to satisfy all wants, somehow society must decide how to allocate scarce outputs, or determine who gets how much of what.

● THE PURE MARKET, OR PRICE, SYSTEM

A market economy is one way that individuals can organize to produce goods and exchange them. A market economy is also

115

known as a *price system*, as we saw in a previous chapter. In the the following few sections, a pure market, or price, system will be explained. This is an ideal, or model. Variations of it do exist in the United States and elsewhere, but for now the ideal will be considered.

In the pure market system, buyers and sellers are allowed complete freedom to exchange in a multitude of markets—from stock markets to flea markets. The economy is completely decentralized. There are no small groups of government-appointed decision makers dictating what should be produced, how it should be produced, and who should receive the output. Rather, millions of individuals buy and sell in markets. The results of such demand and supply are individual market prices. In turn, individuals—producers and consumers—react to the signals that market prices provide. Hence, the notion of a price system. As noted in Chapter 4, via changing prices and profits, a price system directs resources from lower-valued to higher-valued uses.

A **pure market economy** is an economy in which all markets are free to operate without government interference. Remember, a pure market economy is only a theoretical abstraction, but it is useful as a point of departure for analysis.

How a Pure Market Economy Answers the Three Fundamental Questions

Most of what is important in economics relates to how a market economy answers the three fundamental economic questions. How a pure market economy answers these questions may seem complicated because there are so many "players." Nevertheless, the ultimate analysis is actually quite simple.

What and in What Quantities. In a pure market economy, profitability is the most important determinant of what and how much is produced. A businessperson buys factors of production—land, labor, and capital—at a cost that is believed to be less than the price attainable when the finished product is sold. The difference between the amount of money received and the amount of money spent is, of course, profit. Those goods that are most profitable will be produced. Those that are unprofitable will not be produced.

What ultimately determines profitability is consumer demand. Only to the extent that consumer demand exists will profits exist. Simply because a business can produce a particular product does not mean that it will be desired. Rather, in a pure market economy, it is the changing demands of final consumers that dictate the changing mix of goods and services offered for sale.

Note that whether the commodity is ugly, tacky, impractical, or immoral is irrelevant. In a pure market economy, if something is

Pure market economy

An economy without government intervention. Owners of resources buy and sell those resources freely without constraints and use them any way they wish.

116

profitable, it will be produced. Will pornographic movies be produced and exhibited? In a pure market economy, the answer is yes, if moviegoers find such films desirable and are willing to pay for them. The answer is no, if most moviegoers find such films obscene and offensive. Remember, however, that because of the proportional voting system in a pure market economy—dollar votes—only a minority need demand a particular product for it to be offered for sale. Even if only 1 percent of moviegoers find pornographic movies desirable, sufficient demand may exist, relative to the cost of producing such movies, for those movies to be produced and to be produced profitably.

How to Produce.   As has already been noted, resources are substitutable. A particular commodity can be produced either labor intensively, land intensively, or capital intensively. In a pure market economy, what determines how a commodity will be produced?

Suppose that you produce shoes capital intensively and your neighbor produces shoes in a sweatshop, labor intensively. Assuming that the shoes are exactly the same, how will a market economy choose between the two methods? Given that both methods produce shoes of the same quality, the cheaper production method will prevail in the marketplace. If your method is cheaper, you can charge a lower price, still make a profit, and take customers away from your neighbor. If your neighbor responds by lowering prices to compete with yours, his or her profits will fall, perhaps to such a low level (or even to a loss) that your neighbor will be forced either to adopt your cheaper production technique or go out of business. The market has selected the answer to the *how* question.

Let's look at some numbers. Consider the possibility of using only two types of resources—capital and labor. The production costs for 100 units of slippers using two techniques, A and B, are represented in Table 6–1. Two hypothetical combinations of capital

TABLE 6–1
Production Costs for 100 Units of Slippers

Techniques A or B can be used to produce the same output. Obviously, B will be used because its total cost is less than A's.

		A		B	
INPUTS	INPUT UNIT PRICE	INPUT UNITS	TOTAL COST	INPUT UNITS	TOTAL COST
Labor	$10.00	5	$50.00	4	$40.00
Capital	8.00	4	32.00	5	40.00
Total cost of 100 units of slippers			82.00		80.00
Average cost per unit			$ .82		$ .80

117

and labor are given in that table. Consider the market price of slippers as given. Which production technique will be chosen from Table 6–1? Obviously, the one for which total cost for 100 units of slippers is the lowest; in other words, the technique for which average cost per slipper is the lowest. That is technique B. Total costs are $2 less than for technique A; average costs are two cents less.

In the price system, the *least-cost combination*, which is technique B, will in fact be chosen because, given price, profits will be the highest possible. A pure market economy virtually guarantees that the least-cost production technique will be chosen because if any other technique were chosen, firms would be sacrificing potential profits.

Moreover, in a price system, competition will *force* firms to use least-cost production techniques. Any firm that fails to employ the least costly technique will find that other firms can undercut its price. In other words, the firms that choose the least-cost production technique will be able to offer the product at a lower price and still make a profit. The lower price for which they offer the product will induce consumers to shift purchases from the higher-priced firm to them. Inefficient firms will be forced out of business.

This discussion assumes that technology and resource prices are held constant. If the cost of capital remained the same and the cost of labor were to decrease considerably, another production technique, such as A, might then be less costly. Firms would then shift to that production technique in order to obtain the highest profits possible.

For Whom to Produce. The final question that any economic system must solve is distribution—*how* is total output distributed among competing claimants? The problem can be separated into two parts, one relating to the distribution of products to consumers and the other relating to the distribution of money income to individuals.

The distribution of finished products to consumers is based on the consumers' ability and willingness to pay the market price for the products. If the market-clearing price of TV dinners is $2.50, those consumers who are able and willing to pay that price will get those TV dinners. Those consumers who are not, will not.

This refers to the *rationing* function of market-clearing prices in a price system. Rather than have a central political figure decide which consumers will get which goods, those consumers who are willing to pay the market-clearing price will obtain the good. That is to say, relative prices ration the available resources, goods, and services at any point in time among those who would like to have the scarce items. If scarcity didn't exist, there would be no need for any system to ration available resources, goods, and services. Every-

118

one could have everything desired without taking away from what anyone else obtained.

In a price system, a consumer's ability to pay for consumer products is based on the size of his or her money income. That in turn depends on the quantities, qualities, and types of the various human and nonhuman resources that the individual owns and supplies to the marketplace. Additionally, the prices, or payments, for those resources influence total money income. When you are selling your human resources as labor services, your money income is based on the wage rate, or salary, that you can fetch in the labor market. If you own nonhuman resources—capital and land, for example—the level of interest and rents that you would be paid for your capital and land will clearly influence the size of your money income and thus your ability to buy consumer products.

The Pure Market, or Price, System and Efficiency

Consumer sovereignty in a pure market system means that because businesspersons in each industry are competing for the dollar votes of consumers, each firm (and hence the economy taken as a whole) will fully utilize its available resources. It will generate maximum consumer satisfaction by fulfilling the largest number of consumer desires, this being reflected by voluntary money income expenditures.

There are two parts to efficiency—technical efficiency and economic efficiency, both of which are satisfied in a pure market economy.

Technical efficiency relates to utilizing production techniques that do not waste inputs. The assumption is, then, that within the market economy businesses will never waste inputs; they will never use 10 units of capital, 10 units of labor, and 10 units of land when they could produce the same amount of output with only 8 units of capital, 7 units of labor, and 9 units of land.

Economic efficiency relates to maximizing the total subjective valuation of available resources. Thus, resources are moved to their highest-valued uses, as evidenced by consumers' willingness to pay for the final products. As stated earlier, profits signal resources to move around so that economic efficiency occurs. The forces of demand and supply guide resources to their most efficient uses. Individuals as businesspersons seeking their own self-interest end up, consciously or unconsciously, generating maximum economic value from their activities.

An example involving lumber (ash, pine, oak, and redwood), shipping crates, and furniture will clarify the distinction between technical and economic efficiency.

Technical efficiency

The utilization of the cheapest production technique for any given output rate. No inputs are willfully wasted.

Economic efficiency

The use of resources that generate the highest possible value of output as determined in the market economy by consumers.

119

Technical Efficiency.   Oranges will be shipped in crates made with the minimum amount of lumber. No lumber will be wasted. Crates will not, for example, be made with 3-inch thick wood when wood three-eighths of an inch thick will do (and possibly also save on shipping costs because it is lighter).

Economic Efficiency.   Ash or pine will be used for the crates rather than oak or redwood, which have a higher-valued use today for, say, furniture. Perhaps in the past, when the demand for furniture was relatively less compared to the more abundant supply of oak and redwood, it might have been economically efficient to use those types of wood for orange crates instead of ash or pine. How do we know that oak and redwood will now be used for furniture? Because furniture makers will be willing to pay more for those types of wood than will crate makers.

We have been discussing a pure market economy. Understanding the pure market economy is important for understanding capitalist ideology, which we will look at next, and, finally, for understanding that part of the U.S. economy that is indeed a pure market system.

● ANALYZING THE ASSUMPTIONS OF CAPITALIST IDEOLOGY

Capitalism is a type of economic system that is characterized by limited involvement of government in the economy, coupled with individual ownership of the means of production.

Although it is difficult to define capitalism exactly, we can look at many of the assumptions underlying the capitalist ideology. Our analysis will be limited to a discussion of these five assumptions:

1. The system of private property
2. Free enterprise and free choice
3. Self-interest
4. Competition and unrestricted markets
5. The limited role of government

The System of Private Property

Capitalism

An economic system in which individuals privately own productive resources and use them in any (legal) manner they see fit.

The ownership of most property under a capitalist system is usually vested in individuals or in groups of individuals. The state is not the owner of, for example, productive resources that are important forms of property. In the United States, the government does own certain property, but, in general, Americans live in a system in which private property is controlled and enforced through

120

the framework of laws, courts, and police. Under capitalism, individuals have their property rights protected; they are usually free to use their private property as they choose, as long as they do not infringe on the legal property rights of others. Individuals are usually allowed to enter into private contractual agreements that are mutually satisfying.

Free Enterprise and Free Choice

Another attribute of a capitalist system is **free enterprise**, which is merely an extension of the concept of property rights. Free enterprise exists when private individuals are allowed to obtain resources, to organize those resources, and to sell the resulting product in any way they choose. In other words, a government or competitor cannot put up artificial obstacles or restrictions to block a business's choice in purchasing its inputs and selling its outputs.

Additionally, all members of the economy are free to choose to do whatever they wish. Workers are free to enter any line of work for which they are qualified, and consumers can buy the desired basket of goods and services that they feel is most appropriate for them. The ultimate voter in the capitalist system is the consumer, who votes with dollars and decides which product "candidates" will survive; that is, consumer sovereignty exists in that the ultimate purchasers of products and services determine what is produced.

Self-Interest and "The Invisible Hand"

In 1776, Adam Smith, the author of *The Wealth of Nations*, described a system in which government had a limited role and individuals pursued their own self-interest. Smith reasoned that, in so doing, individuals would be guided as if by an invisible hand to achieve maximum social welfare for the nation. In his own words,

> [An individual] generally, indeed, neither intends to promote the public interest, nor knows how much he is promoting it. . . . He intends only his own gain, and he is in this, as in many other cases, led by an invisible hand to promote an end which was no part of his intention. . . . By pursuing his own interest he frequently promotes that of the society more effectually than when he really intends to promote it.[1]

What does self-interest entail? For the businessperson, it normally means maximizing profits or minimizing losses. For the consumer, it means maximizing the amount of satisfaction possible from spending a given amount of money income. From the worker's point of view, it means obtaining the highest level of income possible for

Free enterprise

A system in which private business firms are able to obtain resources, to organize those resources, and to sell the finished product in any way they choose.

[1]Adam Smith, *The Wealth of Nations* [1776] (New York: Random House, 1937), Book IV, chap. 2, p. 423.

121

a given amount of work. For the owner of a resource, it means obtaining the highest price possible when that resource is sold, or the greatest rent if it is rented.

Capitalism, therefore, presumes self-interest as the motivation for the way people operate in the system. Self-interest is the guiding light in capitalism.

Competition and Unrestricted Markets

Competition is rivalry among sellers who wish to attract customers, and rivalry among buyers to obtain desired goods. In general, competition exists among buyers and sellers of all resources who wish to obtain the best terms possible when they transact their business.

Competition requires, at a minimum, two things:

1. A relatively large number of independently acting sellers and buyers
2. The freedom of sellers and buyers to enter or exit a particular industry

The Limited Role of Government

Even in an idealized capitalist system there is still a role for government, for someone has to define and enforce private property rights. Government protects the rights of individuals and businesspersons to keep private property private and to keep the control of that property vested with the owners. Even Adam Smith, the so-called father of free enterprise, described in detail the role of government in a purely capitalist system. He suggested the need for government in providing national defense and in eliminating monopolies that would restrain trade. Smith further suggested that the functions of a government within a capitalist system might include such things as issuing money, prescribing standards of weights and measures, raising funds by taxation and other means for public works, and settling disputes judicially. Government thus is essential to the existence of even a purely capitalist system.

● THE AMERICAN ECONOMY— A MIXED ECONOMIC SYSTEM

We have been talking about the capitalist ideology, or pure capitalism, in theory. How well does this ideal system fit the American economic scene? Does Adam Smith's "invisible hand" perform all of its tasks well and rapidly, resulting in maximum welfare for society? The answers to these questions have to be partly yes and

122

partly no. The United States no longer (if it ever did) has a purely capitalist economy. Rather, through the years it has tended toward one in which the government plays a more influential role. It is a **mixed system**—a market system coupled with government control and intervention.

Increased Government

The role of government in our economic system has expanded greatly, especially since World War II. When we speak of government—federal, state, and local—we are referring to the collective total of all individuals who, in one way or another, are paid by tax dollars, who decide what should be done with other tax dollars, and who regulate private transactions. Not only does government control an important share of total income, but it has entered into many aspects of hitherto private economic dealings. For example, governments step in to help out (subsidize) certain industries (e.g., loan guarantees to Lockheed and Chrysler) or to tax others (e.g., a windfall-profits tax on oil companies). The government has also put many restrictions on the workings of the agricultural sector. Additionally, through its many departments and agencies, the government controls numerous aspects of energy, transportation, communication, and commerce in general. In the last several decades, the government has increased its welfare programs—tax dollars are redistributed to those who are deemed needy. Finally, education has become primarily a government activity.

Mixed system

An economic system in which the *what, how,* and *for whom* questions are answered partly by the private sector and partly by the public, or government, sector.

Market Economies Generate Desirable Income Inequalities

THE ARGUMENT

In a pure market economy, income inequalities occur because of the operation of the price system. Impersonal market forces result in some individuals earning very high incomes and some individuals earning very low incomes. Proponents of a pure market system believe that such income inequalities are desirable.

THE ANALYSIS

In the impersonal marketplace in a pure market economy, millions of buyers cast their dollar votes for goods, and therefore they indirectly determine income inequality. Individuals who do not have productive resources that correspond to those necessary for desired products find themselves with low incomes. If someone has a particular skill that no firm requires, then competition among firms will force each of them to ignore that resource and to choose the least-cost production technique.

At the other end of the income scale, relatively high incomes are necessary in order to get people to take hazardous, risky, and unpleasant jobs. Relatively high incomes are also necessary to induce people to train and educate themselves and to acquire different skills.

In a pure market economy, in the absence of restraints and imperfections in the system, maximum economic value is obtained from a given set of resources at any point in time. Proponents of the price system see such a system as harnessing self-interest in order to provide society with the greatest possible output of desired goods. Additionally, the price system leads to an automatic transfer of resources from lower-valued to relatively higher-valued uses. Thus, resources will not stay in an industry when the demand for its product has withered away because of a change in consumer tastes.

The opponents of the price system, however, point out that even though it might be economically efficient, an undesired, unequal distribution of income results. Perfect economic efficiency may still allow certain individuals to starve to death when they do not have sufficient resources that are valued in the marketplace. Questions of fairness and equity arise. Should those who have the most resources be allowed to reap large benefits from the price system while the less fortunate barely survive? Should the more cunning and entrepreneurial among us be allowed to accumulate, particularly over generations, large holdings of property resources with which tremendous incomes can be earned? For many critics of the price system the answer is no, and that is why they believe the system should not be allowed to work without restrictions and regulations.

124

Finally, what if we accept that income inequalities generated by a market economy are undesirable? How do we eliminate them? If we eliminate income inequality by taxation and redistribution—taking from some to give to others—we interfere with incentives. Individuals will now be rewarded less for taking risks and engaging in hazardous occupations. Some argue that efficiency will suffer to such an extent that the nation will become poor. In other words, the pie will be more evenly divided, but it will be smaller.

DISCUSSION QUESTIONS

1. If everyone were to receive the same income, how would people be induced to take risky or unpleasant jobs?

2. Under what conditions would taxing individuals and redistributing income more equally *not* result in a smaller pie?

● WHAT'S AHEAD

Most of this chapter was concerned with a pure market economy. The next chapter is concerned with the role of government in our mixed economy. You will find out which functions government normally performs in a capitalist system and also what our national goals are.

● CHAPTER SUMMARY

All economic systems must answer three fundamental questions: (1) What and how much will be produced? (2) How will it be produced? (3) For whom will it be produced? In a pure market economy, relative prices and profits dictate what will be produced and in what quantities. Unprofitable activities will wither away; relatively profitable activities will increase in relative size. The question of how to produce is solved by using that combination of resources that generates maximum profits for any given level of output. Who to produce for is a question of the distribution of income, and that is solved in a pure market system by people being rewarded for the amount of output their own resources generate.

A distinction between technical and economic efficiency was made. Technically efficient production is the utilization of the cheapest production technique for any given output rate, whereas economic efficiency involves using resources so that the highest possible *value* of output is generated from a given set of resources.

Within the capitalist ideology the following exist: (1) a system of private property; (2) free enterprise and free choice; (3) self-interest; (4) competition and unrestricted markets; and (5) a limited role for government.

125

● QUESTIONS FOR REVIEW AND STUDY

1. The human condition is one of _____.

2. The three fundamental economic questions to be answered by all economies are: _____ _____ and _____ _____.

3. In an economy in which all wants are completely satisfied all the time because of a superabundance of resources relative to such wants, there is still a *what* question to answer with respect to _____.

4. In a _____ _____ economy, all resources are privately owned, bought and sold, and used without government interference.

5. In a pure market economy, the question of *what* should be produced is determined by _____.

6. In a pure market economy, the question of *how* to produce is answered by using the _____ method possible for any given output, given quality.

7. In a pure market economy, the question *for whom* is answered by how much people _____ into the economy.

8. In a capitalist system, _____ _____ rights are enforced by the legal system.

9. The main motivating force in a purely capitalist system is _____ _____.

10. Producing any given output the cheapest way is an example of _____ efficiency.

11. We can determine what is economically efficient only if we know the _____ of inputs and outputs.

12. The United States is a _____ _____ because it is neither purely capitalistic nor purely command, or planned.

ANSWERS

1. scarcity 2. What? How? For whom? 3. time 4. pure market 5. profitability 6. cheapest 7. put 8. private property 9. self-interest 10. technical 11. prices 12. mixed economy

● ANSWERS TO CHAPTER PREVIEW QUESTIONS

1. Most economists describe the economic system in the United States as a mixed economy. What does that mean?

No advanced economies in the real world are purely capitalistic or purely command, or planned. As a practical matter, all advanced economies are mixed; resource allocation decisions are made by both private individuals and governments. Even under an idealized capitalist economy, important roles are played by the government; it is generally agreed that government is required for (some) income redistribution, national defense, maintenance of competition, protection of property rights, and so on. On the other hand, command economies have found it convenient to allow for private property rights regarding labor, agriculture, and personal property items (clothing, housing, consumer durables, etc.).

2. *What prevents producers and sellers from charging you higher prices for the goods and services that you now buy from them?*

In a private economy, most resources are owned, and owners find it in their self-interest to sell to the highest bidder. But there is a check on the selling prices of goods and services. The check is competition; individual sellers cannot charge higher and higher prices because buyers can buy from competing sellers.

To turn to the other side of the picture, you, as an individual buyer, cannot use any power you might have to squeeze out lower and lower prices from sellers, because sellers have the option of selling to other buyers. It is competition within the unregulated sector of the American economy that acts as a regulating force.

● PROBLEMS

1. Assume that a business has found that its most profitable output occurs when it produces $172 worth of output of a particular product. It can choose from three possible techniques, A, B, and C, that will produce the desired output. The table lists the amounts of inputs these techniques use, along with each input price.

		PRODUCTION TECHNIQUES		
PRICE OF INPUT (per unit)	INPUT	A (units)	B (units)	C (units)
$10	Land	7	4	1
2	Labor	6	7	1i
15	Capital	2	6	3
8	Entrepreneurship	1	3	2

a. Which technique will the firm choose and why?
b. What would the firm's maximum profit be?
c. If the price of labor increases to $4 per unit, which technique will be chosen and why? What will happen to profits?

127

2. Many factors determine how production and exchange occur in the American economy. Can you list some of the institutions through which resources in our economy are used to satisfy human wants? Choose one such institution (e.g., ethics) that has changed over the last several hundred years. How has that change altered our economic system?

● SELECTED REFERENCES

Ebenstein, William, and E. Fogelman. *Today's Isms.* 8th ed. Englewood Cliffs, N.J.: Prentice-Hall, 1980, chap 3.

Haag, E. van den, ed. *Capitalism: Sources of Hostility.* New York: Epoch Books, 1979.

Heilbroner, Robert L. *The Worldly Philosophers.* Rev. ed. New York: Simon & Schuster, 1972.

7

The Role of Government and Our National Goals

Chapter Preview

1. To what extent does government affect your life?

2. If you were asked to pay voluntarily for your fair share of national defense spending, would you be willing to pay?

● KEY TERMS

Antitrust legislation
Economic growth
Free rider
Inflation
Principle of exclusion

Private goods
Public goods
Transfer payments
Transfers in kind

Since the 1930s, the government's influence on our daily lives has increased tremendously. Even if we confine our discussion to the government's *economic* influence, the trend clearly has been toward greater and greater impact. Some critics have suggested that the impact of government is so pervasive that to call the United States a market economy or free enterprise economy is misleading at best.

In this chapter, we assess the government's role in the U.S. economy and how it has changed over time. In addition, we provide at least the flavor of the government's impact on our economic lives.

● THE SIZE OF GOVERNMENT

In the United States, federal, state, and local government spending accounts for a sizable percentage of total national expenditures. These government expenditures are for purchases of everything from missiles to paper clips. Since people produce such goods, it follows that a large percentage of income in the United States is derived from government spending. Graph 7–1 shows how government *purchases*, as a percentage of our economy's total production, have changed over the years. Notice how government spending increased dramatically during World War I and again during World War II. Indeed, during World War II, it reached almost 50 percent of total U.S. expenditures. In recent years, this percentage has remained somewhat above 20 percent. In fact, from 1960 through the 1980s, government expenditures, expressed as a percentage of total gross national product, have increased to about three times their average from the period 1776 to 1916.

Of course, government purchases are not the only government impact on our economy. The government also collects taxes from some individuals and transfers that tax revenue to others in the form of cash, food stamps, or rent subsidies. By some estimates, the ratio of (1) the sum of all government expenditures and *transfers* to (2) total national income has increased from about 25 percent in 1950 to 42 percent in 1983.

Moreover, the indirect, regulatory impact of government on consumers and producers may be even greater than the direct influence

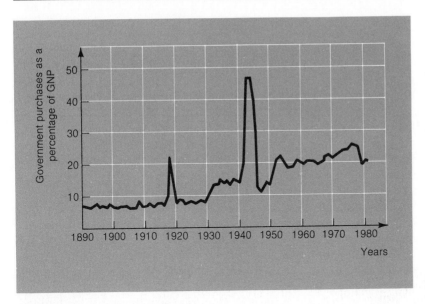

GRAPH 7–1
Rising Government Purchases

Here we show government *purchases* at all levels—federal, state, and local—of goods and services as a percentage of total gross national product. The big jump occurred during World Wars I and II. In recent years, the percentage has leveled off at 20 percent.

SOURCE: U.S. Department of Commerce.

of government expenditures and transfers. Businesses devote a sizable portion of their available labor hours filling out various government forms for such agencies as the Federal Trade Commission, the Securities and Exchange Commission, the Occupational Safety and Health Administration, and the Department of Commerce. Consumers eventually must pay for such activities through higher retail prices.

● THE ROLE OF GOVERNMENT

In modern mixed economies, the role of government is extremely important. Among other things, the government plays a role in the following:

1. Setting and enforcing the rules of the game—that is, providing a legal system
2. Ensuring competition
3. Providing public goods
4. Redistributing income from higher- to lower-income groups
5. Correcting externalities
6. Ensuring economywide stability

131

Setting and Enforcing the Rules of the Economic Game

Part of any economic system is the legal institutions set up to govern exchanges. The courts and the police may not at first seem like economic arms of the government. But their activities have important consequences on the economic activities within any country. People are constantly entering into contracts, whether the contracts are oral or written, express or implied. And when they believe that they have been wronged, they seek redress of their grievances within the legal institutions. Moreover, consider the legal system that is necessary for the smooth functioning of our capitalist system. Our laws define quite explicitly the legal status of businesses, the rights of private ownership, and a system for the enforcement of contracts. In fact, all of the relationships among consumers and businesses are governed by the legal rules of the game. We might consider the government in its judicial function, then, as the referee for disputes in the economic arena.

Many of the laws passed by Congress and the decisions handed down by judges affect economic activities. For example, consider the history of legislation governing the manufacture and sale of therapeutic drugs. Drugs produced today must meet much higher standards than drugs of, say, 75 years ago. The Pure Food and Drug Act of 1906, as well as numerous amendments and acts passed since then, put many strictures on the production and sale of drugs; this is part of the consumer protection role of government.

Ensuring Competition

Many people believe that the only way to attain economic efficiency is through competition. To ensure the existence of a competitive system, Congress and the various state governments have passed **antitrust legislation**. Such legislation makes illegal certain (but not all) economic activities that might restrain trade—that is, prevent free competition among rival firms in the marketplace. The avowed aim of antitrust legislation is to reduce the power and prevent the formation of monopolies. The most famous antitrust legislation was the Sherman Act of 1890, which made "every contract, combination in the form of trust or otherwise, or conspiracy, in restraint of trade or commerce among the several states" illegal. Perhaps because of the vague wording of that act, a large number of other antitrust laws have been passed that prohibit more specific anticompetitive business behavior. Both the Antitrust Division of the Department of Justice and the Federal Trade Commission attempt to uphold these antitrust laws. Moreover, various state judicial agencies also attempt to maintain competition.

Certain industries are exempt from antitrust laws when it is felt

Antitrust legislation

Statutes, or laws, that make it illegal for businesses to engage in anticompetitive (monopolistic) activities.

132

that the public would be better served by only one firm than by several competitive firms. Rather, regulatory agencies are set up to make the firm act *as if* it were competing, or at least behave in a more socially desirable manner. For example, electric utility companies have been granted monopolies in the geographic areas they serve but are regulated by various state and federal commissions. The quality of the service they offer and the prices they charge are the two major variables that public utility commissions regulate. In other industries, government regulation may be provided for a variety of reasons, all under the general rubric "in and for the public interest."

Providing Public Goods

Most goods can be characterized as **private goods**. These goods, when purchased, are consumed privately. That is, when you purchase a pair of shoes, you exclude others from using them. Anyone else wanting to acquire those shoes legally must contract with you. The same idea holds for private goods ranging from hamburgers (at least the part you haven't already eaten) to videocassette recorders. All private goods are bound by the **principle of exclusion**: If they are used by one person, they cannot be used by any others simultaneously.

There is another class of goods for which the principle of exclusion does not apply. These are goods for which exclusion of other individuals is difficult, if not impossible. They are called **public goods**. An example of a public good is national defense. Note that when you reap the benefits of national defense in terms of security, others are simultaneously reaping those same benefits. In fact, all the people in the nation "consume" national defense together. Other public goods are police protection and the legal system. When you partake of them, you do not necessarily take away from someone else's share of these goods.

Characteristics of Public Goods.   Several characteristics of public goods set them apart from all other goods:

1. *Public goods are usually indivisible.* You can't buy or sell $5 worth of our ability to annihilate the world with bombs. Public goods cannot be produced or sold very easily in small units.
2. *Public goods can be used by increasing numbers of people at no additional cost.* Once a television signal has been transmitted from a station, turning on your set does not cost the station anything; the opportunity cost of your receiving the signal is zero.
3. *Additional users of public goods do not deprive others of any of the services of the good.* If you turn on your television set, your neighbors don't get weaker reception because of your action.

Private goods

Goods that are subject to the principle of exclusion; that is, when one person consumes a private good, that person can prevent others from consuming it.

Principle of exclusion

The principle whereby one person's use of a good excludes the possibility of anyone else using it simultaneously.

Public goods

Goods for which the principle of exclusion does not hold. These goods must be, or usually are, consumed collectively.

133

4. *It is very difficult to charge people for a public good on the basis of how much they use*. It is nearly impossible to determine how much any person uses or values national defense. It cannot be bought and sold in the marketplace.

How Public Goods Are Provided.   While public goods are interesting to economists and puzzling to students, they present a real problem for market economies. Since the principle of exclusion does not work well for public goods, they are not likely to be produced in sufficient quantities in pure market economies.

Consider the following example. Suppose that you and your friends go into the national defense business. You pool your money and borrow more from a bank and start building missiles, nuclear warheads, and the like. Now, all of this has cost you quite a bit. You've got to recover this money and make a profit, so you must sell your national defense services. But who will buy them? Eventually, nearly everyone will realize that the principle of exclusion doesn't work here. That is, most people will realize that they can "consume" the same amount of national defense whether or not they pay you for it. To be sure, some individuals will recognize this problem and will therefore pay you to continue your national defense efforts. Perhaps these individuals are superhawks—or perhaps very wealthy. (Wealthy people have valuable possessions to protect and might be willing to contribute, even if others would benefit free of charge.)

Still, when all is said and done, it probably would not be profitable for you or any other private citizen to go into the national defense business. Or, if some firms do enter the business of providing national defense, it's a safe bet that "not enough" will be provided. Because of the possibility of not enough public goods being provided to an economy, such goods are usually financed by government. When government steps in, more public goods are provided than would have been provided by the private sector.

The Free Rider Rides Again.   Since national defense is consumed collectively, it follows that whether or not an individual pays has no bearing on the amount of national defense he or she can consume. Everyone, therefore, has an incentive to be a **free rider**. Of course, if you, as an individual, pay and no one else does, the amount of national defense provided will be insignificant: Your single contribution will not make any difference to the country's security. We can see that this is true from the table on page 135, where we assume that an individual share of the cost of national defense is $75.

Note the implications of this table. If you *do* pay your share, along with everyone else, then total national defense outlays will equal $100,000,075. If you *don't* pay and if everyone else does, total outlays will be $100 million. Of course, $75 isn't going to make much

Free rider

A person who pays nothing for the services of a public good but does indeed derive utility, or satisfaction, from those services nonetheless.

134

	TOTAL OUTLAYS IF YOU PAY	TOTAL OUTLAYS IF YOU DON'T PAY
AND IF EVERYONE ELSE PAYS	$100,000,075	$100,000,000
AND IF NO ONE ELSE PAYS	$75	$0

difference. It therefore follows that whether you pay makes no difference to the country's security. This argument helps to explain why national defense is typically provided by governments; the quantity of national defense supplied by a pure market economy is likely to be insufficient.

Redistributing Income

Another function of government, which has recently become very important, is the redistribution of income. This redistribution is accomplished through two systems: the progressive income tax (described in Chapter 11) and **transfer payments**. Transfer payments are those payments made to individuals for which no services or goods are concurrently rendered. The three primary money transfer payments in our system are welfare, social security, and unemployment insurance benefits, although there are others.

Income redistribution also includes a large number of income **transfers in kind**, as opposed to money transfers. Examples of income transfers in kind are food stamps, Medicare and Medicaid, government-provided health care services, government-provided low-cost public housing, and government-provided education.

There is a substantial amount of income redistribution in the United States. Between 1960 and 1983, income redistribution and programs related to social welfare expanded at the expense of other parts of the federal budget, in particular, national defense. Over those years, the percentage of federal budget allocations related to welfare and welfare-associated expenditures rose from 25 percent to about 45 percent. At the same time, the percentage of the budget allocated to national defense fell from 54 percent to 32 percent.

Correcting Externalities

Chapter 5 was devoted to a discussion of externalities, or spillovers. We pointed out that in a world where there is no government regulation against pollution, it is possible to manufacture too many products that generate pollution during their production and consumption. When there are negative spillovers in a pure market economy, there will be an overallocation of resources to the produc-

Transfer payments
Money payments made by governments to individuals for which no services are concurrently rendered (e.g., welfare and unemployment insurance benefits).

Transfers in kind
Payments made in the form of actual goods and services to individuals for which no goods or services are rendered concurrently.

135

tion of the good in question. (In the example in Chapter 5, too much steel was being produced.) The government can correct negative externalities through special taxes and legislative regulation or prohibition.

Special Taxes through Legislation.   In the example of the steel mill, the externality problem originates from the fact that air (as a dumping place) is costless to the firm. The government could, however, compensate for this flaw by charging a price for the use of the air. In other words, the government could tax the steel mill for dumping its pollutants into the air. This tax could be commensurate with the cost of pollution to third parties. This, in effect, would be a pollution tax.

No matter what type of tax is used, the cost to producers will be increased. Thus, the ultimate effect would be to raise the price to consumers. In this example the equilibrium quantity of the product in question would fall, and so would the quantity of pollution.

Regulation.   To correct the negative externality caused by pollution, the government can simply specify a maximum allowable rate of pollution. This action would require that the producer of pollution install pollution-abatement equipment or reduce its rate of output, or both. In any event, supply in the industry being regulated would decrease.

Ensuring Economywide Stability

Another important government function, especially since the Great Depression, is ensuring economywide stability. Increasingly, the federal government has taken on the job of (1) maintaining price stability, (2) providing for full employment, and (3) encouraging economic growth. Since we will devote full chapters to each of these national goals, we will cover them only briefly here.

Maintaining Price Stability.   Price stability refers to the rate of change of prices. In particular, it refers to the average level of all prices when that average is neither rising nor falling by great amounts. In recent years, there has been a great deal of discussion about **inflation**, defined as a sustained rise in the weighted average of all prices. An important issue today is how to reduce the rate at which prices are rising.

As we explain in the next chapter, when the economy experiences inflation, certain problems arise. When inflation is not anticipated, some groups benefit at the expense of others. And uncertainty about the future usually increases in a world of inflation.

Inflation

A year-in and year-out rise in the average of all prices in the economy.

Providing for Full Employment.   The high unemployment rates dur-

136

ing the Great Depression and the advent of new theories about ways for government to reduce unemployment led to a landmark piece of legislation at the end of World War II. The Employment Act of 1946 clearly specifies the federal government's responsibility for economywide stability:

> The Congress hereby declares that it is the continuing policy and responsibility of the Federal Government to use all practicable means consistent with its needs and obligations and other essential considerations of national policy, with assistance and cooperation of industry, agriculture, labor and State and local governments, to coordinate and utilize all its plans, functions, and resources for the purpose of creating and maintaining, in a manner calculated to foster and promote free competitive enterprise and the general welfare, conditions under which there will be afforded useful employment opportunities, including self-employment, for those able, willing, and seeking to work and to promote maximum employment, production, and purchasing power.

Because the wording of this act was so vague, Congress amended it with the Full Employment and Balanced Growth Act of 1978 — more commonly known as the Humphrey–Hawkins Act, after its sponsors. The Humphrey–Hawkins Act specifies numerical goals for employment and price stability.

In Chapter 9 we discuss the meaning of unemployment, the kinds of unemployment, and the problems involved in its measurement.

Encouraging Economic Growth. **Economic growth** is reflected in the increase in a nation's standard of living over time; hence, it is important to a nation. Sustained economic growth, which has occurred in only a small number of countries, has made it possible for masses of people to be better fed and clothed and to live longer and healthier lives. Nonetheless, in recent years, a movement has been afoot to discredit the desirability of high economic growth rates. Advocates of zero economic growth argue that growth is not an unmixed blessing. Thus far, we have looked only at the benefits of growth. There are costs, also.

The topic of economic growth is discussed in more detail in Chapter 17.

Economic growth

Increase in a nation's standard of living; the average individual has more real goods and services to consume year after year. It can be measured by how fast available goods and services per person grow over time.

The Size of Government Should be Limited

THE ARGUMENT

The role of government in our economy has grown tremendously since the 1930s. The rapid growth of government at all levels has caused some alarm. Indeed, it might be said that the presidential election of 1980 revolved around this issue. Should there be a limitation on government expenditures, say, at some fixed percentage of income (national income for the federal government, state income for state governments)?

THE ANALYSIS

Those who argue in favor of a limitation on the size of government point out that the size of government today is greater, on average, than in any other period in our peacetime history. Today, the average person contributes almost 40 percent of his or her annual income to governments at all levels. A high level of government spending requires relatively high rates of taxation. These high rates of taxation are blamed for reversing the 200-year trend of increased productivity. High tax rates have discouraged productive people in higher income brackets from working as much as they would otherwise.

Not surprisingly, the 1970s and 1980s saw numerous attempts at restricting increases in government spending. For example, in 1976, voters in Michigan were offered Proposal C, which set a limit of 8.3 percent of personal state income as the size of the state government. Then in 1978, voters in Tennessee overwhelmingly approved a tax limitation measure that would keep state tax revenues at the same percentage of total state personal income that existed in 1977. And California's Proposition 13, limiting property taxes, was passed in 1978.

Critics Voice Opinions

Critics of limiting state taxes and spending point out that such a restriction could mean restricting "essential" programs such as police protection and public education. They further point out that putting a specific, absolute number in the state constitution would eventually be as troublesome as it has been in other cases where specific numbers have been embedded in ordinances, building codes, and other legislation.

The Federal Level: A Constitutional Convention

The examples so far have concerned limitations on government spending at the state and local levels. There is also a movement to somehow limit spending at the *federal* level. Part of this movement involves an amendment to the U.S. Constitution that would require a balanced federal budget. The interesting thing about this proposal from a political point of view is that it has not come from Congress, but rather from states demanding that a national convention be convened. Indiana state legislators passed a resolution in 1957 urging Congress to call such a convention. Wyoming sent a similar resolution to Congress in 1961. But the real movement for a constitutional convention started when Virginia called for a balanced-budget amendment in 1973. These states were acting under a provision in Article V of the U.S. Constitution that permits 34 states to force Congress to call a constitutional convention.

A Constitutional Convention Is Unlikely. According to legal experts, even if the required 34 states pass resolutions to force a constitutional convention, there are so many legal uncertainties that a convention may never really come about. There is no precedent and no specific guidelines in the Constitution. Can the convention be limited to one specific issue? Does Congress have the legal authority to set the ground rules? No one really knows. One of the problems is that the resolutions passed by the various states and sent to Congress are not identical. They seek at least 10 different forms of a constitutional amendment to balance the budget.

What Is the "Best" Size of Government?
At both the state and federal levels, voters must determine the "best" size of government. Economics, as a science, cannot tell what percentage of the national economy should be devoted to government expenditures. The percentage of total national income going to government has, indeed, risen in the last two hundred years. Is that bad, or is that good? The answer depends on one's value judgments, not on economic analysis. Indeed, at this juncture, there are no clear-cut answers. Moreover, whatever the size of government, there will always be citizens who believe it is too small and others who believe it is too large.

DISCUSSION QUESTIONS

1. What groups in society would be most in favor of limiting the size of government? What groups would be most against it?
2. Is it possible to limit the size of state government without reducing goods and services provided by each state?

● WHAT'S AHEAD

In the next chapter we discuss the definition and the measurement of inflation. Also analyzed are the various theories of inflation and the problems that inflation inflicts on the economy.

● CHAPTER SUMMARY

The size of government has expanded greatly. It is estimated that in the 1980s, federal, state, and local governments control more than 40 percent of gross national product. In mixed economies, the role of government is important in (1) setting and enforcing the rules of the game—that is, providing a legal system; (2) ensuring competition; (3) providing public goods; (4) redistributing income; (5) correcting externalities; and (6) ensuring economywide stability.

Public goods are those goods that can be enjoyed simultaneously by large numbers of individuals; any one individual's consumption of the good does not exclude anyone else's consumption. In other words, the principle of exclusion does not apply to public goods.

Because of the free-rider problem, public goods would not be provided in sufficient quantities if provided through the private sector. That is why governments typically provide such public goods as national defense.

Redistribution of income involves transfer payments of money and transfer payments in kind, such as food stamps and medical care.

Governments can correct externalities, or market failures, through taxes, legislation, and regulation.

● QUESTIONS FOR REVIEW AND STUDY

1. Government—federal, state, and local—accounts for about _____ percent of our annual production.

2. When a government gives individuals tax revenues in the form of cash or other goods and services, it is making a _____.

3. In addition to government taxing and spending, there is also government _____ in the areas of occupational and product safety, among others.

4. One way that government ensures competition is through _____ legislation.

5. When a government grants a special privilege that gives one firm a competitive edge, the government is fostering _____.

6. An apple or an oil change are examples of a _____ good.

7. Private goods are subject to the principle of _____.

8. The principle of exclusion does not apply to _____ _____.

9. One of the major problems with public goods is the inability to _____ individuals from consuming them.

10. Because of the problem of the _____ _____, it is difficult, if not impossible, for a pure market economy to provide public goods in optimal quantities.

11. When a government provides a transfer to individuals in the form of food stamps, rent subsidies, and medical care, it is providing transfers _____ _____.

12. Economic stability involves at least three factors: _____ _____, _____ _____, and _____ _____.

ANSWERS

1. 40   2. transfer   3. regulation   4. antitrust   5. monopoly   6. private   7. exclusion   8. public goods   9. exclude   10. free rider   11. in kind   12. price stability, full employment, economic growth

140

● ANSWERS TO CHAPTER PREVIEW QUESTIONS

1. *To what extent does government affect your life?*

When you start to work (if you haven't already), the federal government will take part of your paycheck for social security "contributions" and federal withholding taxes. Your state government may also tax some of your money income. In addition, you pay taxes on virtually everything you buy in most states in the form of a sales tax. All told, approximately 40 percent of your annual income will go to the government—federal, state, and local combined. On the other hand, you can expect to receive benefits from your payment of taxes. These benefits include, but are not limited to, public education, national defense, social welfare programs, police protection, and a judicial system. Your life as a citizen, consumer, and producer is greatly affected by government at all levels. For example, you are prevented from entering many occupations unless you obtain a license from a state occupational licensing board. As a consumer, you will find that certain products are prohibited from sale to you (e.g., narcotics). As a worker, you may find that much of your working environment is regulated by a government agency such as the Occupational Safety and Health Administration. In fact, government pervades your life from the moment you are born until the moment you die.

2. *If you were asked to pay voluntarily for your fair share of national defense spending, would you be willing to pay?*

If you thought rationally about the effects of paying for your fair share of national defense, you would see that either way your payment would make little difference. If you were asked to pay voluntarily for extremely expensive public goods, you would probably be tempted to be a free rider. Only in situations where small numbers of people are involved can you rationally see that your payment does have an effect. Consider a homeowners' association for 50 houses in a small community. If you do not pay for crime control, street lighting, and maintenance, the total is reduced by one-fiftieth, certainly a more perceptible amount than that by which the total dollars spent on defense would be reduced if you refused to pay. And, not surprisingly, private homeowners' associations that operate on voluntary contributions function quite well. There is always the problem of the free rider; that we cannot deny. But social pressures against those homeowners who do not pay seem sufficiently persuasive to eliminate, or at least reduce dramatically, the problem of the free, or cheap, rider.

● PROBLEMS

1. Assume that you live in a relatively small suburban neighborhood called Whispering Pines. There is a Whispering Pines Homeowners' Association that collects money from homeowners to pay for upkeep of the surrounding stone wall, lighting at the entrances to Whispering Pines, and lawn maintenance around the perimeter of the area. Each year you are asked to donate $50. No one can force you to do it. There are 100 homeowners in Whispering Pines.
   - **a.** Your annual contribution to the homeowners' association would account for what percentage of its total yearly "take"?
   - **b.** At what level of participation will the absence of your $50 contribution make a difference?
   - **c.** If you do not contribute your $50, are you really receiving a totally free ride?

2. We have used national defense as an example of a public good. Alaska and Hawaii are part of the United States. Is our example still valid? Is local police protection a public good? Explain.

3. Label two columns on your paper *private goods* and *public goods*. List each of the following under the heading that *best* describes it.
   - **a.** Sandwich
   - **b.** Public television
   - **c.** Cable television
   - **d.** National defense
   - **e.** Shirt
   - **f.** Elementary education
   - **g.** College education
   - **h.** Health clinic flu shots
   - **i.** Operas
   - **j.** Museums
   - **k.** Automobile

● SELECTED REFERENCES

Carson, Robert B., et al. *Government in the American Economy*. Lexington, Mass.: Heath, 1973.

Eckstein, Otto. *Public Finance*. 4th ed. Englewood Cliffs, N.J.: Prentice-Hall, 1979, chaps. 1 and 2.

Maxwell, James A., and J. Richard Aronson. *Financing State and Local Government*. 3d ed. Washington, D.C.: The Brookings Institution, 1977.

McKean, Roland N. *Public Spending*. New York: McGraw-Hill, 1968.

Phelps, Edmund S., ed. *Private Wants and Public Needs*. Rev. ed. New York: Norton, 1965.

Schultze, Charles L. *The Public Use of Private Interest*. Washington, D.C.: The Brookings Institution, 1977.

UNIT 2

Inflation, Unemployment, and Income Determination

Contents

8

Inflation

1960 $1.00
1965 93¢
1970 77¢
1975 50¢
1980 35¢
1982 30¢

Chapter Preview
1. Is it possible for inflation to hurt every single person simultaneously?
2. Who is hurt most by inflation?

● KEY TERMS

base year	inflationary expectations
bracket creep, or taxflation	inflationary premium
cost-push inflation	nominal, or absolute, prices
currency reform	nominal interest rate
demand-pull inflation	real income
index number	real interest rate
inflation	relative price

Since the middle 1960s, inflation has been one of the most serious problems facing this nation. Actually, inflation is a worldwide phenomenon. What's more, inflation in the United States is not nearly so severe as it is in many other countries (just look at Table 8–1). Countries in Latin America, such as Brazil, Argentina, and Chile, have annual rates of inflation that range from 20 percent to 105 percent. In Israel, the rate is even higher!

Numerous historical examples place inflation rates at unbelievably high levels. In Germany between 1920 and 1923, the price level increased almost a trillionfold. In other words, the same item that cost the equivalent of $1 in 1920 cost $1 trillion in 1923. People literally pushed wheelbarrows of money to shops. But the record seems to be held by Hungary, where the pre-World War II unit of currency (the pangö) was equivalent to 820 octillion units in 1946. (An octillion is a 1 followed by 27 zeros.) Such dramatic examples give an indication of the serious direction in which our moderate U.S. inflation *could* move—although this is very unlikely. Nevertheless, inflation is a persistent problem in this country, and people in government and industry spend much time and effort predicting it, analyzing it, and attempting to reduce it.

TABLE 8–1
Inflation Rates in Selected Countries

NATION	ANNUAL RATE OF INFLATION (1981)
United States	10.4
Brazil	105.5
Argentina	104.5
Chile	19.7
Israel	116.8
Italy	17.8
France	13.3
Ireland	20.4
Japan	4.9
United Kingdom	11.9
Iran	24.2
Mexico	27.9

SOURCE: *International Financial Statistics*, vol xxxv, no. 8, August 1982, Bureau of Statistics of the International Monetary Fund, p. 51.

● INFLATION DEFINED

The most obvious sign of inflation is rising prices. We have already presented the economist's relatively formal definition of inflation. Essentially, **inflation** is a *sustained* and continual rise in the weighted average of all prices. Of course, during periods of inflation, some prices may actually fall (e.g., prices of hand calculators and microcomputers in recent years). These prices fall because of improvements in production methods, which, in turn, encourage competitors to enter the market. Overall, however, prices rise enough to offset any price declines. Hence, the average of all prices rises. Notice that the emphasis is on the word *sustained*. Thus, a one-time increase in the average of all prices is not considered an inflationary phenomenon. But when the average of all prices is rising year in and year out, as it has been in the United States in recent years, that is definitely inflation.

Nominal, or Absolute, Prices

Inflation is a phenomenon relating to a sustained rise in **nominal, or absolute, prices**. Nominal prices are the prices that are reported in the marketplace. They are called nominal because they are in name only. Consider the following example. In France in January 1960, there was a so-called **currency reform**, in which every 100 francs became equivalent to 1 new franc. The accounting system had changed. All financial statements were changed. How? By moving the decimal point two places to the left. Nominal, or absolute, prices were changed in one fell swoop by the currency reform in France.

Would a currency reform alter the rate of inflation? No, because inflation is a measure of a change in the average of all nominal prices. A currency reform simply changes the base from which inflation is measured. Some people have the mistaken notion that a currency reform causes people's wealth to fall. That is not correct. When a government engages in a currency reform, it is simply changing the accounting system. Everyone's ability to purchase goods and services with his or her existing wealth remains the same. For example, suppose you were living in France on December 31, 1959, and had 50,000 francs in your bank account. If suddenly your bank statement listed your balance at 500 new francs, your ability to purchase goods and services would not be affected. You could still purchase the same amount of goods and services because all market prices would now be expressed in new francs, too.

Relative Prices

Inflation involves the change in the average of nominal, or absolute, prices. A change in one or more specific prices results in a change in **relative prices**. Statements about changes in the price of

Inflation
A sustained and continual rise in the weighted average of all prices.

Nominal, or absolute, prices
The actual market prices at which goods are sold.

Currency reform
Situation in which the government changes the currency accounting system (e.g., 1 new franc equals 100 old francs, or—if it happened—1 new dollar equals 10 old dollars).

Relative price
The price of a good expressed in terms of the price of another good or the average price of all other goods.

gasoline, automobiles, or shoes are statements about relative prices. A relative price is expressed in terms of one price compared with one or more prices.

Moreover, the nominal, or absolute, prices of all goods could increase while the relative prices of some goods fall. As Table 8–2 demonstrates, the prices of both videocassettes and video discs increased in nominal, or absolute, terms during three years of inflation. However, the relative price of video discs increased, while the relative price of videocassettes actually decreased.

Beware of Nominal Prices

In periods of inflation, nominal, or absolute, prices tend to give misleading information. Suppose the rate of inflation is 8 percent per year, but the price of gasoline is rising at 4 percent per year. The unsuspecting might conclude that people will buy less gasoline, since its price is higher. However, a moment's reflection will tell us that even though the nominal price of gasoline rose, the relative price of gasoline actually fell. Since gasoline is now relatively cheaper, other things held constant, people will purchase more. Car pooling will decrease and larger automobiles will reappear on the highways if this trend continues. Note that if incomes are also rising at 8 percent per year (along with all prices), it will take fewer minutes of work to pay for a gallon of gas. In all important respects, gasoline has become cheaper; therefore, its quantity demanded will increase. The evidence (as well as common sense) indicates that people respond to relative, not absolute, prices or income changes.

● HOW WE MEASURE INFLATION

We have defined inflation and talked about changes in the average of all nominal prices. The next step is to find a way to measure these changes in average prices. This is done by constructing a price index. It is easy to determine how much the price of an individual commodity has risen. If last year's light bulb cost $0.50, and this year's light bulb costs $0.75, there has been a 50 percent rise in the price of that light bulb over a one-year period. We can express the change in the price of the light bulb in one of several ways:

1. The price has gone up by $0.25.
2. The price is 1½ (1.5) times as high.
3. The price has risen by 50 percent.

An index number of this price *rise* is simply the second choice multiplied by 100. That is, the price index for light bulbs is 150, assuming a base price index of 100 in the original year.

TABLE 8–2
Nominal versus Relative Price

The nominal prices of videocassettes and video discs have risen. But the relative price of videocassettes has fallen (or conversely, the relative price of video discs has risen).

	NOMINAL PRICE		RELATIVE PRICE	
	Price 3 Years Ago	Price Today	Price 3 Years Ago	Price Today
VIDEOCASSETTES	$50	$150	$\dfrac{\$50}{\$25} = 2$	$\dfrac{\$150}{\$100} = 1.5$
VIDEO DISCS	$25	$100	$\dfrac{\$25}{\$50} = 0.5$	$\dfrac{\$100}{\$150} = 0.67$

You may have read in the newspapers that the consumer price index (CPI) increased by, say, 1 percentage point last month. Or you might have watched the news last night and heard that according to the latest CPI figures, the price level increased at an annual rate of 12 percent. The consumer price index is a special type of price index that is used frequently by government statisticians and economists to measure the rate of inflation.

The Consumer Price Index

Although it is possible to get a precise measure of inflation by regularly (daily or weekly) keeping track of the prices of each of the millions of goods and services produced in the United States, it would be prohibitively expensive and time-consuming. Fortunately, we can get an accurate enough measure of inflation from the monthly changes in the prices of a selected sample of goods and services, provided the sample is "good." In other words, we can select a representative basket of goods and services that the "average" family is likely to purchase during a month. Then we look at how the cost of that specific bundle of goods and services changes each month.

Assume that the representative bundle of goods and services includes bread, eggs, shoes, and jeans, to name a few. It is convenient to represent the *whole list* of prices by just *one number*. This number is known as the consumer price index, or CPI. We will call the year when we begin to measure inflation the **base year**, and we find it convenient to assign to the whole list of prices for that year the number 100. That is, the CPI equals 100 for the base year.

Suppose that one year later the prices of the goods in our sample have increased an average of 10 percent. What number should we

Base year

The year used to compare all other years' prices. The number 100 is arbitrarily assigned to the price index in the base year.

149

now assign to this new list of prices? Since the CPI is 10 percent higher than in the base year, we say that the CPI one year later is 110.

The Weighting Problem.   Suppose the price of a loaf of bread has increased by 12 percent and the price of a pack of chewing gum has increased by 8 percent. Can we say that, on average, prices have gone up 10 percent? Perhaps, but it would probably be misleading to do so. Bread purchases are more important in most family budgets than chewing gum. Therefore, bread purchases should have more influence, or *weight*, on the CPI number than chewing gum purchases do. In general, weights are selected that reflect the *actual* quantities of buyers' purchases.

Index Numbers.   When the weighted average of the prices of goods and services in the representative bundle of goods and services rises by 10 percent, the new CPI number is 110. Another way to interpret this number is as follows: If the representative bundle of goods and services costs $100 in the base (beginning) period, that same bundle now costs $110. The CPI numbers (100, 110, and so on) are referred to as **index numbers**: hence, the name consumer price *index*.

Problems with the Consumer Price Index

The CPI is widely accepted and used to make cost-of-living adjustments (COLAs) in many sectors of our economy. For example, social security recipients occasionally receive upward adjustments in their benefit checks based on a rise in the CPI. So do retirees on private and government pension plans. And many unions have cost-of-living adjustment clauses in their wage contracts, whereby wages are periodically adjusted based on changes in the CPI. With so many people having some benefit tied to a cost-of-living adjustment, the CPI becomes all the more important. But as it turns out, the CPI is an imperfect measure of what is really happening to the cost of living.

Sampling Problems.   One problem with the CPI is that it is based on a *sample*. That is, it is an estimate of the average price increase for a *particular subset* of consumers. Simply because most people do not buy exactly the same goods in that representative bundle, the CPI is an imperfect measure for them. For example, the representative family purchasing the bundle of goods and services is a couple with two children. The bundle of goods purchased clearly does not reflect what is being purchased by younger families without children, nor is it representative of what retired people purchase. Surely, retired

Index number

A *weighted* average of a compilation of other numbers. The CPI, for example, represents an index number of the prices of a representative sample of goods and services.

150

people consume a bundle of goods that is quite different from the bundle on which the CPI is based. For this reason there has been criticism about the use of the CPI to adjust social security and private pension plan payments for elderly individuals.

Taxes Ignored. To some extent, the CPI *overstates* a person's true economic well-being because it does not correctly take account of certain taxes. It does take account of product-specific taxes, such as sales taxes, but it does not take account of changes in social security taxes and federal and state income taxes. To the extent that increases in taxes are ignored by the CPI, this index number is "too low" and people's "true" economic well-being is overstated.

On Net, the CPI Overstates Cost-of-Living Increases.

On balance, however, it is generally agreed that the CPI *understates* the true economic well-being of most groups in society. The CPI as currently measured shows increases that are not reflective of changes in the cost of living. People are really better off than increases in the CPI would lead us to believe.

One way that the CPI understates economic well-being (and overstates the cost of living) is by measuring through time the cost of *given* quantities of goods and services in the representative bundle. However, as prices of all goods change, relative prices change, and some goods in the bundle will have greater price increases than other goods. Therefore, we would not expect people to continue buying that identical bundle. That is, people will buy less of the relatively more expensive goods and services, and more of those goods that have become relatively cheaper. For example, in 1972–1973, a survey of urban consumers was taken. From that survey, a new representative bundle of goods and services was estimated by the Bureau of Labor Statistics for use in a revised consumer price index that started in 1978. But starting in 1973, the price of gasoline increased dramatically and certainly at a much higher rate than the rate of inflation. We know that individuals responded to this higher relative price in gasoline by purchasing smaller quantities. Nonetheless, the original quantities purchased by the average family in 1972–1973 continued to be used in CPI data from 1978 on.

And that leads to another problem with the CPI. Through time, the contents of the bundle of goods that people purchase will surely change. The *quality* of some goods will improve, and *new products* will become available. But the CPI does not take into account quality improvements or the new products that technological advances bring until well after those changes have occurred. Therefore, increases in the CPI overstate actual changes in the cost of living. After all, at the same nominal price, a good is actually cheaper if its quality has been improved.

151

Other Price Indexes

There are numerous other price indexes that economists refer to when discussing inflation. One of the most important is the producer price index (PPI). The PPI used to be called the wholesale price index. It is similar to the CPI except that it measures changes in the average prices of goods sold in wholesale markets by producers of commodities in all stages of processing. At present, it includes price quotations for about 2800 items from producers and manufacturers. No services are included in the PPI market basket.

There are other indexes that relate to personal consumption expenditures and the total value of final goods and services produced in the economy. All indexes suffer from certain problems, particularly those problems outlined with respect to the CPI. In addition, the PPI creates a problem with its double counting system. By counting some prices over and over again, it gives them more weight than they deserve. For example, a change in the price of raw cotton will later be reflected in the price of cloth, and then again in the price of clothing. This pyramiding overemphasizes crude-material price changes and can cause the PPI to behave quite erratically, especially when the prices of raw materials are changing. Also, some prices reported in the PPI represent list prices rather than actual prices, but it is actual prices that undergo more gradual changes. Therefore, the PPI may not reflect the smoother transition that may occur as actual prices change. Instead, the prices shown in the PPI may be overly slow to reflect a change, and when they do change, the change may be very abrupt.

● WHO IS HURT BY INFLATION?

Everyone complains about inflation. Everyone seems to assume that it is "bad." And most people seem to assume that everyone is hurt by it. Consider, for a moment, the fact that inflation, in a real sense, is simply *an annual change in our accounting system*. Instead of saying that this year we will count things in terms of dollars and next year in pesos, and the following year in rubles, we say, for example, that a paperback of constant quality and length costs $2.00 one year, $2.50 the next year, and $3.50 the following year.

But does that mean that everyone is hurt by higher book prices? Not necessarily. After all, if you pay a higher price for that book next year, someone is receiving more income. Indeed, during inflation, some people pay higher prices while other people benefit from those higher prices. The fact is that if inflation were perfect—if every single price in the economy, including wages and other incomes, rose at exactly the same rate—then inflation would have little effect on different groups in the society. All groups would remain rela-

152

tively the same in wealth, because the *fully anticipated* rate of inflation would be reflected in the same price increases everywhere in the economy.

But most people believe that inflation *is* "killing" them, and here is the reason why. Suppose an individual receives a 12 percent salary increase at the end of the year. But that individual learns that prices have risen during the year by 9 percent. The conclusion seems obvious: "If it hadn't been for inflation, my income would have gone up 12 percent, but in fact, my **real income** (or purchasing power) has gone up only 3 percent." The fallacy in this reasoning is that the person probably would not have received the 12 percent salary increase in the absence of inflation. Rather, if inflation had been zero, that person probably would have received a 3 percent salary increase, the typical salary increase during periods of little or no inflation in the United States, such as in the 1950s.

Different groups in society are indeed hurt by inflation, particularly when its rate is unanticipated. Those groups are (1) fixed-income groups; (2) creditors; (3) those who enter into contracts without inflation-protection clauses; and (4) people who hold cash.

Individuals on Fixed Incomes

The most obvious group of individuals to lose out because of inflation is that group living on fixed incomes. If, for example, you are retired and have a fixed retirement income of $600 per month, the purchasing power of that $600 will continue to fall as long as there is inflation. If, over a 10-year period, the CPI doubles, then your purchasing power at the end of the 10 years will be only half of what it was at the beginning. That is, your $600 will buy only half of what it bought 10 years earlier. Thus your standard of living on that fixed income will be half as great as it was when you started.

As a general rule, then, any time you are locked into an income that is fixed in nominal dollars, you will suffer because of inflation. However, many retirees are not in such dire straits as you might think. Of all Americans over 65 years of age, 93.4 percent receive social security payments, which in the last 10 years have increased at a faster rate than the rate of inflation. In fact, the latest data show that while the CPI increased 81.5 percent from 1967 to 1977, Congress raised social security benefits an average of 184.6 percent over the same period. Thus, social security recipients not only kept up with inflation, but actually beat inflation.

Creditors May Lose and Debtors May Gain

Suppose you lend a friend $100 to be repaid one year later. Suppose further that there is no inflation now and none expected during

Real income

Income corrected for price changes, or income corrected for inflation or deflation.

the year. You might charge your friend a **nominal interest rate** of, say, 5 percent. At the end of the year, you will be repaid the $100 plus $5 in interest. If, indeed, no inflation occurs during that period, the $100 will still purchase the same real quantity of goods and services.

On the other hand, if the CPI rises by 5 percent during that one-year period when you did not anticipate a rise, then you will end up making no return at all on your loan. Why? Because the dollars that you are repaid by your friend will have only 95 percent of their original purchasing power. The $100 you are paid back can purchase only $95 worth of goods. The value of your loan in terms of purchasing power will have fallen by 5 percent; the 5 percent interest you would have received will just cover that loss in purchasing power. You will have made a **real interest rate** of 0 percent during that period.

Now consider the possibility that the rate of inflation rises beyond the rate of interest you are charging your friend. What if the inflation rate is 10 percent? At the end of one year, despite the 5 percent interest you receive, the purchasing power of the $100 plus $5 interest will be less than the purchasing power of the $100 you lent your friend at the beginning of the year. You would then receive a negative real interest rate.

The point to understand from this example is that creditors lose and debtors gain whenever inflation rates are unanticipated and *underestimated* for the life of the loan. If, on the other hand, you fully anticipate a 5 percent inflation, you can require your friend to pay you an **inflationary premium** in addition to the 5 percent interest you charge for the use of your money.

During the 1960s and 1970s, there were many years in which the rate of inflation was higher than anticipated. During those years creditors did, on net, lose and debtors did, on net, gain. However, if **inflationary expectations** are correct, inflation will not adversely affect most people.

People who borrow money during periods of anticipated inflation are willing to pay higher interest rates because they know that the dollars they pay back to the creditor will be cheaper—that is, they will have a lower purchasing power. An individual may borrow $20,000 for a luxury car, knowing full well that by the time the loan is due, that same $20,000 might buy only a small compact.

Remember, the crucial distinction here is between *unanticipated* and *anticipated* inflation.

Signing Contracts Without Inflation-Protection Clauses

Let's assume you sign an agreement to work for someone over a two-year period, and that agreement states that you will receive a

---

Nominal interest rate

The apparent or *market* rate charged for borrowing funds.

Real interest rate

The inflation-adjusted rate charged for borrowing funds.

Inflationary premium

A premium that is tacked on to the real interest rate on a loan to take into account expected inflation in the future. The higher the expected rate of inflation, the greater the inflationary premium will be.

Inflationary expectations

Those predictions that individuals make about the future rate of inflation based on available information and "gut" feelings about future price increases.

154

10 percent increase in wages at the end of one year. But if the inflation rate during that period turns out to be 20 percent, you will find yourself with less purchasing power than when you started the job.

It is extremely important in inflationary times not to get locked into long-term contracts that make no allowances for higher rates of inflation than anticipated. There has been a tremendous variation in the rate of inflation in the United States over the last 15 years. Thus, workers increasingly will refuse to be tied down to long-term contracts, or will demand that a clause be added to such contracts to take into account unanticipated changes in the rate of inflation.

Holding Cash Becomes Expensive

Most people carry a certain amount of cash in their wallets. And many individuals maintain checking account balances that may average several hundred or even several thousand dollars per month. Just about everyone, therefore, loses wealth during an inflation. That is, the purchasing power of cash held in a wallet or checking account falls at the rate of inflation.

A simple example will demonstrate this. Assume that you have stashed away $100 in $1 bills underneath your mattress. If at the end of one year there has been a 10 percent increase in the CPI, then the purchasing power of those 100 $1 bills will be only $90. You will have lost value equal to the 10 percent inflation times the amount of cash you kept on hand. In essence, then, the value of the cash we keep on hand depreciates at the rate of inflation. The only way to lessen this type of inflationary tax, as it were, is to reduce cash balances. Unfortunately, this is not always practical. Most people find it convenient to have money in their wallets and checking accounts so they can pay for the things they want when they want them. (Imagine trying to purchase everything on payday so as to minimize the amount of cash in your checking account or wallet.)

● TAXES AND INFLATION

Over the past two decades, Americans have felt a particularly dramatic effect of inflation. Americans have been pushed into higher and higher income tax brackets. Although the topic of taxes is treated in more detail in Chapters 11 and 15, we will discuss it here briefly in relation to inflation.

The federal income tax system is a progressive tax system. In other words, as you earn greater and greater amounts of income, the *additional* income is taxed at higher and higher rates. As taxpayers are put into higher tax brackets, the amount they have to pay on the last few dollars clearly goes up. Individuals have been pushed into higher and higher tax brackets because inflation has caused their nominal incomes to increase. Inflation, therefore, causes the average federal income tax rate to rise simply by putting taxpayers into higher and higher tax brackets. This process is known as **bracket creep, or taxflation**.

The effect of inflation on purchasing power can be dramatic. Purchasing power, or real income, is defined as income corrected for inflation. In other words, if nominal income goes up by 10 percent and our measure of inflation—say, the CPI—also goes up by 10 percent, then purchasing power, or real income, has not risen at all. Consider that example further. You have received a 10 percent salary increase, but inflation has also been 10 percent. Presumably, you are no better off at the end of the year than at the beginning of the year. But actually, you will probably be worse off. Why? Because that extra 10 percent income will be taxed at a higher rate than your previous income. You will be paying more in taxes to the federal government, on average, than you were in the past.

Table 8–3 shows the effects of inflation on take-home pay, where there is a 9.4 percent inflation rate that is just matched by a 9.4 percent pay raise. We see that for all three levels of income—low, medium, and high—the after-tax real income in year 2, expressed in terms of year 1 dollars of purchasing power, is lower. Because of the progressive nature of the federal personal income tax system, Americans must receive raises each year that *exceed* the rise in the average of all prices. Why? Because they must pay the higher taxes caused by their being pushed into higher tax brackets.

TABLE 8–3
The Effect of Inflation on Take-Home Pay

Because of graduated income tax rates, even families that get raises matching the big increase in living costs wind up losing purchasing power. Here we show how a 9.4 percent inflation rate outruns a 9.4 percent pay raise.

		GROSS INCOME	FEDERAL INCOME TAX	EFFECTIVE AVERAGE TAX RATE (PERCENT)	AFTER-TAX REAL INCOME IN YEAR 1 DOLLARS
LOW INCOME	Year 1	$14,000	$1,600	11.4	$12,400
	Year 2	15,316	1,890	12.3	12,164
MEDIUM INCOME	Year 1	20,000	3,010	15.1	16,990
	Year 2	21,880	3,506	16.0	16,646
HIGH INCOME	Year 1	30,000	6,020	20.1	23,980
	Year 2	32,820	7,035	21.4	23,361

Bracket creep, or taxflation

The process by which inflation pushes individuals into higher and higher tax brackets.

The 1981 tax legislation approved by Congress incorporated a wide variety of tax breaks for both businesses and individuals. The legislation includes three one-year, across-the-board marginal tax rate reductions of 5 percent beginning October 1, 1981, with additional reductions of 10 percent on July 1, 1982, and July 1, 1983. Although the cuts in marginal tax rates end with the July 1983 reduction, starting in 1985 personal rates and personal exemptions will be *indexed to inflation* by adjusting them for increases in the CPI. The move is designed to eliminate the effect of bracket creep.

● OTHER EFFECTS OF INFLATION

There are at least three phenomena that result from a variable, or uncertain, rate of inflation.

First, more resources are devoted to predicting the rate of inflation and to avoiding the effects of inflation. Individuals attempt to negotiate escalator clauses into their contracts, a procedure that requires time and effort as well as legal and accounting resources. And witness what has happened in the mortgage market. It seems as if every year a new type of mortgage contract is devised to take account of wildly changing interest rates which, as we will see, are basically a reflection of wildly changing rates of inflation. Since individuals and institutions are relying more and more on inflation escalator clauses, or cost-of-living clauses, additional resources are devoted to more accurate measures of price changes. If 50 million people depend on what has happened to the CPI over the last few months, then more resources must be directed toward ensuring the accuracy of the CPI.

Second, financial planning for the future becomes more difficult. People can no longer determine when to make major purchases if they cannot count on price changes being constant. Moreover, they will have a more difficult time determining what their savings rate should be today, what type of job to take, and so on, if they are uncertain about the rate of inflation in the future.

Third, comparison shopping increases for infrequently purchased items. Consumers make choices on the basis of relative prices. Even during a period of inflation that is variable and uncertain, consumers have little difficulty determining the relative prices of frequently purchased goods, such as food items. However, when consumers enter the marketplace seeking a less frequently purchased item, such as a washing machine, an expensive coat, or a car, they are apt to be shocked at how high the prices are. They cannot believe that such prices reflect the true value of the infrequently purchased item. To obtain further information about prices, these consumers feel compelled to search longer than they would in a world without inflation or in a world of constant inflation. Ulti-

157

mately, consumers will buy infrequently purchased items about as often with or without inflation. But because of inflation, consumers will spend more time and effort in comparative shopping before making the purchase.

● WHY WE HAVE INFLATION

There are as many theories about inflation as there are people who want to express their opinions about inflation. Often we hear that inflation exists because of rising prices. But that is not a theory of inflation. Rather, such a statement merely reflects our definition of inflation as a sustained rise in the weighted average of all prices. It is certainly true that prices will rise in a time of inflation. The question is, why? The informed economic analyst will not fall into the trap of restating definitions in the guise of explaining a concept or phenomenon.

Another attempt to explain inflation focuses on those components of the price index that are rising the fastest and estimates what the index would be if those items were omitted. As expected, the index rises at a lower rate. Sometimes the lower rate is called the *underlying rate of inflation*. Sometimes the argument focuses on special circumstances that cause some prices to rise at a high rate and reasons for believing that the measurement of the high-rising prices is defective. However, the opposite approach, that of removing the least rapidly rising prices from the index, is usually ignored. In addition, the special-circumstances argument is not applied to prices that rise slowly, and it ignores the question of what would have happened to other prices if some had not risen as quickly. For example, if food and energy prices had not risen so rapidly, would other prices have risen faster because more money would have been spent on them instead?

The key point is the distinction between absolute and relative prices, explained previously. Inflation is a rise in the weighted average of *all* prices and is not explained by relative price movements. Some prices rise faster than the average and some rise slower than the average, reflecting *relative* price changes. Arguments that focus on a subset of prices—for example, on some rapidly rising prices—do not explain the phenomenon of inflation. In fact, the effect of some rapidly rising prices, relative to the average of all prices, could be offset by other prices that are falling. On balance, the *relative* price changes could leave the average level of all prices unchanged, or even lower.

We will now explain the two major theories of inflation: **demand-pull inflation** (demand pulls prices up) and **cost-push inflation** (costs push up the prices of final products).

Demand-pull inflation

A sustained rise in the average of all prices caused by increases in total, or aggregate, demand—too many dollars chasing too few goods.

Cost-push inflation

A sustained rise in prices caused by rising input costs.

158

Demand-Pull Inflation

If total demand in the economy is rising while the available supply of goods is limited, demand-pull inflation occurs. Goods and services may be in short supply either because the economy is being fully utilized or because the economy cannot grow fast enough to meet the growing economywide demand. In either case, the general level of prices rises.

Demand-pull inflation, at least in part, has been associated with a full-employment economy. By definition, once the economy reaches full employment, any increase in economywide demand will simply pull up prices. Hence the term *demand-pull inflation*.

A simplified representation of this theory is given in Graph 8–1. Output is measured on the horizontal axis; the price level is mea-

GRAPH 8–1
Demand-Pull Inflation

The economywide supply curve is given as S. It is horizontal until nearly full employment is reached. When full employment is reached, it becomes vertical. No more output is possible from the economy. If the economywide demand curve for all goods and services is D_1, output will be at Q_1 per year. Total demand in the economy can increase to D_2 without any increase in the price level. However, when it increases to D_3, there is some increase in the price level as well as an increase in output to Q_3. After output rate Q_4, however, any increase in demand, such as up to D_4, will merely lead to increases in the price level. Increases in demand pull up prices.

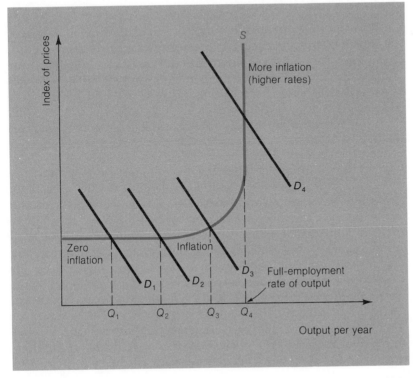

159

sured on the vertical axis. Output and employment can increase without any increase in the general price level, as long as the economy is nowhere near the full-employment level of output. Graph 8–1 shows an economywide supply curve, S; it becomes vertical at the full-employment rate of output—no more can be supplied. The economy is running at full steam at output rate Q_4. D_1 through D_4 represent possible economywide, or aggregate, demand curves. If total demand increases from D_1 to D_2, then output can increase from Q_1 to Q_2 without any increase in an index of prices. If the economywide demand curve increases further to D_3, output will increase to Q_3, but there will be some inflation. Finally, if the total demand curve increases to D_4, output will be at Q_4, but there will be considerable inflation. In fact, any further increases in a total demand curve that intersects the supply curve, S, along its vertical portion will produce inflation, since no increase in output is possible.

A number of factors can cause a shift in the aggregate demand curve, D, outward beyond D_3. In most cases, such a shift is associated with the public's efforts to buy more than the full-employment output. We have observed these shifts during periods of war, during large federal government budget deficits, and during excessive increases in the amount of money in circulation. We will discuss all of these possibilities in later chapters.

Cost-Push Inflation

The cost-push inflation theory has emerged as a popular theory of price increases. It attempts to explain why prices rise when the economy is *not* at full employment. The cost-push inflation theory apparently explains both creeping inflation and the inflation that the United States experienced during its 1969–1970 and 1973–1975 recessions. Essentially three factors are mentioned in the cost-push inflation theory: union power, big-business monopoly power, and higher raw materials prices.

Union Power. Many people feel that unions are responsible for inflation. Their reasoning is as follows. Unions decide to demand a wage hike that is not warranted by increases in the workers' productivity. Because the unions are so powerful, employers must give in to their demands for higher wages. When the employers have to pay these higher wages, their costs become higher. To maintain their usual profit margins, these businesspeople raise their prices. This type of cost-push inflation seemingly can occur even when there is no excess demand for goods, and even when the economy is operating below capacity at under full employment. The union power argument rests on the unions having monopolistic market power in their labor markets. In other words, it is argued that some unions are so strong that they can impose wage increases on employers even when those wage increases are not consistent with increases in labor productivity.

Big-Business Monopoly Power.   Another variant of the cost-push theory is that inflation is caused when the monopoly power of big businesses allows them to push up prices. It is alleged that powerful corporations can raise their prices whenever they want to increase their profits. And each time these corporations raise prices, the cost of living goes up. Workers then demand higher wages to make up for the loss in their standard of living, thereby giving the corporations an excuse to raise prices again. And so goes a vicious cycle of price-wage increases.

Raw Materials Cost–Push Inflation.   Because of rising prices for all forms of energy, a relatively new type of cost-push inflation has been suggested. It is called raw materials cost-push inflation because the cost of raw materials seems to keep rising. Coal is more expensive; so is petroleum; so is natural gas; and so are a lot of other inputs into basic production processes.

Whether caused by union power, big-business monopoly power, or higher raw materials prices, the increased costs of production push prices up; hence the term *cost-push inflation*. One solution offered as a way to stop, or at least slow down, cost-push inflation is wage and price controls. We now analyze these controls to see whether they have done much to cure the inflation that plagues this economy.

Wage and Price Controls Can Reduce the Rate of Inflation

THE ARGUMENT

Since the time of the Roman emperor Diocletian, the response of government to rising prices often has been to impose a ceiling on prices and wages. As recently as 1971, President Nixon imposed such controls. Even after what was widely perceived by economists as the disastrous consequences of these controls and their subsequent

elimination in 1974, a Gallup poll in November of that year showed that 62 percent of the American people favored them. Can wage and price controls effectively eliminate, or at least reduce, the rate of inflation?

THE ANALYSIS

The history of wage and price controls in this country has been long indeed. In 1636, the American Puritans imposed a code of price and wage limitations. Anyone caught violating the code was considered to be as bad as "adulterers and whoremongers." Even before the Declaration of Independence, the Continental Congress had set price ceilings. General George Washington complained of excessive rates of inflation, as did others at that time. Later a few states enacted price-control laws. There were various attempts at controlling prices during World War I, but the big effort came during World War II. The Office of Price Administration, established after the Price Control Act of 1942, put direct controls on numerous prices. These controls were supported by 70,000 paid employees and 350,000 price-control volunteers. But during the war, it became clear that price controls had an undesirable side effect—black markets.

The Black Market

We can analyze the effect of a black market by using the supply and demand analysis presented in Chapter 2. Look at Graph 8–2. Assume that this graph represents the supply and demand schedule for automobiles at the start of World War II. The equilibrium price would be at P_e, where the demand and supply schedules intersect. However, the government sets a maximum legal price of P_1. But at that price the quantity supplied by the manufacturers in Detroit would be only Q_s, and the quantity demanded would be Q_d. Obviously, there would be an excess quantity demanded. The actual supply schedule, if the controls were properly enforced at the manufacturing stage, would now be equal to SS'—that is, the supply schedule slopes up until it reaches the intersection with the legal price, at which point it becomes vertical. The intersection of the new supply curve and the old demand curve

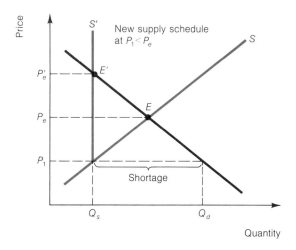

GRAPH 8–2
Black Markets

The demand curve is D. The supply curve is SS. The equilibrium price is P_e. The government, however, steps in and imposes a maximum price of P_1. At that lower price, the quantity demanded will be Q_d, but the quantity supplied will only be Q_s. There is a shortage, and black markets develop. The price is bid up in the black market to P_e' because that is where the new supply curve, SS', intersects the demand curve at E'. Black market prices can be obtained by any number of devices, such as under-the-counter payments to retailers.

is at E', or a price of P_e'. This black market price is obtained when customers make under-the-counter payments to retailers.

Other Problems
Ignoring the black market problem, consider the problem of quality. Take, for example, a loaf of bread. Bread contains a number of ingredients. The baker, in the face of rising costs and a legally imposed price ceiling, has the option of reducing the size of the loaf, reducing the quality of the flour, or reducing the quantity or quality of other inputs. Bread, however, is a relatively simple commodity as compared with, say, an automobile. In the face of price ceilings, the automobile producer has thousands of ways to alter the quality of the automobile. Note

the implications of this point. A reduction in quality at a constant price enforced by the price ceiling is, in fact, a price increase, since what results is an inferior automobile at the same price as before.

But we have only begun to contemplate the impossible task that faces the administrator of price ceilings. What about seasonal variations in the real cost of providing goods? Should the price of lettuce in midwinter be the same as the price of lettuce in summer? If it is, we can be assured that the lettuce will disappear in midwinter if the summer price is imposed. And if we impose the winter price of lettuce, then we are giving windfall gains to summer lettuce producers. And what about the goods that we import? Do we impose a price ceiling on them? If we do and their costs rise, it simply means that we will no longer be able to import them. Then shortages will exist, which, in turn, will either prevent production or raise the cost to other producers along the line who use those goods as inputs into their manufacturing.

Redistribution of Wealth and Income
It should be clear from this discussion that an efficient price-control system is impossible. The number of goods and services required to enforce a wage or price ceiling is staggering. Literally hundreds of millions of individual goods and services are exchanged for which the administrator must devise and enforce a ceiling. And the problem is even more complex because some prices are much easier to force a ceiling upon than others. Wages, for example, are quite visible—they exist in contracts. Therefore, it is easier to enforce a wage ceiling than to enforce the ceiling on a product whose quality can be altered. The result is that certain kinds of prices will be effectively enforced, while others, in fact, will change. Thus, we can have an immense redistribution of real income in the system, favoring those who avoid price ceilings and injuring those whose

163

products or services can be regulated easily and effectively.

DISCUSSION QUESTIONS

1. How do the concepts of supply and demand relate to the analysis of wage and price controls?

2. Imagine a system of price controls that sets maximum retail prices but allows input costs to increase to reflect changing market conditions. If cattle farmers experience rising feed costs due to crop shortages, how will cattle farm operations be affected?

● WHAT'S AHEAD

To many individuals, a more compelling problem in the American economy is continued unemployment. Indeed, since the late 1960s, the terms *inflation* and *unemployment* have been bound together. The United States has had periods of inflation and unemployment, both associated with human suffering and sacrifice. In the next chapter, we will learn about the effects of unemployment throughout our history. We will also look at the way it is measured and some of the reasons it has occurred.

● CHAPTER SUMMARY

Inflation is defined as a sustained rise in the weighted average of all prices. The rate of inflation is commonly measured by changes in the consumer price index (CPI). This price index is derived from changes in the total cost of a representative bundle of goods and services purchased by a representative household. The cost of this representative bundle of goods and services is estimated each month by the Bureau of Labor Statistics. The CPI, however, suffers from numerous flaws, including inadequate accounting for bracket creep, improvements in quality and new products, and changes in expenditure patterns of consumers.

Individuals on fixed incomes certainly are hurt by inflation. But it is not always clear who is actually on a fixed income. For example, all social security recipients and many government and private pension plan recipients have cost-of-living clauses (COLAs) in their contracts and therefore receive payments that increase at least at the rate of inflation, as measured by changes in the CPI. Lenders certainly are hurt by unanticipated inflation because the interest rates they have charged borrowers do not have a high enough inflationary premium to take account of the depreciating purchasing power of the dollars repaid by the borrowers. Finally, anyone who signs a contract that does not fully take account of unanticipated inflation will suffer from inflation. But remember, not everyone suffers from inflation, because increased expenditures by some (due to higher prices) automatically mean a receipt by others of higher income. In effect, inflation is a change in the accounting system every year.

Because of the graduated nature of our federal personal income tax, inflation causes individuals to be pushed into higher tax brackets, even when increases in income match increases in prices. This phenomenon is known as bracket creep, or taxflation. Starting in 1985, assuming current congressional legislation remains in force, this phenomenon will no longer occur because the federal personal income tax system will be indexed to the rate of inflation.

In developing a theory of inflation, we must be careful to distinguish between relative and nominal, or absolute, prices. Price rises of individual commodities do not constitute an inflationary phenomenon nor do they constitute a theory of why inflation exists. Two important theories of inflation are demand-pull and cost-push inflation. Demand-pull inflation predicts that prices will rise whenever total, or aggregate, demand in the economy grows faster than total supply in the economy. Cost-push inflation may be caused by excessive increases in wages due to union power, excessive increases in prices due to big-business monopoly power, or excessive increases in raw materials prices.

● QUESTIONS FOR REVIEW AND STUDY

1. Inflation is defined as a _____ rise in the weighted average price level.

2. Even during periods of overall price stability—zero inflation— tastes change. These changes in taste will lead to changes in _____ prices.

3. Even during a period of inflation, some _____ will fall.

4. During periods of inflation, changes in taste will lead to changes in the relative _____ of price increase for different goods.

5. When the price of gasoline goes up, in absolute terms, by 4 percent and the CPI goes up by 10 percent, the relative price of gasoline has _____.

6. Some measures of inflation require that we collect price data on a _____ bundle of goods and services.

7. To derive a correct index of overall price increases, we must _____ the prices of different goods and services according to the percentage of our total expenditures represented by such purchases.

8. To derive the CPI, we must obtain a _____ of the goods and services purchased by individuals.

9. The CPI does not include _____ and therefore over-states a person's true economic well-being.

10. Since individuals purchase less of those goods whose relative prices have risen, the CPI has a tendency to _____ cost of living increases, because it uses a fixed representative bundle of goods.

11. Inflation typically does not hurt everyone because for every loser, there is often a _____.

12. Individuals usually form _____ _____ about what will happen to prices in the future.

13. It is important to distinguish between _____ inflation and actual inflation.

14. Anyone on a _____ income will suffer when inflation occurs, whether or not the inflation has been _____.

15. There are relatively few groups in society on fixed incomes; even those receiving _____ _____ find that their pay-ments rise at least at the rate of inflation, if not more rapidly.

16. In periods of anticipated inflation, lenders will require _____ interest rates.

17. During periods of inflation, we observe high _____ interest rates.

18. When we correct nominal interest rates for the anticipated rate of inflation, we obtain the _____ _____ _____.

19. Whenever inflation is higher than anticipated, borrowers are _____ _____.

20. Labor contracts are typically signed for periods of three to five years in terms of _____ wages.

21. Whenever the inflation rate rises more rapidly than nominal wages, the _____ _____ _____ falls.

22. Because it is difficult to predict the rate of inflation, inflation causes _____ uncertainty in society.

23. The two major theories of the causes of inflation are _____ _____ and _____ _____.

24. Cost-push inflation can be caused by _____, _____ or _____.

25. Demand-pull inflation is due to _____ demand for goods and services.

26. A common definition of demand-pull inflation is _____ _____ dollars chasing _____ _____ goods.

(For answers see top of facing page)

ANSWERS

● ANSWERS TO CHAPTER PREVIEW QUESTIONS

1. *Is it possible for inflation to hurt every single person simultaneously?*

In a sense, it is impossible for everyone to be hurt by inflation simultaneously. After all, for every expenditure of income there is a receipt of income. That is, expenditures always equal receipts. So when one person is paying more for a product, someone else is receiving more. All we can say is that certain groups will suffer from inflation, while others will gain.

2. *Who is hurt most by inflation?*

Individuals on fixed money incomes lose from inflation. Individuals who have loaned money at an interest rate that does not take sufficient account of inflation also lose. Workers who accept future nominal wage increases that do not compensate adequately for inflation clearly lose. In general, those individuals who do not fully anticipate the future rate of inflation are those who will lose. It is important, therefore, to distinguish between anticipated inflation and unanticipated inflation. But even if a worker or a lender attempts to anticipate inflation, he or she can make an inaccurate prediction. Additionally, those who do not like uncertainty (risk avoiders) will find themselves worse off in a period of inflation, particularly if the rate of inflation varies each year and is very difficult to predict.

● PROBLEMS

1. Study the table at the right and then answer the following questions.

   a. What is the base year for the CPI?
   b. What has been happening to the price level since 1967?
   c. By how much did prices rise from 1977 to 1978?
   d. If the representative bundle of goods and services cost $100 in 1967, what did it cost in August 1980?

2. Who is helped by inflation?

YEAR	CPI
1967	100
1977	181.5
1978	195.4
1979	217.4
August 1980	249.4

● SELECTED REFERENCES

Campbell, Colin D., ed. *Wage–Price Controls in World War Two: United States and Germany*. Washington, D.C.: American Enterprise Institute, 1971.

Collander, David C. *Solutions to Inflation*. New York: Harcourt Brace Jovanovich, 1979.

Heilbroner, Robert L. *Beyond Boom and Crash*. New York: Norton, 1978.

Lekachman, Robert. *Inflation: The Permanent Problem of Boom and Bust*. New York: Random House, 1973.

Schuettinger, Robert, and Eamon Butler. *Forty Centuries of Wage and Price Controls*. Washington, D.C.: The Heritage Foundation, 1979.

9

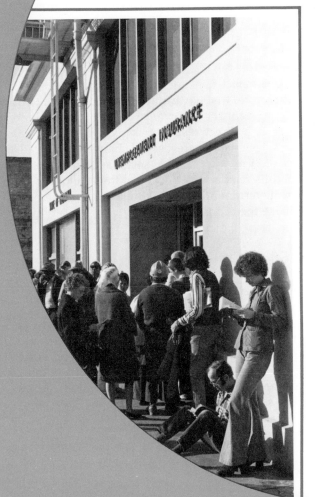

The Business Cycle and Unemployment

Chapter Preview
1. Under what circumstances might you be better off not working, even if you had the opportunity to work?
2. When times get tough, what are the first types of purchases you start doing without?

● KEY TERMS

Business cycle	Expansion
Business investment	Frictional unemployment
Capital goods	Innovation
Cyclical unemployment	Recession
Depression	Seasonal unemployment
Durable goods	Structural unemployment

From 1929 to about 1940, the United States experienced a tremendous economic slump. This period is referred to as the Great Depression. From 1930 to 1932, over 5000 banks went bankrupt as a financial panic gripped the nation. The production of goods and services fell 36 percent. The purchasing power of the average family was no greater than it was in 1908 (which was *itself* a depression year). And unemployment was rampant. The measured unemployment rate went from 3 percent of the labor force in 1929 to almost 25 percent in 1933–1934.

But statistics cannot really tell the story, for the Great Depression was a time of serious economic consequences and human suffering. It is not surprising, therefore, that government should resolve to do everything possible to prevent the recurrence of such an event. As mentioned in Chapter 7, a direct result of this depression was a series of legislative acts designed to effect social change. Specifically, the Employment Act of 1946 was passed, social security was put into effect, and numerous regulations to control the economy were enacted. Basically, the government began taking a much greater role in attempting to stabilize the economy.

● THE BUSINESS CYCLE

Although the general trend of the U.S. economy has been a rise in living standards, economic growth has not been smooth. That is, the U.S. economy (like any growing economy) has not always grown at the same rate. Instead, it grows by fits and starts. Indeed, at times the economy contracts. Thus, the economy experiences identifiable phases of **expansion** (increasing output and employment) and **recession** (decreasing output and employment). Recessions can become very severe and lead to a **depression**, such as the one just described. The aftermath of a recession or depression is an eventual upward trend in employment and output.

Phases of the Business Cycle

The behavior of the economy can be described in terms of the four phases of the **business cycle**. When a *recession* (phase 1) has run

Expansion

The phase in the economy when output and employment are increasing; the date it starts is somewhat arbitrary.

Recession

The phase in the economy when output and employment are decreasing; the date when it starts is somewhat arbitrary.

Depression

An extremely serious recession; the moment in time when a recession becomes a depression is arbitrary.

Business cycle

A general description of the ups and downs of overall economic activity; a business cycle consists of recessions, troughs, expansions, and peaks.

its course, a *trough* phase (phase 2) begins. The trough phase is usually followed by an *expansion* (phase 3), which eventually reaches a *peak* (phase 4). The economy then reverts to a recession phase and the cycle starts all over again.

The phases of an *ideal* business cycle are presented in Graph 9–1. Note how output and employment fall in the recession phase and rise in the expansion phase. In this graph, the economy is growing —the upward trend indicates growth—but growth is not smooth. Thus, over long periods of time, later peaks occur at higher output and employment levels than did earlier peaks. And even the level of successive troughs increases through time. Indeed, in later periods, troughs are at higher output and employment levels than were peaks in earlier periods. Everything is relative.

So far, our discussion has been in terms of an ideal business cycle. In the real world, however, the economy does not move in-

GRAPH 9–1
Phases of the Business Cycle

This graph shows how much output and employment change over the business cycle—and over time. After a recession runs its course, a trough phase begins which is followed by economic expansion. Finally, a peak is reached, which is then followed by another recession.

Note that during a recession, output and employment fall, while during the expansion phase, output and employment rise. But also note that over long periods of time, the *trend* is one of increased output and employment—at least for nations experiencing economic growth. You can see from the graph that each successive peak is at a higher level than the previous one (usually), and so are the successive troughs. Indeed, troughs later in time are higher than *peaks* in earlier time periods. Such is the "typical" path of a growing economy.

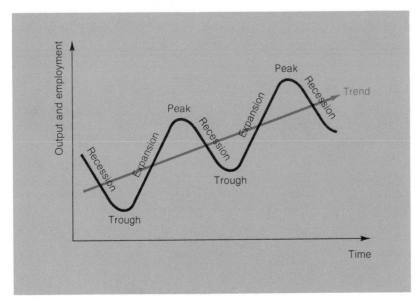

evitably from one phase to another. Nor does each phase of the business cycle last for a fixed period of time. Indeed, an examination of actual data on the U.S. economy in Graph 9–2 shows that real-world business cycles are varied and complex.

Today, it is considered rather archaic to refer to business cycles. Government stabilization policies can certainly change the duration and phases of business cycles—and not always in the right direction.

● WHAT HAPPENS TO DURABLE GOODS DURING A BUSINESS CYCLE?

Durable goods

Goods that last for more than a specified time period, usually a year (e.g., automobiles, stereos, houses, and tractors).

The role of **durable goods** in a business cycle is extremely important. Durable goods are those goods that last longer than a specified time period, usually a year. The output of durable goods

GRAPH 9–2

Business Activity in the United States

Here, note the ups and downs of business activity in the United States from before the Civil War until today. The prosperity during the 1960s was the longest period of a sustained rise in business activity that we have ever had. The ups and downs in business activity are measured as a *percentage change* compared to the long-range trend.

SOURCE: Cleveland Trust Company.

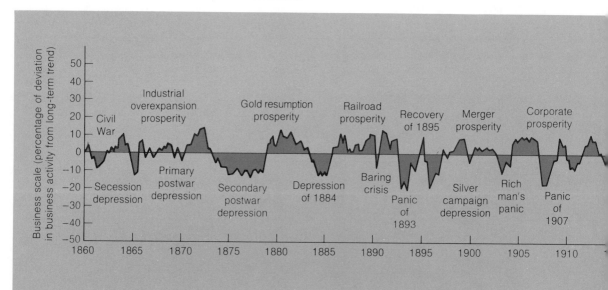

shows greater variability over the business cycle than the output of other goods. For example, an automobile is a durable good that lasts a number of years. Since it is long-lasting, the purchase of a new automobile can usually be postponed for long periods. In a recession, the overall purchases of automobiles (and videocassette recorders, television sets, refrigerators, and so on) will fall dramatically. On the other hand, during an expansion, such durable goods will be in great demand. When times are good, people want to purchase new durable goods. Thus, the production and purchase of consumer durable goods will fluctuate greatly over the business cycle. Bread, milk, and beer sales, on the other hand, will change only minimally over the business cycle. Look at Graph 9–3. In (a), the sales of durable goods fluctuate dramatically relative to national income. In (b), the sales of nondurable goods—food and other short-lived items—do not fluctuate much relative to changes in national income.

The same characteristics apply to durable business goods, otherwise known as **capital goods**. Since machines and buildings are long-lasting, businesses have the option of purchasing them or postponing their purchase almost at will. During periods of recession, many companies find that they have excess capacity—that is, they are not using all the machines and equipment already on hand. These firms will therefore cut back dramatically their purchase of such capital goods.

Capital goods

Durable goods used by business to produce other goods and services; examples of capital goods are machines and equipment.

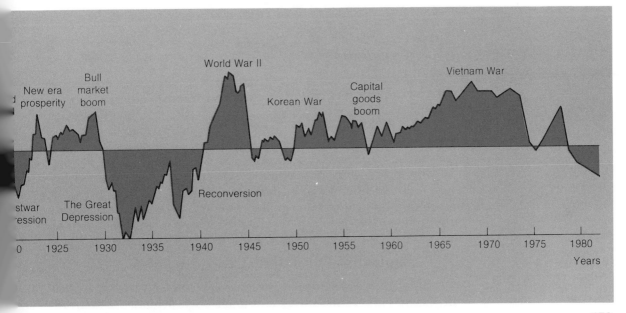

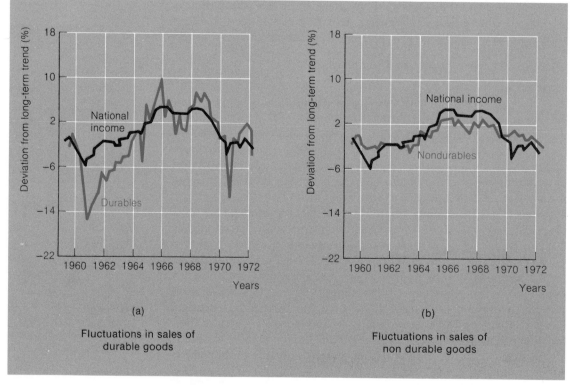

(a)

Fluctuations in sales of
durable goods

(b)

Fluctuations in sales of
non durable goods

GRAPH 9–3
Business Fluctuations and Durability

The change in the demand for durable goods is much more responsive to changes in national income than is the change in demand for nondurable goods. The deviation from durables' long-term trend, shown in (a), is much more pronounced than the deviation from nondurables' long-term trend, shown in (b). In other words, there is more variability in durable goods' demand than in nondurable goods' demand.

● CAUSES OF THE BUSINESS CYCLE

Numerous theories have been proposed to explain what causes the business cycle. The more modern theories are concerned with government spending and taxation as well as alterations in the amount of money in circulation. We will discuss these theories in later chapters. But for now, let's look at three possible theories, those dealing with technological innovation, dynamic growth, and psychological factors.

Innovation

The *adaptation* of an invention to an actual production technique.

Technological Innovation

Although many new products are invented each year, especially in societies where incentives encourage such inventions, **innova-**

174

tions are much rarer. Innovation requires the *adaptation* of an invention to a production technique. In other words, innovations are inventions that can be used or sold to buyers. Most inventions never become innovations.

When innovation does occur, however, it can send shock waves through the economy. For instance, the innovation of the automobile, the telephone, the airplane, radio and television, and the computer led to tremendous increases in the demand for durable capital goods. These increases in demand, in turn, caused expansions in supporting industries such as steel, rubber, plastics, and other capital goods industries. When the expansion phase leveled off (demand was temporarily sated), a peak was reached and the stage was again set for the recession phase.

An innovation like any of those mentioned above provides a tremendous quantity of consumer durable goods to the population. This lends an additional element of instability to the economy, since the future demand for these goods can fluctuate greatly. Clearly, the investment and innovation will taper off as more and more consumers finally own a particular durable good. Later, as the consumer durable good depreciates, a replacement cycle will occur.

Dynamic Growth

Changes in population can set off a change in the demand for consumer durable goods and capital goods. The baby boom of the 1950s is an example, as are the various periods during the 1800s and early 1900s when waves of immigrants came to our shores.

A major discovery of a natural resource, such as the gold rush in the mid-1800s, can also lead to dynamic economic growth. And finally, major moves of a nation's physical frontier can create additional investment opportunities, which, in turn, lead to the boom–bust cycle. For example, in the United States, frontier expansions occurred until, essentially, no more were possible; that is, expansion occurred until the area between the East Coast and the West Coast had been settled.

The dynamic growth theory, in short, uses external factors of the economy as the generators of cycle phases.

Psychological Theory

Another theory suggests that waves of business confidence and pessimism occur, causing large swings in **business investment** (business expenditures on capital goods). Such psychological tremors do affect the economy and can set the business cycle in motion toward one phase or another. For instance, high consumer sales may generate optimism and set off increased capital goods spending by businesses, thus providing more fuel for an expansion phase.

Business investment

Business expenditure on equipment and machinery, that is, on capital goods. Such investment yields more consumer goods in the future.

Low consumer sales, on the other hand, may generate pessimism, causing businesses to postpone capital goods expenditures, thus plunging the economy into a deeper recession.

● UNEMPLOYMENT

The loss of a job can be one of the most devastating events in a person's life. Studies indicate that unemployment can damage a person's confidence and self-image, which can lead to stress, and eventually to physical disorders. Unemployment brings economic harm to the individual, the family, and the economy. The economy suffers because unemployment, in many circumstances, represents wasted resources. In this section we will discuss how unemployment is measured, as well as the various types of unemployment.

Measuring the Labor Force and Unemployment

Consider Table 9–1, which shows how to calculate the number of unemployed people. We start with the total population in the United States and subtract from that number all inmates of institutions and persons under 16 years of age. This gives us the total noninstitutional population, which was estimated at 174,201,000 people in May 1982. From that number we subtract the number of people not in the labor force, which includes students, homemakers, all those unable to work because of mental or physical illness, and all those who are voluntarily idle, retired, or too old to work. In May 1982, the estimate of those not in the labor force was 61,360,000 people. Having derived the total labor force, we subtract from it 2,175,000 members of the armed services, yielding a total civilian labor force of approximately 110,666,000 individuals.

From the total civilian labor force is subtracted the number of employed individuals, people sampled during the survey week who:

(a) worked *at all* as paid employees, in their own business or profession or on their own farm, *or* who worked 15 hours or more as unpaid work-

TABLE 9–1
Calculation of the Number of Unemployed, May 1982

Total noninstitutional population 16 and over		174,201,000
Minus	Not in labor force	61,360,000
Equals	Total labor force	112,841,000
Minus	Members of armed services	2,175,000
Equals	Total civilian labor force	110,666,000
Minus	Employed	100,117,000
Equals	Unemployed	10,549,000

SOURCE: *Employment and Earnings*, June 1982, vol. 9, no. 6, Tables A-1 and A-33, U.S. Department of Labor, Bureau of Labor Statistics.

ers in an enterprise operated by a family member; and (b) were not working but who had jobs or businesses from which they were temporarily absent because of illness, bad weather, vacation, labor–management dispute, or personal reasons, whether or not they were paid by their employers for the time off, and whether or not they were seeking other jobs.

As Table 9–1 indicates, 100,117,000 people were estimated to be in the "employed" category in May 1982. Subtracting the employed from the total civilian labor force gives us the number of unemployed, estimated at 10,549,000 people in May 1982.

To calculate the unemployment rate, we must divide the number of unemployed by the total number of civilian labor force. In May 1982, the unemployment rate was 10,549,000/110,666,000 = 9.5 percent. The unemployment rate since 1929 is shown in Graph 9–4.

Survey Procedures for Determining the Unemployment Rate

The Bureau of the Census and the Bureau of Labor Statistics jointly compile information on the number of unemployed and publish their findings in the monthly *Current Population Survey (CPS)*. Because the surveys taken cannot possibly include every adult in

GRAPH 9–4

Unemployment in the United States

U.S. unemployment has varied from a low of 1.2 percent of the civilian labor force at one point during World War II to almost 25 percent at the depths of the Great Depression. As you can see, the cyclical variations in unemployment are irregular.

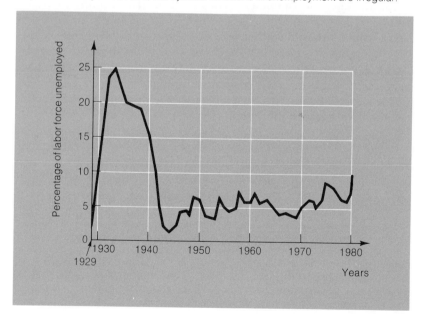

the country, statisticians have designed a sample method to collect the necessary data.

Trained interviewers collect information from a sample of about 65,000 households, representing 629 areas in 1133 counties and independent cities, with coverage in 50 states and the District of Columbia. A certain proportion of the households is changed each month to reduce the effect of any biased answers that might develop in a particular household that is interviewed month after month. The data collected are based on the activity reported for the calendar week, including the twelfth of the month. The number of unemployed is calculated from information obtained in these interviews.

Who Are the Unemployed?   Once the sample is taken, the number of unemployed is computed. A person is considered unemployed if that person:

1. Did not work at all during the survey week but was available for work.
2. Was looking for work.
3. Was waiting to be called back to a job from which he or she was laid off.
4. Was waiting to start a new job within the next month and was not in school.
5. Was temporarily ill and otherwise would have been looking for a job.

Table 9–2 gives a breakdown of the unemployed according to reason for unemployment as of May 1982. In that month, 5,647,000 people, or 5.1 percent of the labor force, were estimated to have lost their last job, and 815,000 people, or 0.7 percent of the labor force, were estimated to have left their last job. Over the same period, 2,332,000 people who had previously left the labor force had apparently reentered and were seeking employment. Finally, 1,113,000 people were estimated to have entered the labor force and for the first time were looking for jobs.[1]

Definition of Unemployed Has Changed over Time.   Government statisticians have not always followed the rules just given for defining the unemployed. During the Great Depression, from 1933 to 1941, unemployment rates officially ranged from almost 25 percent

[1]We show seasonally adjusted data for the total number of unemployed in Table 9–1 and the number of unemployed persons by reason for unemployment in Table 9–2. The number of employed is seasonally adjusted independent of the number of unemployed by reason of unemployment. As a result, the seasonally adjusted number of unemployed by reason of unemployment does not exactly equal the seasonally adjusted total number of unemployed shown in Table 9–1. For the same reason, the total unemployment rates are different in the two sets of data.

TABLE 9-2
Reason for Unemployment, May 1982

NUMBER OF UNEMPLOYED	
Both sexes, 16 years and over:	
Total unemployed	9,957,000
Job losers	6,647,000
On layoff	1,770,000
Other job losers	3,877,000
Job leavers	815,000
Reentrants	2,332,000
New entrants	1,113,000

UNEMPLOYED AS A PERCENT OF THE CIVILIAN LABOR FORCE	
Total unemployment rate	9.1
Job losers	5.1
Job leavers	0.7
Reentrants	2.2
New entrants	1.0

SOURCE: *Employment and Earnings*, June 1982, vol. 9, no. 6, Table A-13, U.S. Department of Labor, Bureau of Labor Statistics.

in 1933 to above 10 percent in 1941. However, these data are deceiving because they include as unemployed the approximately 3.5 million workers in such government work programs as the Civilian Conservation Corps and the Works Progress Administration. It was reasoned that because the government jobs were not permanent, the private sector would eventually have to provide jobs for these individuals. However, since these people were working, the true unemployment rate during that period was probably around 4 to 7 percent lower than that reported by the Bureau of Labor Statistics.

Unemployment by Race, Age, and Sex

Which groups in society typically have a high unemployment rate and which have a low rate? Table 9–3 gives the unemployment rate as measured by race, age, and sex.

It turns out that high unemployment groups typically include teenagers, blacks (especially black teenagers), young adults and senior citizens (as opposed to those between the ages of 25 and 64). On the other hand, married men, where the spouse is present, tend to have lower-than-average unemployment rates.

The Duration of Unemployment

The *duration* of unemployment is the length of time workers remain unemployed. The *rate* of unemployment can rise even when

179

TABLE 9–3
Unemployment by Race, Age, and Sex

By far the greatest percentage of unemployment is found among teenagers, the smallest percentage among heads of households.

Year	Total (All Civilian Workers)	UNEMPLOYMENT RATE (PERCENT OF CIVILIAN LABOR FORCE IN GROUP)								
		BY SEX AND AGE			BY RACE		BY SELECTED GROUPS			
		Men 20 Years and Over	Women 20 Years and Over	Both Sexes 16–19 Years	White	Black and Other	Experienced Wage and Salary Workers	Married Men, Spouse Present	Full-time Workers	Part-time Workers
1975	8.5	6.7	8.0	19.9	7.8	13.9	8.2	5.1	8.1	10.3
1976	7.7	5.9	7.4	19.0	7.0	13.1	7.3	4.2	7.3	10.1
1977	7.0	5.3	6.8	17.3	6.1	13.9	6.6	3.6	6.6	9.7
1978	6.0	4.2	6.0	16.3	5.2	11.9	5.6	2.8	5.5	9.0
1979	5.8	4.1	5.7	16.1	5.1	11.3	5.4	2.7	5.3	8.7
1980	7.1	5.9	6.3	17.7	6.3	13.2	6.8	4.2	6.8	8.7
May 1982	9.5	9.1	9.0	22.5	8.0	16.5	9.2	6.0	9.1	8.6

SOURCE: *Employment and Earnings*, June 1982, vol. 29, no. 6, U.S. Department of Labor, Bureau of Labor Statistics.

the absolute number of workers *becoming* unemployed per week remains constant. Such an anomaly will occur whenever the average duration of unemployment increases, because fewer workers are leaving the ranks of the unemployed. Hence, an increase by a week or two in the average duration of unemployment may increase the unemployment rate by one-half a percentage point.

Some analysts have suggested that a more accurate statistic is the percentage of the unemployed labor force that remains out of work for a certain period of time—say, more than 6 months. It turns out that even during a severe recession, most unemployed workers find jobs within 14 weeks.

Remember, not all unemployed persons are workers who were fired or laid off. About half of those reported as unemployed either left their last job voluntarily, never worked before, or are reentering the labor force after an absence due to illness or pregnancy, for example.

Types of Unemployment

Cyclical Unemployment.   We have already discussed the phases of the business cycle. During the recession and trough phases, output and sales decline, and businesses require less labor; thus, unemployment will increase. During the expansion and peak phases, however, more and more workers are needed to meet increased demand for goods and services; thus, unemployment will fall. **Cyclical unemployment**, then, is related to the cycles of business activity.

Cyclical unemployment

Unemployment that results when total economic demand is insufficient to create full employment of labor resources.

180

Structural Unemployment.   In a dynamic economy, tastes eventually change. Demand increases for some goods and falls for others. This means that there will be long-term increases in the need for some skills and long-term decreases in the need for others.

We refer to these swings in demand as changes in the structure of the economy; the unemployment that results from these changes is called **structural unemployment**. This problem is especially acute for older individuals because they may be more reluctant to learn new skills, and employers are certainly reluctant to hire and retrain them.

In some cases, structural unemployment results from technological changes. With the introduction of labor-saving machines, many laborers become structurally unemployed for long periods, their skills obsolete.

Whole towns or regions may be affected by structural unemployment. This usually happens when an area specializes in the production of a particular commodity (e.g., textiles, coal). When the production of that commodity is no longer in demand, a serious structural problem results. If individuals refuse to leave these geographic areas because of social or family ties, a permanent recession will exist in that region.

Frictional Unemployment.   A certain percentage of unemployment can be attributed to information costs. A worker who leaves one job (whether voluntarily or involuntarily) must spend time, and perhaps money, finding another job. Such individuals must expend their own resources to obtain information on the best alternative sources of work. They may not take the first job offered if they think they can find another job with better wages and/or working conditions. However, a better job may not exist, or information leading to the better job may be unavailable. These situations cause **frictional unemployment**, the continuous flow of individuals from job to job and in and out of employment.

Consider an example. Suppose that unemployment statistics collected for January show that 3 percent of the labor force are frictionally unemployed. That is, during January, 3 percent of the labor force quit, got laid off, or were fired. Suppose that those unemployed individuals are identified as Ms. Johnson, Mr. Smith, Mr. Gonzalez, and so on. Then in February, unemployment data are again collected and again show that 3 percent of the labor force are frictionally unemployed. However, something interesting has happened. Johnson, Smith, Gonzalez, and the others frictionally unemployed in January have since found jobs. Meanwhile, Jones, Henderson, Benson, and so on, have quit, been laid off, or fired. That is, a *new* and *different* 3 percent of the labor force have replaced the original group of frictionally unemployed workers.

Essentially, as long as the frictionally unemployed find jobs

Structural unemployment

Unemployment that results when there is a shift in the demand for a particular product or service such that certain skills and jobs are no longer needed or desired.

Frictional unemployment

The continuous flow of individuals from job to job and in and out of employment; it is due to a lack of perfect information in the job market about all opportunities.

181

rather quickly, there is no real cause for concern. A constant 3 percent unemployment rate poses no real problem as long as the people comprising that 3 percent constantly change. In this sense, a certain amount of unemployment is not necessarily harmful; rather, it is a sign of a dynamic economy.

Seasonal Unemployment. A fourth type of unemployment must be taken into account. It has to do with seasonal changes in the demand for particular jobs. **Seasonal unemployment** rises and falls with the seasons of the year. In cold-weather states, construction workers work overtime during the summer and are idle during the winter. In ski resorts, the opposite occurs. During winter months, employment peaks; during summer months, jobs are scarce. Data gathered on unemployment are usually adjusted for seasonal unemployment.

Further Problems in Measuring Unemployment

Now that we have discussed the methods for measuring unemployment and the various types of unemployment, we must consider some of the factors that make a "true" assessment difficult.

Homemakers' Services. There is general agreement among economists that homemakers' services to their families constitute productive activity. Yet homemakers are not counted in the labor force. If they were, the measured unemployment rate would fall dramatically because the denominator—the measured labor force—would be increased by the total number of homemakers. However, the numerator—the number of officially unemployed—would remain the same because, by definition, homemakers are employed.

Members of the Armed Forces. Another problem centers around members of the armed forces. Although regarded as part of the labor force, they are nevertheless subtracted from the total labor force, thereby leaving an estimate of the civilian labor force. The reported unemployment rate in our economy refers to the ratio of unemployed to the civilian labor force *only*. The ratio of unemployed to the total labor force (including members of the armed forces) would obviously be smaller because over 2 million members of the armed forces would be added to the denominator in our unemployment statistics. However, the numerator would remain the same, since, by definition, members of the armed forces are employed.

Seasonal unemployment

Unemployment caused by the seasonal nature of certain types of jobs, such as construction and resort work.

Discouraged Workers. Another problem in measuring the unemployment rate concerns "discouraged workers." This category includes potential laborers who would like to work, but because of

182

age, race, or lack of skills, have become convinced that they cannot find a job. After repeated unsuccessful attempts, such individuals become discouraged and abandon their search. When polled as to whether they have looked for a job within the last few weeks, they answer no. Thus, they are not counted as members of the labor force. Consequently, they are not counted in the ranks of the unemployed. Estimates on the number of discouraged workers reach upward to 800,000. While this figure represents a relatively small percentage of the total labor force (over 100 million workers), some economists feel that discouraged workers should be counted as unemployed.

Unemployment Compensation Can Cause Unemployment

THE ARGUMENT

Unemployment can lead to extreme hardship for the unemployed and their families. However, each state has a system of unemployment compensation to which employers must contribute. Given to qualified individuals who are unemployed, these benefits are, in the main, nontaxed income. The aim of unemployment compensation is to aid the unemployed until they are able to find jobs. However, critics of the system maintain that in their present form, unemployment benefits create unemployment by inducing workers to remain off the job.

THE ANALYSIS

Not working is the alternative to working. Thus, a person who is currently out of a job has more leisure time. There is a cost associated with leisure time, however, and it is usually measured by the income given up by not working. For example, suppose a person is given the choice of working 5 additional hours a week at $3 per hour. If that person decides not to work the 5 additional hours, the cost of the 5 hours of leisure is $15 ($3 × 5). In essence, the person has "bought" 5 hours of leisure at a cost of $15.

Leisure, like any other good, follows the law of demand. Less will be demanded at a higher price than at a lower price. Thus, the person who decides to "buy" 5 hours of leisure at a cost of $15 might decide to forgo those leisure hours if the wage rate became $4 per hour, since the cost for the 5 hours of leisure would increase to $20. In other words, people are more willing to work at higher wage rates than at lower wage rates.

What does this have to do with unemployment compensation? For those eligible for unemployment compensation, each week without a job means a week of leisure at a cost *less* than the wages forgone. It is less because the unemployed worker receives unemployment compensation.

To illustrate, consider a man who is laid off from a job that pays $100 a week. If he does not receive unemployment benefits, he loses $100 a week for every week not worked. That is, the leisure that he "buys" has a price of $100 per week. Now consider what happens if this same man is eligible for unemployment benefits. Those benefits make up a percentage of his lost income—perhaps as much as 80 percent. If this worker is eligible to receive 80 percent of his lost wages ($100 × 0.8 = $80), then, effectively, the cost of a week's leisure is not $100, but only $20.

If the law of demand holds for leisure, some unemployed workers will respond to this reduced price of leisure by purchasing additional leisure. That is, some workers will remain unemployed longer, taking more time to look for a job.

Unemployment Compensation and the Tax System

The extent to which unemployment compensation can benefit the unemployed becomes more apparent when we consider that no taxes are paid on such compensation. However, taxes must be paid on income earned. Thus, the actual cost of not working can be seen as the difference between the *after-tax* income that a worker was earning and the unemployment compensation to be received.

In many cases, the actual cost of leisure is minimal. That is, the difference between the after-tax income of an employed worker and the untaxed unemployment benefits turns out to be small. According to several studies, the tax savings achieved through unemployment compensation greatly diminish the recipient's incentive to return to work. According to these studies, this lack of motivation will continue as long as the individual continues to receive unemployment benefits.

The New Unemployment

Unemployment resulting from unemployment compensation has been dubbed the "new unemployment." Various studies have estimated that new unemployment accounts for between 1 and 3 percentage points of the overall unemployment rate. If the actual figure is 1 percent, then an overall unemployment rate of 6 percent could be reduced to 5 percent by eliminating unemployment compensation.

Even though such studies indicate that unemployment benefits contribute to a higher unemployment rate, they stop short of calling for the elimination of unemployment compensation. Rather, the studies recommend that the system be altered to reduce the incentive not to return to work.

One suggestion is to tax unemployment benefits as income earned. It is reasoned that since individuals with low incomes do not pay high tax rates, they would be the least affected by such a change in the unemployment compensation system.

Another suggestion is to change the current distribution of unemployment benefits. Today, low-income families receive a small percentage of unemployment benefits. Either they work in industries that aren't covered by unemployment insurance or they don't work long enough to qualify. Since the taxing of unemployment benefits would affect higher-income earners in higher tax brackets more, they would probably take less advantage of unemployment insurance if these benefits were taxed.

DISCUSSION QUESTIONS

1. How does unemployment compensation increase the length of time that job losers search for a new job?

2. How might an increase in the unemployment rate, when it is due to an increase in "new unemployment," overstate the degree of economic hardship that the unemployment rate attempts to measure?

● WHAT'S AHEAD

Price levels and unemployment rates are two important aspects of our nation's economic status. We have now discussed ways to measure inflation and unemployment. In the following chapter, methods for measuring the amount of overall economic activity will be presented, along with a simple model of how goods and services flow throughout the economy.

● CHAPTER SUMMARY

Business activity in the United States can be represented by a business cycle made up of four phases: recession, trough, expansion, and peak. During a recession phase, the output and sales of both consumer and producer durable goods fall dramatically relative to the change in national income. During an expansion phase, the output and sales of durable goods rise more rapidly than the non-durable goods sectors of the economy.

During recessionary phases of the business cycle, unemployment increases. Unemployment is defined as the number of individuals looking for jobs divided by the official number of individuals in the measured civilian labor force. There are three basic types of unemployment: cyclical, structural, and frictional. Cyclical unemployment relates to the ups and downs in the demand for labor caused by the ups and downs in the business cycle. Structural unemployment occurs when the demand for a particular commodity permanently decreases, or technological change permanently reduces job opportunities in certain areas. Frictional unemployment occurs because of the coming and going of individuals in and out of the labor force and is due primarily to a lack of perfect information about job opportunities. If members of the armed forces and homemakers were counted as part of the measured labor force, the measured rate of unemployment would fall. On the other hand, if discouraged workers were counted as part of the labor force the measured unemployment rate would rise slightly.

● QUESTIONS FOR REVIEW AND STUDY

1. A business cycle has alternating periods of _____ and _____.

2. The four phases of the business cycle are: (1) _____; (2) _____; (3) _____; and (4) _____.

3. The ideal business cycle is an analytical fiction. We don't really observe it. Nor is a business cycle of _____ duration, according to each phase.

4. The difference between an invention and an _____ is that an _____ is the adaptation of an invention to some actual production technique.

5. Ups and downs in innovations may lead to ups and downs in the demand for _____ _____.

6. Changes in population, major discoveries of natural resources, and frontier development lead to a _____ _____ theory of the business cycle.

7. Periods of optimism and pessimism are the basis of the _____ theory of business cycles.

8. The highest unemployment groups include _____, _____, and _____.

9. The typical _____ of unemployment for most unemployed individuals is less than _____ weeks.

10. The four types of unemployment are _____, _____, _____, and _____.

11. Cyclical unemployment is caused by the phases of the _____ _____.

12. Structural unemployment is caused by abrupt shifts in _____, so that a person's skills are no longer demanded.

13. Some structural unemployment is caused by _____ _____ when machines replace men and women.

14. We have _____ unemployment because information about job vacancies and requirements is imperfect.

15. Seasonal unemployment is caused by changes in _____ that accompany changes in the _____.

16. Unemployment statistics may be biased upward because the services of _____ and _____ are not counted as employment.

17. On the other hand, unemployment figures may be biased downward because of so many _____ workers who decide that it isn't worth looking for a job.

ANSWERS

1. expansion; recession 2. recession; trough; expansion; peak 3. fixed 4. innovation; innovation 5. durable goods 6. dynamic growth 7. psychological 8. teenagers; blacks; older adults 9. duration; 15 10. cyclical; structural; frictional; seasonal 11. business cycle 12. demand 13. technological change 14. frictional 15. demand; seasons 16. homemakers; servicemen 17. discouraged

● ANSWERS TO CHAPTER PREVIEW QUESTIONS

1. Under what circumstances might you be better off not working, even if you had the opportunity to work?

In all likelihood, you would not accept a job if the combination of working conditions and after-tax wage rates were poor relative to the value you place on leisure time. Indeed, this situation accounts for some portion of measured unemployment. Most unemployed individuals looking for work could probably find a job if they were willing to take a low enough wage rate. But people will not accept wage rates that are "too" low. They would rather wait until a better job comes along. Also, if you are offered continued unemployment benefits, you may be tempted to look longer for another job because you have that "cushion" of benefits on which to rely. Finally, if you are receiving welfare benefits, which could be reduced or completely eliminated if you take a job, you may be tempted to remain out of the labor force.

2. *When times get tough, what are the first types of purchases you start doing without?*

For most people, the first items cut from the budget when times are tough—recessionary times—are large purchases such as cars, refrigerators, washers, dryers, houses, stereos, videotape decks, and so on. Purchases of consumer durable goods are the first to be put off during periods of unemployment and reduced income. People decide that they can "make do" with the consumer durables they now have. It is not surprising, therefore, that there is greater fluctuation in the durable goods industry, relative to fluctuations in overall economic activity, than in other industries.

● PROBLEMS

1. Assume that you are receiving unemployment benefits of $50 a week. You are offered a job that will pay you $100 a week before taxes. Assume further that you would have to pay 7 percent social security taxes plus federal income taxes equal to 19 percent of your salary. What is the opportunity cost of remaining unemployed. That is, how much will it cost you to refuse the job offer?

2. Assume that the labor force consists of 100 people, and that every month 5 people become unemployed, while 5 others who were unemployed find jobs.
    a. What is the frictional unemployment rate?
    b. What is the average duration of unemployment?
Now assume the above *and* assume that the only type of unemployment in this economy is frictional.
    c. What is the unemployment rate?
Suppose that a system of unemployment compensation is instituted, and the average duration of unemployment rises to 2 months.
    d. What will the unemployment rate for this economy be now?
    e. Does a higher unemployment rate necessarily mean that the economy is "sicker" or that laborers are worse off?

● SELECTED REFERENCES

Economic Report of the President. Washington, D.C.: U.S. Government Printing Office. Published annually in January.

Ganaty, John A. "To Be Jobless in America." *American Heritage*, vol. 1, December 1978, pp. 64–69.

Haberler, Gottfried. "Preliminary Remarks." In *Prosperity and Depression*. New York: Atheneum, 1963, pp. 5–13.

U.S. Department of Commerce. *Survey of Current Business*. Published monthly; January issue takes a retrospective view of the economy.

10

GNP Accounting and National Income Determination

Chapter Preview
1. News analysts are constantly referring to GNP. What exactly *is* GNP?
2. If you were a businessperson selling a product, what would be your first clue that the total demand for all goods and services in the economy was slowing down?

● KEY TERMS

Aggregate demand
Aggregate supply
Consumer goods and services
Depreciation
Gross national product (GNP)
Indirect business taxes
Intermediate goods
Inventories

Inventory investment
Investment
National income
Net exports
Net investment
Net national product (NNP)
Profit

To produce goods and services, business firms must use one or more of the four factors of production: labor, land, capital, and entrepreneurship. Payment for the use of these resources is in the form of wages, rent, interest, and **profit**, with each representing income for the owners of the resource. The relationship between production and income in a market economy is clear-cut: by producing goods and services, businesses generate income. Production and income, then, are two sides of the same coin. In this chapter, we will explore the relationship between income and output on a *national* level.

● MEASURING NATIONAL INCOME AND OUTPUT

The news media are constantly referring to national income and GNP. In a little while, we will define these terms. For now, however, it is enough to know that these statistics are official measures of the nation's income and output.

Why We Measure National Income and Output

Why does the U.S. government spend so much time and effort collecting data to measure national income and output? There are a number of reasons, but here are the two most important:

1. To obtain a measure of the economy's overall *productive activity* over a certain period of time, usually one year. (Is national output rising or falling? Has productive activity been increasing or decreasing? Was last year a productive year compared with previous years?)
2. To determine what is happening to the nation's overall economic well-being. (Are living standards rising or falling? Because standard of living is closely related to national output, a change in one implies a change in the other.)

Profit

The income earned by entrepreneurs. It is the difference between total revenues and the total cost of the goods and services sold.

Measuring Productive Activity

Since it is not always easy to decide if a given activity is "productive," measuring productive activity can sometimes be difficult. However, a good rule of thumb is to ask if consumers would be willing to pay for the resulting good or service. That is, does the good or service generate satisfaction or utility?

If a consumer is willing to pay for the output of a particular activity, that consumer incurs an opportunity cost for its purchase. Consider the example of football fans. When they pay money for football tickets, they can no longer use that money to purchase *other* goods and services. Since football fans are only too eager to pay for their tickets, we must assume that professional football provides a worthwhile service to the ticket purchaser. Hence, professional football must be considered a productive activity, even though no physical output results, and even though some people (non-fans) consider it frivolous.

While some may quarrel with this analysis, we stand by our definition. To determine whether an activity is productive, we need only decide if buyers would voluntarily make expenditures for the good or service.

The Problem of Double Counting.   In determining the nation's overall productive activity during a year, we must be careful not to exaggerate the resulting estimate. For example, the measure of national output could include the prices of the resources used to manufacture an automobile (e.g., steel, aluminum, rubber, tires) plus the final selling price of the automobile. However, this calculation would involve *double counting*—that is, adding up the value of certain productive activities twice. The *final* selling price of an automobile reflects the value of all the inputs that go into the making of a car. To count the selling price of the car *and* all of its inputs would be to overstate productive activity. Thus, only the value of final goods and services is counted in the measure of GNP.

Final Versus Intermediate Goods.   Final goods and services are those used by the consumer. **Intermediate goods** and services are those used in the production of final goods and services. For example, the inputs involved in the production of an automobile— steel, tires, and so on—are intermediate goods. The automobile itself is the final good.

Coal, however, may be a final good or an intermediate good, depending on its use. When it is used to produce steel, which is then used to produce an automobile, both the coal and the steel are intermediate goods. On the other hand, when coal is purchased by homeowners for heat in the winter, it is considered a final good. The key to classifying a good as final or intermediate is to determine

Intermediate goods

Goods used in the production of other goods and services (either final or intermediate).

193

if it will be used in another stage to produce another good. If so, it is an intermediate good. If it is purchased in its final stage, it is a final good.

Nonproductive Transactions

When attempting to measure total national productive activity, we must be sure to eliminate nonproductive transactions. Productive transactions involve the *final* purchase of *newly* produced goods or services. But our economic exchanges involve numerous nonproductive transactions (including purely financial ones), as well as transfers of used goods.

Financial Transactions.   There are three general categories of purely financial transactions:

1. *Buying and selling securities.* If you want to purchase a share of stock in General Motors, another individual must sell it to you. In essence, there is a transfer of ownership rights. For example, if you pay $100 in cash to obtain the stock certificate, the seller (through the brokerage system) receives the $100 and relinquishes the stock certificate. This exchange involves no productive activity. Thus, the $100 is not included in the measure of GNP. On the other hand, the brokerage fee is counted because brokers provide a service.
2. *Government transfer payments.* In Chapter 7, we defined transfer payments as those payments for which no productive services are concurrently provided in exchange. The most obvious *government* transfer payments are social security, veterans' benefits, and unemployment compensation. The recipients make no contribution to current production in return for such transfer payments (although they may have made contributions in the past in order to receive them). Thus, such payments cannot be included in GNP.
3. *Private transfer payments.* Are you receiving money from your parents so you can live at school? Has a relative ever given you a gift of money? If so, you have been the recipient of a *private* transfer payment. A private transfer payment is merely a transfer of funds from one individual to another. As such, it does not constitute productive activity and is not included in the measure of GNP.

The Transfer of Used Goods.   If I sell you my two-year-old stereo, no current production is involved. Rather, I transfer to you the ownership of a sound system that was produced several years ago. In exchange, you transfer to me, say, $550. The original purchase price of the stereo was included in the GNP the year I purchased it. To now include the *used* purchase price as part of GNP would be to count the value of the stereo a second time (double counting).

● MEASURING GROSS NATIONAL PRODUCT

The term used to represent the value of all final goods and services produced over a one-year period is **gross national product (GNP)**. GNP can be measured in nominal, or absolute, dollars or it can be measured in inflation-corrected, or real, dollars. Clearly, the most accurate measure of the nation's productive activity is GNP corrected for the rate of inflation.

We will now consider the two methods of measuring GNP, ignoring, for the moment, the problem of inflation. The first approach involves the types of expenditures made in our economy, while the second approach involves the types of income received.

Measuring GNP from Expenditures

Consumer Expenditures.   We've already talked about durable **consumer goods**, such as cars, washing machines, and houses. And we have also made reference to nondurable consumer goods, as well as **consumer services**. Durable goods are arbitrarily defined as items that last more than a year. Nondurable goods include the remaining items, such as food and gasoline. Services include medical care, education, and legal advice. We will use the symbol C to represent all consumer expenditures.

Business Investments.   When businesses invest, they make expenditures on future productive capacity. Indeed, our definition of **investment** is not simply the transfer of asset ownership among individuals. Rather, it relates to an increase in future capacity or the ability to create newly produced goods in the future.

Investment can also involve changes in inventories of finished goods on hand, goods in process, and raw materials. For example, if a firm starts out with $1 million worth of raw materials on hand at the beginning of the year and ends up with $2 million worth of raw materials on hand at the end of the year (and there's been no inflation), then an **inventory investment** of $1 million has been made.

Besides investing in future productive capacity, businesses must also invest in the maintenance of current productive capacity. They do this by repairing and replacing worn-out machines and equipment. In other words, businesses spend money to take care of the **depreciation** of capital stock. In calculating gross national product, we look at *gross investment* — that is, investments that *include* repairing and replacing worn-out equipment. We will use the symbol I to represent gross investment.

We can obtain **net investment** by subtracting depreciation from gross investment. Exhibit 10–1 shows the difference between gross investment and net investment.

Gross national product (GNP)

The total money value of the nation's final goods and services, or output, produced each year. It is the total market value of all final goods and services produced over a one-year period.

Consumer goods and services

Final goods and services purchased by households and nonprofit institutions.

Investment

Expenditures by businesses on new plant and equipment purchases (capital goods) for the purpose of increasing future production.

Inventory investment

Changes in the stocks of finished goods, goods in process, and raw materials.

Depreciation

The reduction in capital goods due to physical wear and tear, and obsolescence.

Net investment

Gross investment minus depreciation.

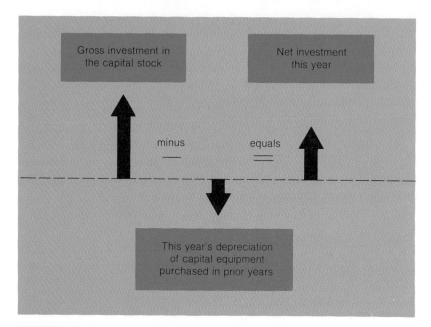

EXHIBIT 10–1

The Derivation of Net Investment

Gross investment includes investment in the maintenance, repair, and replacement of capital equipment that was purchased in previous years and is wearing out. When we subtract this year's depreciation of capital equipment purchased in prior years from gross investment, we obtain this year's net investment.

Government Expenditures.   Expenditures in the economy are not limited to personal consumption expenditures and gross investment. The government purchases goods and services at all levels, and we will use the symbol G to represent these expenditures. Since many government goods and services are provided at no direct cost to the consumer, we cannot use the market value of government services when computing GNP. Therefore, goods provided by government are simply valued as equal to their cost.

The Foreign Sector.   Every country has a foreign sector. The United States purchases goods and services from other countries and other countries purchase goods and services from it. This foreign sector must be considered in order to get an accurate representation of gross national product. The annual difference between what a nation sells abroad—exports—and what it buys abroad—imports— is equal to **net exports** and is normally part of GNP. However, to make the calculations easier, net exports are ignored and it is simply assumed that the United States is a closed economy.

Net exports

The difference between total exports and total imports over a one-year period.

196

Putting It All Together. GNP can now be defined in terms of expenditures made by consumers, businesses, and government. We have the equation

$$GNP = C + I + G,$$

where C stands for consumer expenditures, I stands for gross investment expenditures, and G stands for government expenditures. Look at the historical picture given in Graph 10–1, where nominal-dollar GNP and its components are presented.

Deriving Net National Product. The word "gross" in gross national product refers to the gross investment being included. If we

GRAPH 10–1
Nominal GNP and Its Components

Here we see a display of gross national product, consumer expenditures, government purchases, and gross investment plus net exports, for the years 1929 to 1981. Note that during the Great Depression gross investment plus net exports were negative because the U.S. was investing very little at that time.

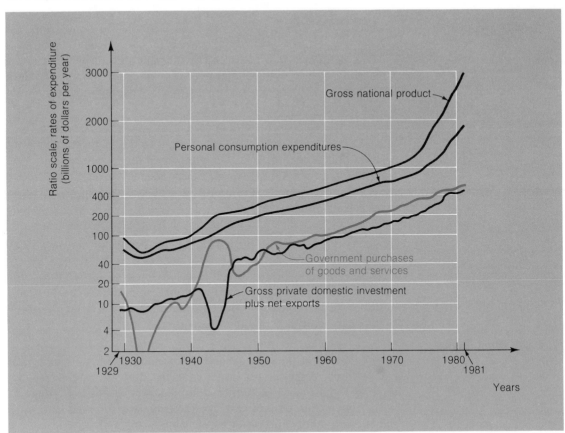

net out, or subtract, depreciation from gross investment, we obtain net investment. When we add net investment to consumer and government expenditures (ignoring the foreign factor), we end up with what is called **net national product (NNP)**. Simply defined,

NNP = GNP − depreciation,

or, using the symbols from before,

NNP = $C + I + G$ − depreciation.

Measuring GNP from Income

For every expenditure of money, there is a receipt of money in the form of income. Indeed, total expenditures must equal total income. Businesses produce goods and services and, in so doing, generate income in the form of wages, interest, rent, and profits.

Perhaps the single most important concept to understand is this: Total expenditures on final goods and services in the nation must equal the sum of all wages, interest, rent, and profits received in the nation:

Total expenditures on
final goods and services = wages + interest + rent + profits.

This definition follows from the ultimate definition of profits as a residual, that is, what is left over after wages, interest and rents have been paid by business firms. Consider these four income categories in more detail.

Wages. The most important category is wages, which also include salaries and other forms of labor income, such as income in kind, incentive payments, and so on. Social security taxes (both the employees' and the employers' contributions) are also counted. Income taxes are also included.

Interest. Here interest payments do not equal the *sum* of all payments for the use of money capital over one year. Instead, net interest is equal to household interest income receipts minus consumer interest payments. In other words, the interest component of national income includes only the net interest received by households plus net interest paid by foreigners.

Net national product (NNP)

The sum of total consumer and government expenditures on final consumption goods plus *net* investment, in a simplified economy.

Rent. Rent is all income earned by individuals for the use of their real (nonmonetary) assets, such as farms, houses, and stores. The implicit rental value of owner-occupied houses must be included here. Also included in this category are royalties received from copyrights and patents and other assets such as oil wells.

198

Profits. Profits are whatever is left over after wages, interest, and rents have been paid. This last category includes total gross corporate profits and so-called proprietors' income. Proprietors' income is that income earned from the operation of unincorporated businesses, which include sole proprietorships, partnerships, and producers' cooperatives.

These four components, added together, equal **national income**. To obtain gross national income (GNI), which will then be equal to gross national product, we must add two other components: **indirect business taxes** and depreciation.

Indirect Business Taxes. Excise taxes, sales taxes, and property taxes incurred by businesses make up indirect business taxes. They are not payments to factors of production. Think of them this way: Businesses actually act as the government's agent when they collect a sales tax. They collect the tax from the consumer and turn it over to the government. The tax is a business expense, but the real burden is likely to be on the customer, who pays a higher price. Such indirect taxes are included in gross national income as a cost item (which does not represent earnings of a resource).

Depreciation. Just as we had to consider depreciation in figuring the difference between NNP and GNP, we must also consider it in figuring gross national income. We must add depreciation to net national income to obtain gross national income. Depreciation is that portion of the current year's GNP used to replace physical capital consumed in the process of production. Since someone has paid for the replacement, depreciation must be added as a component of gross national income. (It represents those expenses of businesses that are not income to resources.)

● THE CIRCULAR FLOW
OF INCOME AND PRODUCT

Exhibit 10–2 shows how money flows from businesses to households and then from households to businesses in an endless circular flow. The upper loops show households paying businesses money in exchange for final goods and services. The lower loops show businesses paying wages, interest, rent, and profit in exchange for the productive services of labor, capital, land, and entrepreneurship. Keep in mind that this is a simplified version of the economy.

The value of the final goods and services purchased (as shown in the uppermost loop) is identical to the total money receipts in the

National income

The yearly amount earned by the nation's resources, which includes wages, rent, interest, and profit.

Indirect business taxes

The excise taxes, sales taxes, and property taxes. Such taxes do not include taxes on corporate profits.

199

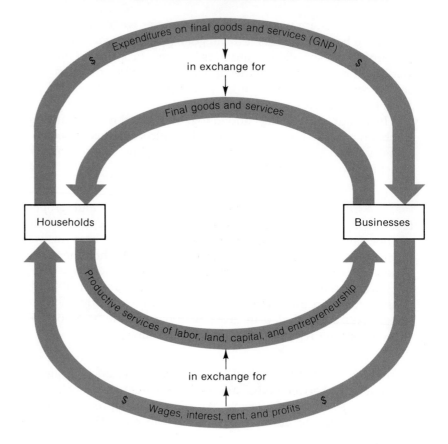

Expenditures on final goods and services (GNP)

in exchange for

Final goods and services

Households

Businesses

Productive services of labor, land, capital, and entrepreneurship

in exchange for

Wages, interest, rent, and profits

EXHIBIT 10–2
The Circular Flow of Income

This figure shows the endless circular flow of income. Money flows via outer loops in a clockwise manner from households to businesses, and from businesses back to households. Goods and services flow, via inner loops, in a counterclockwise manner.

In the upper loops, businesses provide final goods and services to households in exchange for money. This amount of money receipts is equal to the value of final goods and services purchased by households. In the lower loops, another exchange occurs. Households provide productive services to businesses in exchange for income in the form of wages, interest, rent, and profits.

The money value represented by the uppermost loop is equal to the money value represented by the bottommost loop. In other words, the market value of final goods and services produced is *identical* to the money incomes generated from their production. Thus, national income is equal to the money value of the national output of final goods and services.

form of wages, interest, rent, and profits received (as shown in the bottommost loop).

Because profit is a residual—what's left over—it makes the loops always equal; profit is what is left over after the other factors have been paid.

● DETERMINING NATIONAL INCOME AND OUTPUT

Thus far, we have seen that national expenditures equal national income. It really makes no difference whether the *source* of the expenditures is households (consumption, or *C*), businesses (investment, or *I*), or government (*G*) because all of these sources of expenditures are also sources of income generated by output production.

Aggregate Demand and Supply

The sum of all sources of expenditures is called **aggregate demand**. Aggregate demand (AGG *D*) is equal to the sum of consumption spending, business spending on investment, and government spending. That is,

$$AGG\ D = C + I + G.$$

Since expenditures equal income, it follows that changes in aggregate demand lead to changes in national income. Thus, in this simplified version of the economy, national income is determined by the aggregate demand for goods and services.

Aggregate supply refers to the grand total value of all final goods and services supplied by all firms in the economy. It is synonymous with national product.

What quantity of goods and services will be produced during a one-year period? That is, what will be the national output? The eventual level of output will be whatever is most profitable for firms. In general, the most profitable output level will be determined by the aggregate demand for that output. Briefly stated, the primary determinant of national income is aggregate demand. Aggregate supply adjusts to whatever aggregate demand is within an economy's capacity to produce.[1]

Aggregate demand and aggregate supply (or national income and national output) must balance each other for the economy to be in equilibrium. Before we look at how the equilibrium rate of national income is established, let's review the concept of equilibrium introduced in Chapter 2.

Aggregate demand

The total value of all planned expenditures of all buyers in the economy.

Aggregate supply

The total value of all final goods and services supplied by all firms in the economy; it is equal to national product.

[1]Modern emphasis on the supply side is analyzed in Chapter 15, when we discuss supply-side economics.

Equilibrium

The equilibrium price, or market-clearing price, occurs at the intersection of the demand curve and the supply curve. Note that there is no tendency for price or quantity to change once supply and demand are in equilibrium. But when the market price is greater than the equilibrium price, forces act to push the price back down toward equilibrium. For example, producers and retailers may offer unsold "surpluses" at lower prices; and producers respond by reducing output. On the other hand, when market price is below the equilibrium price, there is an excess quantity demanded at that price, and forces are set in motion that cause the price to rise. More-than-willing demanders bid up the price; and this time producers respond by increasing the quantity supplied.

Thus, when the market is *not* in equilibrium, forces will work to reestablish equilibrium. This concept applies both to equilibrium for a single-product market and to equilibrium for the entire market for goods in the U.S. economy. If the aggregate demand for all goods and services is not equal to the aggregate supply of all goods and services, market forces will operate to bring aggregate demand and aggregate supply back into equilibrium. In the process, national income and product will either rise or fall.

Equilibrium is a concept that pervades all of economic analysis. We have already assumed that equilibrium prevails within the circular flow model of Exhibit 10–2. By requiring that all household earnings be spent in the product market and that all business production be offered for immediate sale, we allow for no discrepancy in the basic circular flow between the aggregate demand and the aggregate supply of goods and services, thus automatically keeping aggregate demand and aggregate supply in equilibrium.

Determining the Equilibrium Rate

Suppose businesses in the aggregate *do not know* what the most profitable national output is. Suppose businesses produce $2 trillion worth of goods and services per year because they think that this is the most profitable output rate.

Let us now consider two cases: (1) when the aggregate supply of $2 trillion is *less* than the aggregate demand, and (2) when the aggregate supply of $2 trillion *exceeds* the aggregate demand.

When Aggregate Supply Is Less Than Aggregate Demand. Let's assume that businesses in the aggregate produce $2 trillion worth of goods and services, but aggregate demand equals $2.2 trillion. That is,

$$\$2 \text{ trillion} = AGGS < AGGD = C + I + G = \$2.2 \text{ trillion}.$$

What will happen? Well, since businesses in the aggregate have

202

underestimated the most profitable output level, their **inventories** of finished goods will decline by about $0.2 trillion per year. Because firms cannot satisfy all orders immediately out of current production, they keep inventories of finished goods on hand. Moreover, most firms want to smooth out production activity (rather than experience peaks and lulls) and therefore continue to produce even when demand for their product temporarily slows down. However, there is a certain *optimal* level of inventories that firms wish to keep, and in this case those optimal levels of inventories are declining in the aggregate by about $0.2 trillion per year. (Earlier we talked about inventory investment. Well, negative inventory investment would exist in this example.)

Faced with declining inventories and the realization that they have underestimated the most profitable rate of output, businesses will *increase* their output levels. To do so, they will increase their resources—capital and labor. National output and income will therefore rise. This same process will continue until aggregate supply rises enough to equal aggregate demand. That is, for the economy as a whole, in equilibrium,

$$\$2.2 \text{ trillion of } AGG\,S \; = \; AGG\,D \; = \; C \; + \; I \; + \; G \; = \; \$2.2 \text{ trillion.}$$

Note that aggregate supply expanded to meet aggregate demand because it was profitable to producers for this to occur. Also, it is important to realize that inventory reductions initially gave businesses the clue that they needed to increase output rates.

When Aggregate Supply Is Greater Than Aggregate Demand.   Now consider the opposite case, in which businesses produce $2 trillion worth of goods and services because they think it is the most profitable rate, but aggregate demand is only $1.9 trillion. In equation form, this is seen as

$$\$2 \text{ trillion} \; = \; AGG\,S \; > \; AGG\,D \; = \; C \; + \; I \; + \; G \; = \; \$1.9 \text{ trillion.}$$

What will happen? Businesses will realize that they have overestimated the goods they can profitably produce and sell. How? By observing that inventories are rising at about the rate of $0.1 trillion per year. In other words, businesses are incurring unplanned inventory investment.

Faced with the realization that they have overestimated the amount of goods they can most profitably produce and sell, and faced with inventory increases, businesses will cut back on output rates. They will do so by laying off laborers. National output and income will fall.

This process will continue until aggregate supply declines sufficiently to equal aggregate demand at $1.9 trillion. In equation form, national equilibrium will occur when

$$\$1.9 \text{ trillion} = AGG\,S = AGG\,D = C + I + G = \$1.9 \text{ trillion.}$$

Inventories
The finished goods that firms keep on hand from which they fill orders.

203

Note again that aggregate supply adjusted to aggregate demand. That is, aggregate demand determined the most profitable rate of national output. In this case, unplanned inventory increases (inventory investment) provided the initial clue to businesses that they needed to reduce output rates.

Summary of National Income and Output Determination

The equilibrium level of national income and output will occur where aggregate supply equals aggregate demand. In general, this will be the most profitable output level; in this simplified version of the economy, national income is primarily determined by aggregate demand. Aggregate supply will adjust to the level of aggregate demand within the nation's capacity. It is inventory changes (positive or negative unplanned inventory investment) that tell businesses whether they should expand or contract output rates.

Now let's see what happens when there are changes in aggregate demand.

Changes in Aggregate Demand

Assume for the moment that aggregate demand increases because of, say, an increase in government expenditures. Such a change in aggregate demand will lead to changes in national output and income. If aggregate demand increases, inventories will fall unexpectedly. This unplanned negative inventory investment will eventually cause national output and income to rise. The size of the circular flow depicted in Exhibit 10–2 will increase.

Similarly, a decrease in aggregate demand due to, say, a reduction in government expenditures will cause inventories to pile up initially. Eventually, national output and income may fall.

This concept is important from a policymaking point of view. If government, through its policies on government spending, business investment, or consumer spending, can alter one of the elements of aggregate demand, then the equilibrium level of national income will be affected. Any policy change that affects C, I, or G will change aggregate demand and, hence, national product and income.

In times of recession, national output and income, as well as employment, fall. This process could be reversed by increasing aggregate demand.

Conversely, if aggregate demand could be reduced during periods of excessive business activity (booms and inflation), the equilibrium level of national income and output could also be reduced.

Later chapters will show how government policy can affect C, I, and G.

204

Gross National Product Really Measures Economic Well-Being

THE ARGUMENT

GNP data are used as an index of whether living standards are rising or falling. GNP data are also used by government policymakers to determine whether government activities for the entire economy should be changed. There are numerous critics of the way GNP is measured, however. Consider an example. An increase in GNP occurs one year because of an increase in the production and sale of pollution-control equipment. Pollution-control equipment is now required because producers have been fouling the air and polluting the water, and the cost to society of this activity had thus far been ignored. What exactly does this increase in GNP mean? Critics of GNP measurement would like to know. This is just one example of the many criticisms lodged against our present method of measuring GNP.

THE ANALYSIS

There are indeed many problems with using GNP to represent living standards. Some of these problems suggest that GNP may understate national economic well-being. Still other considerations indicate that GNP and living standards are unrelated.

Homemakers' services, for example, certainly provide productive activity. Yet homemakers' services are not counted in the data that comprise GNP. Every year the Chase Manhattan Bank of New York estimates the value of homemakers' services based on the wage rates that would have to be paid to provide those services if the homemakers did not. By now, the *weekly* value of a homemaker's services is estimated to be approximately $300.

And what about do-it-yourself activities? Do-it-yourself projects certainly constitute productive activities, but they are left out of GNP measurements. If you take your car to a mechanic, the services performed on the car end up as part of GNP. But if you repair your car yourself, these services are not included in GNP. Actually, homemakers' services can be viewed as a category of all do-it-yourself activities.

Increased leisure relative to income must also be taken account of if we are going to obtain a correct measure of GNP. After all, leisure is a good and it is scarce. It has value and generates satisfaction. For the civilian population, average weekly hours worked have fallen from over 48 to around 36 in the last 50 years. This represents a definite increase in the real standard of living of those enjoying more leisure time.

A large share of true gross national product and true well-being in this economy is never measured. It involves the so-called underground, or subterranean, economy, where numerous transactions take place, but no records are kept. All illegal activities are part of the underground economy. So, too, are all trades among individuals that are done in cash and not reported. Such activities increase living standards, but are not counted in the gross national product.

When all is said and done, though, there are many favorable arguments for looking at GNP as an index of economic well-being. It is still the best statistic available for measuring the goods and services that are produced and that ultimately can be consumed. It is true that there are problems in measuring these goods and services. But perhaps the best way to solve those problems is to alter our current measurement of GNP, not ignore it completely.

DISCUSSION QUESTIONS

1. Does an increase in GNP *necessarily* mean that living standards are rising? If not, why not?

2. Why does an increase in group expenditures lead to an increase in group income?

● WHAT'S AHEAD

The next unit examines the way government policy changes the equilibrium level of national income. In particular, the various taxes levied by federal and state governments are explored. We will also examine the way the government alters tax policy to affect aggregate demand.

● CHAPTER SUMMARY

The best estimate of total productive activity generating final output in a nation is gross national product (GNP), defined as the total market value of all final goods and services produced annually. The emphasis is on *final*, indicating an intent to avoid double counting.

The total of all expenditures made by households, businesses, and government on final goods and services gives an expenditure estimate of GNP. Alternatively, the payments generating income from the production of final goods and services (pre-income tax wages, interest, rent, and profits) can be added to indirect business taxes and depreciation to obtain an income estimate of GNP.

Investment by businesses can be used to produce future productive capacity and to replace or repair existing capital equipment. Investment that includes both of these expenditures is called gross investment. When depreciation is subtracted, we have net investment. No investment occurs via the transfer of ownership rights to assets among individuals. In other words, the purchase of stocks does not constitute investment.

If only net investment is used, the result is net national product, or NNP. In other words, net national product is gross national product minus depreciation. The circular flow of income and product shows that households provide labor, land, capital, and entrepreneurship for which they are paid wages, rent, interest, and profit. The circular flow goes from households to businesses and from businesses to households. By assumption, the circular flow is always equated because everything that is earned is spent. However, it is possible for aggregate demand—all planned expenditures—and aggregate supply—the amount of output produced—to be unequal. If aggregate demand exceeds aggregate supply, the circular flow values will tend to grow. If aggregate demand is less than aggregate supply, the circular flow values will tend to get smaller.

● QUESTIONS FOR REVIEW AND STUDY

1. We like to know what is happening to _____ _____ and _____ in order to see what is happening to productive activity between two points in time. In this way we also find out what is happening to living standards.

2. One definition of productive activity is any activity for which someone is willing to _____ for the resulting output or service.

3. When we measure overall productive activities, we try to avoid _____ _____ by counting only expenditures on final goods and services.

4. To avoid double counting, we avoid including the value of _____ goods and services in our calculation.

5. The sum of all pre-tax income receipts—_____, _____, _____ and _____—is called _____ _____.

6. Profits are defined as a _____, which means that they are what is left over from total business receipts after wages, interest, and rents have been paid.

7. In a simplified economy in which there are only households and businesses, we can show a _____ _____ of income in which households spend money income on final goods and services that businesses provide, and businesses spend money income on wages, interest, rents, and profits for which productive services of labor, capital, land, and entrepreneurship are provided from households.

8. Businesses make _____ expenditures on new plant and equipment purchases and on inventories.

9. Machines and equipment wear out. This process is called _____.

10. To obtain net investment, we subtract _____ from gross investment.

11. To obtain _____ we simply deduct depreciation from GNP.

12. Changes in _____ _____ can lead to changes in national income. Thus, national income is largely determined by the _____ _____ for goods and services.

13. The aggregate supply of goods and services is that level of national output that is _____ _____ for businesses to produce.

14. Whenever aggregate demand exceeds aggregate supply, _____ will decline, causing businesses to expand output.

15. Whenever aggregate supply is greater than aggregate demand, inventories will _____, causing businesses to cut back on production.

ANSWERS

1. national income; output   2. pay   3. double counting   4. intermediate
5. wages; interest; rent; profits; national income   6. residual   7. circular flow
8. investment   9. depreciation   10. depreciation   11. net national product
12. aggregate demand; aggregate demand   13. most profitable   14. inventories
15. increase

● ANSWERS TO CHAPTER PREVIEW QUESTIONS

1. *News analysts are constantly referring to GNP. What exactly is GNP?*

Gross national product, or GNP, is a measure of total economic activity. It is defined as the annual total market value of all *final* goods and services produced in an economy. As such, GNP measurement must exclude intermediate goods and services. This avoids double counting. Also, the value of used goods is not included in the measurement of GNP. After all, we have already included the value of the good when it was new, and we do not wish to double count. GNP is typically measured at an annual rate. It expresses the total value of final goods and services produced over a year.

2. *If you were a businessperson selling a product, what would be your first clue that the total demand for all goods and services in the economy was slowing down?*

Most likely, the first thing you would observe during an economic recession is an increase in your finished-goods inventory. This increase would be above the level of inventory you normally keep. Prior to the business slowdown, you would have already determined an optimal, or most profitable, level of inventory, and that level would now be exceeded. Your reaction would probably be to try to reduce your inventory by cutting down on the number of products you purchase or manufacture. As everyone in the economy reacts the way you do, aggregate supply will fall to accommodate a lower aggregate demand.

● PROBLEMS

1. At the top of a piece of paper write the following headings: Productive Activity, Nonproductive Activity. Now list the following events under one of the two headings:
   a. Mr. X sells his used car to Mr. Y.
   b. Joe's used car lot sells a car to Mr. Z and receives a $50 profit for doing so.
   c. Merrill Lynch receives a brokerage commission for selling stocks.
   d. Mr. Arianas buys 100 shares of AT&T stock.
   e. Mrs. Romano cooks and keeps house for her family.
   f. Mr. Gonzalez mows his own lawn.
   g. Mr. Gonzalez mows lawns for a living.
   h. Mr. Smith receives a welfare payment.
   i. Mr. Johnson sends his daughter $500 for a semester of fun at College U.

2. Why are only *final* goods and services evaluated in deriving GNP?

● SELECTED REFERENCES

Mitchell, Wesley C. "The Backward Art of Spending Money." In *The Backward Art of Spending and Other Essays.* New York: Augustus M. Kelly, 1950, pp. 3–19.

Morgenstern, Oskar. *National Income Statistics.* San Francisco: The Cato Institute, 1978.

Peterson, Wallace C. *Income, Employment, and Economic Growth.* 4th ed. New York: Norton, 1978, chap. 4.

U.S. Department of Commerce. *Survey of Current Business.* May issues give annual national income data.

UNIT 3

Taxes, Money, and Macro Policy

11

Taxes

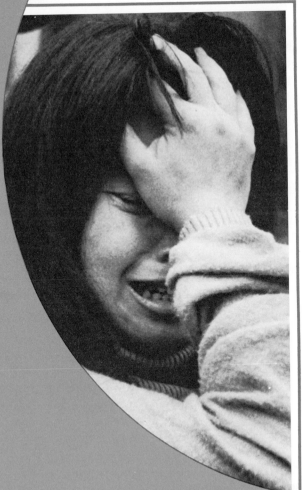

Chapter Preview
1. Many people would like to see corporations pay a larger share of all taxes, so that individuals could pay less. But is this possible?
2. Do you think you will be able to benefit from tax loopholes when you first start working?

● KEY TERMS

Ability-to-pay principle	Proportional tax system
Average tax rate	Regressive tax system
Benefit-received principle	Retained earnings
Marginal tax rate	Tax bracket
Productivity principle	Tax loophole
Progressive tax system	

"As inevitable as death and taxes," goes a familiar cliché.

This nation was founded as the result of a tax rebellion and continues to experience waves of taxpayers' revolts. Some citizens believe that they already bear too large a share of the tax burden; some would prefer fewer government services; and others simply feel they have a right to retain more of their earned incomes. One recent estimate indicates that the average person works from January 1 until mid-May to satisfy federal, state, and local tax requirements. That is, the average person works almost five months of every year just to support the tax system.

In this chapter, we will analyze tax systems and principles of taxation. In Chapter 12, we will explain how changes in taxes can affect the economy.

● AVERAGE AND MARGINAL TAX RATES

Before we can begin discussion of the different types of tax systems, an understanding of some basic tax concepts is needed. These concepts relate to the average tax rate and the marginal tax rate. The **average tax rate** is defined as the total tax bill divided by total income. That is,

$$\text{Average tax rate} = \frac{\text{total tax bill}}{\text{total income}}$$

This is the rate at which income would be taxed if each dollar were taxed at the same rate.

The **marginal tax rate**, on the other hand, is defined as the change in the tax bill divided by the change in income. That is,

$$\text{Marginal tax rate} = \frac{\text{change in tax bill}}{\text{change in income}}$$

The marginal tax rate relates to the tax on *additional* income earned.

To understand the relationship between the average tax rate and the marginal tax rate, we must understand the relationship between

Average tax rate

The total tax bill divided by total income.

Marginal tax rate

The change in the tax bill divided by the change in income.

all marginal and average values. For example, consider your school's basketball team. Suppose that so far this season, your school's team has made 70 out of 100 attempted foul shots. The team has an *average* foul-shooting performance of 70/100 = 0.700 for the year; that simply means that the team has an *average rate* of 0.700, or 70 percent, for its foul shots in all games played so far.

Now, what will happen to the foul-shooting average if this Saturday night the team makes 8 out of 10 foul shots? Note that the *marginal* performance, or the *marginal rate*, is 8 out of 10, or 0.800. That is, corresponding to a change of 10 attempted foul shots is a change of 8 successful foul shots. Since the marginal performance exceeds the average performance prior to the Saturday night game, the new average, which includes Saturday night, will have to rise. Indeed it does; the team would then be shooting 78 out of 110, or 78/110 = 0.709, at the foul line.

On the other hand, suppose the team makes only 5 out of 10 foul shots Saturday night. Since the marginal performance of 0.500 is less than the average performance of 0.700 prior to Saturday night, the team's new foul-shooting average, which includes the Saturday night game, will have to fall, and indeed it does. Seventy-five successful foul shots out of 110 attempts yields a team average of 75/110 = 0.682 at the foul line.

We conclude that the marginal rate pulls and tugs at the average rate. *If the marginal rate is above the average rate, the average rate will rise. If the marginal rate is below the average rate, the average rate will fall.* Of course, if the marginal performance is equal to the average performance, the average will remain the same.

This relationship between marginal and average rates holds whether the issue is foul shots, baseball batting averages, rainfall, or tax rates.

● TYPES OF TAX SYSTEMS

There are three principal types of tax systems:

1. Proportional
2. Regressive
3. Progressive

Proportional Tax System

A **proportional tax system** (also called a *flat-rate* tax system) is one in which the average tax rate remains constant regardless of the amount of income. That is, taxpayers at all income levels pay the same *proportion* of their income in taxes.

Consider an example. If the proportional tax rate were set at

Proportional tax system

A tax system in which the percentage of income paid to taxes is the same for all taxpayers; the average tax rate remains constant as income rises.

215

25 percent, then an income of $1000 would be taxed at $250; a person with an income of $10,000 would pay $2500; and a person earning $50,000 would pay $12,500 in taxes. Note that each person is paying the same average tax rate of 25 percent.

From our discussion of the relationship between marginal and average rates, you should not be surprised to learn that the marginal tax rate also equals 25 percent in this example. Since the average tax rate remains unchanged as income rises, the marginal tax rate must be equal to the average tax rate.

Table 11–1 shows a proportional tax rate structure. You can see that people at all income levels are paying a 25 percent average tax rate. Note also that the marginal tax rate facing all taxpayers is also 25 percent. Look at the income level at $10,000. Twenty-five percent, or $250, of the first $1000 goes to taxes. Twenty-five percent of the next $9000, or $2250, also goes to taxes. Adding the two numbers together gives us a total tax of $2500. But, $2500 divided by $10,000 equals 25 percent, so the average tax rate is equal to the marginal tax rate.

Another way of looking at a proportional tax structure is to figure that double the income means double the tax, and half the income means half the tax. If you were assessed an income tax of 25 percent on every dollar you earned, you would be facing a proportional, or flat-rate, tax structure. You would know that if you earned $10,000, you would pay $2500 in taxes, and if you made $1 million, you would pay $250,000 in taxes. You would be paying more in taxes, but the average tax rate would remain the same.

Regressive Tax System

A **regressive tax system** is one in which the marginal tax rate falls as income increases. That is, a smaller percentage of income is taken in taxes as income increases. Here the marginal tax rate on the last bit of income is below the average tax rate. With a regressive tax structure, as income doubles, taxes increase, but they do not double.

An example of a regressive tax rate structure is presented in Table 11–2. As in Table 11–1, there are three income classes— $1000, $10,000, and $25,000. But this time a regressive tax structure is assumed in which the marginal tax rate is 25 percent on the first $1000 of income, 20 percent on the next $9000 of income, and 15 percent on the next $15,000 of income. That is, the average tax rate declines as income rises. Since the marginal tax rate is below the average tax rate for incomes above $1000, the average tax rate falls, as seen in column 3. The average tax rate falls from 25 percent to 20.5 percent and finally to 17.2 percent. Thus, as the income level rises, the average tax rate gets smaller and smaller. Now consider the matter of the sales tax.

Regressive tax system

A tax system in which higher-income groups pay a smaller percentage of their income to taxes than do lower-income groups; that is, the marginal rate is below the average rate. The average rate falls as income increases.

216

TABLE 11–1
A Proportional Tax Rate Structure

INCOME LEVEL (1)	MARGINAL TAX RATE (2)		TAXES PAID		AVERAGE TAX RATE (3)	
$ 1,000	0.25 × $1,000	=	$ 250		$250 / $1,000	= 25%
10,000	0.25 × $1,000	=	$ 250			
	0.25 × $9,000	=	2,250		$ 2,500 / $10,000	= 25%
			Total $ 2,500			
50,000	0.25 × $1,000	=	$ 250			
	0.25 × $9,000	=	2,250			
	0.25 × $40,000	=	10,000		$12,500 / $50,000	= 25%
			Total $12,500			

The Sales Tax.   It is generally believed that a sales tax on food is an example of a regressive tax. Evidence indicates that lower-income groups spend a higher proportion of their total income on food. Even if low-income groups and high-income groups pay the same 5 percent sales tax on food, the proportion of total income paid in sales taxes on food falls as income rises.

Consider a simple example. Assume that people at an income level of $1000 per year spend 20 percent of their income, or $200, on food. If the sales tax is 5 percent, they pay total taxes of $10, and their average tax rate is $10/$1000, or 1 percent, as shown in Table 11–3. Now consider the situation for individuals with an income of $5000 per year. Assume that they spend 10 percent of their income,

TABLE 11–2
A Regressive Tax Rate Structure

INCOME LEVEL (1)	MARGINAL TAX RATE (2)		TAXES PAID		AVERAGE TAX RATE (3)	
$ 1,000	0.25 × $1,000	=	$ 250		$250 / $1,000	= 25%
$10,000	0.25 × $1,000	=	$ 250			
	0.20 × $9,000	=	1,800		$2,050 / $10,000	= 20.5%
			Total $2,050			
$25,000	0.25 × $1,000	=	$ 250			
	0.20 × $9,000	=	1,800			
	0.15 × $15,000	=	2,250		$4,300 / $25,000	= 17.2%
			Total $4,300			

TABLE 11–3
A Regressive Sales Tax on Food

INCOME LEVEL	FOOD CONSUMPTION	5% SALES TAX	SALES TAX AS A PROPORTION OF INCOME (AVERAGE TAX RATE)
$ 1,000	$200	$10	$\dfrac{\$10}{\$1,000} = 1\%$
$ 5,000	$500	$25.	$\dfrac{\$25}{\$5,000} = \tfrac{1}{2}\%$
$10,000	$750	$37.50	$\dfrac{\$37.50}{\$10,000} = \tfrac{3}{8}\%$

or $500, on food. A 5 percent sales tax on food yields a total tax bill of $25. The average tax rate for this income group is $25/$5000, or one-half of 1 percent. Finally, assume that individuals with $10,000 of annual income spend only 7.5 percent of their income on food consumption. Their tax bill on food is 5 percent of $750, or $37.50. Their average tax rate is $37.50/$10,000, or three-eighths of 1 percent. In this example, the average tax rate fell from 1 percent to one-half of 1 percent to three-eighths of 1 percent, as income increased from $1000 to $5000 to $10,000 per year. In short, this example shows that a sales tax on food is regressive.

Of course, taxes on luxury food such as caviar and imported wines may not be regressive, because the poor are unlikely to purchase such items.

Progressive Tax System

Consider a tax structure in which higher-income groups pay a higher percentage of their income in taxes than do lower-income groups. That is, the average and marginal tax rates rise with income. Such a structure is referred to as a **progressive tax system**.

Consider the example given in Table 11–4. Assume that the first $1000 is taxed at a marginal tax rate of 25 percent, the next $9000 is taxed at a marginal tax rate of 35 percent, and the next $15,000 is subjected to a marginal tax rate of 50 percent. We can think of a progressive tax rate structure as one in which a doubling of income yields more than double the taxes owed.

Table 11–4 shows that the average tax rate rises from 25 percent to 34 percent to 43.6 percent for total income levels that rise from $1000 to $10,000 to $25,000 per year. Since higher-income groups pay a higher percentage of their total income in taxes, this tax struc-

Progressive tax system

A tax system in which the average tax rate rises as income rises. The marginal tax rate is above the average tax rate. Higher-income groups pay a higher percentage of their income to a particular tax than do lower-income groups.

218

TABLE 11–4
A Progressive Tax Rate Structure

INCOME LEVEL (1)	MARGINAL TAX RATE (2)	TAXES PAID	AVERAGE TAX RATE (3)
$ 1,000	0.25 × $ 1,000 =	$ 250	$\dfrac{\$250}{\$1,000} = 25\%$
$10,000	0.25 = $ 1,000 = 0.35 = $ 9,000 =	250 3,150	$\dfrac{\$3,400}{\$10,000} = 34\%$
	Total $ 3,400		
$25,000	0.25 × $ 1,000 = 0.35 × $ 9,000 = 0.50 = $15,000 =	$ 250 3,150 7,500	$\dfrac{\$10,900}{\$25,000} = 43.6\%$
	Total $10,900		

ture is considered progressive. Here the marginal tax rate exceeds the average tax rate above income levels of $1000. Hence, the average tax rate rises.

● PRINCIPLES OF TAXATION

What is a fair taxing policy? What principles should be followed to achieve the "right" taxing policy? The words *should* and *fair* provide the clues: We are dealing with value judgments here. Ultimately, individual tastes dictate what is fair or what should be done.

Most of us realize that the nation requires tax revenues to carry on affairs of state and to pay for public goods and services. But how do we decide how resources *should* be taken from individuals to finance public expenditures?

There are three principles of how tax revenues should be obtained from individuals to pay for public goods and services: the benefit-received principle, the ability-to-pay principle, and the productivity principle. Keep in mind, however, that there is no scientific or objective way to choose which of these principles *should* be followed.

Benefit Received

The **benefit-received principle** of taxation is just what its name suggests. According to this principle, different individuals should be taxed in proportion to the benefits they receive from public expenditures. Thus, those who receive the most benefits from government expenditures should pay the most in taxes. Conversely, those

Benefit-received principle
A principle of taxation whereby individuals pay taxes in proportion to the benefits they receive from government.

219

who receive few benefits from government expenditures should pay the least.

Two examples of the benefit-received principle of taxation are toll roads and gasoline taxes. In each example, those who use the roads (which are built with tax dollars) most often will pay the most. Indeed, nonusers will not pay anything—and rightly so, according to the benefit-received principle of taxation. Presumably, the sales tax on gasoline would provide a cheaper means for collecting road construction taxes. It probably is also a less precise match of benefits received to taxes paid than toll roads are.

Although the benefit-received principle sounds reasonable, in practice, it would be difficult to administer. How do we determine what benefit each individual receives from public goods, such as national defense? Isn't it likely that people will try to hide their actual demand for such goods, thus creating a free-rider problem, as discussed in Chapter 7?

Ability to Pay

The **ability-to-pay principle** maintains that each individual's tax bill should be assessed according to his or her ability to pay. Presumably, higher-income individuals are better able to pay taxes than are lower-income individuals. Most people would agree that a family earning $50,000 per year is in a better position to pay taxes than is a family earning $5000 per year, other things being equal.

While this principle may sound easy to apply, such is not the case. For example, is the ability of the $50,000 family to pay taxes 10 times greater than the ability of the $5000 family, or is it 2 times, 5 times, or 20 times greater? Unfortunately, there is no way to answer this question. This is one reason people continue to argue about which kind of tax structure is fairer: a progressive or a proportional tax structure. Under *both* structures, higher-income groups will pay more *absolute* tax dollars. But under a progressive tax system, higher-income groups pay proportionately more and more. Although this follows the ability-to-pay principle, there is nothing in the principle to indicate that higher-income individuals become increasingly able to pay more.

Ability-to-pay principle

A principle of taxation whereby individuals are taxed according to how much they are able to pay, not how much they are willing to pay, or how much they benefit from government services.

Productivity principle

A principle of taxation whereby individuals are taxed according to their productivity, so that each individual's after-tax income exactly reflects the relative productivity in society.

Productivity

The **productivity principle** of taxation maintains that after-tax relative income should be no different from pretax relative income. If Smith produces twice as much as Jones, then Smith should have twice the after-tax income of Jones. Under this method of taxation, both the pretax and after-tax incomes would accurately reflect relative economic contributions of different people.

220

Each person is due his or her relative share of output—a share relative to that person's productivity. If markets are competitive, wages and other income earnings will reflect a person's productivity or contribution to the production process. For example, if your contribution is valued by the marketplace at $50,000 per year, and your friend's contribution is valued at $25,000 per year, then your contribution is twice as great as your friend's. The productivity principle of taxation maintains that after you and your friend have been taxed, your after-tax earnings should still be twice as much as your friend's.

It is not clear that this principle of taxation is any better or worse than the benefit-received or ability-to-pay principle. Again we must emphasize that we are dealing with value judgments here. Thus, there is no scientific way to choose from among the three alternatives (or any others that are offered).

● THE FEDERAL TAX SYSTEM

The federal tax system is a major force in the economy. When we earn income, we pay federal personal income taxes. If we work for a corporation, that corporation pays federal corporate income taxes, as well as employment and payroll taxes. If we purchase tobacco or liquor or gasoline, we pay what is called an excise tax, which is a type of sales tax. When we die, the estate we leave undoubtedly will be taxed by the federal government.

There are many aspects of the federal tax system, not all of which can be dealt with here. Our discussion will be limited to personal income taxes, corporate income taxes, and social security taxes.

The Federal Personal Income Tax

Federal personal income taxes are by far the largest tax source of the federal government. In 1982, over $250 billion worth of personal income taxes was collected, accounting for over 44 percent of all federal revenues. In that year, marginal tax rates ranged from 0 percent to 50 percent.

A Progressive Tax Structure. Look at Table 11–5, which shows the federal personal income tax for a childless couple in 1982. The federal personal income tax is progressive, since the marginal tax rate goes up as taxable income rises, even though the rates applicable to the *previous* lumps of income stay the same. It is important to understand that the marginal tax rate applies to the last **tax bracket** of income. Many people think that someone in a 50 percent tax bracket pays 50 percent of his or her taxable income to the federal government. This is not the case, even for an honest taxpayer. Con-

Tax bracket

A specified interval of income to which a specific and unique marginal tax rate is applied.

221

sider a childless couple facing the tax rates shown in Table 11–5. If they are already earning $85,600 and are given a bonus of $10,000, the 50 percent tax rate applies to the $10,000, not to any monies earned prior to the bonus. Those monies are taxed at rates from 49 percent down to 0 percent.

Tax Loopholes.   Despite their higher tax rates, most high-income individuals do not pay as much in taxes as one would think. It turns out that tax loopholes for high-income individuals abound. A **tax loophole** is a legal method of tax avoidance. Some examples of loopholes in the federal personal income tax system include tax-exempt earnings on municipal bonds and special tax breaks on real estate, mineral extraction, and farming. The intent of many of these loopholes is to provide investment incentives to increase the amount of resources going to particular activities in the economy.

It is not surprising that only individuals in the higher tax brackets can profitably take advantage of tax loopholes. After all, a tax loophole involves a legal deduction in tax liability. The higher your marginal tax rate, the more benefit you receive from any $1 of income that is exempted from taxes. Consider the example of tax-exempt municipal bonds.

Tax-Exempt Bonds.   The tax-exempt status of interest paid to holders of state and municipal bonds is well known to most investors.

Tax loophole

A legal method of reducing tax liabilities, properly called tax avoidance. Tax avoidance should not be confused with tax evasion, which is illegal and punishable by penalties, fines, and/or imprisonment.

TABLE 11–5
Federal Personal Income Tax for a Childless Couple, 1982

Here we show the different income brackets and the marginal tax rates along with the average tax rates. As you can see, the marginal tax rates go up to a maximum of 50 percent.

NET INCOME BEFORE EXEMPTIONS (BUT AFTER ADJUSTMENTS AND DEDUCTIONS)	PERSONAL INCOME TAX	AVERAGE TAX RATE (%)	MARGINAL TAX RATE (%)
Below $ 3,400	$ 0	0.0	0
5,500	252	4.6	12
7,600	546	7.2	14
11,900	1,234	10.4	16
16,000	2,013	12.6	19
20,200	2,937	14.5	22
24,600	4,037	16.4	25
29,900	5,574	18.6	29
35,200	7,323	20.8	33
45,800	11,457	25.0	39
60,000	17,205	28.7	44
85,600	30,249	35.3	49
Above 85,600	—	—	50

SOURCE: U.S. Treasury Department, Internal Revenue Service.

Tax-exempt bonds are a form of tax shelter in that the interest income that the investor obtains does not have to be reported on federal income tax returns. Hence, taxable income is reduced by the amount of income received from those bonds.

Now, what is the dollar benefit to you of tax-exempt income? You cannot answer that question unless you first determine your marginal tax rate. If your marginal tax rate is 50 percent, then every dollar you receive in tax-exempt interest from a municipal bond is a dollar on which you will *not* have to pay 50 cents in taxes. Therefore, your tax saving from investing in municipal bonds is 50 percent of the interest from those bonds. On the other hand, if your tax bracket is only 20 percent, your tax saving is only 20 cents on every dollar of tax-exempt income.

Bond buyers are aware of this relationship; thus, in their competition to obtain tax savings (that is, tax-exempt income) from these bonds, they bid up the price of bonds, causing relatively low yields. If you look in the financial pages of a newspaper, you will find that the yield listed for tax-exempt bonds is lower than the yield listed for non-tax-exempt bonds of similar quality. Usually, it is lower by between 30 and 40 percent.[1]

Consider the following example. Assume that tax-exempt municipal bonds are selling at a price that yields 7 percent per year, and that non-tax-exempt bonds of equivalent risk are selling at a price that yields 10 percent a year. Which should you buy?

If you are in a relatively high tax bracket, you should probably buy the tax-exempt bond. But if you are in a relatively low tax bracket, you should probably buy the non-tax-exempt bond. To see why, refer to Table 11–6.

Let's say that you are again in the 20 percent tax bracket. If you buy a non-tax-exempt bond yielding 10 percent, the after-tax yield will be 10 percent minus what you must pay to the government. Since you must pay the government 20 percent of that 10 percent, or 2 percentage points, your after-tax yield will be

$$10\% - (0.2 \times 10\%) = 10\% - 2\% = 8\%.$$

Of course, the before- and after-tax yields on the municipal bond are the same, 7 percent, because no taxes are paid on the interest. Since 8 percent is a higher after-tax yield than 7 percent, you are better off buying a non-tax-exempt bond.

If, on the other hand, you are in the 50 percent tax bracket, you will be better off buying the 7 percent tax-exempt municipal bond. The after-tax yield on the non-tax-exempt 10 percent bond is 50 percent of 10 percent, or only 5 percent. But you can keep all of the interest on the tax-exempt municipal bond, and that is equal to

[1]This difference represents the *implicit* taxes that you pay when buying a tax-exempt bond.

223

TABLE 11–6
Tax-Exempt Bonds: To Buy or Not to Buy?

	LOW TAX BRACKET (20%)		HIGH TAX BRACKET (50%)	
	Non-Tax-Exempt Bond (1)	Tax-Exempt Bond (2)	Non-Tax-Exempt Bond (3)	Tax-Exempt Bond (4)
Federal tax rate	20%	20%	50%	50%
Interest rate payable from bond	10%	7%	10%	7%
Percentage points you must pay in taxes	2%	0%	5%	0%
Percentage points you get to keep	8%	7%	5%	7%
After paying taxes, which bond pays more interest and by how much?	Non-tax-exempt pays 8% − 7% = 1% more than tax-exempt			Tax-exempt pays 7% − 5% = 2% more than non-tax-exempt
Which to buy?	In low tax bracket, buy *non*-tax-exempt bonds			In high tax bracket, buy tax-exempt bonds

7 percent—2 percentage points more than on the non-tax-exempt bond.

Thus, because of this nation's progressive tax system, many tax shelters are beneficial only to those in higher income brackets. This is so because competition among investors drives up the price of tax-sheltered, income-earning assets to reflect the tax savings. The purpose of not taxing income from state and municipal bonds is to subsidize state and local governments. The tax-exempt status of these bonds allows such governments to sell their debt (borrow) at a lower interest rate. The subsidy is real and may or may not be desirable, depending on one's point of view. However, its distortion of the progressive nature of the U.S. tax system is perhaps an unwanted side effect.

The Corporate Income Tax

Corporate income taxes account for about 14 percent of all federal taxes collected. Corporations are usually taxed on the difference between their total revenues, or receipts, and their expenses. In 1901, the corporate tax rate amounted to a mere 1 percent of corporate profits, with the first $5000 a year being exempted. By 1932, this

224

exemption had disappeared and the rate had jumped to 13.755 percent. From 1950 to 1978, corporations paid a "normal" tax on the first $25,000 of profit per year in addition to the tax on profits in excess of $25,000 per year. Starting in 1984, the corporate profit tax structure will be set up as follows:

0—$25,000	15 percent
$25,000—$50,000	18 percent
$50,000—$75,000	30 percent
$75,000—$100,000	40 percent
$100,000 and up	46 percent

The Double Taxation on Corporate Earnings. The after-tax profits of a corporation are taxed again when stockholders pay taxes on dividends received or on realized capital gains. For example, if you receive $1000 in dividends, you must declare it as income and pay taxes at your marginal rate. But before the corporation paid you those dividends, it had to pay taxes on all of its profits, including any that it put back into the company or did not distribute in the form of dividends. Eventually, the new investment made possible by those **retained earnings**—profits not given out to stockholders—will be reflected in the increased value of your stock. When you sell your stock, you will have to pay a capital gains tax on the difference between the amount you paid for the stock and the amount for which you sell it. In this sense, corporate profits are taxed twice.

Consider the following example. The sale of a product yields $2 in revenues, and the cost of producing it is $1. Thus, the before-tax profit is $1. If the tax rate on corporate profits is 46 percent (or 46 cents on the dollar of profit), the after-tax profit is 54 cents. If this amount is given to stockholders as a dividend, they must pay, at the very least, the federal personal income tax on it. If that tax is 50 percent, they have to pay 27 cents of the dividend in taxes. Thus $1 of corporate profit yields 27 cents in stockholders' pockets.

Who Really Pays Corporate Taxes? Corporations can exist only as long as consumers buy their products, employees make their goods, stockholders (owners) buy their stocks, and bondholders buy their bonds. Corporations, per se, do nothing. They exist only insofar as they have customers, employees, stockholders, and bondholders. Who, then, really pays the tax on corporate income? There is considerable debate on this subject. Some economists maintain that corporations pass their tax burdens on to consumers by charging higher prices. Other economists believe that it is the stockholders, the people who purchase shares of ownership, who bear most of the tax. Still others believe that employees pay at least part of the tax by receiving lower wages than they would otherwise. This debate is likely to remain unsettled. Suffice it to say, though, that you should

Retained earnings

Those earnings that a corporation saves for use in investment. These earnings are not distributed to the stockholders of the corporation.

be cautious about advocating an increase in corporation income taxes. You may be the one who ultimately pays the increase.

Social Security Taxes

The social security system was established in 1935 when it became clear that many individuals had not provided for their retirement years. Even those who did provide apparently did not have enough to sustain themselves in the face of the Great Depression. Many changes have occurred in the social security system since 1935. Tax rates have increased rapidly. Indeed, an increase in the percentage of total federal tax receipts is accounted for each year by taxes levied on payrolls. Known under the rubric of social security, or FICA (Federal Insurance Contribution Act), the benefits covered by these taxes are social security, retirement, survivors' disability, and old-age medical insurance (Medicare).

In 1985, the social security and Medicare total tax rate percentage of covered earnings will be 7.05 percent on a projected base of $38,100. The 7.05 percent is paid by both the employer and the employee. That is, the employer matches your "contribution" to social security. Individuals who are self-employed must pay a self-employment tax equivalent to three-fourths of the combined employer and employee rate. Thus, in 1985, self-employed individuals will have to pay 0.75×14.1 percent $= 10.575$ percent of their earnings.

Social security taxes seem to correspond to the benefit-received principle of taxation, since it is the workers who pay the taxes and the workers who receive the benefits. Critics of social security, however, note that the amount of social security taxes paid bears little relationship to the payments that individual workers receive. Moreover, the social security system is a regressive system. After the cutoff point, or covered earnings base, no social security contribution is paid. Thus, the higher one's income after the cutoff point, the lower the average social security tax rate on total income. Consider an example at the 1985 rate. An individual earning exactly $38,100 will pay exactly 7.05 percent, or $2,686.05, in contributions. But a person earning twice that amount, or $76,200, will also pay $2,686.05. That person's average social security tax rate will fall from 7.05 percent to 3.525 percent.

In recent years, it has been argued that the social security system faces a potential bankruptcy problem. This issue is discussed in more detail in the following Controversy.

The Social Security System is Going Bankrupt

THE ARGUMENT

The trust funds of the social security system have been approaching the zero point over the last few years. This has brought the specter of a bankrupt social security system to the fore. Can the social security system actually go bankrupt? If it can, will current and future recipients of social security benefits find that no checks will be forthcoming from the federal government?

THE ANALYSIS

It is true that benefits have been increasing rapidly relative to the rise in taxes. In 1972, social security benefits were increased by 20 percent. After that, increases were tied to the consumer price index (CPI) to prevent benefits from being eroded by inflation. But because of some quirk in the system, benefits have actually risen faster than the rate of inflation. The net result was that between 1970 and 1980, social security benefits per recipient increased 55 percent more than increases in the consumer price index. That means that real purchasing power of social security benefits went up 55 percent. During the same time period, the real purchasing power earnings for private, non-agricultural workers rose only 2 percent. Thus, the increase in benefits received by social security recipients was more than 50 percent greater than the increase in earnings by those workers who were paying the taxes to support the social security system. And it appears that the problem will become more pronounced as the population, on average, gets older. Today, every retiree receives benefits that are paid for by four active workers in the labor force. If the social security system continues on its present course, by the year 2030 each retiree will be financed by only two laborers. The distinct possibility exists that future generations will not be willing or able to subsidize the older generation.

To understand why it is the current generation that subsidizes the retired generation, you must realize that the social security system is simply a pay-as-you-go transfer system. Current workers subsidize already-retired workers. It is not an insurance policy because social security benefits are legislated by Congress. As our population gets older, more individuals will be reaping social security benefits relative to the number of individuals in the labor force. The only way to obtain more benefits for retired individuals is to tax working individuals more. But at higher and higher tax rates, individuals in the labor force have less and less incentive to work: thus the problem of the *ability* of future generations to finance social security payments to retired generations.

227

On the bright side of the picture, the system ultimately can be made financially sound if the federal government would assume the obligations—the benefit payments. The federal government can meet social security payments out of general taxes rather than earmarked taxes. There are also numerous ways to slow down the rate of increase of benefits paid. For example, the indexing method could be changed; the age of retirement could be increased; and eligibility requirements could be strengthened. In brief, there are many measures that can be taken to solve the short-run problem facing the social security system. Ultimately, however, the body politic must decide to what extent the work force should provide transfer payments to retired individuals.

DISCUSSION QUESTIONS

1. Is it possible that people currently in the 30-, 40- and 50-year-old age brackets will have to pay higher social security taxes only to find that *their* benefits will fall when they retire? Why?

2. A private pension plan is one to which you contribute yearly and, in a sense, own. To what extent does a U.S. worker who must pay social security taxes own his or her social security retirement plan? Can he or she voluntarily opt out?

● WHAT'S AHEAD

Now that you have some idea of how the federal income tax system works, we will examine how changes in the amount of federal taxes collected can affect the equilibrium level of national income and output. In other words, we will see how our government's policymakers can change fiscal policy either to pull the economy out of a recession or cool off an overheated economy.

● CHAPTER SUMMARY

There are three types of tax systems—proportional, regressive, and progressive. Whenever the marginal tax rate is equal to the average tax rate, a proportional tax system is in effect. If the marginal tax rate is less than the average tax rate, there is a regressive tax system. And finally, when the marginal tax rate is greater than the average tax rate, there is a progressive tax system.

There are at least three principles of taxation. The benefit-received principle states that individuals should be taxed according to the benefits they receive from government services. The ability-to-pay principle states that individuals should be taxed according to their ability to pay. And finally, the productivity principle states that individuals should have after-tax income that reflects their relative productivity in the economy.

Individuals in high tax brackets do not pay high marginal tax rates on all of the income that they earn. They pay high tax rates only on the last tax bracket, defined as the intervals of income over which a specific and unique marginal tax rate applies.

Higher-income individuals can benefit from legal avoidance of taxes, called tax loopholes. One of the most common is the purchase of tax-exempt municipal bonds. Yields on such bonds, however, are lower than on taxable bonds. Therefore, only individuals in the highest tax brackets can benefit by their purchase. Others are better off buying non-tax-exempt bonds.

Corporations pay a tax on their profits. When after-tax profits are distributed as dividends, they are taxed again as ordinary personal income, thus leading to double taxation. Corporations never pay taxes; only people in the form of stockholders, customers, and employees can pay taxes.

● QUESTIONS FOR REVIEW AND STUDY

1. We define the _____ tax rate as the total tax bill divided by total income.

2. We define the marginal tax rate as the _____ in the tax bill divided by the _____ in income.

3. Whenever the marginal rate is _____ the average rate, the average will rise.

4. Whenever the marginal rate is _____ the average rate, the average will fall.

5. Another name for a _____ tax system is a flat-rate system.

6. With a proportional tax system, your income level does/does not affect the percentage of taxes you pay.

7. A tax system in which you pay a smaller percentage in taxes as your income goes up is a _____ system.

8. A progressive tax system is one in which you pay _____ and _____ marginal tax rates as your income rises.

9. Every principle of taxation involves a _____ judgment.

10. Three possible principles of taxation are _____ _____, _____ _____ _____, and _____.

11. The federal personal income tax system is _____.

12. The rich are able to take advantage of _____ _____ to reduce their tax liabilities.

13. Corporations are taxed on their earnings, and then those same

229

earnings are again taxed as personal income in the form of dividends. Thus, corporations suffer from _____ _____.

14. The three groups that can pay corporation taxes are _____, _____, and _____.

15. The social security system is/is not an insurance system.

ANSWERS

1. average 2. change; change 3. above 4. below 5. proportional 6. does not 7. regressive 8. higher; higher 9. value 10. benefit received; ability to pay; productivity 11. progressive 12. tax loopholes 13. double taxation 14. stockholders; consumers; employees 15. is not

● ANSWERS TO CHAPTER PREVIEW QUESTIONS

1. *Many people would like to see corporations pay a larger share of all taxes, so that individuals could pay less. But is this possible?*

It would be nice if corporations could be taxed more heavily so as to reduce individual taxes. Remember, though, that corporations are "things" and, as such, cannot be taxed. Only people can be taxed. Therefore, corporation taxes ultimately are paid by people. Three groups pay for higher corporate taxes. Owners of corporations can pay in the form of reduced dividends and less stock appreciation for stockholders. Consumers of corporate products can pay in the form of higher prices for the goods they buy. And laborers working for corporations can pay in the form of lower wages than they would otherwise receive.

2. *Do you think you will be able to benefit from tax loopholes when you first start working?*

In all probability, you will not be earning enough at your first job to put you into a high enough marginal tax bracket to justify taking advantage of tax loopholes. Tax loopholes are a benefit to those who receive significant tax reductions by using them. When you first start working, your marginal tax rate may be only 20 percent. That means that the benefit to you of having $1 of your income not taxed is only 20 cents. Compare this to the benefit received by someone earning so much income that he or she is in the 50 percent tax bracket. That person receives a 50-cent benefit by not having $1 of income taxed. Consequently, the rich bid up the prices of any assets that allow a tax loophole. You will, in fact, be worse off if you try to take advantage of these tax loopholes, unless you are in virtually the highest tax brackets.

● PROBLEMS

1. Consider the following tax structure:

Income Bracket	Marginal Tax Rate
$0–$1500	0%
$1501–$2000	14%
$2001–$3000	20%

Mr. Smith has an income of $2500 per year.
    a. Calculate his tax bill for the year.
    b. What is his average rate of taxation?

2. In 1983, social security tax payments on wages were 6.70 percent of wages, on wages up to $33,900. No *further* social security payments were made on earnings above this figure. Calculate the average social security tax rate for annual wages of
    a. $4000
    b. $33,000
    c. $50,000
    d. $100,000.
Is the social security system a progressive, proportional or regressive tax structure?

● SELECTED REFERENCES

Break, George F., and Joseph A. Pechman. *Federal Tax Reform: The Impossible Dream?* Washington, D.C.: The Brookings Institution, 1975.

Clark, Lindley H. *The Secret Tax.* New York: Dow Jones Books, 1976.

Groves, Harold M., and Robert L. Bish. *Finance in Government.* New York: Holt, Rinehart & Winston, 1973.

Laffer, A. B., and J. P. Seymour, eds. *The Economics of the Tax Revolt: A Reader.* New York: Harcourt Brace Jovanovich, 1979.

Pechman, Joseph A. *Federal Tax Policy.* 3d ed. Washington, D.C.: The Brookings Institution, 1977.

Setting National Priorities. Available every year, usually in May, from The Brookings Institution, Washington, D.C.

12

Fiscal
Policy

Chapter Preview
1. How can the federal government's fiscal policy
—the way government spending and taxes are
determined—affect you personally?
2. What is automatic fiscal policy and how does it
help stabilize an economy?

● KEY TERMS

Automatic stabilizers

Balanced budget

Budget deficit

Budget surplus

Fiscal policy

Multiplier effect

National, or public, debt

Suppose that you learned that taxes were going to fall significantly and that this tax reduction would remain in force for many years to come. Do you think that this "permanent" tax reduction would encourage you and others to increase spending on goods and services? And suppose that your unemployed cousin was just hired by a construction company that had just received a government contract to build a road over a 10-year period. Would you expect your cousin to start spending more income on goods and services? Would his life-style change?

Most economists believe that the answer to both questions is yes. In this chapter, we will try to analyze the effects on the *whole economy* of changes in federal taxes and federal expenditures.

In Chapter 10, we learned that aggregate demand (AGG *D*) is equal to planned or desired expenditures for consumption (consumer goods), investment, and government goods and services. That is,

$$\text{AGG } D = C + I + G.$$

It was also shown that the economy is in equilibrium when total planned expenditures on final goods and services are equal to national income. Increases in aggregate demand will cause the equilibrium level of national income to rise as businesses increase output to meet the increase in aggregate demand. Conversely, if aggregate demand falls, the equilibrium level of national income will fall as businesses react by reducing output.

Since changes in aggregate demand lead to changes in national income, the federal government can deliberately change aggregate demand to affect the business cycle. We've already noted that government activity is an important part of our economy. Government expenditures on goods and services are a sizable source of national income, and taxes play an ever-increasing role in economic events. Indeed, some statisticians believe that every dollar of GNP is taxed at approximately 40 percent when we include all taxes at the federal, state, and local levels.

In recent years, government policy has had a growing influence on the economy. Through its ability to change aggregate demand, the government has increased its role in the *attempt* to stabilize overall economic activity.[1] Aggregate demand can be altered directly by

[1]Some critics of government stabilization policies contend that the policies ultimately are destabilizing, rather than stabilizing.

a change in government expenditures and indirectly by a change in taxes. Tax changes affect aggregate demand indirectly through changes in consumption and investment expenditures.

● DISCRETIONARY FISCAL POLICY

The federal government can deliberately alter aggregate demand; it can change government expenditures and/or taxes to affect national income and output. This is called **fiscal policy**.

Changes in Government Expenditures

If government expenditures on goods and services increase, then aggregate demand will increase directly. Suppose that government expenditures increase by $10 billion a year for interstate highway construction. Assume that people who were previously unemployed are hired as a result of the highway program and that national income rises by $10 billion. But those workers won't take that $10 billion of new income and hoard it. Rather, they will probably spend some of their additional income and save some. Since one person's *expenditure* is another person's *income*, the part of the $10 billion that is spent will become an increase in income for another group.

Suppose the group that receives the $10 billion increase in income for building the road spends, say, $5 billion of it on goods and services. The next group—producers of the extra $5 billion in goods and services purchased by the road builders—will then receive a $5 billion increase in its income. Again, however, that next group will not hoard the $5 billion. It will spend some and save some of this additional income. The process continues and ultimately results in what is known as the **multiplier effect**.

The Multiplier Effect.   In our example, a $10 billion increase in government expenditures eventually increased national income by more than $10 billion. Income expansion occurred. First, $10 billion was spent, then $5 billion was spent. If we assume that each group spends only half of what it receives and saves the rest, then the group that received $5 billion will spend $2.5 billion, which will become income for some other group. And that group will spend $1.25 billion, and so on. Each time part of the increase in income is respent, it produces an income increase for another group.

It appears that every $1 increase in aggregate demand, coming about by a $1 increase in government expenditures, can cause national income to rise by *more* than $1. This is the multiplier effect at work. Look at Exhibit 12–1 for a picture view of the multiplier effect as it relates to our example. A more detailed and mathematical pre-

Fiscal policy

The changing of government expenditures and/or taxes to affect national income and output.

Multiplier effect

The impact of changes in aggregate demand on the equilibrium level of national income; a $1 change in aggregate demand may cause the level of national income to change by *more* than $1.

235

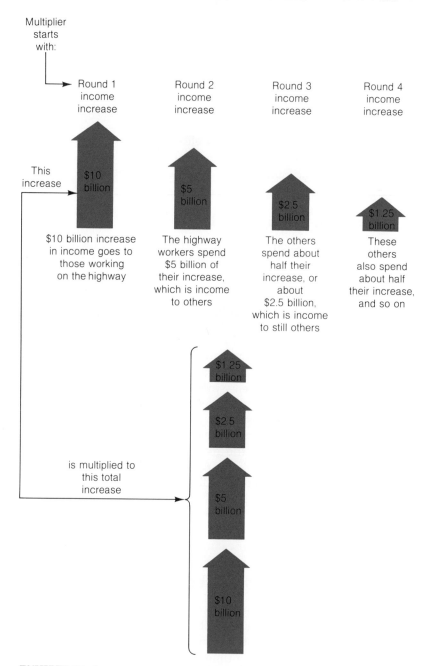

Multiplier starts with:

Round 1 income increase

Round 2 income increase

Round 3 income increase

Round 4 income increase

This increase

$10 billion

$5 billion

$2.5 billion

$1.25 billion

$10 billion increase in income goes to those working on the highway

The highway workers spend $5 billion of their increase, which is income to others

The others spend about half their increase, or about $2.5 billion, which is income to still others

These others also spend about half their increase, and so on

$1.25 billion

$2.5 billion

is multiplied to this total increase

$5 billion

$10 billion

EXHIBIT 12–1
The Multiplier Effect

sentation of the multiplier effect is presented in the Appendix immediately following this chapter.

The Multiplier Effect Works in Both Directions.   In our definition of the multiplier effect, we referred to a "change" in aggregate demand, and not specifically to an "increase." The implication is that a $1 *decrease* in aggregate demand may cause the level of national income to fall by more than $1.

Suppose that the government decided to cancel its *annual* $10 billion interstate highway expenditure. In effect, income would fall by $10 billion in the first round, and those people with less income would spend less on goods and services. Since one person's expenditure reduction represents another person's income reduction, a second-round income reduction would occur, and so on. In short, the multiplier effect is a two-edged sword; the multiplier effect works in both directions.

Changes in Taxes

If the federal government changes taxes, it can affect aggregate demand *indirectly* through changes in household consumption expenditures. If the government raises taxes, and people expect the tax increase to be permanent, they will reduce their consumption expenditures on goods and services. Similarly, "permanent" tax reductions will motivate households to increase their consumption expenditures.

The Taxation Multiplier.   It follows that changes in taxes will lead to changes in aggregate demand indirectly through changes in consumption (and through changes in investment if business taxes are changed). Since tax changes lead to shifts in aggregate demand, we would expect a multiplier effect to occur. Indeed, a $1 increase in taxes will lead to a more than $1 reduction in national income. Similarly, a $1 decrease in taxes will cause national income to rise by more than $1. Look at Exhibit 12–2 for a diagrammatic view of fiscal policy.

Fiscal Policy during Inflation

When producers are unable to keep up with aggregate demand, temporary shortages for most goods will result. This, in turn, causes the general price level to rise; we refer to this as inflation. Inflation can occur when the demand for goods and services exceeds the economy's ability to produce those goods and services. Using our new vocabulary, we can say that inflation will occur if the aggregate demand for goods and services at current prices exceeds the aggregate supply of goods and services at current prices.

237

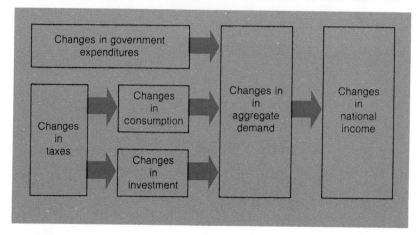

EXHIBIT 12–2
Fiscal Policy

How should fiscal policy be applied to fight inflation? The government has two options: changes in government expenditures and changes in taxes.

Government Expenditures during Inflation.   Since the problem during inflation is that aggregate demand exceeds aggregate supply, you can probably guess the fiscal policy prescription: reduce government expenditures. As the government reduces its expenditures, we can expect a multiplier decrease in aggregate demand and national income. It is hoped that a decrease will occur only in prices, or in the rate of inflation. Output might also fall, however, and this is one of the undesirable effects of restrictive fiscal policy.

Taxes during Inflation.   What about taxes? Remember, our object is to reduce aggregate demand due to inflation. Therefore, the fiscal policy prescription is an increase in taxes. This, in turn, will reduce household consumption expenditures. Aggregate demand will fall and the equilibrium level of national income will fall by some multiple of the tax increase. In other words, a tax *increase* will lead to the same kind of result that a government expenditure decrease will lead to: a decrease in national income.

Balanced budget

Government receipts equal government outlays; that is, the government is spending exactly what it is taking in.

Budget surplus

Government revenues (tax receipts) exceed government expenditures.

Fighting Inflation by Budget Surpluses.   What is the result of a reduction in government expenditures and/or an increase in taxes? If the government had been running a **balanced budget** previously, a **budget surplus** would now exist. During periods of inflation, fiscal policy presumably should aim for budget surpluses. This would indicate that the government is taking spending power out of the economy. That is, a budget surplus demonstrates that the govern-

238

ment is reducing aggregate demand, which is the desired policy prescription during periods of inflation.

Fiscal Policy during Recessions

During a recession, national income is not growing and may actually be falling. Aggregate demand is not sufficiently high to ensure a national income level that keeps pace with the potential productive capacity of the nation.

Government Expenditures during Recessions.   The problem during a recession is that at a given price level, aggregate demand is insufficient to achieve full employment. Therefore, fiscal policy calls for an increase in government expenditures. It is hoped that increases in government expenditures will lead to a multiple increase in the equilibrium level of national income. This will help get the economy out of the recessionary phase of the business cycle. As aggregate demand rises, the resulting increased output will require higher employment levels.

Taxes during Recessions.   What should be done about taxes during a recession? Since our goal is to increase aggregate demand, the government should reduce taxes, thereby encouraging increased household expenditures. Aggregate demand will rise and the equilibrium level of national income will rise by some multiple of the tax reduction. As national output rises, there will be an increase in employment.

Fighting Recessions by Budget Deficits.   What is the result of increased government expenditures and/or reduced taxes? Assuming a previously balanced budget, there will now be a **budget deficit**. In short, recessions are fought by budget deficits, for it is through deficit spending that the government adds to aggregate demand and thereby increases the equilibrium level of national income, output, and employment.

The Historical Record

Graph 12–1 presents the historical record of budget deficits and surpluses (the few that we've had) over the last 51 years. Budget deficits seem to be growing, but that may be because prices are rising and the economy is getting bigger. Budget deficits expressed as a percentage of gross national product show a different story. Deficits represent only a few percentage points of GNP.

Do not conclude that every year there was a budget deficit, the federal government was engaging in fiscal policy to fight recessions.

Budget deficit

Government outlays exceed government receipts; that is, government expenditures exceed tax receipts.

GRAPH 12-1
Historical Record of Budget Deficits and Surpluses

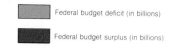

Federal budget deficit (in billions)

Federal budget surplus (in billions)

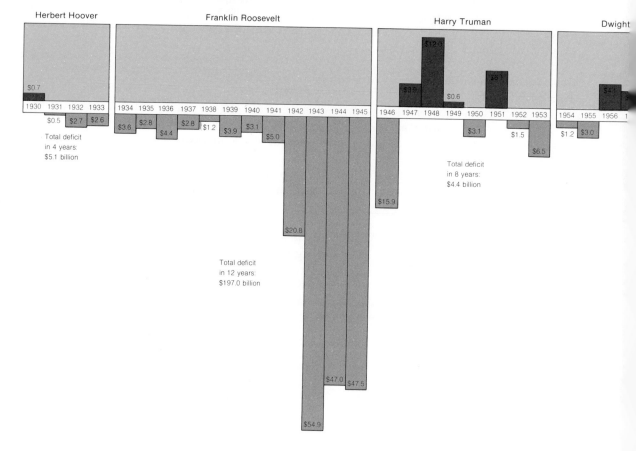

Herbert Hoover

$0.7
1930 1931 1932 1933
$0.5 $2.7 $2.6

Total deficit
in 4 years:
$5.1 billion

Franklin Roosevelt

1934 1935 1936 1937 1938 1939 1940 1941 1942 1943 1944 1945
$3.6 $2.8 $4.4 $2.8 $1.2 $3.9 $3.1 $5.0
$15.9
$20.8

Total deficit
in 12 years:
$197.0 billion

$47.0 $47.5
$54.9

Harry Truman

$12.0
$3.9 $6.1
$0.6
1946 1947 1948 1949 1950 1951 1952 1953
$3.1 $1.5
$6.5

Total deficit
in 8 years:
$4.4 billion

Dwight

$4.1
1954 1955 1956 1
$1.2 $3.0

240

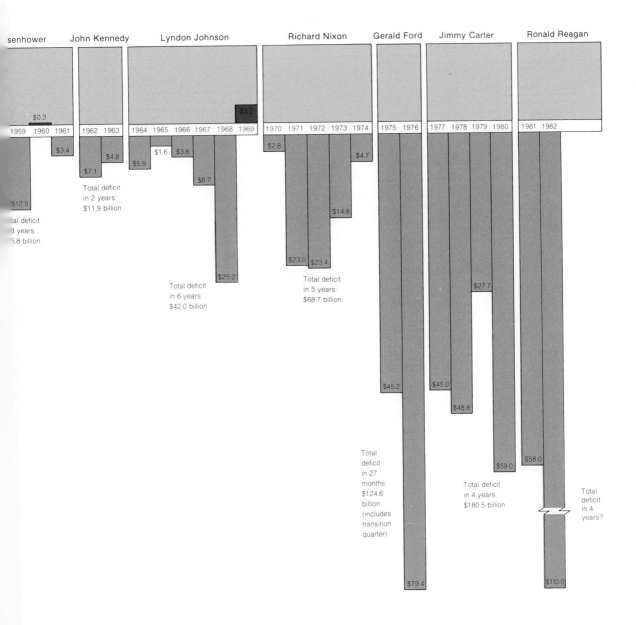

senhower | John Kennedy | Lyndon Johnson | Richard Nixon | Gerald Ford | Jimmy Carter | Ronald Reagan

$0.3

1959 1960 1961 | 1962 1963 | 1964 1965 1966 1967 1968 1969 | 1970 1971 1972 1973 1974 | 1975 1976 | 1977 1978 1979 1980 | 1981 1982

$3.2

$3.4

$4.8

$5.9 $1.6 $3.8

$7.1

$4.7

$2.8

$8.7

Total deficit
in 2 years:
$11.9 billion

$12.9

tal deficit
8 years:
6.8 billion

$14.8

$23.0 $23.4

$25.2

Total deficit
in 6 years:
$42.0 billion

Total deficit
in 5 years:
$68.7 billion

$27.7

$45.2 $45.0

$48.8

$59.0 $58.0

Total
deficit
in 27
months:
$124.6
billion
(includes
transition
quarter)

Total deficit
in 4 years:
$180.5 billion

Total
deficit
in 4
years?

$79.4

$110.0

241

Some part of all budget deficits occurs without the federal government explicitly changing fiscal policy. After all, if everything is going along smoothly and the federal budget is balanced, a recession will cause a budget deficit without any action on the part of the president or Congress. By assumption, government spending remains the same, but the recession lowers income. Many of the taxes collected by the government will therefore fall; hence, a deficit will occur.

● THE NATIONAL, OR PUBLIC, DEBT

Fiscal policy is presumably symmetric—it calls for budget deficits during recession and budget surpluses during inflation. But the historical experience is far from consistent with this symmetric view of fiscal policy. Look again at Graph 12–1. The United States has had only a handful of budget surpluses since 1930. Since that time, the federal government has run mostly budget deficits. The result of this almost constant deficit spending has been an increase in the **national, or public, debt**.

The government borrows by selling bonds (securities) to the public. The federal government has almost continuously run budget deficits, the size of the public debt has increased dramatically over time. By 1983, the public debt had reached the staggering sum of about $1.3 trillion. This figure, however, is somewhat exaggerated. Approximately $400 billion of that $1 trillion is owed by one government agency to another, so it really does not represent the debt that the government owes to the public. Also, since 1970, the ratio of the public debt to GNP has remained approximately constant at about 30 percent. In relative terms, therefore, the growth in the public debt has not been great.

National, or public, debt

The total value of all outstanding federal government securities (bonds). It is the sum of past budget deficits that have not yet been repaid.

Automatic stabilizers

Changes in government expenditures and taxes that occur naturally and do not require any action on the part of Congress or the president of the United States; they occur because of changes in economic conditions.

● AUTOMATIC STABILIZERS

Up to this point, our focus has been on *discretionary* fiscal policy, where the government *deliberately* changes expenditures and taxes to fight recessions or inflations. Some changes in government expenditures and taxes occur automatically, however, over the course of the business cycle. In other words, they are not discretionary and occur without legislation. These changes in taxes and government expenditures are called **automatic stabilizers**. Examples of automatic stabilizers are the progressive income tax system and unemployment compensation. As explained in Chapter 7, unemployment compensation benefits are a form of transfer payments.

Automatic Changes in Expenditures

In times of recession, as more and more individuals are laid off from jobs, the total sum of unemployment compensation automatically increases. Total welfare payments and food stamp outlays are also likely to rise automatically during a recession because more people meet the eligibility requirements. All of this happens automatically and without any act of Congress.

Precisely the opposite occurs in the expansion phase of the business cycle. During boom times, fewer people are unemployed. Thus, unemployment compensation benefits fall, as do welfare and food stamp benefits, because fewer people meet eligibility requirements.

Automatic Changes in Taxes

In times of economic expansion, people move into higher marginal tax brackets. Because of the progressive tax structure, the average tax rate rises as incomes rise. Boom times, therefore, automatically generate higher taxes; legislation is not required. Note that the same thing applies to corporate and other taxes that are assessed progressively. In short, boom times automatically generate a more-than-proportionate increase in tax payments.

Of course, precisely the opposite occurs during the recession phase of the business cycle. As national income, output, and employment fall, individuals move into lower tax brackets and the average tax rate falls. Again, because of the progressive nature of the federal personal income tax, recessions automatically generate a more-than-proportionate decrease in tax revenues. And again, corporate income taxes and other progressive taxes also fall automatically, proportionately more than the reduction in income.

Why are these automatic changes referred to as *stabilizers*? Recessions automatically give rise to increased government spending and decreased taxes; thus, the recession's impact is cushioned. On the other hand, when the economy is expanding rapidly, the expansion is choked off somewhat by automatically increased taxes and decreased government expenditures. These automatic changes move to counteract the phases of the business cycle, thereby providing an element of stability; hence the term *automatic stabilizers*.

● SOME RECENT FISCAL POLICY ACTIONS

There have been a number of discretionary fiscal policy actions since the 1960s. We will discuss some of them here.

The Kennedy – Johnson Tax Cut of 1964

As part of his campaign platform in 1960, John F. Kennedy made a commitment to "get this country moving again." The country was, in fact, still pulling itself out of a recession that had begun in 1958. When Kennedy took office, the country did start "moving again"; but his economic advisers cautioned the president that unless there was a tax cut, the momentum that was building would soon die and the economy would lapse into another serious recession. Starting in 1961, the administration began prodding Congress for a tax reduction.

After Kennedy's assassination in 1963, Lyndon B. Johnson took over and continued to prod Congress for a tax cut. Finally, in 1964, federally collected taxes were cut by some $11 billion. Unemployment fell from 5.2 percent in 1964 to 4.5 percent in 1965. Investment and consumer spending were stimulated.

The Johnson 1968 Tax Surcharge

The escalation of the war in Vietnam caused national defense expenditures to rise at a relatively rapid rate. From 1965 to 1967, they increased from $50 billion to $70 billion per year; in 1968, they increased by another $10 billion. The unemployment rate remained below 4 percent during the entire 1966–1969 period. At the same time, prices started to rise. Inflation seemed to be getting out of hand. In an effort to "cool down" the economy, President Johnson proposed and got a *tax surcharge*—a tax on a tax. Tax liabilities increased by 10 percent because of the surcharge.

While policymakers were delighted with the apparent success of the 1964 tax cut in helping expand the economy, they could not take similar delight in the effect of the 1968 surcharge. Inflation did not slow down one bit; in fact, it increased. Many argue that the Johnson surcharge came too late, since the economy started "overheating" around 1965 or 1966.

Fiscal Policy in the 1970s

Fiscal policy actions during the 1970s were not as dramatic as some of the tax changes of the 1960s. Nonetheless, there were a number of minor fiscal policy actions after the Johnson 1968 tax surcharge.

In March of 1975, a series of tax reductions and rebates was put into effect. A large percentage of the taxpaying population was paid a $100–$200 rebate on 1974 taxes. There was an individual tax credit of $30 per person instituted in 1975. Additionally, there was an extension of the investment tax credit with some minor changes.

The period 1974–1975 was considered by many to be the worst

244

recession of the post–World War II period. For this reason, fiscal policy was structured to be highly stimulative for those years. By the spring of 1975, this recession had bottomed out, and President Gerald Ford was concerned with making a gradual and long-lasting economic recovery. Moreover, he was determined that this recovery would be fueled by advances in the private sector—not by expansion of the public sector. Thus, Ford's fiscal proposals during 1975–1976 stressed (1) fiscal stimulus via tax cuts, not government expenditure increases, (2) permanent tax cuts, and (3) a balance between increased consumer spending and increased business investment.

In 1977, Jimmy Carter became president, and with the new president came a new direction for fiscal policy. The Carter administration wanted to cure the unemployment problem through such devices as employment tax credits to employers, job training programs, and expenditures for public service employment.

During 1978, the focus of fiscal policy shifted; unemployment fell faster and inflationary rates increased faster than had been anticipated. As a consequence, fiscal policy moved toward "restraint" —defined as continuing fiscal stimulus but gradually reducing its *rate* of growth. Thus, the president decided to revise his tax reduction program, scaling down the amount from $25 billion to $20 billion, and then postponing the effective date until January 1979.

By 1979, fiscal policy had again shifted as inflation became the number one concern. Fiscal policy was now aimed at restraining aggregate demand (monetary policy and price–wage guidelines were to help). The federal budget deficit dropped from over $48 billion in 1978 to $27.8 billion in 1979. Inflation did not abate; the CPI increased by 6.4 percent in 1976, 7.1 percent in 1977, 7.65 percent in 1978, and 11.2 percent in 1979.

Fiscal Policy in the 1980s

In 1980, the rate of inflation was about 12 percent, and the federal budget deficit was almost $60 billion—more than $20 billion higher than anticipated. People were beginning to wonder if the federal budget was running out of control. President Ronald Reagan promised to give new direction to fiscal policy during his tenure in office. Reagan vowed to reduce permanently and significantly taxes and government expenditures. His aim was to generate economic expansion and reduce inflation by a tremendous growth in the private sector.

In 1982, the rate of inflation was falling; indeed, during the spring, the CPI actually fell for the first time since 1966. Unemployment, however, was rising, hitting 10 percent. The size of the budget deficit was getting larger and larger, and there was a great deal of pressure on the Reagan administration to increase taxes, after having gotten the largest tax cut ever passed, in 1981.

In August 1982, this pressure resulted in a tax increase—new or increased taxes on cigarettes, phone calls, and travel, along with a new tax structure for capital gains and interest income.

Reagan boldly announced a program he called the New Federalism. His plan was to have the states take over a larger share of the federal government's transfer program, including health care, welfare, and food stamps. He proposed that a temporary trust fund be set up to help the states pay for these added responsibilities. The fund was to be phased out between 1987 and 1999. At that time, the states were to decide themselves whether they wanted to continue each of the transfer programs. If not, the programs would be eliminated. Reagan's goal under the New Federalism was to limit the federal government's concerns to national security, health care for the poor, programs for farmers and the elderly (including Social Security), and fiscal stabilization policies. He hoped to achieve this by 1991. One major complaint by critics of the New Federalism was that it would eliminate a major set of automatic stabilizers. After all, if the states eventually phased out welfare, food stamps, and the like, then aggregate demand would not be cushioned in the face of falling income during recessions.

The Public Debt Is Too Large and It Is a Burden on Future Generations

THE ARGUMENT

Recently, the government has been running relatively large deficits, thereby adding to the size of the public debt. Concerned policymakers and laypersons alike question the advisability of carrying such a large debt. They talk about a burden of the public debt and argue that the federal government could go bankrupt and that future generations will have to pay for current activities.

THE ANALYSIS

Opponents of a large public debt point out that if firms always ran in the red—just as government spends more than it receives—those firms would eventually go out of business; they would go bankrupt. But the analogy between firms and the government is not valid. The government will go bankrupt only when it loses its ability to raise taxes. Interest on the public debt will always be paid as long as the government has revenue-raising powers. Moreover, the public debt never has to be paid off. It can be, and indeed is, refinanced as it comes due. Every month, some of the debt reaches maturity; it is then "rolled over," as they say in the financial trade. For example, if a $1 million Treasury bond came due tomorrow, the U.S. Treasury would simply pay it off by reissuing another $1 million bond.

Making Future Generations Pay

Did future generations pay for World War II? Not really. The resources used to fight World War II were taken away from that popu-lation. Recall the production possibilities curve from Chapter 1. There is a trade-off between civilian goods and military goods. During World War II, this nation used a relatively large share of its resources to make military goods. The people at that time had to give up consumption and private investment.

The same argument holds today. If the federal government runs a deficit of $100 billion and finances it by increasing the public debt by the same amount, future generations will not be paying for the government resources used today. After all, if the government commands, say, $900 billion worth of current resources, it doesn't matter that part of government spending was financed by the issuance of debt. The production possibilities curve between private goods and government goods will always show a trade-off during any given year.

Interest must also be paid on increases in the public debt. How are higher interest payments paid for by government? By in-

247

creased taxes. But that is not in itself a burden, because the taxes are paid by some Americans and the interest is received by others. In principle, this is merely a re-distribution, not a burden on *all* of society.

Possible Real Burdens of the Debt

So far we have been dealing with internal public debt. But if part of the debt is held by foreigners, the nation no longer owes all the debt to itself. (Foreigners now own about 20 percent of the net public debt.) Increased taxes will again be used to pay the interest on the public debt; but now a portion of this interest will leave the country. Nonetheless, this still may not constitute a burden on future generations.

Assume that the U.S. is straining pro-ductive capacity and can get no more output from available resources. However, if it borrows resources abroad by selling public debt to foreigners, it can increase available resources. Future generations must pay foreigners the interest that allows for this increased use of resources today. If, however, the government takes some of those bor-rowed resources and uses them to invest in buildings, dams, and electric plants, future generations may still be better off. They will be assessed higher taxes to pay the in-terest on this externally owned public debt, but they will also be receiving the benefits of more buildings, dams, and electric plants.

DISCUSSION QUESTIONS

1. In recent years, a greater percentage of the U.S. public debt has been financed by borrowing from foreigners. Do foreign-held claims on the public debt place a burden on future generations? Why or why not?
2. The federal government seems to be in debt all the time. Do private business firms constantly stay in debt also?

● WHAT'S AHEAD

So far, we have dealt with the government's use of fiscal policy to stabilize aggregate economic activity. In the next chapter, we turn to money and the banking system to prepare for an examination of monetary policy.

● CHAPTER SUMMARY

When the government attempts to change aggregate demand by altering expenditures or taxes, it is engaging in fiscal policy. In principle, changes in government expenditures and changes in taxes lead to a multiple change in the equilibrium level of national income. In other words, if government spending increases by $10 billion, the equilibrium level of national income may increase by $20 or $30 billion.

Fiscal policy can be used to fight recessions through increased government expenditures and decreased taxes. Fiscal policy can be used to fight inflation through decreased government expenditures and increased taxes. During recessions, expansionary fiscal policy may bring about a federal budget deficit. During inflations, contractionary fiscal policy may bring about a federal budget surplus.

The national, or public, debt is the sum of past budget deficits that have not yet been repaid. Part of the public debt is owned by the government itself and therefore is not important. The remaining $800 billion or so is, however, significant.

Automatic stabilizers involve expenditure and tax changes that occur automatically when there are changes in overall business activity. Some automatic stabilizers include the progressive income tax system and unemployment compensation benefits.

● QUESTIONS FOR REVIEW AND STUDY

1. Whenever the government deliberately alters aggregate demand by changing taxes or expenditures, it is engaging in _____ _____ policy.

2. An increase in government expenditures leads to a(n) _____ in aggregate demand.

3. An increase in government expenditures leads to a _____ increase in national income and output.

4. Because of the _____ effect, a $1 change in aggregate demand will cause the level of national income to change by _____ than $1.

5. A $1 decrease in government expenditures will lead to a _____ _____ $1 _____ in national income.

6. Changes in federal personal income taxes will lead to a more-than-proportional change in national income; therefore, we say that there exists a tax _____.

7. During periods of inflation, federal fiscal policy includes _____ in income taxes.

8. If the government starts out with a balanced budget, an increase in income taxes will lead to a budget _____.

9. The federal government might fight a recession by _____ taxes; this could lead to a federal budget _____.

10. Federal government budget deficits lead to increases in the _____ _____.

11. When there is a recession, unemployment compensation benefits increase without an act of Congress. This is just one example of an _____ _____.

12. If the U.S. did not have a _____ personal income tax system, then taxes would not automatically fall during a recession and rise during a boom time.

ANSWERS

1. discretionary fiscal   2. increase   3. multiple   4. multiplier; more   5. more than; decrease   6. multiplier   7. increases   8. surplus   9. decreasing; deficit   10. national debt   11. automatic stabilizer   12. progressive

● ANSWERS TO CHAPTER PREVIEW QUESTIONS

1. *How can the federal government's fiscal policy—the way government spending and taxes are determined—affect you personally?*

The federal government's fiscal policy consists of changes in taxes and changes in government expenditures. Both of these changes can affect you personally.

In the first place, an increase or decrease in federal personal income taxes will affect your take-home pay if you are working. Moreover, if the tax change is temporary, it will affect you differently than if it is permanent. You will react more strongly to a permanent change than to a temporary change.

Direct government spending can also affect you personally. You may be the recipient of a government contract to produce a good or perform a particular service. Or perhaps you are learning a skill in a federally sponsored job training program.

In short, federal government fiscal policy can affect you in many ways.

2. *What is automatic fiscal policy and how does it help stabilize an economy?*

With discretionary fiscal policy, government spending and taxing policies are deliberately applied to stabilize an economy. Automatic fiscal policy, on the other hand, does not require deliberate policy and congressional legislation; automatic fiscal policy results from changes in national income. Thus, a progressive tax structure and an unemployment compensation system (which are already in force) automatically change taxes and government outlays as national income changes. As national income falls in a recession, government outlays for unemployment automatically increase and tax revenues fall as lower incomes push people into lower marginal tax brackets. These automatic stabilizers counteract a declining national income. Similarly, in an inflationary period, tax revenues automatically rise (as people are forced into higher marginal tax brackets), and unemployment compensation outlays fall. Thus, the inflation is automatically counteracted by higher tax revenues and decreased government outlays. Since income increases or decreases are automatically countered (somewhat) by a progressive tax system and an unemployment compensation program, we say that automatic fiscal policy lends stability to the U.S. economy.

● PROBLEMS

1. Assume that all individuals save 100 percent of any extra income they receive. In other words, they do not spend any part of any extra dollars in income due to an increase in government expenditures.

    a. How big do you think the multiplier will be?

    b. What will happen to the multiplier as people spend a larger and larger percentage of any extra dollar generated by government expenditures?

2. What is the multiplier effect? How does it work, and what is the main determinant of the multiplier?

● SELECTED REFERENCES

Carson, Robert B. *Macroeconomic Issues Today: Alternative Approaches*. New York: St. Martin's Press, 1980.

Heller, Walter W. *New Dimensions of Political Economy*. New York: Norton, 1967.

Lerner, Abba P. "The Burden of the National Debt." In *Public Debt and Future Generations*. Edited by James M. Ferguson. Chapel Hill: The University of North Carolina Press, 1964, pp. 16–19.

Stein, Herbert. *The Fiscal Revolution in America*. Chicago: University of Chicago Press, 1969.

APPENDIX TO CHAPTER 12
The Multiplier Effect

For a more detailed understanding of the multiplier effect, you must first learn some terminology. In the chapter, we talked about people spending only part of their additional income and saving the rest. The degree to which a family spends additional income is called the *marginal propensity to consume*, or MPC. The term *marginal* means small change in, or incremental, or decremental. The degree to which a family saves additional income is called the *marginal propensity to save*, or MPS.

The marginal propensity to consume, then, is defined as

$$\text{MPC} \equiv \frac{\text{change in planned consumption}}{\text{change in disposable income}}$$

The marginal propensity to save is similarly defined:

$$\text{MPS} \equiv \frac{\text{change in planned saving}}{\text{change in disposable income}}$$

The MPC and MPS tell us the percentage of an increase or decrease in income that will be spent or saved. The emphasis here is on the word *change*. The marginal propensity to consume indicates how you will change your planned rate of consumption if there is a change in your disposable income. If your marginal propensity to consume is 0.8, that does not mean that you will consume 80 percent of *all* disposable income. An MPC of 0.8 means that you will consume 80 percent of any *increase* in your disposable income.

● THE MULTIPLIER PROCESS

The multiplier process involves the amount by which national income changes when there is a change in government spending or taxation. The multiplier is the number by which a change in government spending is multiplied to obtain the change in equilibrium national income. Let's take a simple numerical example, where the marginal propensity to consume (MPC) is equal to 0.8, or 4/5. The marginal propensity to save (MPS) must therefore be 0.2, or 1/5, since whatever percentage (out of 100%) is not consumed must be saved.

Now let's say that the government decides to *increase* expenditures by $100 billion a year. We see in Table 12–1 that during the first round, government expenditures increase by $100 billion; this also means an increase in income of $100 billion, because spending by one group represents income for another. Column 3 gives the resultant increase in consumption by households that receive this additional $100 billion in income. This is found by multiplying the MPC by the increase in income. Since the MPC equals 0.8, during the first round consumption expenditures increase by $80 billion.

But that's not the end of the story. This additional $80 billion increase in household consumption will provide $80 billion of additional income for still other individuals. Thus, during the second round, we see an increase in income of $80 billion. Now, out of this increased income, what will be the resultant increase in consumption expenditures? It will be 0.8 times $80 billion, or $64 billion. We can continue these rounds of induced expenditure indefinitely. And if we do, we will find that because of an initial increase in government expenditures of $100 billion, the equilibrium level of national income will increase by $500 billion. A $100 billion increase in government spending will induce an additional $400 billion increase in consumption spending, for a total increase in GNP of $500 billion. In other words, the equilibrium level of national income will change by an amount equal to 5 times the change in government spending.

TABLE 12–1

The Multiplier Effect of a $100 Billion per Year Increase in G

We trace the effects of a $100 billion increase in government spending on the level of national income. If we assume a marginal propensity to consume (MPC) of 0.8, then such an increase will eventually elicit a $500 billion total increase in the equilibrium level of national income.

	ASSUMPTION: MPC = 0.8 OR 4/5		
Round	Increase in Income (billions of dollars per year)	Increase in Planned Consumption (billions of dollars per year)	Increase in Planned Saving (billions of dollars per year)
1 ($100 billion per year increase in G)	100	80	20
2	80	64	16
3	64	51.2	12.8
4	51.2	40.96	10.24
5	40.96	32.768	8.192
.	.	.	.
.	.	.	.
All later rounds	163.84	131.072	32.768
Totals	500	400	100

● THE MULTIPLIER FORMULA

It turns out that the multiplier is equal to the reciprocal of the marginal propensity to save. In our example, the MPC was 4/5; and since MPC + MPS = 1, the MPS was 1/5. The reciprocal of 1/5 is 5— the same number as the multiplier. Thus, we can find the multiplier in our simple example by the following formula:

$$\text{Multiplier} \equiv \frac{1}{\text{MPS}} \equiv \frac{1}{1 - \text{MPC}}.$$

We can always figure out the multiplier if we know either the MPC or the MPS. For example, if MPS = 1/4, then we simply substitute 1/4 in the formula to get

$$\text{Multiplier} \equiv \frac{1}{1/4} = 4.$$

And if we are given the MPC instead of the MPS, we can still use the formula. For the example above, MPC $\doteq$ 3/4. Substitute 3/4 in the formula, we get

$$\text{Multiplier} \equiv \frac{1}{1 - (3/4)} = \frac{1}{1/4} = 4,$$

the same answer as before.

By working out a few numerical examples, you will soon discover an important property of the multiplier. That property is:

The smaller the marginal propensity to save,
the larger the multiplier.

Otherwise stated:

The greater the marginal propensity to consume,
the larger the multiplier.

Prove this to yourself by computing the multiplier for MPS = 3/4, MPS = 1/2, and MPS = 1/8. What happens to the multiplier as the MPS gets smaller?

● THE TAXATION MULTIPLIER

What we have just described is the government expenditure multiplier. There is also a taxation multiplier that is somewhat different. An increase in taxes leads to a reduction in equilibrium national income, and a decrease in taxes leads to an increase in equilibrium national income. Thus, we know that the taxation multiplier is opposite in sign from the government spending multiplier; but we also can determine that it is smaller in size. We just found that a

254

government spending multiplier is 5 if the marginal propensity to consume is 0.8 and the marginal propensity to save is 0.2. Given the same marginal propensity to consume, the taxation multiplier turns out to be negative 4. What accounts for this difference?

Let's compare a $100 billion increase in government spending with a $100 billion decrease in taxes. Intuitively we can understand why the difference occurs by looking at the first-round effect of the change. An increase in government spending of $100 billion adds a full $100 billion of additional income to the circular flow of income and product. Remembering our discussion of the multiplier, we know that this is just the first round of a long series of increases in income, because part of that $100 billion is saved and the rest is spent, thus starting the second round of increases in income, which then starts the third round, and so on. But what about a $100 billion decrease in taxes? The decrease in taxes translates into $100 billion of additional disposable income for households to spend. But now look at the first round in the series of increases in equilibrium income. In our previous example of an increase in government spending, the first round started with the full $100 billion. An increase in disposable income due to a tax cut, however, finds first-round spending just equal to some fraction of the $100 billion in tax cuts. That fraction, of course, is the marginal propensity to consume. In our example, MPC = 0.8, so the first round starts out with only $80 billion of spending. Herein lies the difference between the government multiplier and the taxation multiplier. The first round of spending is smaller for a $100 billion tax reduction than it is for a $100 billion increase in government spending.

Another way of looking at the difference between the government multiplier and the taxation multiplier is that during first-round spending due to a tax cut, there is a *leakage* into saving. No such leakage occurs with an increase in government spending. In other words, because some increased disposable income will be allocated to saving in the case of a tax cut, expenditures will *initially* increase by the MPC times the decrease in taxes (0.8 × $100 billion = $80 billion) and not by the full amount of the tax cut ($100 billion). Alternatively, because some taxes will be paid out of saving in the case of a tax increase, expenditures will *initially* drop by the MPC times the increase in taxes (0.8 × $100 billion = $80 billion) and not by the full amount of the tax increase ($100 billion).

To get the taxation multiplier, we must correct the standard formula for the leakage into saving. As indicated above, the correction factor is equal to the marginal propensity to consume. The taxation multiplier is equal to the negative of the marginal propensity to consume times the government spending multiplier. That is, the taxation multiplier equals the negative of the MPC × (1 ÷ MPS). In our example, the government spending multiplier is 5, since MPC = 0.8 and MPS = 0.2, or 1/5. If we multiply (negative) 5 times an MPC of 0.8, we get a taxation multiplier of (negative) 4. Notice that the taxation multiplier is always negative. In other words, an *increase* in taxes leads to a *decrease* in the equilibrium level of national income, and a *decrease* in taxes leads to an *increase* in the equilibrium level of national income. In the formulas below, we show the negative sign to indicate this inverse relationship between tax changes and changes in the equilibrium level of national income. We label the government spending multiplier M_g and the taxation multiplier M_t. The formulas are

$$M_g = \frac{1}{MPS}$$

and

$$M_t = -MPC \times \frac{1}{MPS}$$

13

Money and Our Banking System

Chapter Preview
1. Take a dollar bill and look at it. What "backs" that United States dollar?
2. Our banking system involves only fractional reserves. What are the characteristics of this fractional reserve banking system?

● KEY TERMS

Asset	Fiduciary monetary standard
Barter	Float
Central bank	Fractional reserve banking system
Commercial bank	Liquidity
Electronic funds transfer system	Required reserves
Excess reserves	

Money. All your life, you have heard about money; some people seem to talk about little else. People work for it, fight for it, and a few even kill for it. In this chapter, we will look at money per se. At some time in our lives, all of us make money *income*. Only the banking system and counterfeiters make money.

● WHAT IS MONEY?

Over the years, many things have been used as money. Gold and silver come to mind first. But wampum, cows, salt, and even boulders, which were eventually covered by the sea, have also been used as money. So have diamonds, cigarettes, and pearls. We can define money by its functions, that is, by the duties it performs. Money is anything that is generally accepted as

1. A medium of exchange
2. A unit of accounting
3. A store of value

A Medium of Exchange

The most important function of money has always been its ability to serve as a medium of exchange. That is, buyers can use it as payment in making transactions, and sellers will readily accept it. Thus, consumers purchase goods and services with money; sellers exchange their goods and services *for* money. Similarly, sellers of labor or of other productive services will accept money in exchange for their resources.

Consider a world without money as a medium of exchange. In such a world, individuals would have to engage in **barter**, which is the exchange of goods and services for other goods and services without the use of a medium of exchange. That is, to acquire bread and butter, you would have to offer either your own productive services or some other goods that you own in exchange for bread and butter. In barter situations, individuals trade labor, land use, and natural resources for goods and services.

Barter

The exchange of goods and productive services for other goods and productive services, without the use of money.

258

Considering how difficult it would be for anyone to be totally self-sufficient, barter is preferable to no exchange at all. Nonetheless, trade is greatly hindered under a barter system because of the improbability of wants being simultaneously in accord with each other. For example, what is the probability that a fisherman who wants bread and butter will find bakers and dairy suppliers who also want fish that same day? And what is the probability that salt producers who want shoes will find shoemakers who want salt at the very same time? Thus, barter is a difficult method of exchange because of the difficulty of finding a double coincidence of wants. Also, if you take payment in goods rather than money, you may have to hold inventories of those goods until you find a trading partner. Maintaining inventories can be costly, particularly if the goods are perishable.

Finally, under a system of barter, people usually do not specialize in one productive activity. For example, an individual may have a comparative advantage in producing a particular good whose demand is spread out over a large geographic area. But in spite of that comparative advantage, the individual may decide not to specialize because of the physical difficulty in exchanging his or her output with other people. Thus, changing from a barter system to a money economy greatly increases specialization and economic development.

Since the benefits of using money for exchange are so great, it is not surprising that societies throughout the ages eventually abandoned barter for a system that used various "things" as money.

A Unit of Accounting

Money enables individuals to compare the relative value of goods and services. Prices for goods and services can easily be expressed in the form of money. That is, instead of valuing, or pricing, a loaf of bread in terms of pounds of salt, people can value, or price, it in terms of money. Valuing everything with respect to a unit of accounting greatly simplifies price comparisons. Consider an economy with only 1000 goods. Each good can be expressed in terms of units of the other 999 goods. Keep in mind, though, that this applies each time we look at a separate good. It turns out that relative price comparisons number almost 500,000 for a 1000-good economy. The same information, however, can be derived from 1000 money prices if that economy uses some type of money as a unit of accounting. Using money as a unit of accounting greatly reduces the number of prices that must be listed, and no information is lost. Therefore, another benefit of a money economy is that less time is needed to find out information about relative values.

Note that in earlier chapters, final goods and services were valued at market value. Money was used implicitly as a unit of accounting to value national income. In effect, final goods and services were weighted by their relative money prices.

Money as a Store of Value

Consider the following situation. A fisherman comes into port after two days of fishing. At the going price of fish that day, he has $1000 worth of fish on board his boat. But those fish are not a very good store of their own value. If the fisherman keeps them on board for any length of time (assuming he has no refrigeration system), they will probably rot. If he attempts to barter them with other tradespeople, at least some of the fish may rot before he has time to barter the entire catch. On the other hand, if he sells the entire catch for money, he is storing the value of his catch in the money that he receives.

Money is an **asset**—something of value—that accounts for part of one's wealth. Wealth in the form of money can be exchanged later for some other asset. Although money is not the only form of wealth that can be exchanged for goods and services, it is the one most widely accepted. This additional attribute of money is called **liquidity**. We say that an asset is liquid when it can be easily acquired or disposed of without high costs and with relative certainty as to its value. Money is, by definition, the most liquid asset there is. Just compare it with a share of stock listed on the New York Stock Exchange. To buy or sell that stock, you must first call a stockbroker, who will place the buy or sell order for you. Of course, this must be done during normal business hours. Also you will have to pay a percentage commission to the broker. Moreover, when you sell the stock, there is a distinct possibility that you will get more or less for it than you originally paid. This is not the case with money. You can easily convert money to other asset forms—and without paying a commission. Therefore, most individuals hold at least a part of their wealth in the form of this most liquid of assets—money.

Asset

Something that has value and is owned. In other words, it is something to which a bank, business, or household holds legal claim.

Liquidity

The degree to which an asset can be acquired or disposed of without danger of intervening loss in nominal value. Money is the most liquid asset, by definition. A liquid asset can be used easily as a means of payment without risk of gain or loss in nominal value.

● THE COST OF HOLDING MONEY

Although money serves a number of important functions, it is a non-interest-earning form of wealth. In other words, you are not paid an interest rate for holding dollar bills. If you took those dollar bills and invested them, however, you could earn an interest rate. So why do people hold money? People continue to hold money because of the convenience of being able to make transactions easily and because of the security money provides for future emergencies. Thus, even though there is an *opportunity cost* of holding money (e.g., the foregone interest that could have been earned by putting it in a savings and loan account), people normally regard this opportunity cost as a worthwhile expenditure.

Note that we have talked about the cost of *holding* money. The cost of money itself is not the interest rate that could have been earned had the money been put into a savings and loan account, for example. Rather, the cost of money is its *opportunity cost*. That is, the cost of money is what you have to give up to own money. What does it cost you to keep a $10 bill? It costs you whatever you could have bought with that $10, such as a book or record album. The purchase price, as it were, of money is the goods and services given up to obtain it. In other words, the price of money is its purchasing power.

● THE DISTINCTION BETWEEN MONEY AND CREDIT

It is important to understand the distinction between money and credit. Money is merely the most liquid asset in which people choose to hold part of their wealth. Credit, on the other hand, is funds or savings that are made available to borrowers. In other words, the credit market is basically a market where those who are willing to wait to have purchasing power provide funds at a cost (the interest rate) to those who want to have purchasing power now.

To further understand the distinction between money and credit, consider a barter society in which no money exists. Nonetheless, credit can still exist. In such an economy, a man might lend you his lawn mower for a year. In return, you might promise to give him back the lawn mower at the end of one year, plus 5 bushels of tomatoes that you will have grown, as payment for the credit he is extending to you. Does credit here depend on the amount of money in society? No, for in a barter society, no money exists.

● DEFINING THE MONEY SUPPLY

Although we have referred to money often in this and previous chapters, we haven't actually defined it. The definition of money is somewhat elusive. If we define money simply as those items used as a medium of exchange, our definition of the U.S. money supply will take on one particular meaning; if we define money as a store of wealth, our definition of the U.S. money supply will mean something else entirely. Let's first look at the narrowest definition of the money supply, used by the banking authorities in the United States until 1982.

The Narrowest Definition of the Money Supply

By the narrowest definition, the money supply consists of the value of coins, paper currency, and checking accounts owned by the nonbanking public.

Currency.   Currency refers to the value of coins and paper bills outstanding, not held by banks. Although it is what most people *think of* as "money," currency is really only one component of the total money supply in the United States. Today, currency consists mainly of paper bills with denominations of $1, $5, $10, $20, $50, and $100. At various times, $2 bills have circulated widely, as have higher-denomination bills—all the way up to $10,000. Our coins consist of 1-cent, 5-cent, 25-cent, 50-cent, and $1 pieces. All of the circulating coins today are made with metals whose market values are less than the face values of the coins. Older coins whose face values are less than the market values of the metals in the coins usually do not circulate. Rather, they are kept by owners as an asset for sale later on. For example, older dimes containing silver must be purchased from coin dealers. You will rarely find one given to you as change.

Checking Account Balances.   Since money is partly defined as a medium of exchange, checking account balances certainly belong in the official definition of the money supply. Checking account balances are also called *demand deposits* because the deposits can be transferred or converted to currency on demand. Note that it is the account *balance* that is considered part of the money supply, and not the checks themselves.

Until 1981, only certain types of financial institutions were allowed to issue demand deposits. These were called **commercial banks**, and their special attribute was their ability to offer demand deposits. Consequently, the narrowest definition of the money supply until 1981 was simply currency plus demand deposits held in commercial banks. Times have changed, however, and that definition no longer applies, since a variety of financial institutions now offer checking accounts.

Commercial bank

A private, profit-seeking institution that was, until recently, the only financial institution that could accept demand deposits against which checks could be written. Today, many other financial institutions are legally allowed to offer checking accounts.

An Enlarged Definition of the Money Supply

If you can open an account in a savings and loan association or a mutual savings bank or a credit union and write checks against that account, shouldn't your account balance be included as part of the money supply? The answer is yes. Consequently, the official definition of the money supply now includes all checking accounts at so-called thrift institutions, such as credit unions, savings and loan associations, and mutual savings banks. Savings and loan associations and mutual savings banks offer what are called NOW accounts, or negotiable orders of withdrawal. Credit unions offer credit union share draft accounts. The various names of these accounts have little meaning in and of themselves because, in effect, they are all checking accounts now. The reason thrift institutions didn't offer checking accounts in the past was a legal one. Until the passage of the Depository Institutions Deregulation and Monetary Control Act of 1980, only commercial banks were allowed to offer checking accounts. Actually, prior to 1980, a few mutual savings banks in the Northeast were offering NOW accounts. Effective 1981, the Monetary Control Act of 1980 (as it is normally called) authorized the majority of thrift institutions to offer checking accounts. Additionally, that act authorized commercial banks to offer interest on checking accounts. As a result of the Monetary Control Act of 1980, the difference between commercial banks and thrift institutions will be virtually indistinguishable in the future.

Recognizing the similarity among checking accounts in all depository institutions, the official definition of the money supply now includes account balances in both thrift and commercial banks. This money supply is labeled M1. In the United States it is the sum of the value of all currency and checking account balances held by the non-banking public.

Still Broader Definitions of the Money Supply

Broader definitions of the money supply include additional forms of wealth that can easily be converted into a means of payment. For example, money market mutual funds often allow check-writing privileges if the check is larger than $500 or $1000. A money market mutual fund is an investment company that takes investors' dollars and reinvests them in money market securities, such as U.S. Treasury bills (T-bills) and debt issued by corporations. Thus, broader definitions of the U.S. money supply include account balances in money market mutual funds.

● WHAT BACKS THE U.S. DOLLAR?

Students are often surprised to learn that the U.S. dollar is not backed by anything. That is, if you look at a dollar bill, you will find nothing on it to indicate that it is exchangeable for some specific amount of gold or silver or any other commodity. Rather, the U.S. economy has a **fiduciary monetary standard**. In essence, then, the

Fiduciary monetary standard

A monetary standard in which the value of the currency rests upon the public's confidence that the currency can be exchanged for goods and services. The word *fiduciary* comes from the Latin *fiducia*, which means "trust" or "confidence."

U.S. dollar is backed only by faith. In other words, when people use dollar bills in their transactions, they indicate the following:

1. That they have faith in the U.S. government.
2. That they believe the government won't print so much money that the dollar will become worthless.
3. That they have *confidence* that the dollar can be exchanged for goods and services.

Of course, this faith is not without limits. Should people's confidence in the dollar fall, and should people fear that dollars will not be accepted as a medium of exchange, then something else will replace the dollar as money. However, this is not likely to happen in the near future in the United States. Although we have experienced inflation in recent years, it has not been so erratic and so tremendous that we have been unable to predict reasonably the purchasing power, or value, of dollars in the future. The U.S. inflation rate may seem high, but compared with many other countries, it is mild. Besides, people are quite reluctant to stop using a country's *fiat* currency (paper bills and coins whose intrinsic value is less than the face value). Even in countries with very high inflation rates, people still use paper currency and coins to make transactions. Clearly, alternatives to using currency are not very appealing. The return to a barter system, for example, would be both costly and inefficient.

● THE U.S. BANKING SYSTEM

The U.S. banking system consists of numerous financial institutions and a monetary authority. The financial institutions consist of commercial banks, savings and loan associations, credit unions, and mutual savings banks.

Commercial Banks and Other Financial Institutions

A commercial bank is a privately owned, profit-seeking institution that accepts demand deposits against which checks may be drawn. Savings and loan associations, credit unions, and mutual savings banks are implicitly profit-seeking, privately owned financial institutions that, as of 1981, are able to accept a form of demand deposits. All of these financial institutions are regulated in one way or another by various state and federal banking regulatory agencies. Regulations are numerous and dictate how much readily available cash must be held in reserve, what assets the financial institution can buy, what types of loans it can make, and so on.

264

Our Monetary Authority— The Central Bank

At the head of the entire U.S. banking system is a **central bank**, an official banking institution that regulates the banking system and serves as a banker's bank. The central bank typically holds deposits of other banks and financial institutions and normally regulates and controls the supply of money in circulation. Our central bank is called the Federal Reserve.

● THE FEDERAL RESERVE SYSTEM

Our central bank was established by the Federal Reserve Act, signed on December 23, 1913, by President Woodrow Wilson. The act was the outgrowth of recommendations from the National Monetary Commission, which had been authorized by the Aldridge–Vreeland Act of 1908. Basically, this commission was trying to find a way to counter the periodic financial panics that had occurred in the United States. The Federal Reserve System (also known as the Fed) was set up to aid and supervise banks and also to provide banking services for the U.S. Treasury.

Organization of the Federal Reserve System

Exhibit 13–1 shows the Federal Reserve organization chart. There is a Board of Governors, composed of seven salaried, full-time members appointed by the president with the approval of the Senate. There are 12 Federal Reserve District Banks, which have a total of 25 branches. In addition, there is the very important Federal Open Market Committee (FOMC), which determines monetary policy for the Fed. This committee is composed of the Board of Governors plus five Federal Reserve bank representatives who are rotated periodically (with the exception of the president of the New York Fed, who is always a member). The FOMC determines the future growth of the money supply and other important variables.

Depository Institutions

The banks and other depository institutions that make up our monetary system consist of approximately 15,000 commercial banks, 4700 savings and loan associations, 23,000 credit unions, and 463 mutual savings banks. Formerly, there was a distinction between member and nonmember commercial banks. Commercial banks that were members of the Federal Reserve System enjoyed certain benefits not allowed nonmember banks; these member banks had to pay

Central bank

A banker's bank, usually controlled and operated by the government.

EXHIBIT 13–1

The Federal Reserve System

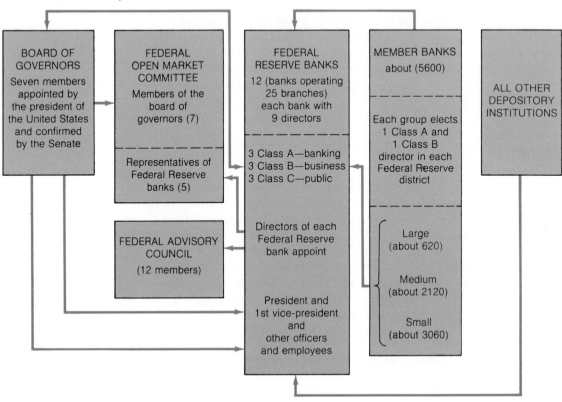

Source: Board of Governors of the Federal Reserve System.

a price to be part of the Federal Reserve System, however. The Monetary Control Act of 1980 has changed that distinction. By around 1986, all depository institutions, including member and nonmember commercial banks, as well as savings and loans, credit unions, and mutual savings banks, will be able to purchase services from the Federal Reserve System on an equal basis. Also, all depository institutions will be required to keep a certain percentage of their deposits on reserve with the Federal Reserve District Banks.

The Functions of the Federal Reserve System

The Federal Reserve System performs many functions in the economy. Some important ones are described below.

The Fed Supplies the Economy with Fiduciary Currency.   The Federal Reserve District Banks supply the economy with paper currency called Federal Reserve Notes. These Notes are printed at the Bureau of Printing and Engraving in Washington and then shipped to the 12 District Banks. Each Note is assigned a code indicating from which of the 12 Federal Reserve District Banks it "originated."

The Fed Provides a System of Check Collection and Clearing.   The Federal Reserve System establishes a mechanism for the clearing of checks. Exhibit 13–2 demonstrates how a check clears. Consider an example. Suppose that John Smith, who lives in Chicago, writes a check to Jill Jones, who lives in San Francisco. When Jill Jones re-

EXHIBIT 13–2
How a Check Clears

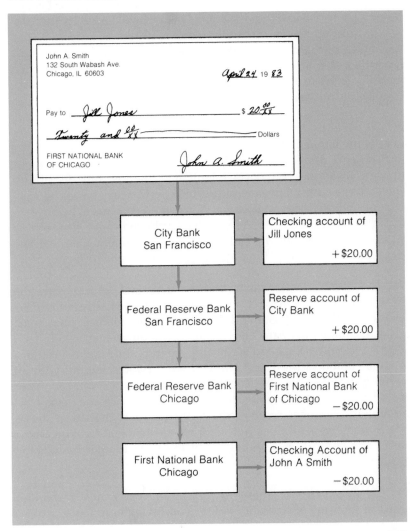

ceives the check in the mail, she deposits it at her commercial bank. Her bank then deposits the check in the Federal Reserve Bank of San Francisco. In turn, the Federal Reserve Bank of San Francisco sends the check to the Federal Reserve Bank of Chicago. The Chicago Fed then sends the check to Smith's commercial bank. There the amount of the check is deducted from John Smith's account. All member banks and depository institutions in a particular Federal Reserve district can send deposited checks to one location—their district Fed—thereby reducing the cost of check clearing. (The Fed's check collection and clearing operations compete with private clearinghouses. Since the Fed will now be charging for these services, we can expect to see a shift of some of this business back to the private sector.)

The Fed Holds Depository Institutions' Reserves.   The 12 Federal Reserve District Banks hold the reserves of depository institutions. By law, all depository institutions are required to keep a certain percentage of their deposits in reserves. For example, a bank with deposits of over $25 million must keep 12 percent of all of its demand deposits in the form of reserves held in its district Federal Reserve Bank or in vault cash.

The Fed Acts as the Government's Fiscal Agent.   The Federal Reserve is the banker and fiscal agent for the federal government. The government, as we are all aware, collects large sums of money through taxation. The government also spends and distributes equally large sums. Consequently, the U.S. Treasury has a checking account with the Federal Reserve. Thus, the Fed acts as the government's banker, along with commercial banks that hold government deposits. Additionally, the Fed helps the government collect certain tax revenues and aids in the purchase and sale of government bonds.

The Fed Supervises Member Banks.   The Fed (along with the Comptroller of the Currency and the Federal Deposit Insurance Corporation) is the supervisor and the regulator of member commercial banks. (Nonmember banks are regulated by other agencies. In fact, there is virtually no unregulated bank, savings and loan association, or credit union in the U.S.) The Fed will periodically and without warning examine member commercial banks to see what kinds of loans have been made, what has been used to back the loans (collateral), and who has received them. If such an examination shows that a member bank does not comply with current banking standards, the Fed can exert pressure on the bank to alter its banking practices.

The Fed Regulates the Money Supply.   The Fed's most important function in terms of its ability to influence overall economic activity is its regulation of the money supply. The Federal Reserve System regulates the money supply through a variety of methods, all of which will be explained in Chapter 14.

The Fed is an Independent Agency

The Federal Reserve System is an independent agency. That is, it is not subject to presidential or congressional controls. The Fed was designed as an independent agency so that it would not be hampered by political pressures from the executive and legislative branches. For example, prior to an election, there might be strong political pressure on the Fed to engage in expansionary monetary policy to pump up the economy. This would create in voters' minds a more favorable impression of the incumbent at election time and aid in his or her reelection.

Nonetheless, Congress has attempted to influence the Fed on occasion. For example, in 1975, Congress passed a resolution requesting the Fed to increase substantially the supply of money. Although the Fed was under no obligation to do as Congress requested, its members may have felt political pressure. Also, numerous presidents have been known publicly and privately to put pressure on the chairman of the Board of Governors of the Federal Reserve System to change the course of monetary policy.

Of course, Congress always has the right to amend the original legislation that created the independent Federal Reserve System. It could, for example, make the Federal Reserve part of the United States Treasury (i.e., merge the two agencies).

● HOW THE BANKING SYSTEM AS A WHOLE CAN CREATE MONEY

An individual bank cannot create money. It merely takes in a certain amount of deposits and loans out a fraction of those deposits to customers. But the banking system *as a whole*, including the Federal Reserve, can create or destroy money and hence can increase or decrease the supply of money. To understand how, we must first understand the fractional reserve banking system.

Fractional Reserve Banking

In earlier centuries, goldsmiths and moneylenders owned the safest vaults. Other people recognized this and began leaving their valuables with these two groups—for a small fee, of course. Eventually, goldsmiths and moneylenders noticed an interesting pattern: Over any given period of time, only a small fraction of the total stock of assets would be withdrawn. Although some people would withdraw gold and other assets, others would simultaneously put some in. Vault owners soon realized that they could earn handsome profits by holding only a small percentage of these "deposits" on reserve —and by lending out the rest at interest. The small amount held in reserves served as a guard against the possibility of a "run" on the vault. Thus was the beginning of the modern **fractional reserve banking system**. Modern banks know that they can earn profits by holding only a small fraction of total deposits—enough to meet withdrawals. The rest is loaned out to earn interest. We refer to the practice of holding only a portion of total deposits on reserve as fractional reserve banking. Such banking practices form the basis for the banking system's ability to create and destroy money.

Increasing the Money Supply

Suppose that you are digging in your garden and you discover $1000 worth of gold and sell it to the U.S. Treasury. Now suppose that you take this $1000 to your bank (bank A) and deposit it into your checking account. Assume that your bank is required by the Federal Reserve System to hold 20 percent of its total deposits on reserve (i.e., its **required reserves** are 20 percent). That means that your bank must hold $200 of your $1000 deposit on reserve. It now has $800 of what are called **excess reserves**. That $800 is not earning interest as it sits in reserve. We would expect profit-seeking banks to keep their excess reserves down as close to zero as possible by loaning them out at interest.

Let's say that bank A decides to loan out the $800 and earn interest. Suppose John Jones goes to bank A and wants to borrow $800. Bank A finds him creditworthy and therefore credits $800 to his account. (If he doesn't have an account with bank A, it will insist that he open one.) But, of course, Jones doesn't want to borrow money just for the privilege of paying interest; he wants to spend it. Suppose he buys a machine for his business from Jackson's Machine Supply, which has its checking account at bank B. Bank B will credit $800 to Jackson's checking account balance. Bank B's reserves rise immediately by $800: $160 (20 percent of $800) are required reserves, and the remaining $640 are excess reserves on which bank B is not earning interest.

Bank B wants to earn profits, so it will loan out its excess reserves. Suppose Ms. Smith wants to borrow $640. She obtains the loan from bank B. It credits her account with $640. She, in turn, buys something from Mr. Miller, who does his banking at bank C. Bank C now has $640 in new deposits, but only $128 are required reserves. Bank C, therefore, can loan out $512, which it does, to Mrs. Pulsinelli. Mrs. Pulsinelli buys something from Mrs. Powell, and the process goes on and on and on. Table 13–1 demonstrates how this process works. The end result is that a deposit of $1000 in

Fractional reserve banking system

A banking system in which banks keep only a fraction of their deposits on reserve in the form of cash or deposits with the central bank.

Required reserves

The minimum amount of reserves that must be held as required by the Fed; the Fed requires banks and other financial institutions that accept deposits to hold specified minimum reserves in the form of vault cash or deposits with the nearest Federal Reserve District Bank.

Excess reserves

Those reserves held by depository institutions over and above required reserves; excess reserves equal total reserves held minus required reserves.

TABLE 13–1
The Deposit Expansion Multiplier

This table indicates that you and the fractional reserve banking system together have caused the money supply to rise by $5000 because of your $1000 garden discovery. This result follows from the assumption that (a) banks hold zero excess reserves and (b) check recipients deposit their *entire* check—they don't withdraw any cash. Your original deposit set in motion a series of lending and depositing transactions.

This table indicates a multiple deposit (and therefore money) expansion.

ROUND	DEPOSITED BY	AMOUNT OF DEPOSIT	REQUIRED RESERVES (20%)	EXCESS RESERVES (80%)	LOANED TO	PAID TO
1	Student (You)	$1000	$ 200.00	$800.00	John Jones	Jackson's Machine Supply
2	Jackson's	800	160.00	640.00	Ms. Smith	Mr. Miller
3	Mr. Miller	640	128.00	512.00	Mrs. Pulsinelli	Mrs. Powell
4	Mrs. Powell	512	102.40	409.60	Houchen's Grocery	Mr. Ed
5	Mr. Ed	•	•	•		
6	•	•	•	•		
7	•	•	•	•		
8	•	•	•	•		
Eventual totals		$5000	$1000.00			

new money that was originally outside the banking system generates a $5000 increase in the money supply. This is called the *multiple expansion* of the money supply.

The above procedure demonstrating the multiple expansion of the money supply should look familiar. Although applied to a different subject, it is basically the same arithmetic we used in Chapter 12 to show the multiple expansion of the equilibrium level of national income due to an increase in government expenditures or a decrease in taxes.

This is a highly simplified version of what was formerly called the deposit expansion multiplier. In our example, to arrive at an increase in money supply that is 5 times the original new deposit of "fresh" money, each bank had to loan out all deposits over and above its required reserves. That is, we had to assume that there were zero excess reserves. We also had to assume that the recipients of the loans deposited the entire loan amounts and then spent the money by writing checks to others. In other words, we assumed that no cash was withdrawn. In the real world, these assumptions don't hold; consequently, the real-world money supply multiplier is not 5, but rather closer to 2½.

We Are Headed for a Cashless Society

THE ARGUMENT

Because of technological changes in our banking system, many transactions occur without the physical use of currency or checks. Does that mean we are headed for a cashless society?

THE ANALYSIS

We have stated that the U.S. money supply is defined as the sum of the values of currency and checking accounts. In recent years, a tremendous technological change has taken place in our monetary system and in financial markets in general. It is now possible in many cities to have funds electronically transferred from a checking account to a local retailer. An **electronic funds transfer system** (EFTS) has been developed. An electronic funds transfer system is a checkless money transfer system in which sums of money are transferred from one account to another by means of electronic signals. In this way, individuals' banking accounts are automatically credited and/or debited. Paper bills, currency, and checks are not involved. An EFTS allows people to (1) make deposits or withdrawals using computer terminals located in stores, and (2) transfer funds (equal to the value of purchases) from their own accounts to the store's account by using a computer terminal located at check-out counters.

Electronic banking verifies that the customer has the proper computer identification card and that there are sufficient funds in the customer's account. Moreover, the customer's account is instantly debited and the store's account simultaneously credited for the value of the purchase. Electronic transfer systems almost completely eliminate the problem of "**float**" in the banking system. Float occurs when a check has been used and value received without the check being collected, that is, without the checking account of the person who wrote the check being debited for the amount of the check. Float can occur, for example, when you write a check and receive goods in return, but the store receiving the check does not get credited and your account does not get debited until two or three days later. Float occurs any time there is an excess of payments over and above the deposits actually in the banking system. For example, people often write checks for purchases on a Friday, planning to put sufficient funds into their checking account on Monday. With the EFTS, this won't work.

Currently, there are about 35 billion checks written a year. All of these checks have to be cleared. That is, all of them have to be sent to different banking institutions so that some accounts can be credited and some accounts can be debited. An EFTS eliminates the physical necessity of having paper flow throughout the banking system.

Thus, the use of electronic banking will reduce the overall cost of banking and transactions.

Clearly, an EFTS reduces the need to hold coins and paper currency, and it cuts down on the use of physical check writing. Because of this, some people maintain that electronic banking eliminates the need for money. They feel that in the future, we will have a cashless society, with all or most transactions handled by an EFTS.

We will not, however, end up with a cashless, moneyless society. Only the *form* of money will change; the total money supply will still be the same. Though its components may be different, money is here to stay!

DISCUSSION QUESTIONS

1. Why is there a demand for money?
2. Who will benefit from an EFTS? Who will lose?

● WHAT'S AHEAD

Now that you understand how the money supply is defined and how the fractional reserve banking system allows for a multiple expansion of money, you are ready for an analysis of the Federal Reserve System's monetary policies. Typically, Federal Reserve monetary policy consists of changing the amount of reserves in the system, thereby ultimately changing the total money supply in circulation.

● CHAPTER SUMMARY

Money can be defined by its three major functions as a medium of exchange, a unit of accounting, and a store of value. When money is not used, barter is used. Since barter requires a double coincidence of wants, it turns out to be an inefficient system that leads to less specialization.

The cost of holding money is its opportunity cost, or the interest that could have been earned if invested in an interest-earning asset. The price of money is its purchasing power.

Money is not the same thing as credit. Credit is the transfer of current command over goods and services from one party to another for a time period at a particular cost, called the interest rate. Money is an asset like any other asset.

The narrowest definition of the money supply today includes currency in the hands of the public plus all checking account balances held by the nonbanking public in all depository institutions. We have a fiduciary monetary standard in which nothing physical backs the U.S. dollar. Rather, it is the faith that people will continue to accept the dollar in exchange for goods and services that keeps the dollar as our monetary standard.

Electronic funds transfer system

A system whereby checking account balances, credits and debts are all done via electronic signals rather than through the use of paper memos.

Float

The time it takes a credit or debit to be actually recorded on an account after a transaction takes place.

Our monetary system consists of a central bank (called the Federal Reserve), commercial banks, and thrift institutions such as savings and loan associations. All depository institutions must keep reserves on hand at their Federal Reserve District Bank. The Federal Reserve System supplies the economy with fiduciary currency, provides a system of check collection and clearing, holds reserves for depository institutions, supervises member banks, and acts as the government's fiscal agent. Its most important function in monetary policy is to regulate the money supply.

Because we have a fractional reserve banking system, an increase in new money available in the system will lead to a multiple increase in the supply of money in circulation.

● QUESTIONS FOR REVIEW AND STUDY

1. Money can be defined by its three functions. They are
(1) _____ _____ _____ _____,
(2) _____ _____ _____ _____,
and (3) _____ _____ _____ _____.

2. In a system without money, individuals must _____ to make exchanges.

3. Compared with a money economy, a barter economy is necessarily _____ because information and transactions costs are very high in such a system.

4. In a barter economy, people do not _____ as much as they do in a money economy.

5. Money serving as a unit of accounting allows us to express prices both for current transactions and for those in the _____.

6. As a store of value, money is more/less safe than other forms of wealth, such as real estate and stocks and bonds.

7. Individuals who keep part of their wealth in the form of currency receive no interest. Therefore, they are paying a(n) _____ _____ because of the lost interest they could have earned.

8. The narrowest definition of the money supply consists of _____ and all _____ _____.

9. The only thing that backs the U.S. dollar is _____, which is why we call our monetary system _____.

10. At the head of our banking system is the _____ _____ _____, typically called the _____.

11. The main function of the Fed is to regulate the _____ _____.

12. The Fed is an _____ agency, controlled by neither the executive nor legislative branch of government.

13. Any banking system in which the financial institution is not required to keep 100 percent of its deposits in the form of cash is called a _____ _____ system.

14. In a legally controlled fractional reserve banking system, all member institutions must keep _____ _____, which are defined as a certain percentage of total reserves.

15. Sometimes banks keep more reserves than are required. These reserves are called _____ _____.

16. Since excess reserves do not earn interest, banks incur a(n) _____ _____ by holding them.

17. The increase in the total money supply will be greater than any injection of newly found money because of the _____ _____ system.

18. Newly found money injected into the banking system will lead to a _____ expansion of the money supply.

ANSWERS

1. a medium of exchange; a unit of accounting; a store of value   2. barter   3. inefficient   4. specialize   5. future   6. more   7. opportunity cost   8. currency; checking accounts   9. faith; fiduciary   10. Federal Reserve System; Fed   11. money supply   12. independent   13. fractional reserve   14. required reserves   15. excess reserves   16. opportunity cost   17. fractional reserve   18. multiple

● ANSWERS TO CHAPTER PREVIEW QUESTIONS

1. Take a dollar bill and look at it. What "backs" that United States dollar?

Most students think that the U.S. dollar is "backed" by gold, but (some experts say fortunately) that is not the case. The United States is presently on a fiduciary monetary standard, and as such the U.S. dollar is backed by faith—the public's confidence that the dollar can be exchanged for goods and services. This confidence comes from the fact that *others* will accept the dollar in transactions, because—despite the inflation rates in recent years—the U.S. dollar still retains the characteristic of reasonable predictability of value.

2. Our banking system involves only fractional reserves. What are the characteristics of this fractional reserve banking system?

A fractional reserve banking system is one in which the reserves kept on hand by the depository institutions are only a fraction (or percent) of total deposits owned by the public. In general, depository institutions accept funds from the public and offer their depositors interest and/or other services. In turn, the depository institutions loan out some of these deposits and earn interest. Since at any given time, new deposits are coming in while people are drawing down on old deposits, prudent banking does not require a 100 percent reserve/deposit ratio. Because U.S. depository institutions keep less than 100 percent of their total deposits in the form of reserves, the U.S. banking structure is called a *fractional* reserve system.

● PROBLEMS

1. Several types of assets are listed below. Consider each of them in terms of its potential use as (1) a medium of exchange, (2) a unit of accounting, and (3) a store of value.
   a. A painting by Renoir
   b. A 90-day U.S. Treasury bill
   c. A checking account in a bank in Reno, Nevada
   d. One share of IBM stock
   e. A $50 Federal Reserve Note ($50 bill)
   f. A MasterCard credit card
   g. A lifetime pass to the Los Angeles Dodgers' home baseball games

2. What happens to the total money supply when a person deposits in one bank a check drawn on another bank?

● SELECTED REFERENCES

Angell, N. *The Story of Money*. London: Stokes, 1929.
Bernstein, Peter L. *A Primer on Money, Banking, and Gold*. New York: Random House, 1968.
Galbraith, John Kenneth. *Money: Whence It Came, Where It Went*. New York: Bantam, 1976.

14

Monetary Policy

Chapter Preview
1. What is monetary policy, and what tools does the Federal Reserve System have to carry out monetary policy?
2. Will a change in the interest rate affect your decision to purchase goods?

● KEY TERMS

Discount rate

Equation of exchange

Income velocity of money

Monetary policy

Open market operations

Quantity theory of money and prices

The Federal Reserve System has been blamed for high rates of inflation, high interest rates, high unemployment, and just about everything else that has gone wrong with the economy. The critics of the Fed claim that it has not proved to be a stabilizing force in the economy. In this chapter, we will look at how the Fed can carry out its monetary policy. We will also discuss recent monetary history in this country.

● WHAT IS MONETARY POLICY?

The Fed can alter the money supply by changing the available reserves in the banking system and by changing reserve requirements. A change in the money supply can lead to changes in interest rates. When interest rates change, households may respond by changing their consumption expenditures (C), and businesses may respond by changing their investment expenditures (I). Also, changes in the money supply may lead directly to changes in desired aggregate expenditures.

Essentially, this means that changes in the money supply can change (shift) aggregate demand. **Monetary policy** is therefore defined as those actions by the Fed that change the money supply.

Interest Rates and Consumption

How are interest rates and consumption related? Perhaps you have heard prospective home buyers complain about how they cannot afford to purchase a new house because interest rates on mortgage loans are too high. Even people who can make a sizable down payment feel that they "must" wait until interest rates on housing mortgages drop.

Clearly, interest rates are important to those shopping for a home; even small changes in the interest rate can make a large difference in monthly housing payments. To a lesser extent, the same can be said about consumer purchases of any long-lasting, or durable, goods. Automobiles, refrigerators, and so on, are not usually purchased with cash. Most purchasers of these durable goods borrow part of the purchase price from a bank or other lending institution, such as a finance company or credit card company. The pur-

Monetary policy

All those actions that the Fed engages in to change the supply of money in circulation.

278

chase of these goods with borrowed money involves a payment of interest.

The higher the interest rate, the less likely it is that consumers will purchase durable goods. They will postpone their purchases, continuing to use older durable goods for longer periods of time. Higher interest rates lead to reductions in household expenditures, which in turn lead to a reduction in aggregate demand. As pointed out in Chapter 10, this reduction in aggregate demand may cause a multiple contraction in the equilibrium level of national income.

The opposite occurs when interest rates fall. Consumers purchase more durable goods, which in turn leads to an increase in aggregate demand. This increase in aggregate demand due to a fall in interest rates may lead to a multiple expansion of the equilibrium level of national income.

In summary, there is an inverse relationship between the level of interest rates in the economy and household expenditures for durable goods. Thus, there is an inverse relationship between interest rates and aggregate demand. Ultimately, then, a change in interest rates will lead to a change in the equilibrium level of national income.

Interest Rates and Investment

Some businesses make enough profits to cover their entire purchasing costs of machinery, equipment, and maybe even entire buildings. Nevertheless, most businesses must borrow in order to make such large investment expenditures.[1] Since businesses borrow to make investments, they, too, must keep an eye on interest rates. After all, from the profits businesses earn on investments, they must pay back principal *and* interest. At relatively low interest rates, businesses will find more investment projects for which they can borrow money, make the investment, pay back principal and interest—and still have some profit left in the deal. On the other hand, at very high interest rates, businesses will find fewer profitable investment projects. Therefore, an inverse relationship between the level of interest rates in the economy and overall business expenditures on investments, I, is expected.

The conclusion is that as interest rates rise, business investments will fall, and so, too, will aggregate demand, leading to a decrease in the equilibrium level of national income. As interest rates fall, on the other hand, business investments will increase, as will aggregate demand and the equilibrium level of national income. The relation-

---

[1]Even when businesses don't borrow, they are implicitly incurring an interest cost when they use their retained earnings to invest. The implicit interest cost is what they could have earned had they used those retained earnings to buy, for example, U.S. government bonds that yield a specific rate of interest.

ship between changes in interest rates and changes in consumption and investment is shown in Exhibit 14–1.

● THE MONETARY POLICY TOOLS OF THE FED

We have just seen the link between interest rates, aggregate demand, and national income. We know that changes in aggregate demand can lead to changes in national income, output, employment, and the average price level. Now it is important to see how, in fact, the Fed changes the money supply, which in turn changes the level of interest rates in the economy. In this section, we show that the Fed has three tools at its disposal to affect money supply and interest rates. They are (1) changing reserve requirements, (2) changing the discount rate, and (3) engaging in open market operations.

Changing Reserve Requirements

In Chapter 13, we gave an example of how money expansion and contraction can take place. In that example, it was assumed that the Fed required all depository institutions (commercial banks, savings

EXHIBIT 14–1
The Relationship between Interest Rates, Consumption, Investment, and National Income

There is an inverse relationship between the level of interest rates, i, in the economy and desired consumption and investment expenditures. Thus, a change in the interest rate will change both consumption and investment, which will change aggregate demand, thereby changing the equilibrium level of national income.

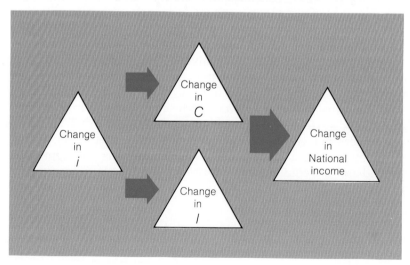

and loan associations, mutual savings banks, and credit unions) to hold 20 percent of their customers' total demand deposits as reserves. For simplicity, it was also assumed that the banks held no reserves above those required. That is, excess reserves were zero, with all reserves above minimum required reserves loaned out to earn interest.

When the Fed Lowers the Reserve Requirement.   To understand what actually happens when the Fed lowers or raises the reserve requirement, consider the following examples. Assume that the reserve requirement is lowered from 20 percent to 10 percent. In that case, all depository institutions will have reserves over and above those required. That is, all depository institutions will now have excess reserves.

Assume that total demand deposits for bank A equal $100,000. Further assume that bank A has made loans equal to $80,000 and is holding $20,000 in reserves to meet its 20 percent legal reserve requirement. If the Fed's reserve requirement is lowered to 10 percent, what happens to the bank's required reserves and excess reserves? With a total of $100,000 in demand deposits, bank A is now required to hold just $10,000 on reserve. But it is holding $20,000. Excess reserves have increased from zero dollars to $10,000.

There is an opportunity cost for holding this $10,000 in excess reserves, and it is the interest that could be earned from loaning out the $10,000. Therefore, bank A will loan out $10,000 to one of its customers, increasing its demand deposits. Remember what happened in our example in Chapter 13 when you found $1000 worth of gold in your garden? In essence, bank A has just "found" $10,000 of "fresh" money or, in this case, reserves. This will result in a multiple expansion of the money supply.

The person who borrows the $10,000 from bank A will soon write a check to pay for his or her expenditures. The person who sells the borrower the good or service will deposit the check in bank B, which will now receive a $10,000 increase in deposits. Only $1000 of those deposits must be held to meet the 10 percent reserve requirement. Bank B will loan out $9000 by creating a new demand deposit—and away we go to a multiple expansion of the money supply.

Effects on Interest Rates.   How does this expansion of the money supply due to a reduction in reserve requirements affect interest rates? To understand the effect on interest rates, we must look at the credit market.

Banks with excess reserves loan them out. Thus, loans make up one side of the credit market—the supply of credit, or the supply of loanable funds. The demand for credit, or demand for loanable funds, is the other side. In other words, a typical supply and demand relationship determines price—in this case, the price of credit, or loanable funds. That price is, of course, the interest rate (actually, an average of all interest rates involved). Since the reduction in reserve requirements has increased the supply of loanable funds, the only way that banks and other depository institutions can induce borrowers (demanders) of credit to demand a larger quantity is to lower interest rates (the price of credit).

In summary, if the Fed lowers its reserve requirement, two things will tend to occur: (1) the supply of money will rise, and (2) the interest rate will fall.

When the Fed Raises the Reserve Requirement.   If the Fed raises the reserve requirement, depository institutions that previously had zero excess reserves will now find that they have "negative" excess reserves. That is, they don't have enough reserves on hand to meet the minimum legal requirements. As loans come due, banks will not renew them. Indeed, they may even have to tell some of their customers to pay off loans earlier than expected. As loans are not renewed and some are called in, the overall total of demand deposits falls. That is, the money supply falls by a multiple contraction process. Meanwhile, interest rates will tend to rise. The supply of credit, or loanable funds, will have fallen as a result of this multiple contraction of the money supply. A reduction in supply with the same demand leads to a higher "price" of credit (i.e., a higher interest rate).

In reality, the Fed does not change reserve requirements very often. Any small change in reserve requirements leads to dramatic changes in the total money supply in circulation. Thus, this tool is alleged to be too powerful for short-run monetary policy. In any event, the Fed has the authority to change reserve requirements from a minimum of 3 percent to a maximum of 14 percent.

Changing the Discount Rate

Another policy tool that the Fed has at its disposal is its ability to change the discount rate. The Fed can loan money to depository institutions if it so chooses; the interest rate the Fed charges is called a **discount rate**. When the Federal Reserve first came into being, changes in the discount rate were the heart of the Fed's control over the banking system; the discount tool is still important to Great Britain's central bank.

Fed lending to depository institutions is for short periods of time. It is understood that borrowers must put their finances in order and not depend on this source of funds to meet reserve requirements indefinitely. Borrowing from the Fed's discount window at the stated discount rate is considered a privilege, not a right, of depository institutions.

Discount rate

The rate of interest that the Fed charges to depository institutions to borrow reserves.

Nonetheless, many believe that depository institutions borrow from the Fed more aggressively. Whenever the discount rate has been significantly lower than the market rate of interest that banks would have to pay, borrowing from the Fed has become very profitable indeed, and depository institutions have acted predictably.

In principle, when the Fed wants to engage in expansionary monetary policy, it can lower the discount rate. This will encourage more depository institutions to borrow Fed money, thereby adding new reserves, or "fresh" money, to the banking system. These new reserves will lead to a multiple expansion of the money supply, and interest rates will tend to fall via the same mechanism outlined earlier. On the other hand, when the Fed wants to engage in contractionary monetary policy, it can raise the discount rate. This tends to discourage depository institutions from borrowing reserves from the Fed's discount window. This depletion of reserves causes a contraction of the money supply and also causes other interest rates to rise.

In reality, today the Fed does not use the discount rate aggressively as a policy tool. The changes in the discount rate tend to lag behind the rest of the economy. In other words, the Fed has typically lowered or raised the discount rate after other interest rates in the economy have already changed in the same direction.

Engaging in Open Market Operations

The third and most important major policy tool at the Fed's disposal involves what are called **open market operations**. Open market operations occur when the Fed buys and sells U.S. government securities, such as U.S. Treasury bills (short-term bonds), in the open market. There is a large and very active market in U.S. government securities. The U.S. Treasury sells U.S. government securities directly to individuals, banks, pension plans, and foreign governments whenever the federal government has run a budget deficit that must be financed by borrowing from the public. The Federal Reserve cannot issue U.S. government securities directly —only the U.S. Treasury can do that. Rather, the Federal Reserve operates in what is called the secondary market for U.S. government securities. It buys and sells U.S. government securities already in existence.

The Fed's purchase and sale of U.S. government securities directly affect the amount of reserves outstanding in the banking system and thereby affect the money supply in circulation. Open market operations also affect interest rates.

When the Fed Buys Bonds from a Depository Institution.   Suppose the Fed buys a $200,000 bond from bank A. Bank A, like all depository institutions, holds reserves with its district Federal Reserve

Open market operations

Refers to the Fed's buying and selling of U.S. government securities in the open market.

283

Bank. When the Fed buys the $200,000 bond from bank A, it credits $200,000 to the reserve account of bank A. Assuming that bank A had zero excess reserves prior to the sale of the $200,000 bond, it will now have excess reserves equal to $200,000, which it will want to loan out to earn interest. As in the situations described previously, a multiple expansion in the money supply will result.

The people who borrow the new money from bank A will write checks as they buy goods. The people who sell the goods will deposit these checks in banks B, C, D, and so on. Based on what Chapter 13 indicated, assuming that the reserve requirement is 20 percent, and assuming that none of this new money leaks out into currency and that no depository institutions keep excess reserves, the money supply will increase by 5 times $200,000, or $1 million. Moreover, the increased supply of loanable funds will lead to lower market interest rates.

Thus, when the Fed buys U.S. government securities on the open market, the money supply will increase by some multiple of the purchase, and interest rates will tend to fall.

When the Fed Sells Bonds to a Depository Institution.   The opposite process will occur when the Fed sells a bond to a depository institution. Suppose that the Fed sells a bond to bank A and that bank A has zero excess reserves at the time of the sale. The Fed will debit its reserve account by $200,000. Thus bank A will find that it cannot renew loans and must call others in to make up for its $200,000 *negative* excess reserve position. A multiple contraction process will ensue. Given the same assumptions as before, the money supply will contract by 5 times the amount of the bond sale to bank A, or $1 million. This will lead to a reduction in the supply of loanable funds and therefore to an increase in interest rates.

A Summary of Open Market Operations.   The Fed can change the supply of money and interest rates through open market operations. By purchasing bonds in the open market, the Fed can initiate a multiple expansion of the money supply (of the bonds' purchase value) and a reduction in interest rates. By selling bonds in the open market, the Fed can initiate a multiple contraction of the money supply and an increase in interest rates.

● MONETARY POLICY AND THE BUSINESS CYCLE

We can now apply the tools of monetary policy to the phases of the business cycle. What should the Fed do during a recession, for example, and what should it do during inflation?

Monetary Policy during a Recession

During a recession, national output and overall employment are not rising as rapidly as they should, and may even be falling. How can the Fed get the economy on the right track? The problem is that the growth in aggregate demand is not sufficient to encourage a full employment of resources. Therefore, the Fed should try to increase aggregate demand.

In this situation, the Fed can attempt to stimulate the economy by a "loose," or expansionary, monetary policy. It can buy bonds on the open market, lower the discount rate, and/or lower the reserve requirement. The tool used most often by the Fed in this situation is the purchase of bonds in the open market.

Such bond purchases create excess reserves. As indicated earlier, excess reserves stimulate lending, causing the money supply to increase and interest rates to fall. Lower interest rates will induce households to purchase more durable consumer goods (C will rise). Lower interest rates will also induce businesses to increase investments (I will rise). The overall effect will be a rise in aggregate demand, which will increase the equilibrium level of national income, output, and employment. (See Exhibit 14–2 for a schematic of how this works in the economy.)

EXHIBIT 14–2
Monetary Policy during a Recession

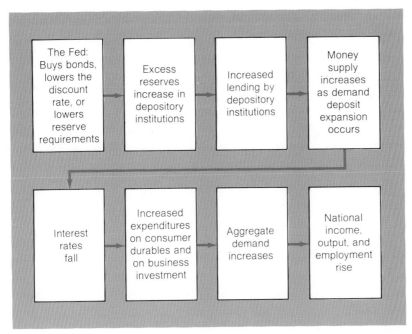

Monetary Policy during Inflation

Periods of inflation occur when too many dollars are chasing too few goods. In other words, the growth in aggregate demand exceeds the growth in aggregate supply. What should the Fed do to reduce the disparity between aggregate demand and aggregate supply?

The Fed can pursue a "tight," or contractionary, monetary policy. It can sell bonds on the open market, increase the discount rate, and/or increase the reserve requirement. By doing any one or a combination of the above, the Fed will cause the money supply to contract and interest rates to rise.

As interest rates rise, households will reduce their expenditures on consumer durables (*C* will fall), and businesses will reduce their investment expenditures (*I* will fall). The result is that both aggregate demand and the equilibrium level of national income will fall. Inflation will be brought under control. (This process is presented schematically in Exhibit 14–3.)

The Dynamics of Monetary Policy

We live in a world of change. We live in a world of rising incomes and rising population. The money supply grows as the economy around us grows and monetary policy changes. The Fed is contin-

EXHIBIT 14–3
Monetary Policy during Inflation

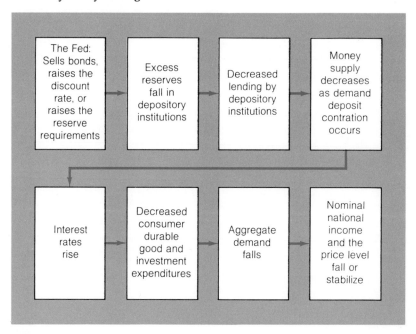

ually changing the *rate of growth* of the money supply. For example, the money supply may be growing at 6 percent a year when the Fed decides to "tighten up." Then, by its open market operations, the Fed may cause the money supply to grow at only a 4 percent rate per year. Thus, contractionary monetary policy refers to a *decreasing rate of growth* of the money supply. Expansionary monetary policy refers to an *increasing rate of growth* of the money supply. The dynamics of monetary policy, however, do not essentially change the analysis given above.

● THE QUANTITY THEORY AND THE EQUATION OF EXCHANGE

By viewing the economy through aggregate demand and aggregate supply, we can gain insight into how national income, output, employment, and price levels change. As we have seen, the aggregate demand–aggregate supply approach also gives us clues as to how monetary policy and fiscal policy can cure the "diseases" of unemployment and inflation. But there is an alternative approach to understanding the national economy. It is referred to as the equation of exchange. This alternative approach provides its own insights as to how a national economy operates and what the effect of monetary policy can be on output and prices.

The Equation of Exchange

The **equation of exchange** states that expenditures by one person will equal income receipts by another. Expenditures and income receipts are simply the opposite sides of the same coin. When you go to a stereo center and buy a cassette for $10, your expenditure represents a $10 income receipt for the stereo center.

Dollars that you have in your wallet or checking account usually don't stay there. They are eventually spent and in the process change hands. It is difficult to see how fast individual dollars are spent, but we can compute the average number of times per year that a dollar is used to purchase final goods or services (NNP). We call this the **income velocity of money**, which is designated by V. The income velocity of money is equal to NNP divided by the money supply. If we let M stand for the total money supply, then our formula for the income velocity of money is

$$V \equiv \frac{\text{NNP}}{M1}.$$

Consider an example. Assume that in 1982 national income is $2.5 trillion and the money supply is $500 billion. The income ve-

Equation of exchange

The number of monetary units times the number of times each unit is spent on final goods and services is identical to the prices times output (or national income).

Income velocity of money

The average number of times per year a dollar is spent on final goods and services. It is equal to NNP divided by the money supply.

locity of money, V, would equal $2.5 trillion divided by $500 billion, or 5. In other words, each dollar would change hands an average of five times a year, or approximately once every two and one-half months. In this sense, then, the income velocity of money is a measure of the economy's nominal output per dollar.

Transposing the Equation.   Let's multiply both sides of the equation by M. This gives us

$$M1V \equiv NNP$$

Now, let's break down NNP into its separate components—quantities and prices. Let P stand for the average price of final goods produced during the year, and let Q stand for the quantity of final output. Thus, the value of final output is price times quantity, or $NNP = P \times Q$. The equation can be rewritten as

$$M1V \equiv PQ$$

In fact, this is the standard form in which the equation of exchange is presented.

Consider a numerical example involving a one-commodity economy. Assume that in this economy, the total money supply, M1, is $100, the quantity of output, Q, is 50 units of a good, and the average price of this output is $10 per unit. Using the equation of exchange,

$$
\begin{aligned}
M1V &\equiv PQ \\
\$100V &\equiv \$10 \times 50 \\
\$100V &\equiv \$500 \\
V &= 5
\end{aligned}
$$

Thus, each dollar is spent an average of 5 times a year.

The Equation of Exchange Is an Identity.   The equation of exchange always has to be true: It is called an *accounting identity*. The equation of exchange states that the total amount of money *spent* on final output, $M1V$, is equal to the total amount of money *received* for final product, PQ. Thus, a given flow of money can be seen from either the buyers' side or the producers' side. The value of goods purchased is equal to the value of goods sold.

Quantity theory of money and prices

The theory that changes in the price level are directly related to changes in the money supply. The quantity theory is based on the equation of exchange.

Quantity Theory of Money and Prices

If we make some assumptions about certain components of the equation of exchange, we can actually come up with one of the oldest theories of inflation—the **quantity theory of money and prices**. This theory states that the level of prices in the economy is directly proportional to the quantity of money in circulation per unit of out-

288

put. To state this theory in symbols, we divide both sides of the equation of exchange by Q:

thus $M1V \equiv PQ$

becomes $P \equiv M1 \times \dfrac{V}{Q}$.

Assuming that both V and Q are fairly constant, then as $M1$ increases or decreases, so, too, does P, and at the same rate. Classical (or 19th century) economists believed that V was indeed constant because they believed that the long-run money-holding habits of firms and households were fairly stable. They also believed that Q was fairly constant because of their prediction that the economy tended toward full employment. If V and Q were indeed constant, then we could predict, for example, that a 10 percent increase in M would cause a 10 percent increase in P. Empirical evidence indicates that while $M1$ and P are highly correlated, they are not proportional; if $M1$ is doubled, P will rise less than twofold.

● A HISTORY OF MONETARY POLICY

We start our history of monetary policy with the Great Depression. In retrospect, the Great Depression can, in part, be blamed on the failure of monetary policy. From 1929 to 1933, the Fed failed to support banks during that financial panic. In one three-month period, 500 banks failed; from 1929 to 1933 over 5,000 failed. The closure of numerous banks and the failure of the Fed to provide liquidity to faltering banks caused the money supply to fall by over one-third during that 1929–1933 period. This was the greatest contraction ever in the supply of money in circulation. The Great Depression has been called the Fed's most dismal hour.

From 1934 to 1941

Recovery from the Great Depression did not begin until late 1934. From 1934 to mid-1937, the money supply grew about 5 percent per year. National income and output also grew steadily. Then, from mid-1937 until 1938, the money supply fell. The Fed thought that because banks were holding excess reserves, nothing would happen if the reserve requirements were raised. But something did happen: The banks built up their excess reserves *again* when reserve requirements were raised. The banks were so worried about another financial panic that they wanted to hold more reserves than required. Not surprisingly, the increase in reserve requirements caused the money supply to fall, and the expansion that started in 1934 was stopped in its tracks, at least partly because of this contractionary monetary policy.

From 1941 to 1960

During World War II, the Fed made numerous open market purchases of bonds; consequently, demand deposits increased from $38 billion to $76 billion, and currency in the hands of the public tripled. In 1947, the Fed sold bonds aggressively and the money supply fell. From 1948 through 1960, the money supply increased steadily as the Fed made a conscious effort to control the supply and interest rates by "leaning against the wind," that is, by using monetary policy to counter the business cycle.

The 1960s

During the 1960s, the United States wanted to increase economic growth to finance unemployment, help the war in Vietnam, and maintain a strong economic advantage over the Soviet Union. The Fed financed these expansionist goals with an easy-money policy. What seemed to occur was an overall business expansion accompanied by a rising rate of inflation that ended the decade at a rate of 6.1 percent per year.

Two Credit Crunches.   In 1966 and again during the 1969–1970 period, two exceptions to the general expansion in both money and the economy occurred in the form of credit crunches.

The Fed became concerned with fighting inflation during 1965–1966. It instigated a tight-money policy that almost seems, in retrospect, an overreaction. Interest rates soared until the Fed eased off.

Another credit crunch appeared in 1969–1970 for exactly the same reasons. The Fed reduced the rate of monetary expansion dramatically, but the housing market was hurt because of the resulting high interest rates.

The 1970s

The 1970s will go down as the period with the most variability in the rate of growth of the money supply. During that period, the Fed consistently—and abruptly—changed the rate of growth of the money supply. In 1971, for example, when President Richard Nixon put into effect wage and price controls, the Fed reduced the discount rate and reserve requirements and made huge open market purchases. After the 1972 elections, monetary policy became restrictive and interest rates increased: The Fed had decided to fight inflation again. In 1973–1974, another credit crunch appeared.

As the 1976 elections approached, monetary policy again became expansionary, with the money supply increasing rapidly and interest rates falling. But as soon as the election was over, the Fed changed to a restrictive policy. In 1978, another credit crunch arose.

290

The 1980s

Monetary policy for the first few years of the 1980s has been characterized by relatively restrictive actions on the part of the Fed, with resulting high interest rates. Indeed, the Chairman of the Board of Governors of the Federal Reserve System has come under constant criticism because of these high interest rates. It remains to be seen whether the Fed will stick to its guns and maintain stable monetary policy.

The Fed Should Be Controlled

THE ARGUMENT

The Fed is an independent agency. Critics of the Fed have maintained that its independence has allowed it to do everything wrong, including cause the Great Depression and numerous reces- *sions from 1960 up to the present. Moreover, the Fed's critics claim that it is to blame for all our inflation problems. Given these complaints, should the Fed be controlled?*

THE ANALYSIS

Because of these complaints, Congress has already passed a resolution imposing some control on the Federal Reserve. Currently, the Chairman of the Board of Governors of the Federal Reserve System must report to the House every six months and also to the Senate every six months, but starting three months later. Thus, every three months, the Fed is required to present to Congress its explicit goals in terms of its "targeted" growth rate of the money supply and how well it has succeeded in reaching those goals. Some observers contend that such explicit reporting of goals and accomplishments by the Fed to the Congress at regular three-month intervals will prevent the Fed from greatly overshooting or undershooting a "reasonable" long-run growth rate of the money supply, as it has done so many times in the past.

There is no question that the atmosphere has changed in Washington. The Fed is no longer a sacred cow. The question of whether the Fed should remain independent is really a question about the past and future per-

formance of the Fed. Even if we agree that the Fed has indeed been responsible for many recessions and inflations, it does not necessarily follow that the Fed should be more answerable to Congress. Indeed, one might argue the opposite approach. The solution might be to isolate completely the Fed from Congress, the president, and any other political body, thereby protecting the Fed from all efforts at political manipulation. Such independence for the Fed could be achieved by what some have called a *monetary rule*. A monetary rule would require the Fed to increase the money supply at specific rates, say, 3 or 4 percent a year, rates consistent with long-term productivity and population growth. (Often in the past, the actual growth of the money supply has been *pro*cyclical—falling during recessions and rising during boom times.) In the long run, there is little question that the money supply can be controlled by the Fed through its control over member bank reserves and reserve requirements. If a monetary rule were instituted, it would become impossible

292

for Congress, the president, or the Fed to amplify any boom or bust condition in the economy.

Certainly, not everyone thinks that a monetary rule is the answer to the Fed's problems. Those who oppose it contend that the Fed should "lean against the wind" to cut down on the ups and downs in the business cycle. Furthermore, they contend that the elimination of the discretionary power of the Fed would remove a valuable and flexible tool of the policymakers.

DISCUSSION QUESTIONS

1. Would the Federal Reserve System be under political control if it were merged with the U.S. Treasury?

2. Why would a monetary rule negate the policymaking function of the Federal Reserve System?

● WHAT'S AHEAD

Now that we have looked at traditional theories concerning macroeconomic (or economywide) problems, it is time to move on to some current controversies and theories that relate to the national economy. In the next chapter, we will examine stagflation and supply-side economics, as well as the problem of higher taxes due to the combination of inflation and a progressive tax structure.

● CHAPTER SUMMARY

Monetary policy involves those activities that ultimately alter the rate of growth of the money supply in circulation. Monetary policy affects interest rates, which affect consumption and investment. At lower interest rates, there will be more purchases of durable consumer goods and more investment. At higher interest rates, there will be less purchases of consumer durable goods and less investment.

The Fed can alter the money supply by changing the reserve requirement, by changing the discount rate, and by engaging in open market operations. Whatever tool is used, the resulting change in excess reserves will cause a multiple change in the supply of money in circulation.

In principle, monetary policy should be contractionary during periods of inflation and expansionary during periods of recession.

The equation of exchange states that one person's income receipts must be matched by another person's expenditures. From the equation of exchange we get the quantity theory of money and prices, if we assume that the number of times each dollar changes hands per year and output remain constant.

● QUESTIONS FOR REVIEW AND STUDY

1. A goal of Federal Reserve monetary policy is to change the _____ _____.

2. The higher the rate of interest, the less/more consumers are likely to purchase durable goods.

3. Typically, when interest rates rise, consumers _____ their purchases of durable goods.

4. There is a(n) _____ relationship between the level of interest rates and overall business expenditures on investment.

5. Increases in interest rates _____ both consumption and investment, thereby _____ aggregate demand.

6. The three monetary policy tools of the Fed are: _____ _____ _____, _____ _____ _____, and _____ _____ _____ _____ _____.

7. A reduction in reserve requirements increases _____ reserves.

8. An increase in excess reserves typically causes banks to _____ credit and deposits.

9. When reserve requirements are lowered, the increased supply of credit causes interest rates to _____.

10. If the Fed lowers the _____ rate below the rate banks have to pay elsewhere, banks will attempt to borrow more reserves from the Fed.

11. Increased borrowing from the Fed by depository institutions will lead to a(n) _____ in the money supply.

12. If the Fed wants to lower the money supply, it can _____ the discount rate.

13. The buying and selling of U.S. government bonds by the Fed is called _____ _____ _____.

14. The Fed's purchase of a bond from a bank or other depository institution will _____ excess reserves and thereby _____ the money supply. The same thing will occur if the Fed buys a bond from the public.

15. When the Fed sells a bond to a depository institution or to the public, it will _____ the money supply.

16. In order to counteract a recession, monetary policy should be _____.

17. During an inflation, monetary policy should be _____.

18. In all economic transactions, expenditures by one person automatically equal _____ by another.

19. The symbolic way to describe the equality in (18) is by the

_____ _____ _____.

20. In an economy where people's spending habits are relatively stable (i.e., the velocity of money is constant), a change in the money supply will lead to a change in _____ _____.

21. In a world of full employment, an increase in the money supply will lead to _____.

ANSWERS

1. bank reserves 2. less 3. postpone 4. inverse 5. reduce; decreasing
6. changing reserve requirements; changing discount rate; engaging in open
market operations 7. excess 8. expand 9. fall 10. discount 11. increase
12. increase 13. open market operations 14. increase; increase 15. decrease
16. expansionary, or loose 17. contractionary, or tight 18. receipts 19. equation
of exchange 20. nominal income, or the price level 21. inflation

● ANSWERS TO CHAPTER PREVIEW QUESTIONS

1. What is monetary policy, and what tools does the Federal Reserve System have to carry out monetary policy?

Monetary policy consists of all those actions that the Fed engages in to change the supply of money in circulation. There are three main tools that the Fed has at its disposal to carry out monetary policy: engaging in open market operations, changing the discount rate, and changing reserve requirements. Open market operations refer to the Fed's buying and selling government securities in the open market; this activity changes depository institutions' reserves and therefore changes the money supply. The discount rate is the rate the Fed charges on loans it makes to depository institutions, lowering the discount rate encourages institutions to borrow from the Fed, and thus reserves (and therefore the money supply) are increased; increasing the discount rate produces the opposite effect. Finally, by changing reserve requirements, the Fed does not directly alter depository institutions' total reserves, but does change excess reserves, which in turn affects the money supply.

2. Will a change in the interest rate affect your decision to purchase goods?

An increase in the interest rate that you have to pay on loans may indeed affect your spending behavior. If, for example, you were planning to buy a car, a stereo, or a house on credit, you may reconsider your decision in view of the higher interest costs you must incur. Conversely, a decrease in the interest rate may induce you to make a purchase of a house, a car, or a stereo sooner than you would have otherwise.

● PROBLEMS

1. What is expansionary monetary policy and how does it work?

2. Show in the form of a diagram the process by which the Fed can reduce inflationary pressures by raising the discount rate.

● SELECTED REFERENCES

Friedman, Milton. *Dollars and Deficits: Inflation, Monetary Policy, and the Balance of Payments.* Englewood Cliffs, N.J.: Prentice-Hall, 1968.

Friedman, Milton, and Walter Heller. *Monetary Versus Fiscal Policy.* New York: W. W. Norton & Company, 1969.

Humphrey, Thomas M. "The Quantity Theory of Money: Its Historical Evolution and Policy Debates." *Economic Review*, Federal Reserve Bank of Richmond, May/June 1974, pp. 2–19.

Laidler, D. E. W. *Essays on Money and Inflation.* Chicago: University of Chicago Press, 1979.

Prager, Jonas. "The Fed Wasn't Always Independent." *New York Times*, October 30, 1977, sec. 3, p. 16.

15

Stagflation, Taxflation, and Supply-Side Economics

Chapter Preview
1. There is a sizable underground economy in this nation. Why didn't it exist 100 years ago?
2. What is supply-side economics all about?

● KEY TERMS

Laffer curve	Supply-side economics
Phillips curve	Taxflation, or bracket creep
Stagflation	Underground, or subterranean, economy

Suppose Mr. Gonzalez received a 7 percent increase in his total yearly income last year. Is he better off because of this increase? By now you know that you do not have enough information to answer this question. All you know is that Gonzalez received a 7 percent increase in his *nominal* income. Before you can tell whether he is better off, you need to know, at the very least, what last year's rate of inflation was.

If the rate of inflation last year was 10 percent, Gonzalez is probably worse off. After all, his money, or nominal, income rose by only 7 percent. It is his real income that matters. His real income went down by approximately 3 percent (+7 percent − 10 percent). Moreover, even if the rate of inflation had been only 7 percent, Gonzalez probably still would have been worse off because he would have paid more taxes to the federal government. Indeed, the issues of high taxes and high rates of inflation have been in the news for a number of years. So, too, has the problem of unemployment existing simultaneously with inflation. In this chapter, we will take a closer look at these issues.

● THE PHILLIPS CURVE

Several decades ago, a British economist, A. W. Phillips, observed an inverse relationship between the percentage change in wage rates and the percentage of unemployment in Great Britain. He found that when wage rates were rising, the unemployment rate was low, and when wage rates were rising only slowly if at all, the unemployment rate was relatively high. Other economists altered this relationship. Instead of changes in wage rates, they substituted rates of inflation. They found that there existed an inverse relationship between rates of inflation and rates of unemployment: High inflation corresponded to low unemployment, low inflation corresponded to high unemployment. This relationship seemed to exist for a number of countries. It is now referred to as the **Phillips curve**. Graph 15–1 shows a hypothetical Phillips curve. It suggests that high inflation rates are consistent with low unemployment, and low inflation rates with high unemployment. As a policy tool, this relationship suggests to some economists a *trade-off* between inflation and unemployment. That is, the nation can "buy" less inflation only

Phillips curve

An inverse relationship between the percentage change in prices (rate of inflation) and the rate of unemployment.

298

with more unemployment. Or, unemployment can be lessened only at the expense of increased inflation. On the Phillips curve shown in Graph 15–1, if the rate of inflation is 6 percent, the rate of unemployment is 3 percent. If the nation wishes to lower the rate of inflation from 6 percent to 4 percent, presumably it must be willing to put up with a 1 percent increase in the rate of unemployment, raising the unemployment rate to 4 percent. Finally, if it wishes to get the inflation rate down to 2 percent, according to this Phillips curve it must be willing to accept 10 percent unemployment.

In a sense, then, the Phillips curve is a policy menu, but only to the extent that the way it is drawn represents a reality that does not change over time.

Shifts in the Phillips Curve

The measured Phillips curve relationship for the United States has been far from stable. The trade-off numbers seem to be changing, so that policymakers can't really be sure that a given level of inflation will repeatedly allow the same rate of unemployment. The

GRAPH 15–1
A Hypothetical Phillips Curve

This diagram indicates an inverse relationship between inflation rates and unemployment rates. Presumably a trade-off exists between inflation and unemployment. Society must put up with more inflation if it wants to reduce unemployment. Similarly, if it wants to reduce inflation, it must pay for any such reduction with increased unemployment.

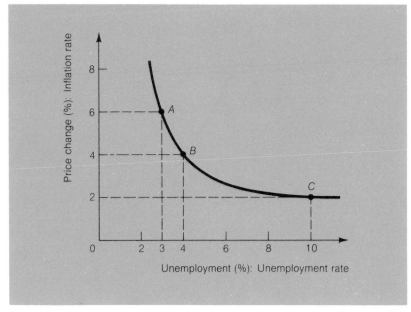

trade-off between unemployment and inflation has become increasingly worse since the mid-1950s. In 1955, for example, a 6 percent unemployment rate implied a 1 percent rise in prices, but the same unemployment rate in 1974 was associated with an almost 12 percent rise in prices. The problem of a shifting Phillips curve is seen in Graph 15–2.

Factors Shifting the Phillips Curve

There has been much talk about the worsening trade-off between unemployment and inflation. The cost of reducing unemployment seems to be rising in terms of higher and higher rates of inflation. We are talking here about a shift to the right in the Phillips curve. There are a number of reasons for this apparent shift to the right.

Increased Unemployment Compensation and Welfare Payments.   If the restrictions on receiving unemployment benefits are reduced, and if the benefits are raised and paid for a longer period, then it is reasonable to expect a higher unemployment rate, other things be-

GRAPH 15 – 2

A Shifting Phillips Curve

When the Phillips curve shifts rightward, any given level of unemployment is associated with a higher inflation rate. Alternatively, any given rate of inflation is associated with a higher unemployment rate. In other words, the trade-off between unemployment and inflation appears to worsen.

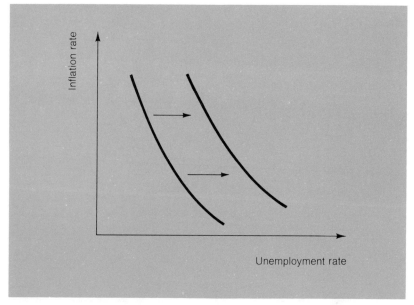

ing equal. This is because unemployed workers will take longer to look for a job. More specifically, if, at a particular rate of growth of aggregate demand (and its related rate of inflation), the unemployed can receive unemployment benefits sooner, for a longer period, and with higher benefits, then the unemployment rate will be higher at that rate of growth of aggregate demand (and its related rate of inflation), all other things being equal. At every level of inflation, the unemployment rate will be higher; thus, increased unemployment benefits and welfare payments will shift the Phillips curve rightward, causing a worse trade-off between unemployment and inflation.

Increase in Labor Force Participation Rate.   Over the last several decades, this nation has observed a larger percentage of its total population choosing to become part of the labor force. That is, there has been an increase in the labor force participation rate. In 1960, 59 percent of the population was in the labor force. Today, 64.5 percent of the population is in the labor force. This means that the economy must absorb a rising percentage of the population into the labor force. Therefore, for any given rate of growth of aggregate demand (and rate of inflation), there will be a higher rate of unemployment when the labor force participation rate is increasing. The Phillips curve trade-off between unemployment and inflation will therefore be worse, other things being equal.

Changes in Labor Force Composition.   It is possible that the shift to the right in the Phillips curve has been due to important changes in the composition of the labor force. There is an increasingly higher percentage of teenagers and women in the labor force. Historically, the rate of unemployment among teenagers and women has been greater than among other groups in the labor force. Therefore, as women and teenagers occupy a larger share of the labor force, the result is a higher rate of unemployment, other things being equal. Otherwise stated, for any given rate of growth of aggregate demand (and rate of inflation), an increase in the percentage of teenagers and women in the labor force will cause a worsening in the Phillips curve trade-off between unemployment and inflation.

Other Possible Causes.   There are a variety of other factors that may have shifted the Phillips curve outward to the right. An increasing minimum wage can cause higher rates of unemployment among the unskilled, particularly teenagers. Greater difficulty in matching unemployed workers with available jobs can also cause a worsening Phillips curve trade-off. This difficulty can be caused by demographic shifts over time. Large numbers of individuals may leave areas where their skills were matched to available job requirements and move to areas where their skills do *not* suit available job requirements. A movement of people from farms to cities may be a case in point.

Recent U.S. Historical Experience

Look at Graph 15–3, which shows the actual rates of inflation and unemployment in the United States since 1954. It looks as if there is a series of loops rather than some inverse relationship between unemployment and inflation. In fact, higher inflation seems

GRAPH 15–3

Relationship between Unemployment and Inflation in the United States, 1954–1982

Since 1954, there has been no simple inverse relationship between inflation and unemployment in the United States. Instead of a typical Phillips curve, we see a series of circular-type loops. Rather than more inflation buying less unemployment, it appears that more inflation has been associated with more unemployment.

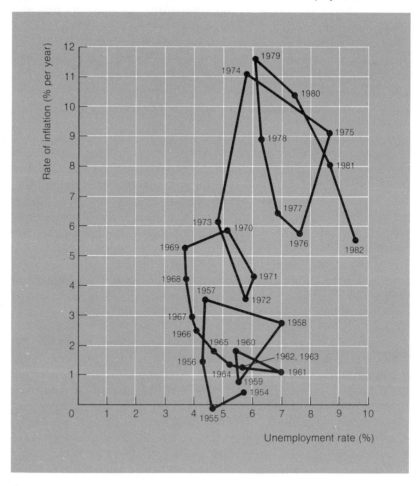

to be associated with higher unemployment. The Phillips curve is apparently too unstable to be useful as a policy tool.

● UNEMPLOYMENT + INFLATION = DISCOMFORT

Table 15–1 shows unemployment and inflation in the United States from 1960 to 1982. The late Arthur Okun of The Brookings Institution and former chairman of the Council of Economic Advisers constructed a discomfort index arrived at by adding the percentage rate of unemployment and the annual percentage rate of inflation. Over the past two decades, the discomfort index has grown dramatically. In 1960 it was only 7.0. By 1980 it had grown to 19.5. In 1981, the index started falling (to 17.0) in what economists hope is a trend.

TABLE 15–1

An Index of Discomfort

Former Chairman of the Council of Economic Advisers Arthur Okun once suggested that we could measure "discomfort due to both inflation and unemployment." All we need to do is add the annual inflation rate and the rate of unemployment.

YEAR	PERCENTAGE RATE OF UNEMPLOYMENT	ANNUAL PERCENTAGE RATE OF INFLATION	DISCOMFORT INDEX
1960	5.5	1.5	7.0
1961	6.7	0.8	7.5
1962	5.5	1.3	6.8
1963	5.7	1.4	7.1
1964	5.2	1.2	6.4
1965	4.5	2.1	6.6
1966	3.8	3.2	7.0
1967	3.8	3.3	7.1
1968	3.6	4.8	8.4
1969	3.5	6.1	9.6
1970	4.9	5.5	10.4
1971	5.9	3.4	9.3
1972	5.6	3.4	9.0
1973	4.9	8.8	13.7
1974	5.6	12.2	17.8
1975	8.5	7.0	15.5
1976	7.7	4.8	12.5
1977	7.0	6.8	13.8
1978	6.0	9.0	15.0
1979	5.8	13.3	19.1
1980	7.1	12.4	19.5
1981	7.6	9.4	17.0

● STAGFLATION

The previous chapter accounted for inflation by the aggregate demand–aggregate supply approach. If aggregate demand exceeds aggregate supply at or near the full-employment output rate, inflation will result. This demand-pull inflation can account for relatively high rates of inflation.

But how can the aggregate demand–aggregate supply approach be used when high rates of unemployment are associated with high rates of inflation, as shown in both Graph 15–3 and Table 15–1? The high rate of unemployment is an indication that the economy is definitely not at the full-employment rate of output. Thus, there should be no inflation according to the aggregate demand–aggregate supply approach. This phenomenon of economic stagnation (high rates of unemployment) and continuing inflation has been labeled **stagflation**.

The first serious period of stagflation in the United States occurred in 1969 and has occurred intermittently since then, both here and abroad. It occurred here again in 1973–1974 and in 1978, and reappeared in the early 1980s.

The existence of stagflation invalidates the Phillips curve, or at least shows that it is not stable. Economists see a major policy problem here. If the Phillips curve is not stable, then how can rising unemployment be fought? If expansionary policies are used, they may lead to an increase in inflation. Indeed, this is the basic problem with traditional monetary and fiscal policy measures during stagflation. Inflation is not desired, but policymakers fear that contractionary policies will only lead to further economic stagnation.

How can the existence of stagflation be explained? One major theory involves the diminishing incentives to work, save, and invest resulting from the high tax rates facing more and more individuals. To understand this explanation, it is helpful to take another look at the concept of taxflation, or bracket creep, which was first discussed in Chapter 8.

● TAXFLATION, OR BRACKET CREEP

Stagflation

The simultaneous existence of both recession (economic stagnation) and inflation.

Taxflation, or bracket creep

The process by which inflation pushes income earners into higher marginal tax brackets.

Taxflation, or bracket creep, refers to the way individuals are pushed into higher and higher marginal tax brackets simply because inflation increases their money, or nominal, incomes. We started this chapter with Mr. Gonzalez receiving a 7 percent increase in nominal income. And we said that even if the inflation rate was also 7 percent, he still might be worse off. Why? Because he might be pushed into a higher marginal tax bracket. Remember, the U.S. has a progressive federal personal income tax system. Table 8–3 showed that an equal increase in income and inflation would leave most

304

individuals worse off. By being pushed into higher marginal tax brackets, their average tax rates increase. For every 1 percent increase in the rate of inflation, the federal government collects 1.5 percent more personal income taxes.

The Stress on Tax Rates

The word *rate* has been used often. Instead of thinking in terms of taxes, think in terms of tax rates. The underlying assumption is that individuals, in their capacities as workers, savers, and investors, respond to changes on the margin.

What is important to the worker contemplating more or less work is the after-tax, or take-home, pay, which is a function of that worker's marginal tax rate. What is important to the saver is the after-tax rate of return on additional saving, which is a function of that saver's marginal tax rate. Finally, what is of interest to the businessperson contemplating investment in new plant and equipment is the expected after-tax rate of return. Again, that is a function of the marginal tax rate.

Tax Rates and the Labor—
Leisure Choice

From labor's point of view, there is always a choice between more work (more pay) and more leisure (less pay). As we just stated, the choice at the margin is a function of the after-tax rate of return to working. The higher the marginal tax rate, the lower the after-tax wage and hence the lower the opportunity cost of leisure. And as shown in Graph 15–4, the lower the opportunity cost (i.e., the greater the marginal tax rate), the greater the quantity of leisure demanded.[1]

Ways to Increase Leisure or Reduce Work Effort.   There are a number of ways in which individuals can respond to higher marginal tax rates. They include

1. Longer vacations
2. Fewer supplemental jobs (less moonlighting)
3. Earlier retirement
4. Greater absenteeism
5. Refusal of higher-paying positions that require more work effort or a location change
6. Lower participation rates for teenagers and older people

[1]We are ignoring so-called income effects in this simplified example. Income effects suggest that higher wages allow laborers to "purchase" more labor since they make the laborer richer. To some extent, these income effects might offset the effect discussed above.

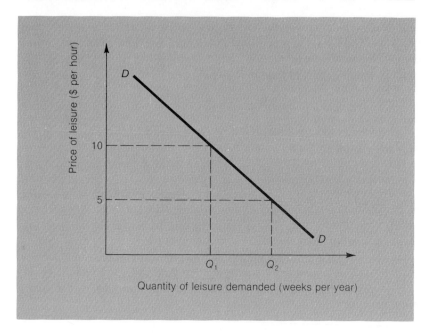

GRAPH 15–4
The Demand for Leisure

The demand for leisure (not working) is related to its price. Its price, however, is an individual's after-tax wage rate because when the individual does not work—that is, "buys leisure"—his or her opportunity cost is the after-tax income loss. Assume that with a zero marginal tax rate, the individual makes $10 an hour. The quantity of leisure demanded will be Q_1. If the individual's marginal tax rate increases to 50 percent, then the after-tax wage rate will be $5 an hour (given a pretax wage rate of $10 per hour) and the quantity of leisure demanded will increase to Q_2.

There have been relatively few studies on the degree to which Americans respond to higher marginal tax rates. We know that work effort is less, but the crucial question of how much less has not yet been answered definitively.

Avoiding Taxes: The Underground Economy

A system of high marginal tax rates encourages individuals to seek ways to avoid paying taxes. Each year, billions of dollars are paid out to lawyers and accountants who help high-income individuals legally reduce their tax liabilities. In addition, there is a growing number of resources devoted to *illegally* avoiding tax liabilities.

It seems that bracket creep has encouraged the so-called **underground, or subterranean, economy**. There is, in fact, a whole sector of economic activity in the United States in which income that is earned goes unreported and therefore is untaxed. To be sure, the

Underground, or subterranean, economy

The cash economy in which no taxes are paid and no official government statistics are kept.

306

underground economy includes the basic criminal elements—organized and unorganized crime, gamblers, prostitutes, drug pushers, and so on. Surprisingly, however, it also includes many otherwise legal activities that go unreported so that people can evade taxes. For example, numerous self-employed carpenters, plumbers, bookkeepers, and babysitters receive payments in cash that they do not report. The same is true for many self-employed businesspersons, physicians, and attorneys. And waitresses and waiters who hide some of their tips from the IRS are also part of the underground economy, as are musicians working "off the books."

What does the underground economy have to do with stagflation? Well, numerous resources go into seeking "off the book" cash transactions. Presumably, these exchanges would be done more efficiently (less costly) if they were part of the normal economy. They would become part of the normal economy if marginal tax rates were sufficiently reduced. After all, the lower the marginal tax rate, the less benefit there is in trying to seek out cash deals to avoid income taxes. Also, those who evade taxes risk fines or prison sentences. Moreover, the existence of a large and growing underground economy may mean that the economy is not suffering from as much stagnation as it seems. In 1976, the IRS attempted to estimate the size of the underground economy. It found that illegal activities represented only a small proportion of the underground economy. According to the study, the tax loss was due mainly to intentional failures to report income earned from legal activities. The IRS estimated that in 1976, people failed to report almost $135 billion in income. More recent estimates place the size of the underground economy at anywhere from 10 to 20 percent of GNP. This means that the nation has a real standard of living that is actually higher than GNP figures indicate and that the actual number of unemployed individuals is considerably less than officially reported. It also means that the actual labor force is greater than the measured labor force.

● SUPPLY-SIDE ECONOMICS AND THE LAFFER CURVE

Taxflation has pushed more and more individuals into higher tax brackets. Consequently, the incentive to work, save, and invest has been reduced, at least theoretically. Moreover, these high tax brackets have increased the incentive to devote resources to avoiding taxes. But what if a change in the tax system could induce Americans to work more, save more, and invest more? In other words, what if a reduction in marginal tax rates led to higher productivity? These propositions are at the basis of what has been called **supply-side economics**. The term comes from the emphasis on aggregate supply.

Supply-side economics

The theory that a reduction in marginal tax rates will lead to more productivity and, hence, higher economic growth. Supply-side economics utilizes the proposition that individuals respond to incentives or, more specifically, to changes in the after-tax rate of return to working, saving, and investing.

307

If productivity is increased, then supply will be increased. Presumably, this will allow the lower rates of inflation and economic growth to occur simultaneously, instead of the opposite, as occurs with stagflation.

Some supply-side economists go one step further and claim that a reduction in tax rates will not reduce tax revenues. To understand how this is possible, we must look at the relationship between tax rates and tax revenues. After some "high" marginal tax rate is reached, individuals reduce their work effort, spend more time seeking ways to reduce tax liabilities, and engage in more nonreported (nontaxed) exchanges. This relationship between tax rates and tax revenues has been popularized by Professor Arthur Laffer of the University of Southern California. His now famous **Laffer curve** demonstrates a relatively simple proposition: After some point, an

GRAPH 15–5
The Laffer Curve

The Laffer curve is a representation of the relationship between tax rates and tax revenues. The maximum tax revenues collectable, R_{max}, result when the tax rate T_1 is utilized. If the government insists on having a tax rate of T_2, tax revenues collected fall from R_{max} to R_2. Thus, if we believe that the real-world relationship between tax rates and tax revenues is as depicted here, and if the nation's rates are above tax rate T_1, then a reduction from current tax rates of, say, T_2 toward tax rate T_1 will *increase* tax revenues from R_2 to some greater amount, with the maximum reachable at R_{max}. In other words, a tax-rate reduction leads to an increase in tax revenues. The validity of this proposition rests on the empirical relationship between reductions in tax rates and changes in the amount of work effort, investment, saving, and attempts at tax avoidance.

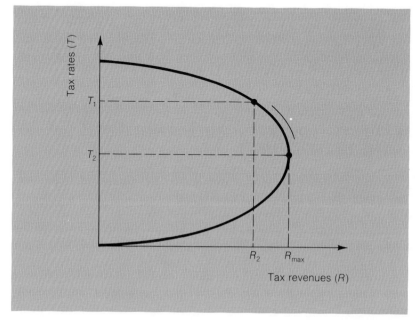

Laffer curve

A representation of the relationship between tax rates and tax revenues, showing that after a certain high tax rate, an even higher tax rate will yield smaller tax revenues. Alternatively, in certain situations, a reduction in tax rates can lead to higher tax revenues.

increase in tax rates actually reduces tax revenues. Look at Graph 15–5 which measures tax rates, T, on the vertical axis and tax revenues, R, on the horizontal axis. According to this curve, tax rate T_1 is the maximum rate that the government can impose before the relationship between tax rates and revenues becomes negative, or inverse. For example, at tax rate T_2, revenues will have dropped from R_{max} to R_2.

The policy implications of the Laffer curve are clear: If the economy is already at or above tax rate T_2, a reduction in tax rates will actually lead to an increase in tax revenues. This reasoning is the basis for numerous current proposals to cut tax rates.

While few argue with the theoretical existence of the Laffer curve, there is much disagreement about where the economy is on the Laffer curve. Many economists and policymakers, as well as concerned citizens, believe that a cut in tax rates would stimulate the economy. However, very few believe that such a tax cut would stimulate the economy so much that the government would actually *increase* its tax revenues. Perhaps the strongest case that can be made for a tax cut is that even if it doesn't increase tax revenues in the short run, it may do so in the *long run* by creating a higher rate of growth in the economy. For example, suppose all *marginal* tax rates are cut by 30 percent. In the first two years following the cut, federal tax revenues may fall by 10 percent. But in the third year, as a result of improved productivity, increased saving, and increased investment, the growth in the economy may increase so much that tax revenues actually increase by 20 percent.

Can Supply-Side Economics Work?

THE ARGUMENT

Even before supply-side economics became popular, it had its critics. Current critics point out that the Reagan tax cut did not reduce unem- *ployment very quickly. In 1982, the economy experienced 10 percent unemployment, the highest since the Great Depression.*

THE ANALYSIS

Although perhaps already suffering from an early death, supply-side economics is still occasionally in the news. President Ronald Reagan was elected in 1980, to a large extent, on the platform that reductions in tax rates can increase productivity, income, output, employment, and saving. Some of his supporters went so far as to argue that a reduction in tax rates could even lead to an *increase* in total federal tax revenues.

You have already been introduced to the concepts of incentives, marginal tax rates, and loopholes. Briefly, the higher the marginal tax rate, the greater the incentive to avoid paying taxes, either through legal tax avoidance, illegal tax evasion (joining the underground economy), or less work, saving, and investment. This simple proposition dating back perhaps several thousand years has been reborn as the Laffer curve. Basically, the Laffer curve contends that people do respond to incentives.

Not surprisingly, at some rate, an increase in the marginal tax rate will lead to a reduction in total tax revenues rather than an increase. Why? Because at some high marginal tax rate, any further increases will cause an overreaction by taxpayers. That overreaction will consist of more-than-propor-

tional attempts to avoid and evade taxes owed to the government.

As a theoretical proposition (or perhaps even a truism), the Laffer curve cannot be denied. What becomes important, rather, is where the economy is on the Laffer curve. Are marginal tax rates so high in the United States that they are past the point of maximum tax collection? If so, then the Laffer proposition is correct, and a reduction in marginal tax rates will lead to an *increase* in total tax revenues. But what if rates haven't yet reached the point of maximum tax collection? In that case, wouldn't a tax rate reduction *reduce* tax revenues?

At the time that President Reagan pushed through his so-called monumental tax cut in 1981, there was little research to show that a cut in the tax rate would, in fact, lead to a tax revenue increase. Some research, however, has shown that secondary workers, such as women and teenagers, are more responsive to changes in the tax rate than are prime-age males. It has been estimated that a 1 percent increase in after-tax income will lead to a 0.9 percent increase in hours worked by adult women, but only a 0.15 percent increase in work effort by the overall work force. Other research has indicated that over the last 20 years, increases in income taxes and payroll taxes have reduced the labor supply of married males by 8 percent and of married females by almost 30 percent.

Little work has been done to predict just how much of the underground economy will come above ground if marginal tax rates are reduced below what they are today. *Some* underground economic activity will start being reported, but the question is, how much? And the same question applies to investment behavior. If the after-tax rate of return to investment increases, more investments will be undertaken. But again, how much? Supply-siders have just begun to document the empirically predicted effects of reductions in marginal tax rates on underground versus reported activity and on investment activity.

But perhaps a more rational approach to supply-side predictions can be found. Although it may be wishful thinking that a cut in the tax rate will increase federal revenues in the short run, it may not be wishful thinking in the long run. A reduction in marginal tax rates today may lead to increased federal budget deficits today. But, if properly structured, reductions in marginal tax rates will increase economic growth through increasing labor force participation, increasing work effort, increasing saving, and increasing investment. Eventually, this increased economic growth will cause the "pie" to grow so much that even at the lower marginal tax rates, the federal government will ultimately end up taking in more in total tax revenues.

No sooner was the ink dry on Reagan's tax cut legislation in 1981 than critics pointed out that it was not working. Supply-side economics quickly fell into disrepute because the economy did not immediately pull out of its recession as predicted. And federal government deficits soon reached the $100 billion mark. Dispassionate analysis of what the Tax Reduction Act of 1981 really did, however, shows that supply-side

economics was never really given a chance. The so-called tax cut package of 1981 was merely a reduction in tax *increases* that would have occurred in its absence. In other words, the tax bite by the federal government stayed about the same, whereas supply-side economics requires that tax rates fall. But, you may wonder, how could tax rates remain the same when marginal tax rates were to be cut by 25 percent over a three-year period? The answer has to do with already scheduled increases in Social Security taxes and bracket creep, or taxflation, a subject we have previously discussed. The press may have hailed the 1981 tax cut as the largest ever, but it is not turning out that way.

DISCUSSION QUESTIONS

1. Beginning economics students learn that supply curves slope upward from left to right. What does this have to do with supply-side economics and the Laffer curve?
2. Why does the word *"marginal"* usually come before *tax rate* throughout this chapter?
3. Why will indexing the federal income tax system in 1985 eliminate the problem of bracket creep?

● WHAT'S AHEAD

So far, we have only examined the domestic economy. In the next chapter, we will review the international economy. You will discover that the exchanges made across national boundaries can be analyzed the same way we analyze exchanges within our own boundaries. That is, trade arises between nations for the same reasons that it does between people within a nation.

● CHAPTER SUMMARY

The Phillips curve expresses the relationship between the rate of inflation and the rate of unemployment. Presumably, there is a trade-off between the two. Empirically, however, the trade-off seems to have worsened over the last several decades, perhaps because of increased unemployment compensation and welfare benefits, because of a structural change in the labor force that caused any given rate of inflation to be associated with a higher rate of unemployment.

Simultaneous existence of recession (high unemployment) and inflation has been called stagflation. One explanation for the existence of stagflation is a reduction in the incentives to work, save, and invest because of the high marginal tax rates facing individuals and businesses. These high marginal tax rates have been a result of taxflation, or bracket creep. Presumably, a shift to lower marginal tax rates would lead to a smaller underground economy, more work, more saving, and more investment.

The relationship between tax rates and total tax revenues has been called the Laffer curve. At 0 percent and 100 percent tax rates, zero tax revenues are collected. At rates in between, various amounts are collected. In theory, there is a tax rate that yields the maximum tax revenues. If the economy finds itself above that tax rate, a reduction in taxes will actually lead to an increase in total tax revenues.

● QUESTIONS FOR REVIEW AND STUDY

1. Some economists believe that a trade-off exists between the rate of inflation and the rate of unemployment. This trade-off is represented by the _____ _____.

2. It is possible to simultaneously have economic stagnation and inflation. This is called _____.

3. The existence of stagflation seems to negate the _____ curve concept because both unemployment and inflation have been rising simultaneously.

4. A progressive tax structure combined with inflation leads to _____ _____.

5. Bracket creep has caused marginal tax rates to continue to rise in the United States. Higher and higher marginal tax rates increase the _____ to not report income.

6. Those who engage in activities in which earned income is not reported are members of the _____ economy.

7. The majority of activities in the underground economy are legal/ illegal.

8. Supply-side economics involves increasing the _____ to work, to save, and to invest.

9. Supply-siders place heavy emphasis on reducing _____ tax rates.

10. Presumably, workers are interested in _____-_____ salaries.

11. The higher the marginal tax rates, the more people wish to "purchase" _____ by working less.

12. Individuals can partake in more leisure through the following: _____ _____, _____ _____, _____ _____, _____ _____.

13. Savers look at a special type of return. It is the _____-_____ real return.

14. The relationship between marginal tax rates and total tax revenues is represented by the _____ _____.

15. According to the Laffer curve, if an economy has extremely high marginal tax rates, a reduction in tax rates will lead to a(n) _____ in tax revenues.

ANSWERS

1. Phillips curve 2. stagflation 3. Phillips 4. bracket creep 5. incentive 6. subterranean (or underground) 7. legal 8. incentive 9. marginal 10. after-tax 11. leisure 12. longer vacations; earlier retirement; no overtime; no moon-lighting; lower participation rates 13. after-tax 14. Laffer curve 15. increase

● ANSWERS TO CHAPTER PREVIEW QUESTIONS

1. There is a sizable underground economy in this nation. Why didn't it exist 100 years ago?

The subterranean economy was not really a problem 100 years ago because marginal tax rates were not nearly so high then for most people. Taxes have increased for two reasons. First, Congress has legislated higher and higher marginal tax rates. For example, during World War II, marginal tax rates reached 94 percent on very high incomes. Currently, marginal tax rates hit their maximum at 50 percent, which is still high by pre-war standards. The other reason that taxes have gone up is because bracket creep, or taxflation, has pushed people with average incomes into relatively high marginal tax brackets in recent years.

2. *What is supply-side economics all about?*

Supply-side economics is a relatively recent reaction by some economists to what they feel is an overemphasis on the role that aggregate demand plays in an economy. Traditional monetary and fiscal policies concern themselves with generating a multiple increase or decrease in aggregate demand, thereby changing the equilibrium level of national income. Supply-side economics, on the other hand, looks at aggregate supply and deals with the way changes in taxation, for example, can influence productivity so that the aggregate supply curve shifts outward. More specifically, supply-side economists maintain that laborers, savers, and investors react rationally to marginal tax rates. A laborer compares his or her after-tax earnings (benefits) to foregone leisure (costs) at the margin. Lower marginal tax rates may well encourage laborers to work more hours and be more productive—that is, to increase the *supply* of labor and output. And lower marginal tax rates on interest earnings may well encourage households to decrease consumption and increase their *supply* of saving. Also lower marginal tax rates on business earnings may well encourage increases in the *supply* of capital equipment for investment purposes—which will lead to increases in productivity, employment, and the *supply* of goods and services.

● PROBLEMS

1. Answer the following questions based on the graph below.

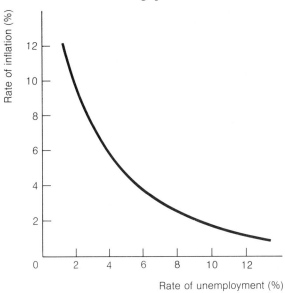

Rate of unemployment (%)

a. To reduce inflation to 2 percent per year, unemployment will "cost" what percent?
b. To reduce unemployment to 4 percent, what is the minimum rate of inflation that must be accepted?
c. What would cause this curve to "worsen," that is, to shift to the right?

2. Answer the following questions based on the graph below.

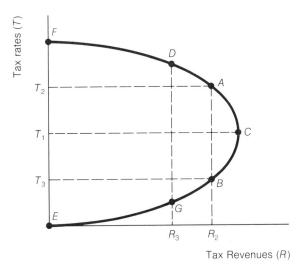

Tax Revenues (R)

    a. What two letters indicate zero tax revenues? How can this situation exist?

    b. What two letters indicate tax revenues equal to R_2?

    c. If the economy is at point A (tax rate T_2 yielding tax revenues R_2), what will happen to tax revenues if the tax rate falls below T_2?

    d. If the economy is at point B (tax rate T_3 yielding tax revenues R_2), what will happen to total tax revenues if the tax rate falls below T_3?

    e. What letter indicates the highest tax rate above which further tax rate increases will yield lower tax revenues?

● SELECTED REFERENCES

Blinder, Alan S. *Economic Policy and the Great Stagflation*. New York: Academic Press, 1979.

Laffer, A. B., and J. P. Seymour. *The Economics of the Tax Revolt*. New York: Harcourt Brace Jovanovich, 1979.

Miller, Roger LeRoy, and Raburn M. Williams. *Unemployment and Inflation: The New Economics of the Wage–Price Spiral*. St. Paul, Minn.: West Publishing, 1974, chap. 8.

Thurow, Lester C. *The Zero Sum Society*. New York: Basic Books, 1980.

UNIT 4

World Economics and Growth

Contents

16

International Trade and Finance

Chapter Preview

1. As a citizen of the United States, are you affected by international trade?

2. What are some of the arguments against unrestricted international trade (free trade)?

● KEY TERMS

Balance of payments	Freely floating, or flexible, exchange
Balance-of-payments deficit	rate system
Balance-of-payments surplus	Import quota
Comparative advantage	Imports
Exports	Infant industry argument
Fixed, or pegged, exchange rate	Tariff
system	Trade balance
Foreign exchange market	Trade deficit
Foreign exchange rate	Trade surplus

Have you ever wondered what your life would be like without international trade? If you take a moment to consider the products that you and your family use, you will probably find that you are affected by international trade every day of your life. If you use microcomputers or hand calculators, for example, there is a good chance that they were manufactured in Japan. The car you drive may be imported. The shirts, shoes, sweaters, and other articles of clothing that you wear may come from Korea, Thailand, or perhaps somewhere in Latin America. The raw materials necessary to produce chalk, erasers, pens, pencils, staplers, and other office supplies have probably been purchased in part from other countries. Certainly, many of the exotic foods and beverages on your grocer's shelves have been imported. And the TV you watch or the radio or stereo you listen to were at least partially produced outside the United States. International trade affects your daily life—of that there is no question.

● THE LANGUAGE OF FOREIGN TRADE

You are probably already familiar with the terminology of international trade. Nevertheless, we will now review certain frequently used terms.

Imports are goods and services purchased from other countries. U.S. imports include petroleum, automobiles, and steel, to name a few.

Exports are those goods and services produced domestically but sold to other countries. Just as we purchase foreign-made goods, other countries purchase our goods. Examples of U.S. exports are food, machinery and equipment, chemicals, and automobiles.

Nations pay for their imports with their exports. For example, nations are not going to produce goods and services for the United States free of charge. And payment in U.S. dollars is really useless to the outside world unless those U.S. dollars can eventually be

Imports

Goods and services purchased from abroad.

Exports

Goods and services made domestically but sold abroad.

320

exchanged for goods and services produced in the United States. Ultimately, a nation makes payment in exported goods and services for what it imports.

When the value of a country's imports just equals the value of its exports, a **trade balance** exists. When the value of a nation's exports is greater than the value of its imports, a **trade surplus** exists. And when the value of a nation's imports is greater than the value of its exports, a **trade deficit** exists.

If one nation has a trade surplus, another nation must have a trade deficit. In other words, no nation can export more than it is importing unless another nation is importing more than it is exporting. At any given time, the *world* must always be in trade balance. That is, world exports must always equal world imports. To see this, consider a simple example. Suppose that there are only two countries in the world—the United States and England. Suppose further that the United States is exporting $100 worth of goods and services to England and importing $150 worth of goods and services from England. The United States is therefore experiencing a trade deficit. At the same time, England must be exporting $150 worth of goods to the United States and importing $100 worth of goods from the United States. Thus, England has a trade surplus. It is important to recognize that even though neither country is in trade balance, the world is. That is, world exports equal $250 and so do world imports.

● THE GAINS FROM WORLD TRADE

In Chapter 1, we used the concepts of **comparative advantage** and specialization to explain how individuals benefit from trade. If every individual did whatever he or she had a comparative advantage in doing, then the value of total output would increase and everyone would benefit. In the same way, each nation gains by doing what it can do best relative to other nations. Thus, the United States benefits by specializing only in those endeavors in which it has a comparative advantage. Remember that cost is measured in opportunities that must be foregone. For example, if the United States decides to produce roller skates, it foregoes part of its opportunity to produce, say, computers, because the resources used in producing roller skates cannot be simultaneously used for computers.

The reason there is comparative advantage among individuals, companies, cities, counties, states, countries, and continents is that opportunity costs vary. It costs less for different parties to engage in different types of economic activities. Opportunity costs for different countries vary, just as they vary for different individuals. Let's examine some of the reasons why opportunity costs, and hence comparative advantages, differ among nations.

Trade balance

The value of exports equals the value of imports.

Trade surplus

The value of exports exceeds the value of imports.

Trade deficit

The value of imports exceeds the value of exports.

Comparative advantage

The ability to produce a good at a lower opportunity cost in terms of other goods than one's trading partners.

321

Differing Resource Bases

Different nations have different resource bases. For example, Australia has a great deal of land relative to its population, whereas Japan has very little land relative to its population. Other things being equal, we would expect countries with relatively more land to specialize in products that require more land. Thus, we would expect Australia, rather than Japan, to engage in extensive sheep raising, since the opportunity cost of raising sheep in Japan is much higher. (Since land in Japan is relatively scarce, its use carries a higher opportunity cost.)

Differences in climate also determine comparative advantage. For example, we would not expect countries with cold, dry climates to grow bananas. And yet, the limitations of a resource base do not *always* restrict a country's actions. Watermelons require tremendous amounts of water, but they are nonetheless grown in Arizona. (The federal government subsidizes water to watermelon growers in that state.)

Advantageous Trade Will Always Exist

Since the beginning of civilization, trade has existed among individuals. Since these acts of exchange have usually been voluntary, we must assume that individuals have generally benefited from the trade. Individual tastes and resources vary tremendously. As a result, there are sufficient numbers of different opportunity costs in the world for exchange to take place constantly.

As individual entities, nations have different collective tastes and different collective resource endowments. We would expect, therefore, that trading among nations will always offer potential gains. Furthermore, the more trade there is, the more specialization there can be. Specialization, in turn, leads to increased output and—if we measure well-being by output levels—to increased happiness. When individuals are self-sufficient, they must forego more opportunities to consume than if they were not self-sufficient. Likewise, self-sufficiency on the part of a nation will lower its consumption possibilities and therefore lower the real income levels of its inhabitants. Imagine life in Delaware if that state were forced to become self-sufficient!

Costs of Trade

Trade does not come without cost. If one state acquires a comparative advantage in farming, then other states may not be able to succeed as centers of agricultural production. As a result, farm workers in states that are less efficient at farming will suffer decreases in their incomes until they find other occupations or move to higher-paying jobs.

322

As tastes, supplies of natural resources, prices, and so on, change throughout the world, different countries may find their areas of comparative advantage changing. For example, Japan has become increasingly competitive with the United States in the production of steel, and U.S. steelmakers are being hurt. The stockholders and employees in U.S. steel companies are feeling the pinch from Japan's ability to produce steel products at lower costs. In summary, foreign trade raises average and total income in each country, but *certain groups* may experience ups and downs in their individual incomes.

● RESTRICTIONS ON WORLD TRADE

Despite the arguments in favor of free trade, restrictions on world trade are numerous and varied. The major restrictions are import quotas, tariffs, and quality restrictions.

Import Quotas

An **import quota** limits the amount of a commodity that can be imported. This type of restriction on trade clearly aids domestic producers. Goods for which import quotas have been enforced by the United States include sugar, meat, textiles, and color television sets.

Tariffs

A **tariff** is a tax on imported goods. Tariffs can be set as a specific money tax per unit (say, 10 cents per pound), or they can be set as a percentage of the value of the imported commodity.

Tariffs have been used at various times in the nation's history to raise revenues for the government and to protect specific industries. Graph 16–1 shows that since 1820, tariffs have varied from a low of less than 10 percent to a high of almost 70 percent. Currently, tariffs are around 10 percent when measured in terms of all tariff duties collected as a percent of all dutiable imports.

A particular tariff cannot simultaneously raise revenues and protect specific industries. After all, if a tariff is set too high, it will discourage trade and therefore lead to lower revenues. This relationship between tariffs and trade is similar to a relationship discussed in Chapter 15—the relationship between tax rates and work incentives reflected in the Laffer curve. If taxes are raised too high, individuals will work less and find ways to avoid taxes. Similarly, if tariffs are too high, individuals will not import as much. Tariffs intended to discourage trade, then, will necessarily be higher than those used to raise revenues.

Import quota

A limit on the quantity of a particular commodity that can be imported into the United States.

Tariff

A tax levied on imports.

323

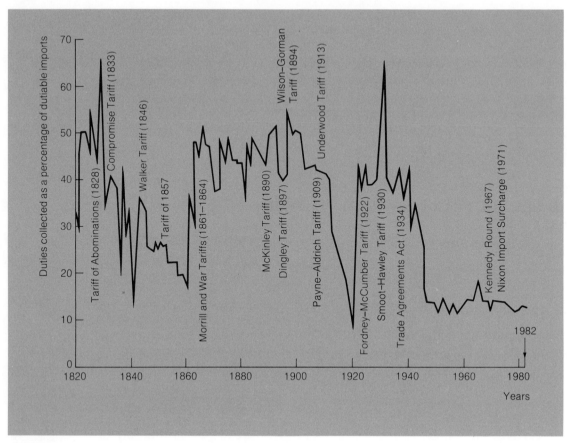

GRAPH 16–1
Tariff Rates in the United States Since 1820.

Tariff rates in the United States have fluctuated tremendously. In the twentieth century, the highest tariff was the Smoot–Hawley Tariff of 1930, which was almost as high as the Tariff of Abominations in 1828.

SOURCE: U.S. Department of Commerce

Quality restrictions

In addition to quotas and tariffs, other restrictions are imposed on imports to discourage potential foreign sellers from entering domestic markets. The most common examples are qualitative standards, such as requirements for meat quality or tomato size; import license delays; ever-changing standards of performance; and laws that force the domestic government to "buy American."

● ARGUMENTS IN FAVOR OF TRADE RESTRICTIONS

There are numerous arguments against free trade. However, these arguments are frequently one-sided. They point out the costs of trade, but they do not consider the benefits of trade or the possible alternatives for reducing costs while still reaping benefits.

Infant Industry Argument

A nation may feel that if a particular industry were allowed to develop domestically, it could eventually become efficient enough to compete effectively in the world market. Thus, if restrictions were placed on imports, native producers would be given enough time to develop their efficiency to the point where they could successfully compete in the domestic market in the absence of restrictions. When and if the protected industry does achieve that greater efficiency, the supply curve would shift outward to the right so that the domestic industry could produce larger quantities at each and every price.

This **infant industry argument** has some merit in the short run and has been used to protect a number of American industries. Such a policy can be abused, however. Often the protective import-restricting arrangements remain in force even after the infant has "matured." If other countries can still produce more cheaply, those who benefit from continued protection are clearly the stockholders and laborers in the protected industry. The people who lose out are the consumers, who must pay a price that is higher than the world price for the product in question. In any event, it is very difficult to know *beforehand* which industries will eventually survive. In other words, no one can predict which infant industries should be protected. (Note that when we talk about which industry *should be* protected, we are in the realm of normative economics; that is, we are stating a value judgment.) Finally, critics of the infant industry argument point out that there really aren't any so-called infant industries threatened by foreign competition in the United States today.

National Security

It is often argued that the United States should not rely on foreign sources for many of its products because in time of war these sources might be cut off and the U.S. will have developed few, if any, substitute sources. A classic example of using a national security argument to justify a trade restriction involves oil exploration. In 1959, for national defense reasons (supposedly), President Dwight D. Eisenhower instituted at first a voluntary, and then a mandatory, oil-import quota system, thereby restricting the amount of foreign oil that could be imported into the United States. The idea was to keep domestic prices up and thereby create an incentive for more exploration of American oil. Thus, in time of war, the United States would have a ready and available supply of oil for its tanks, ships, and bombers. Clearly, this argument for protection can be easily abused. Alternative solutions, such as stockpiling strategic resources, might be less costly.

Infant industry argument
The argument that tariffs should be imposed to protect a domestic industry while it is trying to develop.

Stability

Many people argue that foreign trade should be restricted because it introduces an element of instability into the U.S. economic system. They point out that the vagaries of foreign trade add to the ups and downs in the domestic employment level. Following this argument to its logical conclusion, however, trade among the various states would have to be restricted as well. After all, the vagaries of trade among particular states sometimes cause unemployment in other states. And although these problems are sorted out over time, workers suffer during the adjustment period. Nonetheless, trade among the states is not restricted. In fact, there is a constitutional stricture against taxing exports and imports among states (*inter*state commerce).

However, many individuals seem to feel that adjusting to the vagaries of *international* trade costs more than adjusting to the vagaries of domestic *interstate* trade. Perhaps those individuals believe that foreign trade doesn't benefit the nation that much; thus, they argue against it, claiming that the stability of aggregate economic activity is at stake. (It may also be that individuals derive personal satisfaction from knowing that citizens in other states are benefiting from trade, whereas they do not derive such satisfaction from knowing that unrestricted trade has benefited those in other countries.)

Note one difference between domestic and international trade, however, that does lend some truth to this argument. Labor is far more mobile among states than among nations. Immigration laws prevent workers from moving to countries where they can earn the most income. And differences in language and customs also prevent workers from moving freely from country to country. Therefore, the adjustment costs to a changing international situation may in fact be higher than the adjustment costs to a changing domestic situation. However, this may be an argument in favor of eliminating (or at least relaxing) immigration laws, rather than restricting international trade.

Protecting American Jobs

Perhaps the most popular argument against free trade is that foreign competition will eliminate American jobs because labor is cheaper in other countries. This is indeed a compelling argument, particularly for members of Congress from areas that might be threatened by foreign competition. For example, a congressperson representing an area with a large concentration of shoe factories would certainly be concerned about the possibility of constituents losing jobs because of competition from lower-priced shoe manufacturers in Brazil and Italy. However, this argument against free trade can also apply to trade among the states. After all, if labor in the South is less expensive than labor in the North, southern industry may put northern workers out of jobs. But again, the government does not, and constitutionally cannot, restrict trade among states (at least not overtly).

It should be pointed out here that total American jobs depend on aggregate demand. Even though foreign competition may alter the *structure* of the demand for labor, it does not automatically change the *total* demand for labor. Thus, foreign competition just forces domestic labor to change jobs, it doesn't really eliminate jobs.

Finally, you should be aware that virtually every attempt at protecting American jobs by imposing tariffs, quotas, and other restrictions on international trade leads to retaliation from our trading partners. In other words, they start imposing similar restrictions on trade with the United States. The result is that the nation has less productive employment at the expense of more productive employment. Moreover, measures that protect domestic jobs from imports end up destroying jobs in U.S. export industries. Remember, imports are ultimately paid for by exports; measures that cause a nation to import less will cause it to export less.

● THE POLITICS OF TRADE RESTRICTIONS

The main reason international trade restrictions exist is that a relatively small number of individuals reap large benefits from such restrictions, while a larger number of individuals each incur small losses. Consider an example. Suppose a high tariff or an import quota is set on textiles. Who gains? Owners and laborers in the textile industry of the importing nation gain by higher profits and wages. Who loses? All those individuals who purchase textiles domestically, since they pay a slightly higher price, perhaps only a few pennies. Thus, even though purchasers of textiles may suffer a relatively large *total* loss, individually they have little incentive to fight trade restrictions.

The concentrated benefits and diffuse costs of trade restrictions, together with the numerous arguments against free trade already presented, account for the worldwide restrictions. Mark Twain once pointed out that in the world of politics, the free traders win all of the arguments, but those who want to restrict trade win all of the elections.

● THE FINANCIAL SIDE OF INTERNATIONAL TRADE: EXCHANGE RATES

Nations make numerous transactions with each other. However, each nation has a different national currency (e.g., the U.S. dollar, the French franc, and the German mark). Foreigners who sell goods to the United States don't want our dollars. They want their own currencies so that they can purchase goods in their own countries. Similarly, when U.S. citizens send gifts of money to relatives in the "old country," the relatives want their own currency, not dollars. Fortunately, there is a way to exchange dollars for other currencies and other currencies for dollars. Those transactions take place in the **foreign exchange market**, where a particular exchange rate exists between all currencies. This exchange rate is called the **foreign exchange rate**, and it is determined by the supply and demand of different currencies throughout the world. For example, if the foreign exchange rate for Swedish krona is 5.7608, that means that it takes 5.7608 krona to buy one U.S. dollar. Alternatively, the value of one krona is 17.36 U.S. cents.

The Demand and Supply of Foreign Currency

Suppose you wish to import some Japanese bicycles. To do so you must go to the foreign exchange market to obtain Japanese yen. Your desire to buy the Japanese bicycles therefore provides a supply of dollars to the foreign exchange market. In other words, your demand for Japanese yen is equivalent to your supply of American dollars in the foreign exchange market. Indeed, every transaction made concerning the importation of foreign goods constitutes a supply of dollars and a demand for some foreign currency—in this case, a demand for Japanese yen.

Now suppose that a Japanese citizen is interested in importing some American blue jeans. In our example, we will assume that only two goods are being traded—Japanese bicycles and American blue jeans. Thus, the American demand for Japanese bicycles creates a supply of dollars and a demand for yen in the foreign exchange market. Similarly, the Japanese demand for American blue jeans creates a supply of yen and a demand for dollars in the foreign exchange market. In a **freely floating, or flexible, exchange rate system**, the supply and demand of dollars and yen in the foreign exchange market will determine the equilibrium foreign exchange rate. The equilibrium exchange rate will tell us how many yen a dollar can be exchanged for—that is, the yen price of a dollar—or how many dollars (or fractions of a dollar) a yen can be exchanged for—that is, the dollar price of yen.

Exchange rates reflect the law of demand. For example, you buy so much coffee when the price is 25 cents a cup. If the price goes up to $1 a cup, you will probably buy less coffee. If the price goes down to 5 cents, you might buy more. In other words, the demand curve for coffee, expressed in dollars, slopes downward, following the law of demand. In the example above, the demand curve for yen also

Foreign exchange market

A market in which foreign currencies are bought and sold.

Foreign exchange rate

The price of foreign currency in terms of domestic currency, or vice versa.

Freely floating, or flexible, exchange rate system

A system in which exchange rates are allowed to fluctuate in response to changes in the supply and demand.

328

slopes downward in the foreign exchange market.

Fixed Exchange Rates and the Adjustable Peg

Today, much of the world is on a flexible exchange rate system, although governments do occasionally intervene to prop up the world price of their currency. On the other hand, a **fixed, or pegged, exchange rate system** exists when a country's central bank is willing and able to step into the foreign exchange market to ensure that the price of foreign exchange does not change. A fixed exchange rate system is, in principle, no different from a system of price supports for agricultural products. In a system of price supports, the government buys up the surplus at the supported price when there is an excess quantity supplied. Remember, in a world of flexible exchange rates, dollars, francs, marks, and pounds are just like any other goods and services—their prices fluctuate, depending on changes in supply and demand.

In 1944, at Bretton Woods, New Hampshire, a system was devised to establish fixed exchange rates for most countries in the world, with the exchange rates being allowed to vary slightly around a particular value. Thus marked the formation of the International Monetary Fund (IMF). Each Fund member established a par value for its currency in terms of dollars. (*Par value* simply means "official.") Foreign exchange values were set at that time on a system called the *adjustable peg*. For example, if it were decided that the par value of the franc was 5 francs to $1, or 20 cents a franc, then the exchange rate was set at that level. Exchange rates were, however, allowed to fluctuate under the influence of supply and demand within a narrow band. From 1944 to 1971, the band was 1 percent above par value to 1 percent below par value. From 1971 until 1973, the band was 2.25 percent above par to 2.25 percent below par.

Under the rules established at Bretton Woods, a government was committed to intervene to prevent the value of its currency in the foreign exchange markets from staying at the lower limits. When there was an excess quantity supplied of its currency—that is, when the below-par limit was reached—the deficit government was obligated to buy the excess with dollars in order to prop up the price of its own currency.

Adjusting the Peg

The pegged (or par) value of a country's currency was occasionally adjusted by the IMF. For example, suppose that because of recurrent deficits, the value of the franc in the foreign exchange market was hovering for long periods at the lower limit of its band, say, one franc for 19.8 cents, compared with the par value of one franc for

Fixed, or pegged, exchange rate system

A system in which a unit of each nation's domestic currency can be exchanged for a unit of every other nation's domestic currency at a fixed price.

329

20 cents. In such a situation of recurrent "weakening" of the franc in the foreign exchange market, the IMF might allow France to adjust the par value. For example, France might be allowed to declare a new par value at one franc for 19.8 cents.

Graphic Analysis of the Band Around the Peg

Graph 16–2 shows a graphic analysis of the band around the peg. Consider French francs with a price pegged at 20 cents a franc, the designated par value. One percent par value limits have been drawn in at $0.202 and $0.198. Initially, the supply of French francs is S and the demand is D. If the demand curve (which, remember, is *derived* from the demand for French goods and services) falls to D', it is within the acceptable limits, since the foreign exchange rate for French francs will fall to $0.198 a franc. And if the demand for French francs shifts upward to D'', it, too, is within the limits of the

GRAPH 16–2

The Bank around the Peg

Assume that France's currency is pegged at 20 cents per franc. Its value is allowed to fluctuate in foreign exchange markets by 1 percent. The "bands" are drawn in at $0.202 and $0.198. Assume that supply is stable. The demand curve can go anywhere from D' to D'' without any central bank intervening to push the market price of francs back to 20 cents.

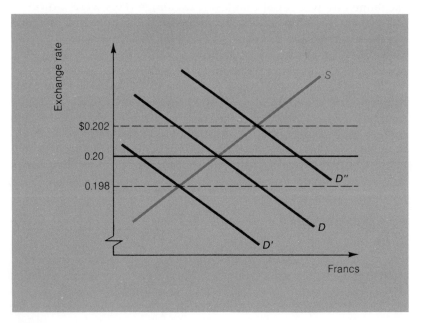

par value, since the market price for French francs will rise to $0.202 a franc. Only if the intersection of supply and demand lays outside the shaded band is the "guilty" country's government supposed to intervene in the foreign exchange market. The French central bank would buy francs with dollars if their price stayed too low; the United States government would buy dollars with French francs if the dollar's value were chronically low.

Other Duties of the IMF

Besides administering the system of exchange rates, the IMF was also authorized to lend funds to member countries in balance-of-payments deficits. These loans were to come from IMF holdings of gold and currency arising from subscriptions by its members in relation to their "quotas." Each member's quota was set according to a formula that took into account its importance in the world economy. But the obligation of the surplus countries to lend to deficit countries was limited. For example, America's obligation to lend to deficit countries was limited to the size of America's quota in the IMF, and no more.

How Can Rates Remain Fixed?

In a world of fixed exchange rates, some mechanism must be available to guarantee that the price of dollars in terms of francs, the price of marks in terms of pesos, and the price of pounds in terms of guilders remain fixed. That mechanism was the intervention by the world's central banks. If the value of the dollar started to weaken in the foreign exchange market, the United States central bank[1] would step in to prop up the value of the dollar by buying dollars in the foreign exchange market, using foreign reserves held in the Federal Reserve. If the value of the German mark started to fall, the German central bank—the Bundesbank—would step in and buy more marks on the foreign exchange market. In this manner, central banks were able to keep the value of their respective currencies relatively stable—as long as reserves were adequate.

England's Recurrent Currency Crises

Unfortunately, it was not always possible for a country to maintain the value of its currency. England, for example, experienced continued pressure on the value of the pound in the foreign

---

[1]The Federal Reserve Bank of New York represents the Federal Reserve System and the U.S. Treasury in the foreign currency market.

exchange market. To keep the pound from losing its value, England had to purchase pounds on the foreign exchange market with other countries' currencies or gold. However, England's central bank did not have an unlimited supply of foreign currency and gold. Therefore, when it was about to run out of foreign exchange funds, it would declare a currency crisis. Usually, the IMF would then call a special meeting to decide how to bail England out. The IMF would do so, in effect, by convincing countries that were selling pounds not to sell them, or by convincing countries to loan foreign currency to England so that England could continue to prop up its own currency.

● THE BALANCE OF PAYMENTS

We have already referred to the balance of trade, which refers to the value of exports and the value of imports. When a country's foreign trade is in balance, the value of exports will equal the value of imports. The **balance of payments** is a more general term that reflects the value of all transactions between two nations, usually for a period of one year. In a flexible exchange rate system, the balance of payments is always nearly in balance because of automatic adjustments in exchange rates. But for most of recent history, the world has not experienced a truly freely floating foreign exchange rate system in which the supply of and demand for currencies were accurately reflected by exchange rates. Therefore, the balance of payments is an important topic in international finance. World leaders worry when their countries run payment deficits or surpluses for very long.

In addition to buying and selling goods, Americans transact other business with foreign nations, such as investing and borrowing. In the earlier example of two countries exchanging two products, the balance of trade was equal to the balance of payments. The value of the transactions the United States had with Japan was equal to the value of the transactions Japan had with the U.S. However, when a **balance-of-payments deficit** occurs (as it has in the United States for almost 20 years), it means that foreign countries are sending the U.S. more value than it is sending them. A **balance-of-payments surplus** occurs for the U.S. when the U.S. is sending other nations, as a group, more than those nations are sending it. This "value" includes all possible types of raw materials, products, services, investments, gifts, and so on. A balance-of-payments deficit or surplus occurs under a special set of circumstances, because with freely floating exchange rates the balance of payments will, by definition, always be in balance. That is, the exchange rate will change if an imbalance occurs; that adjustment will restore a payments balance.

Balance of payments

Refers to the annual value of a nation's transactions in goods, services, financial assets, and military goods (and all other transactions) in the world market.

Balance-of-payments deficit

The value of U.S. transactions with other countries is such that they are sending the U.S. more value than it is sending them.

Balance-of-payments surplus

A U.S. balance of payments surplus occurs when the U.S. is sending other nations, as a group, more value than they are sending it.

332

How To Measure the Balance of Payments

Balance of payments can be measured in a number of ways. Table 16–1 lists three of the most common measures and/or components applied to the United States for various years over the last decade. These measures are described below.

Merchandise Trade Balance Account. The merchandise trade balance is merely the difference between exports and imports of tangible items. For the better part of the last 30 years, the United States had a surplus in its merchandise trade account. However, the situation reversed in the 1970s, when this country began to import more than it exported, due to the fact that the price of imported oil increased rapidly.

Goods and Services Account. The goods and services account is the same as the merchandise trade balance account except that services and intangible items have been added. These items include shipping insurance, tourist expenditures, and income from foreign investments. Note that these items are *net* in the sense that they represent the difference between foreigners' purchases in the United States and Americans' purchases abroad. Thus, the investment income aspect of the goods and services account indicates the difference between the income received by Americans from direct investments abroad and the income received by foreigners from investments in the United States. Direct investment involves putting up money capital for businesses in other countries.

Current Account. The current account differs from the goods and services account in that it includes net government and private transfers. In other words, it includes foreign aid (government gifts) by the United States to other countries, private gifts to those living in other countries, and military expenditures.

TABLE 16–1
U.S. Foreign Accounts (Billions of dollars)

	1961	1966	1971	1976	1980
Merchandise trade balance (goods)	5.6	3.8	−2.3	−9.3	−27.4
Goods and services	5.6	4.5	2.3	9.4	7.1
Current account	3.0	1.6	4.0	4.4	.1

SOURCE: U.S. Department of Commerce.

How Can There Be a Balance-of-Payments Problem in a World of Flexible Exchange Rates?

You may now be wondering how the United States can have balance-of-payments deficits or surpluses in a world of flexible exchange rates. By definition, the balance of payments in such a world is always in balance because of the fluctuation of exchange rates. Actually, though, we do not live in a world of purely flexible exchange rates. Numerous countries engage in what is called a "dirty float," in which central banks intervene to alter the value of foreign currency in the foreign exchange market.

The term *dirty* is used to distinguish from a freely floating exchange rate situation, where government intervention does not occur at all; freely floating exchange rates are "clean" of government intervention. However, the dirty float still has not put the world back on the fixed exchange rate system that existed for so many years beginning with the formation of the International Monetary Fund.

Should the United States Go Back to the Gold Standard?

THE ARGUMENT

Nothing backs the U.S. dollar because, as pointed out in Chapter 13, the U.S. has a fiduciary monetary system. Many observers of both the domestic and international monetary scene have argued that the U.S. should return to the gold standard. A gold standard means that gold coins would be minted and used as a medium of exchange, and exchange rates among nations would be pegged to specific gold prices. Thus, a gold standard is a specific form of a pegged exchange rate system. Most of the industrialized nations were on the gold standard before the IMF system replaced it; in fact, most were on some form of gold standard from 1792 until the mid-1930s.

THE ANALYSIS

Going back to a gold standard would probably require that gold coins be minted and used. In addition, there would have to be gold warehousing, with gold warehouse receipts circulating as a medium of exchange. (After all, gold is cumbersome and subject to theft, and it must be cared for.) The gold warehouse receipts would be directly convertible to gold, since it would be quite awkward and time-consuming for individual merchants to weigh and assess the gold content of coins used as a medium of exchange. Also, many merchants do not possess such skills. Thus, warehouse certificates would probably be used in some form if a gold standard were reestablished in this country.

Does Gold Perform All the Functions of Money?

Gold certainly performs the first function of money; it is a medium of exchange. Money also has proved to be an excellent store of purchasing power in that, *over the long run*, the purchasing power of gold has held up relatively well.

Now comes the problem. It would be difficult, if not impossible, to use gold as a unit, or standard, of accounting. Moreover, even with depreciating currencies (due to inflation), fiduciary money in the United States and in other countries has served its function as a unit of accounting. The dollar as a unit of accounting has been serviceable.

How Accurate Would Gold Be as a Standard of Accounting?

During a typical period, the price of gold fluctuates often. Now, assume that the unit of accounting for gold is going to be 1 ounce. In that case, a house valued at 10,000 ounces of gold one month might be worth 8000 the next month and 15,000 ounces the following month. This example illustrates the major problem with using gold or any other commodity as money—*the market value sometimes fluctuates wildly*. On the other hand, the value of a dollar in terms of its exchange capabilities decreases as inflation increases. But at least it doesn't fluctuate wildly.

In sum, it is difficult to imagine an

efficient economic system in which *any* commodity is used as the *only* money. It would be very difficult to compare relative values of goods and services if the unit in which the valuations were made kept changing unpredictably in purchasing power.

Putting Gold Behind the Dollar

One way, perhaps, to keep people from *losing* faith in the U.S. fiduciary monetary system—those essentially worthless paper dollars and checking account balances—is to reinstate the requirement that a certain percentage of the money supply be backed by gold. While such a requirement doesn't prevent inflation, it may nevertheless reduce the Federal Reserve's ability to create money at will. Some critics of the Federal Reserve contend that right now the Fed can do almost anything it wants with the money supply. These critics argue that if gold backing were required for a given percent of the money supply, the activities of the Federal Reserve would be somewhat constrained.

Such a system couldn't grant full gold convertibility to dollars, otherwise every time the price of gold rose relative to the dollar, people would rush to exchange their extra dollars for gold. And every time the price of gold fell, people would try to sell their gold back. It would be a chaotic system, to say the least.

Gold and Inflation

Most people talk about returning to a gold standard to avoid inflation. It is probably safe to assume that had the U.S. been on a gold standard for the last several hundred years, it would have experienced less inflation. A return to the gold standard, however, would not necessarily eliminate the possibility of inflation. As a matter of fact, there were times in this nation's history when it was on the gold standard but still experienced inflation because of the discovery of gold or of cheaper methods of mining gold.

Basically, the purchasing power, or exchange rate, of gold would be determined by the supply of gold relative to its demand. In other words, if, for whatever reason, the quantity of gold supplied exceeded the quantity demanded, the price of gold in terms of dollars would fall. Thus, inflation would still occur.

Where does gold come from? Most of it comes from the Soviet Union and South Africa, although recently, new ore discoveries have been reported in North America. The worldwide supply of new gold is therefore largely a function of the mining operations of the Soviet Union and South Africa. Either in concert or alone, those countries could—if this country were on a gold standard—create an inflation in the United States simply by mining more gold than they normally do.

DISCUSSION QUESTIONS

1. Is gold different from silver or platinum? If so, in what way would a silver or platinum standard be different?
2. What is the difference between a gold standard and the current domestic and international monetary system now used?

● WHAT'S AHEAD

Now that you have been introduced to the workings of international trade and finance, we will proceed to a discussion of the economic growth of a nation. We will examine the determinants of economic growth, see how economic growth is measured, and compare international growth rates for selected countries.

● CHAPTER SUMMARY

In world trade, when the value of imports equals the value of exports for a nation, that nation is experiencing a trade balance. When the value of a nation's imports exceeds the value of its exports, it is in a trade deficit. And when the value of its exports exceeds the value of its imports, it is in a trade surplus.

International trade is advantageous because each country has a comparative advantage. Each country has a different comparative advantage because of different resource mixes, different tastes, and thus different opportunity costs. Whenever there is a restriction of international trade, countries cannot fully specialize in their comparative advantage.

The major restrictions on international trade involve tariffs, quotas, and quality restrictions. Often the infant industry argument, as well as the national defense argument, is used in favor of restricting international trade.

The financial side of international trade involves the foreign exchange market, where different currencies are traded. In an unrestricted foreign exchange market (floating exchange market), the underlying forces of supply and demand determine foreign exchange rates. In a fixed exchange rate system, governments arbitrarily set exchange rates at a specific level. To keep the exchange rates at that level, government central banks are ready to enter the foreign exchange market to buy or sell their own currency to keep the price constant. In a world of fixed exchange rates, it is possible to have a balance-of-payments deficit or surplus. There are different ways to measure these deficits and surpluses.

● QUESTIONS FOR REVIEW AND STUDY

1. Whenever the value of goods and services sold to other nations by U.S. residents equals the value of goods and services purchased by the United States from other nations, the U.S. has a _____ _____ _____.

2. When import values equal export values, there is a _____ _____ _____.

3. When the value of imports exceeds the value of exports, there is a _____ _____.

4. In the world, at any one time, there must be a world _____ _____ _____.

5. Because of the advantages of trade, individuals and nations tend to _____ in whatever they have a _____ _____.

6. Two important restrictions to international trade are _____ _____ _____ and _____.

7. One argument in favor of restrictive tariffs involves industries that need time to mature. This is called the _____ _____ argument.

8. Regarding the necessity of having strategic materials domestically available, as an alternative to import restrictions, a nation can _____ strategic goods.

9. Transactions involving investments, gifts, and military spending, in addition to imports and exports of goods and services, affect the _____ _____ _____.

10. In a world of freely floating exchange rates, whenever a country suffers a balance-of-payments deficit, the value of its currency, in terms of foreign currencies, will _____.

11. A fixed exchange rate system inevitably leads to monetary _____ because it is difficult to fight the forces of supply and demand that constantly change.

12. The International Monetary Fund (IMF) involved a system in which each country fixed its currency in terms of _____.

13. The 1970s saw a massive balance-of-payments _____ in the U.S. because of a(an) _____ in the price of imported oil.

ANSWERS

1. balance of trade 2. balance of trade 3. trade deficit 4. balance of trade 5. specialize; comparative advantage 6. import quotas; tariffs; quality restrictions 7. infant industry 8. stockpile 9. balance of payments 10. fall 11. crises 12. U.S. dollars 13. deficit; increase

● ANSWERS TO CHAPTER PREVIEW QUESTIONS

1. *As a citizen of the United States, are you affected by international trade?*

The direct impact of international trade on the United States, as measured by the ratio of exports to GNP, is relatively small (only about 8 percent), compared with many other nations. Yet it is hard to imagine what life would be like without international trade. Initially, many prices would rise rapidly, but eventually, domestic production would begin on many goods presently imported. However, consider life without coffee, tea, bananas, and all foreign wines, motorcycles, automobiles, televisions, videotape recorders, and hundreds of other goods from food and clothing to electronics—not to mention vital imports such as bauxite, chromium, cobalt, nickel, platinum, tin, and asbestos.

2. *What are some of the arguments against unrestricted international trade (free trade)?*

Many economists agree that free trade would generate an efficient allocation of world resources; each country would produce those commodities in which it has a comparative advantage and import those commodities in which it does not. This would lead to higher average and total incomes for all countries. Yet, despite this, there are many people who offer arguments *against* free trade.

There is the infant industry argument, which maintains that new industries developing domestically need protection from mature foreign competitors until they can compete with those foreign competitors—at which time protection would be removed. One problem with this argument is that it is difficult to tell when an infant industry has in fact matured, and domestic industries will fight against such weaning. Moreover, this argument is hardly one that U.S. industries can presently use.

Another popular argument against free trade is the national security argument, which maintains that certain inputs or outputs are strategically important and should be developed domestically, even if the cost of doing so is greater than the cost of importation. This will limit the domestic country's reliance on foreign sources, which could be hazardous in time of crisis. This argument is easily abused and is particularly attractive to domestic producers who stand to profit from protection. Moreover, alternatives exist, such as finding substitutes and/or stockpiling "strategic" resources.

Finally, it is alleged that free trade leads to instability for specific domestic industries, as comparative advantage changes in a dynamic world. Nations that traditionally have held a comparative advantage in the production of certain goods occasionally lose that advantage (while necessarily gaining others). Regional hardships are a result, and protection of domestic jobs is demanded. Yet, if carried to its logical conclusion, this argument leads to restriction of trade among states, and then among cities and towns *within* states! A measure of insecurity is the price that nations must pay for higher average and total incomes; nothing is free in this world.

● PROBLEMS

1. If the rate of exchange between the pound and the dollar is $2.45 for one pound, and the United States then experiences a very severe inflation, the exchange rate (under a flexible rate system) would shift and be:

   a. Greater than $2.45 for one pound
   b. Less than $2.45 for one pound
   c. More than one pound for $2.45
   d. None of the above

2. The dollar, the pound, and the mark are the currency units of the United States, England, and Germany, respectively. Suppose these nations decide to go on a gold standard and define the value of their currencies in terms of gold as follows: $35 equals 1 ounce of gold; 10 pounds equals 1 ounce of gold; and 100 marks equals 1 ounce of gold. What would be the exchange rate between:

   a. The dollar and the pound?
   b. The dollar and the mark?
   c. The mark and the pound?

● SELECTED REFERENCES

Friedman, Milton. *Dollars and Deficits*. Englewood Cliffs, N.J.: Prentice-Hall, 1968.

Friedman, Milton, and Robert V. Roosa. *The Balance of Payments: Free Versus Fixed Exchange Rates*. Washington, D.C.: American Enterprise Institute, 1967.

Pen, Jan A. *Primer on International Trade*. New York: Random House, 1967.

Schmidt, Wilson E. *The U.S. Balance of Payments and the Sinking Dollar*. New York: New York University Press, 1979.

Snider, Delbert A. *Introduction to International Economics*. 7th ed. Homewood, Ill.: Irwin, 1979, chaps. 1–6.

17

Economic Growth

Chapter Preview
1. What are some of the ways you can experience economic growth, either for yourself or for your family?
2. How is economic growth measured?

● KEY TERMS

Economic growth   Rule of 72
Real income

Many people in the United States take their living standards for granted. They further assume that their living standards will be higher than their parents', and that their children's living standards will be higher still. The expectation is for **real income** to rise over each person's lifetime. Finally, most people in the United States believe that they are not likely to witness mass starvation or general malnutrition in this country.

Although the chances are quite good that these expectations will be met, a fundamental point is being missed. Throughout history, the economic lot of humankind has been generally miserable. Until quite recently, life for most individuals was "short, nasty, and brutish," as a nineteenth-century scholar once noted. This condition was accepted by poor and rich alike. Indeed, even the "rich" of years past suffered in comparison to some of our "poor" today. The masses expected little more than a short, violent, filth- and poverty-ridden life. Food was in short supply, and more often than not, it was spoiled. Water was dangerous to drink and disease was common.

Then, a few centuries ago, something of an economic miracle began to occur. For the first time in history, a few nations began to experience sustained increases in living standards. Living standards grew steadily, if not spectacularly, in these few countries, and the masses were lifted from a condition of bare subsistence. Life expectancies increased dramatically, infant mortality dropped, and health standards improved. Advances were made in sanitation, as well as in medical and dental care. Food became more abundant and of better quality. And much tedious factory work and housework were replaced by technological innovation.

This economic miracle occurred in only a relatively small number of countries, however. For most people in today's world, conditions aren't much better than they were centuries ago. The question still facing the world today is why some countries have developed and others have not. In other words, what is the secret behind economic growth?

Real income

A measure of the real purchasing power of nominal income; real income is nominal income adjusted for changes in the general price level.

Economic growth

The annual percentage increase in a nation's real per capita GNP.

● DEFINING ECONOMIC GROWTH

What do economists mean when they refer to a nation's economic growth? **Economic growth** refers to the rate of increase in an economy's real per capita gross national product. GNP was defined in Chapter 10 as the market value of all final goods and services produced over a one-year period. To get from GNP to real GNP, an appropriate index of inflation is used to correct for price changes. Finally, to obtain real per capita GNP, real GNP must be divided by the size of the population.

A country's rate of economic growth gives some clue as to its changing living standards. The higher a country's economic growth rate, the more rapidly material living standards are rising. This makes sense because living standards have much to do with a nation's output of goods and services. Increased real per capita output allows for more and more consumption by everyone. And the consumption of goods and services is what the living standard is all about.

Problems with the Definition of Economic Growth

There are problems with this definition of economic growth and how it relates to living standards. First of all, nothing is stated about the distribution of output and income. A nation might grow very rapidly in terms of total or real per capita output, but the nation's poor people might remain poor or become even poorer. For example, certain Central American countries have been experiencing relatively high rates of growth in both total and real per capita output. Guatemala is a case in point. Not everyone in that country, however, is sharing in the increases in output. Some observers maintain that the Indians of Mayan origin in Guatemala are just as poor now as they were 100 years ago. Therefore, in assessing the economic growth record of Guatemala, we must be careful to pinpoint which income groups have benefited the most from such growth.

Also, nothing in this definition of economic growth relates to the spiritual, cultural, and environmental aspects of the "good" life. GNP is not a measure of happiness or satisfaction. Thus, a nation could conceivably be experiencing slow (or no) economic growth, as measured by the lack of increase in real per capita GNP, and at the same time more individuals could be finding more spiritual happiness.

Nevertheless, the definition of economic growth used here does help evaluate the change in living standards through time. It also helps in comparing the living standards of different countries at a given period in time. The measures are not perfect, but if used wisely, they can give a fairly good reading of changes in living standards.

● THE U.S. GROWTH EXPERIENCE

There is an old quip that the Quakers came to America to do good and ended up doing well. There is a grain of truth in this. But the Quakers were not the first to arrive on American shores.

343

The first British outpost in North America was set up by Sir Walter Raleigh in the 1580s. It was located at Roanoke, North Carolina, for the purpose of harassing the Spanish treasure fleets. It stands as one of history's teasing mysteries, because after a short absence, Raleigh returned in 1590 to find no trace of the people— living or dead. This "lost colony" forcefully accents the great hardships that were faced by new settlers in America. The majority of the settlers in the early seventeenth century died within two years. Starvation, disease, Indian attacks, and other calamities were commonplace.

By 1775, however, the colonists had experienced an extraordinary rise in their standard of living, due in part to the hard work and economic freedoms. And in the more than 200 years since then, this nation has seen almost constant improvements in its standard

GRAPH 17–1

U.S. Economic Growth

This graph indicates that the trend in economic growth has been upward; real per capita GNP has risen dramatically since 1869. Note that this economic growth record is neither smooth nor always rising. For example, real GNP fell during the Great Depression, and in the 1970s and 1980s, the rate of growth of real per capita GNP has been relatively low (percentage-wise).

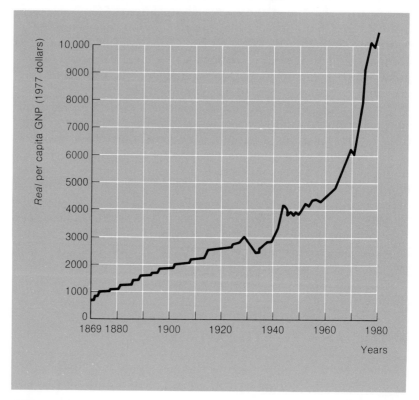

of living. For the time following 1840, the year of the first U.S. national income estimate, it is possible to calculate with fair precision the nation's record of economic growth. Thus, Graph 17–1, expresses economic growth in rates of change of real per capita income since 1869. This rate, although clearly not steady, has followed a long-run trend of approximately 1.6 percent per year.

● COMPARING INTERNATIONAL GROWTH RATES

Table 17–1 shows the average annual growth rates of real per capita income in selected countries for the period 1929–1980. Note the column showing *doubling times*. When something is growing at a certain rate, that "something" will eventually double in size. For example, with an annual growth rate of 2 percent, France will double its real per capita income in 36 years. At a 5.2 percent annual growth rate, Greece will double its real per capita income every 14 years.

One of the easiest ways to approximate doubling time is to use the **rule of 72**. By this rule, we simply divide the number 72 by the coefficient of the annual percentage rate of growth of real per capita

TABLE 17–1

Growth Rates for Selected Countries, 1929–1980

This table compares economic growth rates among different countries. Although the U.S. growth rate is not relatively high, the United States has been growing economically over a very long period of time. Thus, its *base* (starting level) real per capita income level is considerably higher than any other country's. Other things constant, it is more difficult for already-developed nations, such as the United States, to grow rapidly than it is for less-developed nations. Also, the United States has largely been a pioneer, creating new technology, whereas newly developing countries are able to borrow technology.

COUNTRY	AVERAGE ANNUAL GROWTH RATE OF PER CAPITA INCOME (in Percent)	DOUBLING TIME (in Years)
Brazil	1.8	40
Canada	2.1	34
France	2.0	36
Germany	3.0	24
Greece	5.2	14
Italy	2.5	29
Japan	4.9	15
Mexico	3.1	23
United Kingdom	1.7	42
United States	1.9	38
U.S.S.R.	4.4	16

SOURCE: U.S. Department of Commerce and Statistical Office of the United Nations.

Rule of 72

A method to approximate doubling time; divide the number 72 by the coefficient of the annual percentage rate of growth.

income. That's how we found the doubling time for France. Annual growth rate is given as 2 percent, so the doubling time is 72 divided by 2, or 36 years.

Although the current growth rate of the United States isn't particularly rapid, it must be noted that it has been growing for a much longer time than the economies of most other countries. (The United States is definitely no "flash in the pan" in the growth area.) Because the United States has a higher standard of living base on which to build, it is naturally more difficult for it to grow rapidly. In addition, the United States has been a pioneer in technology. Late starters, on the other hand, have had the advantage of "borrowing" technology from both the United States and Europe.

Of course, simple arithmetic shows that if other nations continue to grow at a faster rate than the United States, eventually they will overtake it in living standards. In fact, there is already some evidence that per capita income is higher in several countries, such as Kuwait, Switzerland, and Sweden. The Controversy for this chapter addresses that issue.

● DETERMINANTS OF ECONOMIC GROWTH

There are numerous theories to account for why some nations grow and others do not. These theories typically concern the following topics: natural resources, capital accumulation, labor, technology, and well-defined property rights.

Natural Resources

A large supply of natural resources does not guarantee economic growth. Many of the less-developed countries are much richer in natural resources than some developed nations. However, they have not been too successful in exploiting these resources. To enhance economic growth, natural resources must be converted to useful forms. In the United States, the Indians had many natural resources available to them, but they were unable to increase their standard of living or experience economic growth.

People must devise the methods to convert natural resources to usable forms. This is where the United States has been more successful than other countries. (The U.S. also benefited from large capital investments—machines and funds—from England and other Old World countries.) The founders of our nation were a biased sample. Many of the "criminals" who were transported to the Colonies were guilty of such crimes as religious heresy, debt, evasion of a nation's economic laws, and disagreement with the government itself. In other words, they were people who either wanted to, or were forced to, escape the regimentation of a much more structured

346

society. These were just the kinds of people who were likely to devise new methods to utilize the natural resources in America. And that they did.

This is not to say, of course, that if the U.S. transplanted a cross section of Americans to some less-developed country, the growth rate in that country would suddenly soar. However, the United States did utilize more than just abundant natural resources to reach its current level of development; its people had the ingenuity to transform those resources into useful things. Less-developed countries will also require this type of human resource.

Capital Accumulation

It is often said that a necessary prerequisite for economic development is a large capital stock—machines and other durable goods that can aid in the future production of consumption goods and capital goods. It is true that developed countries have larger capital stocks per capita than less-developed countries. It is also true that the larger the capital stock for any given population, the higher the possible level of real income. This fact is the basis of many foreign aid programs. The United States and other nations have attempted to add to the capital stocks of less-developed countries so that they, too, might grow.

The Relationship between Capital Stock and Economic Growth. What is the relationship between capital stock and a nation's growth rate?

Look at the production possibilities curve in Graph 17–2. There is indicated the trade-off between present goods and future goods, or between present consumption and future consumption. The production possibilities curve, you may recall, represents the *maximum* combinations of the two kinds of goods that a nation can produce at any point in time. If a nation is at point *A*, it can simultaneously have an output of *X* present goods and *Y* future goods. By decreasing the amount of present goods, it can increase the amount of future goods. This means that if it consumes less today, it can have more tomorrow. A nation has to sacrifice present consumption to have more future consumption, given the state of technology.

The size of the capital stock helps determine the maximum amount of income that can be generated at any time. If very few machines are available, fewer goods and services can be produced and income will be lower. The more machines there are, the more income that can be generated. Therefore, the larger the capital stock, the larger the income pie. But how does the capital stock grow? It grows by people making the decision not to consume all their income today. The more households save and the more firms invest (as a percentage of total income), the larger will be the capital stock

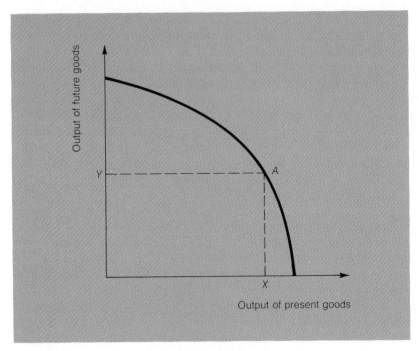

GRAPH 17–2

The Trade-off between Present Goods and Future Goods

This graph shows the production possibilities curve between present goods and future goods for given technology. If a nation wants to have more goods in the future, it has to economize goods today. In other words, there has to be more saving and capital formation if a nation is to have more future goods. At a point in time—for example at point *A*—the nation could consume *X* present goods and, at a maximum, have *Y* future goods.

and the higher will be possible future income. This relationship is demonstrated by again using a production possibilities curve.

Graph 17–3, shows two potential production possibilities curves for the year 2000 and one for the year 1984. The horizontal axis is again labeled present goods, but now the vertical axis is labeled capital goods—just another way of describing future consumption. If an economy is operating at point *A* in 1984, where there are relatively more capital goods being produced than at point *B*, the production possibilities curve in 2000 would be farther to the right (curve *AA*) than it would be if that economy were producing at point *B* in 1984. Clearly the rate of growth achieved by producing at point *A* is greater than the rate of growth achieved by producing at point *B*. The pie gets potentially larger the more people are willing to save today. Thus, the United States might be able to increase its rate of growth drastically if the saving rate of the population were somehow increased and this saving led to the production of more capital goods.

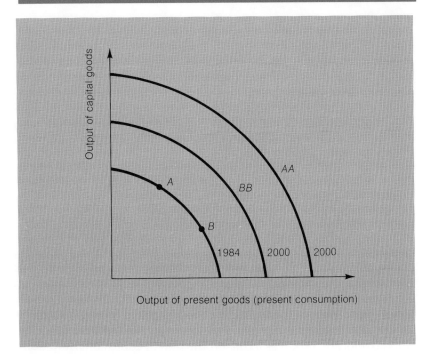

GRAPH 17–3
The Importance of Capital for Growth

This graph shows a production possibilities curve with two points on it, A and B. At point A, the nation is consuming less today and providing for more consumption tomorrow in the form of capital goods. At point B, it is consuming more today and providing less for future consumption. If it operates at point A, it may end up on a production possibilities curve of AA in year 2000. However, if it is at point B, it may end up at a production possibilities curve of only BB in year 2000. In other words, there will be less growth during the next decades if the nation consumes more goods today instead of saving and investing in capital goods that provide for more future consumption.

Can Poor Nations Save?   Because capital seems to be such an important determinant of economic growth, there is a strong argument for giving foreign aid in the form of capital. But this argument is based on the assumption that less-developed nations are "too poor" themselves to save and invest. That is, these nations are so poor that they must devote all their meager resources to the production of present consumption goods; they cannot afford to allocate resources to capital accumulation. This argument maintains that individuals have to spend all their income merely to survive; they cannot afford to save.

There are some flaws in this argument. On an individual level, saving exists even for people considered to be at a subsistence level. After all, these people must provide for the future, too. The saving, however, is sometimes in a form that is not easily recognizable. For

349

instance, very poor families in primitive societies often store food. On a national level, there is much evidence that saving (in the form of income not spent for current consumption or resources not allocated to the production of consumer goods) has occurred in all societies throughout history. Resources have been allocated to pyramids, cathedrals, great walls (China), forts, and government buildings—all examples of national saving. Indeed, historically, the ratio of national saving to national income does not change significantly as the level of national income rises.

Labor

The quantity and *quality* of labor can significantly help to determine a nation's economic growth rate. Notice the emphasis on the word *quality*. Certainly, the quantity of labor is not the only deciding factor. The skill level of that labor force is also important. Skill levels are increased by what is called an investment in human capital. An investment in human capital occurs whenever individuals obtain skills, education, and training that will improve their productivity. Some students of economic development believe that a society should allocate resources to the production of educational and training services.

Technology

When technological progress takes place, it is possible to obtain more output from the same amount of input. Technological progress results in outward shifts in the production possibilities curve. Thus, technological progress determines, at least in part, a nation's rate of economic growth. The ability of a nation to effect and sustain technological change depends on (1) the scientific capabilities of the population, (2) the quality and size of the nation's educational and training system, and (3) the percentage of income that goes into basic research and development each year. Technological progress is not limited to the industrial sector of developed nations.

In the less-developed countries, technological change has involved the use of improved pesticides, higher-yielding hybrid seeds, and improved irrigation techniques. Much of the technological change that first occurred in the developed countries has been transferred to the less-developed countries, thereby allowing them to increase their rates of growth. Consider the invention and widespread use of "miracle" rice, which has caused a "green" revolution in less-developed countries. Miracle rice, although requiring more fertilizer, has much greater yields per acre planted than any previously existing strain of rice. The innovation and use of miracle rice have increased the potential output from the limited capital and skilled labor available to less-developed countries.

Property Rights

If you were in a country where bank accounts and businesses were periodically taken over by the government, would you be willing to leave your money in a savings account or to invest in a business? Certainly, you would be less willing than if such takeovers never occurred. Periodic expropriation of private property rarely occurs in developed countries. It *has* occurred in numerous less-developed countries, however. For example, private property was once "nationalized" in Chile and still is in Cuba. In some cases, former owners are compensated, but rarely for the full value of the property taken over by the state.

Other things being equal, the more confidence there is in private property rights, the more private capital accumulation there will be. People are more willing to invest money in endeavors that will increase their wealth in future years. They have property rights in their wealth that are sanctioned and enforced by the government. In fact, some historians have tried to show that it was the development of well-defined private property rights that allowed Western Europe to increase its growth rate after many centuries of stagnation. The degree of certainty with which one can reap the gains from investing also determines the extent to which businesspersons in *other* countries will invest capital in less-developed countries. The threat of nationalization that hangs over many Latin American nations probably discourages much of the foreign investment that might aid these nations in their development.

CONTROVERSY

Other Countries are Richer than the United States

THE ARGUMENT

The latest per capita GNP figures seem to indicate that the United States is slipping behind other industrialized nations. Some people argue, however, that the GNP figures used to compare living standards across nations cannot tell the whole story. These people claim that the citizens of the United States still experience the highest standard of living in the world.

THE ANALYSIS

There are many problems in using comparative per capita GNP statistics to compare living standards. In the first place, one must take account of what people actually purchase and the prices they pay for those goods and services.

Cost of Living

The cost of living, as measured by the relative cost of buying a market basket of goods, is different in different regions of the United States. For example, the average market basket of goods in Honolulu may be 20 percent higher than the same market basket in Phoenix. Does that mean that if you move to Honolulu with the same income, you will be 20 percent poorer? Probably not, because you would substitute *away from* the more expensive items in Honolulu toward the cheaper ones such as pineapples. You would eat less fresh meat and substitute more frozen imports from New Zealand. You would tend to substitute frequent picnics on the beach for more expensive restaurant meals. The same is true when you shift from one country to another. Individuals react to changes in relative prices by substituting more of the relatively cheaper commodities.

Thus, it is important to look at what individuals actually buy, as opposed to those items some official statistic uses as the typical market basket of goods throughout the world. There is no such thing as a typical market basket that is the same in *all* countries.

Consumer Durable Goods

To get a better picture of the standard of living in a country, other measures besides average per capita income should be used. Living standards should also be measured in terms of the property that people own, how much they own, and the satisfaction, enjoyment, pleasure, usefulness, and so on, that they enjoy. In some countries, per capita income may be higher than in the U.S., but the average person typically owns less property. If one includes the satisfaction, pleasure, and so on, derived from the property individuals own in the United States (which in a way can be considered income — it's implied income from the satisfaction it generates), this country's standard of living is still higher than those of other countries. In the United States, people own more houses, swimming pools, cars, stereos, golf clubs, and records than people in other countries do. That is, the average U.S. citizen has a larger stock of consumer durables from which satisfaction is derived. This satisfaction is a form of income; it is real, because to duplicate that satisfaction, an individual would have to rent the services from the consumer durables that he or she now owns.

Taking Account of Buying Power and Ownership of Durable Goods. Yet another alternative measure of relative living standards has been devised by a team of economists headed by Professor Irving B. Kravis at the University of Pennsylvania. Professor Kravis and his associates compare living standards by comparing the actual consumption of goods

and services. Thus, they attempt to take account of different costs of living and ownership patterns of consumer durable goods. They also take account of the fact that in some countries, health care is paid for by the government. Graph 17–4 shows their findings for several countries. According to these calculations, for example, the French consume, on a per capita basis, only 68 percent of what the average American consumes.

No matter how we attempt to measure living standards in the United States or among nations, we will never be able to answer the question, Is the United States better off than other countries? What is important to this question is the individual level of satisfaction or happiness. We have, at best, imperfect measures of satisfaction. Real per capita GNP is one; the Kravis index is another. But no index can tell us how happy people really are.

DISCUSSION QUESTIONS

1. Can you determine if you would be better off living in another country rather than the United States?

2. If you moved to another country where relative prices were different than in the U.S.—meat was relatively expensive compared to fruit, consumer durable goods were relatively expensive compared to manual labor—how would you change your consumption "bundle" of purchases? Why?

GRAPH 17–4
A Comparison of Relative Living Standards

This bar chart shows that the United States is still way ahead of many countries in terms of relative living standards, at least according to Professor Irving B. Kravis and his associates at the University of Pennsylvania. The calculation of relative living standards takes account of different costs of living and ownership patterns of consumer durable goods, as well as the fact that in some countries health care is paid for by the government.

SOURCE: Irving B. Kravis et al.

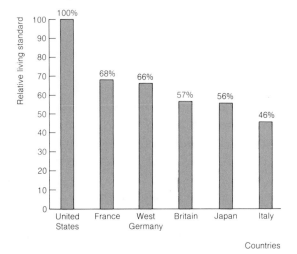

● WHAT'S AHEAD

Now that you have looked at international economics and theories of economic growth, it's time to examine some of the major economic questions facing the United States today. The next unit will look at problems associated with big business and monopoly, as well as the economics of crime and other important issues of the day.

● CHAPTER SUMMARY

Economic growth is measured by calculating the rate of change in a nation's real per capita GNP over time. Any definition of economic growth will have its problems, but this one does serve as an approximate measure, particularly if comparisons of international growth rates are desired.

There are numerous determinants of economic growth, including natural resources, the ability to accumulate capital, the quality and quantity of the labor force, and the amount of technology. It has been argued that the extent to which property rights are well defined also determines the economic growth rate of a country.

● QUESTIONS FOR REVIEW AND STUDY

1. For most people during most periods in the world's history, their _____ or _____ did not rise over their lifetime.

2. Economic growth is defined as the rate of increase in _____ _____ _____ GNP.

3. Economic growth does not necessarily indicate an increase in *everyone's* real standard of living. After all, real per capita GNP may grow rapidly, but most of the higher income can go to a _____ or _____ group of individuals.

4. The United States has had economic growth for so long that it now has the highest standard of living _____ in the world.

5. Even though the U.S.S.R. and Brazil have been blessed with a large supply of _____ _____, they have real living standards that are half that of the United States.

6. Capital accumulation involves a trade-off between _____ consumption and _____ consumption.

7. The opportunity cost of more capital today is sacrificed _____ _____ today.

8. Even the poorest nation and the poorest individuals in that nation must, by necessity, _____ to provide for the future.

9. Forms of saving that we have seen in the past, even in poor countries, include _____ and _____.

10. Technological progress is one determinant of economic growth. Such progress depends on _____ and _____.

11. A system of well-established _____ _____ rights increases an individual's incentive to save and invest.

ANSWERS

1. real income or living standard 2. real per capita 3. small, or elite 4. base 5. natural resources 6. present; future 7. consumer goods 8. save 9. cathedrals; forts; pyramids; national defense expenditures; government buildings (any two answers are acceptable) 10. scientific capabilities of a nation; educational system; allocation of resources to research and development (any two answers are acceptable) 11. private property

● ANSWERS TO CHAPTER PREVIEW QUESTIONS

1. What are some of the ways you can experience economic growth, either for yourself or for your family?

You can experience economic growth only if you are willing to sacrifice something. When you continue to go to school, you are sacrificing your current ability to earn and consume income. But in exchange for that sacrifice, you are developing skills and talents that will allow you to have a higher income in the future. You are investing in yourself by sacrificing current consumption now.

If you wish to accumulate much wealth during your lifetime, you must be willing to sacrifice current consumption. You do this by not consuming all of your income—that is, by saving part of it. The more you save, the more you can accumulate. In particular, if you invest your accumulated savings in wise savings outlets, you will be rewarded by a compounded rate of growth, so that in the future you will have accumulated large amounts of wealth.

2. How is economic growth measured?

This is a much debated question. Many people try to make inferences about changes in a nation's economic well-being from its economic growth rate. Presumably, higher growth rates imply more rapid increases in living standards. Yet, others have argued that increased income inequality may accompany rapid economic growth; that is, a relatively small percentage of the population may benefit from economic growth, while many others do not experience economic improvement. Critics also point out that rapid economic growth is not necessarily consistent with increases in the spiritual, cultural, and environmental *quality* of life. On the other hand, since per capita increases in real GNP do not measure the increased leisure that usually accompanies economic growth, this measure may *understate* the economic well-being of a nation. Economic growth, therefore, is a rather crude measure of changes in well-being and is perhaps a better indicator of productive activity.

● PROBLEMS

1. What are the determinants of economic growth?

2. If a country is experiencing a 5 percent per annum economic growth rate, how many years will it take for that country's real per capita GNP to double?

● SELECTED REFERENCES

Beckerman, Wilfred. *Two Cheers for the Affluent Society*. New York: St. Martin's Press, 1976.

Denison, Edward F. *Accounting for Slower Economic Growth: The United States in the 1970s*. Washington, D.C.: The Brookings Institution, 1979.

Kuznets, Simon. *Growth, Population, and Income Distribution*. New York: Norton, 1979.

Olson, Mancur, and Hans H. Landsberg, eds. *The No Growth Society*. New York: Norton, 1973.

Rostow, W. W. *The Stages of Economic Growth*. 2nd ed. New York: Cambridge University Press, 1971.

Schumacher, E. F. *Small Is Beautiful: Economics as if People Mattered*. New York: Harper & Row, 1973.

UNIT 5

Economic
Issues
in the
1980s and 1990s

18

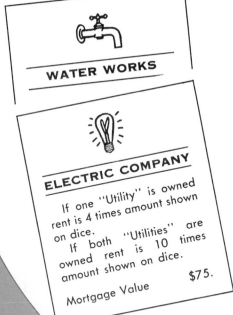

WATER WORKS

ELECTRIC COMPANY

If one "Utility" is owned rent is 4 times amount shown on dice.

If both "Utilities" are owned rent is 10 times amount shown on dice.

Mortgage Value $75.

Big Business and the Threat of Monopoly Power

Chapter Preview

1. In some industries, a few large firms sell most of the output. What are some of the ways these large firms compete?

2. To prevent possible abuses of market power, the government has regulated many forms of business activity. In recent years, there has been a reevaluation of such economic regulation. Why?

● KEY TERMS

Diseconomies of scale
Economies of scale
Industry concentration ratio

Merger
Oligopoly

Some U.S. businesses are gigantic, with billions of dollars in sales and assets and hundreds of thousands of employees. In the face of such big business, many feel that the consumer is powerless. To be sure, there is some truth in this opinion. But the issue is more complicated. In this chapter, we will look at big business—its size, characteristics, and how it is controlled.

● THE STRUCTURE OF AMERICAN INDUSTRY: OLIGOPOLY

Consider the following facts about big business in the United States. In the manufacturing sector, the largest 200 corporations employ about 12 percent of the labor force and own about 25 percent of the income-producing wealth in this nation. The largest 500 industrial corporations account for more than one-half of all sales. As much as 70 percent of total national profits is accounted for by these large corporations. In the banking arena, the 50 largest banks own over 40 percent of all banking assets.

Because such a significant percentage of current assets and sales is concentrated in such a small percentage of corporations and banks, many observers are convinced that productive capacity in the nation is becoming more and more concentrated in a smaller and smaller percentage of large corporations.

Monopoly and Oligopoly

Chapter 4 presented a discussion of the extremes of pure competition and pure monopoly. You may recall that under pure competition, all parties to an economic transaction—all suppliers and all demanders—are *price takers*. No firm or buyer can affect price by its own actions. In a purely competitive world, profits are competed down to the point where they are just normal, that is, just high enough to keep resources in the industry.

In the pure monopoly model, there is only one supplier. The single supplier is indeed the entire industry. A successful monopolist will be able to make higher-than-normal long-run profits, that is, profits that are higher than in a purely competitive industry. By definition, monopolists tend to restrict output and charge higher prices. That is the major complaint against monopolies: Too few resources are being allocated and consumers are paying too high a price for the product.

The model of pure monopoly does not fit most of American industry, however, because a single supplier of a product is the exception rather than the rule. Usually, a few large suppliers dominate an industry, and this type of market structure is called an **oligopoly**. Oligopolists are neither purely competitive nor purely monopolistic.

Within any oligopolistic industry, there are only a few dominant firms. The term *dominant* refers to a percentage of total industry output accounted for by the few top firms. The domestic automobile industry is dominated by three firms. The steel industry is dominated by eight firms. Both are examples of oligopolistic market structures.

Interdependence of Oligopolies

When only a few large firms dominate an industry, they cannot act independently of each other. In other words, they must recognize a mutual interdependence. Each firm will react to the other firms' decisions on output and price, as well as to changes in quality and product differentiation. Remember, in a perfectly competitive model, each firm ignores the reactions of other firms because each firm can sell all that it wants at the going market price. In the pure monopoly model, the monopolist does not have to worry about the reaction of rivals, since, by definition, there are none.

Note that the mutual interdependence of oligopolies results from so few firms in the industry producing a large share of total industry output. In fact, it can be said that in an oligopoly market structure, firms must try to predict the reactions of rival firms. Otherwise, poor business decisions might be made that would result in lower profits.

The Way Oligopolists Compete

One way to compete for additional business is by price competition. Another way is by nonprice competition. Nonprice competition is an attempt to attract customers by means other than price difference. Two types of nonprice competition are considered here —advertising and quality variation.

Advertising.   Advertising allows the seller, whether it be an oligopolist or a monopolist, to increase the demand for its product and therefore sell more of the product at each and every price. Advertising also has the effect of differentiating the product and making the product's availability better known. A firm will advertise as a way of gaining a nonprice competitive advantage over other firms.

Oligopoly

A market structure in which a small number of firms dominate an industry's output and sales; under oligopoly, each firm must take into account its rivals' reactions to its pricing, advertising, and quality variation policies.

361

Quality Variation.   Quality variation, or differentiation, results in a division of one market into a number of submarkets. The prime example of product differentiation is the automobile industry. There are physically definable differences between different automobile models within one single firm. A Citation and a Seville are certainly not the same car. Thus, competition among oligopolistic firms creates a continuous expansion and redefinition of the different models that are sold by any one company. There is competition to create new quality classes and thereby gain a competitive edge. Being the first in the market with a new quality class has often meant higher profits: Witness the phenomenal success of the original Ford Mustang. The strategy doesn't always work, however: Witness the dismal failure of Ford's Edsel! Still, oligopolists are always looking for that best-selling new model.

How Oligopolies Are Formed

Much of U.S. manufacturing can be described as oligopolistic. But how are oligopolies formed? At least two factors account for the existence of oligopolies: economies of scale and mergers.

Economies of Scale.   In some situations, it is very advantageous for a firm to expand. As some firms become larger, that is, increase their rate of output, they can gain advantages over smaller firms. This will happen when an increase in output results in a less-than-proportionate increase in the cost. Stated another way, a doubling of output results in less than a doubling of total costs. When this occurs, **economies of scale** are said to exist.

How do economies of scale arise? As the scale of output increases, it is possible to use machines that embody the latest technology, thus lowering per-unit cost. Also, advertising expenditures per unit of output tend to fall, and this, too, lowers per-unit cost.

However, there are limits to economies of scale. As a firm gets larger and larger, there is usually an increase in red tape. Paperwork multiplies and communication problems increase. One division of a firm may not have any idea what the other divisions are doing. It is possible, therefore, that at a very high rate of output and scale of operation, cost per unit will increase. This situation creates **diseconomies of scale**.

Mergers.   Another reason oligopolies are so common is that a number of firms have merged. A **merger** is the joining of two or more firms under single ownership or control. Relatively large firms can buy or merge with other firms in the industry. If two firms, both producing shoes, merge into one, the concentration of output will increase in the industry.

Economies of scale

The situation in which unit costs fall as the scale of operations and output rise.

Diseconomies of scale

The situation in which increasing output and increasing scale of operations cause unit costs, or average costs, to rise.

Merger

The joining together of two separate firms.

362

Although we've talked about industry concentration, we have not yet explained how to measure it. Let's turn to that subject now.

● INDUSTRY CONCENTRATION

An oligopoly has been defined as a market structure in which very few interdependent firms control a large part of total output in an industry. That is, there is high industry concentration. But how high? How is industry concentration measured?

Concentration Ratio

The most popular way to compute industry concentration is to determine the percentage of total sales or production accounted for by, say, the top four or top eight firms in an industry. Such a computation is called an **industry concentration ratio**. An example of an industry with 25 firms is given in Table 18–1. That exhibit shows that the four largest firms account for almost 90 percent of total output in that industry. Clearly, an oligopoly exists.

U.S. Concentration Ratios

Now that we have explained what a concentration ratio is, we can look at some actual ratios for the United States. Table 18–2 shows the ratios for a selected number of U.S. industries in 1976. Note that ratios are given for both the largest four and the largest eight companies in each industry. Which of these industries can be classified as oligopolies? It's hard to say. Some economists like to use a four-firm concentration ratio of 50 percent as the cutoff point. In that case, in 1976, the motor vehicles, primary copper, aircraft, and synthetic rubber industries were oligopolistic. On the other

TABLE 18–1
Computing the Four-Firm Concentration Ratio

	ANNUAL SALES (in dollars)	
Firm 1	$150,000,000	
Firm 2	100,000,000	
Firm 3	80,000,000	= $400,000,000
Firm 4	70,000,000	
Firms 5–25	50,000,000	
Total	$450,000,000	
4-firm concentration ratio	$= \dfrac{\$400,000,000}{\$450,000,000}$	= 88.9 percent

Industry concentration ratio

The percentage of total industry sales accounted for by either the top four or the top eight firms in an industry.

363

TABLE 18–2
Concentration Ratios (Percent) for the United States

	SHARE OF VALUE OF SHIPMENTS IN 1976 ACCOUNTED FOR BY THE:	
	LARGEST FOUR COMPANIES	LARGEST EIGHT COMPANIES
Motor vehicles	93	99
Primary copper	72	*
Aircraft	66	86
Synthetic rubber	62	81
Blast furnaces and steel mills	45	65
Industrial trucks and tractors	50	66
Construction machinery	43	54
Petroleum	31	56
Paper mills	24	40
Meatpacking	22	37
Newspapers	17	28
Fluid milk	18	26

*Withheld by Commerce Department to avoid disclosing figures for individual companies.
SOURCE: U.S. Department of Commerce.

hand, some economists like to use the eight-firm concentration ratio. Using the same 50 percent cutoff point, a larger number of industries listed in Table 18–2 would be considered oligopolistic. As yet, there is no general agreement on when an industry should be classified as an oligopoly and when it should not.

To add to the difficulty, the concept of an "industry" is necessarily arbitrary. Thus, concentration ratios rise as the definition of an industry is narrowed, and fall as the definition is broadened. For example, the concentration ratio falls as we move from the subcompact to the automobile to the transportation "industry." We must therefore be satisfied with our definition of a particular industry before jumping to conclusions about whether the industry is too concentrated, as measured by a high concentration ratio.

● WHAT'S WRONG WITH OLIGOPOLY?

A major complaint about monopoly is that output is restricted and consumer prices are increased. The same complaint can be made about oligopolies; instead of one seller, however, there are several major sellers controlling most of the industry output. But what does the word "most" mean? Is there some specific concentration ratio above which an oligopolistic industry starts harming society? Critics of big business in America claim there is, suggesting that perhaps any four-firm concentration ratio above 60 percent is indicative of harm being done to the economy. What harm? Again, the harm associated with restricting output and raising prices. And other complaints have also been made against oligopolists, including complaints of excessive advertising and excessive product variations. The Controversy in this chapter will examine the arguments against advertising, particularly as they apply to less-than-perfect competitors, such as oligopolists and monopolists.

Oligopolistic and monopolistic behavior is considered sufficiently detrimental that the federal government and numerous state governments have attempted to control business tactics that lead to either more oligopoly or monopoly. The federal government's efforts to control and prevent oligopolistic and monopolistic behavior have led to the enactment of antitrust laws.

● ANTITRUST POLICY

If the courts can prevent sellers from getting together to decide on output and prices, then monopoly prices will not result. That is the major aim of antitrust legislation—to prevent firms from restraining trade. The major federal antitrust, or antimonopoly, laws are the Sherman Act, the Clayton Act, and the Federal Trade Commission Act.

The Sherman Act

The first antitrust law in the United States was passed during the greatest merger movement in American history. That is, a large number of firms were monopolizing and merging with other firms. When a number of firms merged together, the business organizations were called "trusts." A copper trust, a steel beam trust, an iron trust, a sugar trust, a coal trust, a paper bag trust, and the most famous of all, the Standard Oil trust, were formed. However, there was an increasing public outcry for legislation against these large trusts.

The Sherman Antitrust Act was passed in 1890. It was the first attempt by the federal government to control the growth of monopoly in the United States. Here are the most important provisions of that act:

Section 1: Every contract, combination in the form of trust or otherwise, or conspiracy, in restraint of trade or commerce among the several states, or with foreign nations, is hereby declared to be illegal.

Section 2: Every person who shall monopolize, or attempt to monopolize, or combine or conspire with any other person or persons to monopolize any part of the trade or commerce . . . shall be guilty of a misdemeanor.

Although admittedly vague, this act was used to break up the famous Standard Oil of New Jersey trust in 1906. At the time, that trust controlled over 80 percent of the nation's oil-refining capacity.

The Clayton Act

The Sherman Act was so vague that in 1914, a new law was passed to sharpen its antitrust provisions. This law was called the Clayton Act. It prohibited or limited a number of very specific business practices, which again were felt to be "unreasonable" attempts at restraining trade or commerce. Here are some of the more important sections of that act:

> *Section 2*: [It is illegal to] discriminate in price between different purchasers [except in cases where the differences are due to differences in selling or transportation costs].
> *Section 3*: [Producers cannot sell] on the condition, agreement or understanding that the . . . purchaser thereof shall not use or deal in the goods . . . of a competitor or competitors of the seller.
> *Section 7*: [Corporations cannot hold stock in another company] where the effect . . . may be to substantially lessen competition.

The activities mentioned in the Clayton Act are not necessarily illegal. In the words of the law, they are illegal *only* when their effects "may be to substantially lessen competition or tend to create a monopoly." It takes the interpretation of the court to decide whether one of the activities mentioned actually has the effect of "substantially" lessening competition.

The Federal Trade Commission Act of 1914

The Federal Trade Commission Act came about in an effort to prevent unfair competition. The act was designed to stipulate acceptable competitive behavior. In particular, it was supposed to prevent cutthroat pricing—that is, overly aggressive competition that could eliminate too many competitors. One of the basic features of the act was the creation of the Federal Trade Commission (FTC). That commission is charged with investigating unfair competitive practices. It can do so on its own authority or at the request of firms that feel they have been wronged. The commission can issue cease and desist orders where "unfair methods of competition in commerce" are discovered. In 1938, the Wheeler–Lea Act amended the 1914 Federal Trade Commission Act to prohibit expressly "unfair or deceptive acts or practices in commerce." Pursuant to that act, the FTC engages in what it sees as a battle against false or misleading advertising, as well as the misrepresentation of goods and services for sale in the marketplace.

366

Regulation

Another way to control the activities of business is through direct regulation of prices, quantities produced, customers, and so on. Indeed, there is a large sector of American industry that is regulated by the government. For example, public utilities—electric companies, natural gas companies—are regulated in terms of the geographic area they can serve, the prices they can charge, the profits they can earn, and so on. Most states have a public utility commission whose members hear arguments for and against changing customer rates. At the federal level, there are numerous agencies that regulate the way businesses can operate. For example, the Federal Communications Commission determines which companies or individuals are allowed to own television and radio stations. Until the late 1970s, the Civil Aeronautics Board controlled not only the prices charged for airline tickets, but also which routes different airlines could use.

Recent Trends in Regulation

Regulation is intended to create more competitive industry structure. In the late 1970s and early 1980s, however, there was much more interest in deregulation than in regulation. Numerous studies have attempted to show—and apparently have convinced many people—that regulated industries behave more like monopolies than do nonregulated industries. The reason for this problem may be that the regulated industries "capture" their regulatory agencies. That is, regulatory agencies seem to be more concerned with protecting the members of the regulated industry than with protecting the interests of consumers.

Numerous economists and politicians have called for deregulation of the banking, trucking, airline, railroad, and communications industries. Indeed, that is exactly what has been happening over the last few years. The banking industry is gradually being deregulated, subsequent to the Monetary Control Act of 1980. And the airline industry has found itself in a more or less competitive situation, where prices can be altered at will without the permission of the Civil Aeronautics Board.

Curiously, while economists tend to favor eliminating the older regulatory agencies, there is less agreement about the newer regulatory agencies, such as the Environmental Protection Agency and the Occupational Safety and Health Administration.

Some Recent Changes in Antitrust Policy

The early 1980s can be viewed as a time when antitrust policy took a different direction. Numerous pending cases against major firms were either dropped or settled during the Reagan administration. For example, the Federal Trade Commission dropped its lengthy case against the major breakfast cereal producers. It had argued for a number of years that the three major cereal producers had a "shared monopoly," even though they did not explicitly contact each other about setting prices or output. And the Justice Department dropped a number of cases brought by President Carter's administration, including a case involving Mack Trucks and another case involving the brick industry. Two additional cases gave a clear indication of a change in antitrust policy. These cases involved IBM and the American Telephone and Telegraph Company.

The IBM Case.   In January 1982, the Antitrust Division of the Justice Department dropped its case against IBM, initiated under President Lyndon Johnson in 1969. After 13 years, it became clear that the computer industry was becoming more, not less, competitive. New products had been introduced and prices were falling rapidly. IBM faced competition from manufacturers of large computers, such as Burroughs, Control Data, Fujitsa, and Honeywell. Moreover, the microcomputer business was taking off, and IBM was forced to enter into competition with Apple, Wang Labs, and hundreds of software companies.

The American Telegraph and Telephone Company.   The same day the IBM case was dropped, the decade-old AT&T case was settled out of court. At the time the lawsuit was initiated, AT&T was organized into three main divisions: (1) Bell Labs, (2) Western Electric, and (3) 22 telephone-service-operating companies. Bell Labs was responsible for research and development; Western Electric was responsible for manufacturing telephone equipment. The original antitrust suit called for splitting up all three divisions. The court settlement split the 22 telephone-service-operating companies from the other two divisions. Bell Labs and Western Electric were not divided. In agreeing to the out-of-court settlement, AT&T got a plum. Its remaining two divisions are now able to enter the data processing and telecommunications industries. Critics of the out-of-court settlement claim that the benefits of increased competition in those two industries will be lost through poorer service at the local level because of the unevenness in the quality of management for the 22 different telephone companies.

Advertising Is Detrimental to Society

THE ARGUMENT

Some critics of advertising claim that much of it is self-canceling, and is therefore wasteful. Others maintain that advertising convinces people to buy goods that they don't want, and that it spreads misinformation.

THE ANALYSIS

Critics of advertising contend that it is self-canceling, as in the cigarette industry. That is, cigarette companies just advertise because *other* cigarette companies do. Everyone (except advertising agencies) would be better off without such costly and wasteful ads. Critics do not accept the argument that expanded production through advertising results in a lower unit cost. Although each advertiser must continue to spend money on flashy billboards and magazine ads, the tobacco industry as a whole attracts no additional customers with all members advertising at once. Moreover, even if advertising can cause a firm to realize gains from mass production through increased growth, at some point the firm may incur diseconomies of scale.

Additionally, critics point out that some advertising attempts to impute a glamorous image to activities that are "undesirable." For example, billboard and magazine ads for cigarettes presumably are aimed at young people in an effort to portray smoking as glamorous and thereby induce additional customers to the industry.

Even though advertising accounts for less than 2 percent of national income, critics contend that advertising expenditures divert human and other resources away from much more pressing needs. Advertising, in short, gives rise to a misallocation of resources. The most telling argument along these lines is the claim that advertising causes people to consume more private goods and fewer "public" goods—such as schools, hospitals, and better streets. Although the critics may be right, it should be noted that private businesses are not the only ones that advertise. Consider the amount of advertising done by universities in need of funds, or the amount of advertising that the government does to "sell" its new programs.

Advertising has also been attacked as a means by which producers create artificial wants. Numerous books have been written about both subtle and more blatant forms of advertising that can alter consumers' attitudes and desires. Analyzing this particular contention is difficult because economics can say very little about the creation of wants. However, there is no doubt that advertisers compete; therefore, it would seem difficult for one manufacturer to induce consumers to buy an unwanted product when numerous other manufacturers are attempting exactly the same thing. Moreover, there is plenty of advertising for nonconsumption—that is, for saving. How many ads have you seen—both on television and

369

in the newspaper—inviting you to open a new savings account? And there are countless ads for U.S. savings bonds. In fact, consumers are constantly being bombarded with ads asking them to do everything imaginable with their income and time. Thus, the question is whether some forms of advertising are more persuasive than others, and, if so, does one particular industry have a monopoly on that form of advertising? This is a question no one has yet answered.

DISCUSSION QUESTIONS

1. Assume that advertising for cigarettes was banned completely. Assume further that after the ban, profits increased. Would that necessarily be good for everyone?
2. Some critics of advertising make a distinction between informative advertising and competitive advertising, where the latter means that no true information is given about the product. How would you distinguish between informative and competitive advertising?

● WHAT'S AHEAD

In the following chapter, we will look at the important problem of differences in income that exists in our economy. We will try to determine to what degree those differences in income are a result of discrimination in the labor market against minorities and women. Finally, the topic of poverty and how to eliminate it is discussed.

● CHAPTER SUMMARY

Much of American industry is characterized by oligopolies, that is, several large firms that dominate different industries. One of the main features of an oligopolistic market is that the several large firms in that market must take account of each other's reactions to changes in price. But oligopolists do not necessarily compete solely on the basis of price; they can compete on the basis of advertising and quality variation.

Oligopolies may be formed because of economies of scale or because of mergers.

One way to measure the degree to which an industry is dominated by several firms is to look at the industry concentration ratio, which is computed as the percentage of total annual sales accounted for by the top four or top eight firms.

American antitrust policy is based on the Sherman Act, the Clayton Act, the Federal Trade Commission Act of 1914, and other acts. In the 1980s, antitrust policy has changed, to some extent, to allow for more mergers among large businesses.

● QUESTIONS FOR REVIEW AND STUDY

1. A perfect competitor can be described as a _____ _____.

2. A monopolist faces the entire _____ demand curve.

3. An oligopolist is one of several large firms that _____ an industry's output.

4. One characteristic of oligopolies is that they are independent/dependent/interdependent.

5. One reason an oligopoly may form is because of _____ of _____.

6. When average cost per unit of output falls as output and the size of the firm increase, a firm is experiencing _____ of _____.

7. At some point, however, as output and the size of the firm increase, the firm experiences _____ _____ _____ since its cost per unit rises.

8. Whenever economies of scale are large relative to market size, there will be _____ firms in the industry.

9. If two firms producing the same product join forces, this is a _____.

10. When we look at a percentage of output accounted for by the largest four (or eight) firms, we are observing a measure of the industry _____ _____.

11. The more narrowly an industry is defined, the higher/lower will be its concentration ratio.

12. The first antitrust legislation was the _____ _____ in 1890.

13. Two practices prohibited by the Clayton Act are _____ _____ and _____ _____.

14. The Federal Trade Commission Act of 1914 prohibits _____ competition.

15. In the past decade, economic studies have shown that many regulated industries have _____ their regulatory agencies.

ANSWERS

1. price taker 2. industry 3. dominate 4. interdependent 5. economies; scale 6. economies; scale 7. diseconomies of scale 8. few 9. merger 10. concentration ratio 11. higher 12. Sherman Act 13. price discrimination;exclusive rates; owning stock in a competitive company (name two only) 14. unfair 15. captured

● ANSWERS TO CHAPTER PREVIEW QUESTIONS

1. *In some industries, a few large firms sell most of the output. What are some of the ways these large firms compete?*

These firms do not necessarily compete solely on the basis of price. They may try to differentiate their products and compete by advertising the small differences in these products. For example, automobile manufacturers introduce new models all the time. Each model has specific attributes that are touted in expensive advertising campaigns. In addition, large firms dominating a market can compete on the basis of service after having sold the product. They can also compete on the basis of credit terms, delivery dates, and the like.

2. *To prevent possible abuses of market power, the government has regulated many forms of business activity. In recent years, there has been a reevaluation of such economic regulation. Why?*

Presumably, regulation is an attempt to prevent monopoly abuses and to simulate a competitive market structure where one would not otherwise exist. But research indicates that this is not the case. Regulated industries behave more like monopolies than do nonregulated industries. It is claimed that the regulated firms sooner or later "capture" the regulatory agencies; before long, regulated industries have the protection and sanction of the regulatory bodies! More and more economists are favoring deregulation by the older agencies for such industries as the airlines, trucking, common motor carrier, and communications industries. There seems to be less consensus regarding the degree of desired regulation by the *newer* agencies, such as the Environmental Protection Agency (EPA) and the Occupational Safety and Health Administration (OSHA).

● PROBLEMS

1. The table below gives some information for industry A.

	Annual Sales (in dollars)
Firm 1	$200,000,000
Firm 2	150,000,000
Firm 3	100,000,000
Firm 4	75,000,000
Firms 5–30	300,000,000

    a. What is the four-firm concentration ratio for this industry?

    b. Assume that industry A is the steel industry. What would happen to the concentration ratio if we redefined industry A as the rolled steel industry? As the metal industry?

2. What are the characteristics of an oligopoly market structure?

● SELECTED REFERENCES

Bork, Robert H. *The Antitrust Paradox*. New York: Basic Books, 1978.

Brozen, Yale, ed. *The Competitive Economy*. Morristown, N.J.: General Learning Press, 1975.

Clarkson, Kenneth W., and Roger LeRoy Miller. *Industrial Organization*. New York: McGraw-Hill, 1982.

MacAvoy, Paul W. *Regulated Industries and the Economy*. New York: Norton, 1979.

Mansfield, Edwin, ed. *Monopoly Power and Economic Performance*. 4th ed. New York: Norton, 1978.

Weiss, Leonard W. *Case Studies in American Industry*. 3rd ed. New York: Wiley, 1979.

19

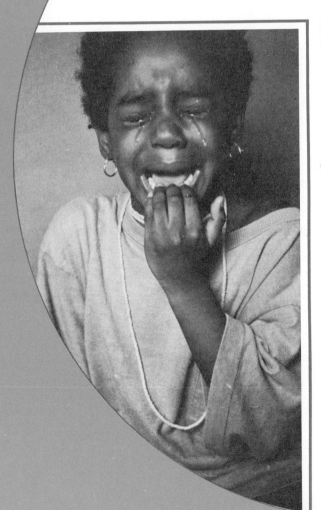

Income Differences, Discrimination, and Poverty

Chapter Preview
1. Why do different individuals earn different incomes?
2. What do you think would be the best way to distribute income in the United States?

● KEY TERMS

Productivity theory
Racial discrimination
Sexual discrimination

In only a few countries in the world has economic growth provided the means for the masses to enjoy living standards considerably above subsistence levels. The United States is certainly one of those fortunate nations. Yet, amid all this plenty, a certain amount of poverty exists even in this country. In this chapter, we explore the reasons for income differences among different people and discuss the issues of poverty and economic discrimination.

● INCOME DIFFERENCES
IN THE UNITED STATES

Amazingly, *money* income differences measured before taxes among different families in the United States have not changed much since the 1940s. Despite the common notion that "the rich get richer and the poor get poorer," the data seem to indicate that in the United States, most of the population gets "richer" through time. In other words, the relative differences among the rich and the poor haven't changed much.

Consider Table 19–1, which divides the U.S. population into five income groups for different years. This table groups families according to whether they are in the lowest 20 percent of income distribu-

TABLE 19–1

Pretax Percentage Shares of Money Income for Income Groups in the United States*

This table indicates the percentage of total pretax money income received by each of five income groups. Notice that the percentage of the total pie going to each income group remains fairly constant. For example, since 1947, the lowest 20 percent of the population has received about 5 percent of total money income before taxes, while the highest 20 percent of the population has received about 40 percent of the total pretax money income pie.

INCOME GROUPS	1947	1960	1973	1981
Lowest fifth	5.1	5.1	5.5	5.9
Second fifth	11.8	12.2	11.9	13.2
Third fifth	16.7	17.8	17.5	17.3
Fourth fifth	23.2	24.0	24.0	25.5
Highest fifth	43.3	41.3	41.0	38.2

*Columns may not total to 100 percent because of rounding.

376

tion, the second lowest 20 percent, and so on. For example, in 1947, the lowest 20 percent of income earners received 5.1 percent of total money income in the United States before taxes. That is, for the group beginning with the poorest family and ending when 20 percent of the total population is reached, the total amount of money income earned in 1947, relative to the total "money pie," was 5.1 percent. By 1981, this percentage had increased, although only slightly, to 5.9 percent.

Similarly, Table 19–1 indicates that the highest fifth (the upper 20 percent of income earners) accounted for 43.3 percent of total pretax money earnings in 1947. By 1981, this percentage had fallen slightly to 38.2 percent. Examination of the other three income groups shows that they, too, experienced only a slight change in the percentage of total pretax money income obtained.

Overall Incomes

It is important to understand what Table 19–1 does and does not imply. A quick glance at Table 19–1 may lead to the conclusion that no one's income has changed significantly from 1947 to 1981. Actually, the table gives no indication of changes in overall income, that is, of economic growth, stagnation, or decline. Table 19–1 gives only the *relative shares* of income going to different groups in the economy, and it shows that the relative shares of pretax money income have not changed significantly since World War II. However, as discussed in Chapter 17, there has been substantial economic growth since 1947. Therefore, even those in the lowest fifth of all income earners were richer in 1981 than they were in 1947, but not relative to other income classes.

Table 19–1 Reconsidered

To a large extent, Table 19–1 overstates the divergence between lower-income groups and higher-income groups, largely because *the table is not adjusted for age*. Over 20 percent of the income earners in the lower fifth are teenagers or people in their early 20s, as well as retired people, whose pretax annual earnings are lower than their average lifetime pretax annual earnings. The upper two-fifths of income earners include large numbers of individuals at the peak of their average annual pretax lifetime earnings.

Also, individuals who have experienced an exceptionally bad year because of illness, union strikes, accidents, and so on, will *temporarily* be relegated to the lower groups. Similarly, individuals who have experienced an exceptionally good year will be advanced to the upper-income groups—temporarily.

Finally, the distribution of pretax money income does not tell the complete story about total income. Numerous individuals obtain in-kind transfers, already referred to in Chapter 7. These transfers involve food stamps, public housing, and health care. There is much debate about the degree to which these in-kind transfers should be considered when calculating income differences in the United States. If all in-kind transfers are included in total income, then the income differences shown in Table 19–1 diminish over time. The lowest one-fifth income group in 1960 received 5 percent of the nation's *total* pretax money income. By 1973, however, a number of government programs had been implemented to aid the poor. In 1973, the lowest one-fifth of income earners received 5.5 percent of pretax money income. But when in-kind transfers were added, their share of *total* income more than doubled to 12 percent.[1] Indeed, when in-kind transfers are included, the relative position of the poorest fifth of families improved by over 100 percent between 1960 and 1973.

● WHY INCOME DIFFERENCES EXIST

Even if we adjust for age, in-kind transfers, and exceptionally good or bad years for individuals, considerable income differences still exist in the United States. We will now examine why this is so.

Productivity Differences

One of the major theories that attempts to explain income differences is the **productivity theory**. The productivity theory states that each individual will be paid according to the increase in revenues that a firm obtains by hiring that individual. The increase in revenues to the firm is obtained by multiplying the price received per unit produced by the number of additional units produced when an individual is hired. Another way of looking at the productivity theory is that individuals will be paid the amount of revenues that a firm would lose if that individual were fired or laid off. A worker's productivity relates to the worker's contribution to the value of output received by the bearer.

Consider a simple example. Suppose that you are hired by T-Shirt Manufacturing. As a result of hiring you, the total output of T-shirts increases by 4 per day. If your company sells each T-shirt for $5, then the additional contribution (or productivity) due to your labor is $20 a day. This is your value to the firm. In a competitive situation, the firm will end up paying you a wage rate of approximately $20 a day. It will not willingly pay you more. If you insisted on getting $40 a day, the T-shirt factory would not hire you, because

Productivity theory

The prediction that individuals are paid only according to their productivity; those with high productivities will be paid more than those with low productivities.

[1]Edward K. Browning, "How Much More Quality Can we Afford?" *The Public Interest* (Spring 1976), pp. 90–110.

that rate would be double the value of your output. Only if your output increased would the firm be able and willing to pay you more than $20 a day. On the other hand, suppose that the T-shirt factory insisted on paying you only $10 a day. In a competitive market, *another* firm would hire you for more than $10 a day. If you are worth $20 a day, both you and the firm that hires you away will be better off.

We can conclude, then, that in a market economy, individuals will be paid a rate close to the value of the additional output that they provide to a firm or employer. Any significant difference between wage rate and productivity worth will result in people changing jobs until most of the difference is eliminated.

There are many factors that account for different productivities and therefore different incomes, including inherited abilities, education, experience, training, risk taking, job unpleasantness, and inherited wealth.

Inherited Abilities.   Innate abilities and attributes can be very strong determinants of a person's potential productivity. Strength, good looks, coordination, mental alertness, and so on, are all facets of nonacquired human capital and therefore have some bearing on an individual's ability to earn income. If a person is extremely tall, that person has a better chance of becoming a basketball player than does someone who is short. If a person is born with a superior talent for abstract thinking, then he or she has a better chance of earning a living as a mathematician or philosopher than does someone who is not born with that talent. The list of inherited abilities and attributes that give some people an "edge" is long indeed.

Education.   Schooling, or education, improves one's productivity by increasing the human capital one has available for use in the labor market. If you have been taught to read, write, work with mathematics, understand scientific problems, do engineering or drafting, lay out advertisements, design clothes, or edit manuscripts, you are of more value to a potential employer than a person who is illiterate and unknowledgeable, except in the area of manual labor. Schooling usually enhances an individual's versatility in the job market.

Experience.   Acquiring experience at particular tasks is another way to increase one's productivity. Consider the example of a person going to work on an assembly line at General Motors. At first, the individual is able to screw on three bolts every two minutes. Then the worker becomes more adept and can screw on four bolts in the same time, as well as insert a rubber guard on the bumper. After a few more weeks, even another task can be added. Experience allows this individual to improve his or her productivity.

The more proficient that people become at a task, the quicker they can do it. Hence, experience leads to higher rates of productivity. And people with more experience tend to be paid more than people with less experience. More experience, however, does not guarantee a higher wage rate. The *demand* for one's services must also exist. Spending years to become a first-rate archer in modern society will probably add very little to an archer's income. And a more experienced pianist in a primitive society may earn the same as an inexperienced pianist—virtually nothing at all—since there is little demand for such talent. Experience has value only if the output is demanded by society.

Training. Training is similar to experience but is more formal. Much of a person's increased productivity is due to on-the-job training programs provided by many companies. New employees may learn to operate machinery, fill out forms, and do other tasks required for the new job. On-the-job training is perhaps responsible for as much of an increase in productivity as is formal schooling beyond grade school.

Risk Taking. Individuals who do dangerous jobs will earn more, on average (but not necessarily over a lifetime), than individuals of equal skills who work at less risky jobs. People who wash windows in tall buildings or who walk on high steel beams earn relatively higher incomes because of the danger involved in such work.

Job Unpleasantness. If two people work on jobs that require similar skills, but one job is more unpleasant (dirtier or smellier, for example) or less prestigious, then, other things being constant, the person working on the more unpleasant job will earn more. That person will require higher wages to compensate for the job's unpleasantness.

Inherited Wealth. Individuals who inherit wealth can earn income on that wealth and, other things being constant, earn higher incomes than those who have no inheritance. In the United States, inherited wealth accounts for less than 10 percent of income differences. In other countries, particularly the less-developed countries, inherited wealth is more important in determining income differences.

Discrimination

So far, it has been hypothesized that individuals tend to get paid an income that reflects their productivity. There is evidence, however, that income differences can exist even among people with similar productivities doing similar jobs with similar risk and similar unpleasantness. Such discrimination exists only because of *market imperfections*. When two groups with equal productivities receive, on average, significantly different incomes for doing similar work, discrimination is said to exist. It is widely believed that **racial discrimination** exists against blacks and other minority groups and that **sexual discrimination** exists against women.

Racial Discrimination. Research shows that even after adjusting for differences in productivity between blacks and whites (that is, differences in age, education quality, training, experience, and so on), an unexplained difference remains between the average incomes of blacks and whites. Presumably, this difference is accounted for by racial discrimination.

In one study, for example, Professor Gary S. Becker found that the incomes of black workers are reduced by 16 percent as a result of racial discrimination.[2] He also came to the following conclusions:

1. Discrimination is related to the relative number of blacks and whites. For a given-sized city, the larger the proportion of blacks, the more discrimination there will be. Further, discrimination is more prevalent when large numbers of blacks are involved in non-market activities, such as attaining a formal education.
2. Discrimination is less evident against blacks seeking temporary work as opposed to permanent work.
3. Discrimination is greater against those blacks who are older and better educated.
4. Discrimination has deterred blacks from entering professions such as law because of their competitive disadvantage in arguing before white juries.

It should be stressed that racial discrimination exists in forms other than income differences. There is evidence that the amount and quality of schooling offered blacks and other minorities have been inferior to the amount and quality offered whites. Studies have shown that even if minorities attend school as long as whites, their scholastic achievement is usually less because they typically are allotted fewer school resources than their white counterparts. Analysis of census data reveals that a large portion of white/nonwhite income differentials has resulted from differences in both the quality of education received and in scholastic achievement, which is more or less a function of the quality of education received. One study showed that nonwhite urban males received between 23 and 27 percent less income than white urban males because of lower-quality education. This means that even if employment discrimination were

---

[2]Gary S. Becker, *The Economics of Discrimination*, rev. ed. (Chicago: University of Chicago Press), 1971.

Racial discrimination

In regard to income, refers to the practice whereby members of different races with similar jobs and similar productivities receive significantly different incomes.

Sexual discrimination

In regard to income, refers to the practice where women are paid less than men even though they have similar productivities and are doing similar jobs.

reduced substantially, we would still expect to see a difference between white and nonwhite incomes because of the low quality of schooling received by nonwhites and the resulting lower level of productivity.

Sexual Discrimination.   Research also shows that, on average, urban white females earn about 40 percent less than urban white males. As in racial discrimination studies, even after we adjust for productivity differences, income differences still exist between males and females. However, these adjusted income differences are less than those of blacks. Sexual discrimination seems to be less powerful an income discriminator than racial discrimination.

One major factor contributing to differences between male and female wages is the different *roles* assigned to men and women. According to one researcher,

> Role differentiation, which begins in the cradle, affects the choice of occupation, labor force attachment, location of work, post-school investment, hours of work, and other variables that influence earnings. Role differentiation can, of course, result from discrimination. [A reduction in role differentiation] would require the combined efforts of men and women at home and in school, as well as the marketplace, and would probably result in a narrowing of earnings differences over the long run.[3]

Evidence supports this contention that role differentiation may be one of the reasons behind male–female wage differentials in this country. One reason American women do not earn a percentage of total wage payments equal to the percentage of their participation in the labor force is that many of them are in low-paying, low-productivity occupations—a situation due, in part, to our value system. In Germany, more than 12 percent of all executive positions are held by women; in France, the figure is at least 9 percent. In the United States, however, female executives represent only 2 percent of the total executive population.

In regard to physically demanding labor, role playing seems to be rampant in the United States. American women are not found doing stevedoring, for example. In many African countries, however, very heavy physical labor is regarded as "women's work." And if you ever take a trip to the Soviet Union, you will see women sweeping the streets and using pneumatic drills to break up sidewalks. And in Asia, you will see women tilling the fields. Obviously, occupational distribution by sex is not strictly a function of the physical differences between men and women.

---

[3]Victor R. Fuchs, "Differences in Hourly Earnings Between Men and Women," *Monthly Labor Review*, vol. 94, number 1 (May 1971), pp. 9–15.

● POVERTY

The United States has "waged a war on poverty" ever since the late 1960s. Since then, it has introduced many programs to help eliminate poverty. The fact that these programs have not been successful can be seen in Graph 19–1. The number of individuals officially classified as poor fell steadily from 1959 to 1969, but since then, there has been relatively little change in the absolute number classified as poor.

On Defining Poverty

The threshold income level, which is used to determine who falls into the poverty category, was originally based on the cost of a nutritionally adequate food plan designed by the Department of Agriculture for emergency or temporary use. The threshold was determined by multiplying the food plan cost times 3, on the assumption that food expenses comprise approximately one-third of a poor family's income. In 1969, a federal interagency committee looked at the calculations of the threshold and decided to set new standards. Until then, annual revisions of the threshold level were based purely

GRAPH 19–1

The Official Number of Poor in the United States

The number of individuals classified as poor fell steadily from 1959 to 1969. But since then, there has been little change in the absolute number classified as poor.

SOURCE: U.S. Department of Commerce.

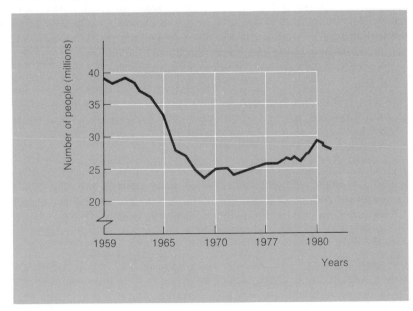

on price changes in the food budget. After 1969, the adjustments were made on the basis of changes in the consumer price index.

The low-income threshold thus represents an absolute measure of income needed to maintain a specified standard of living as of 1963, with the real-dollar value, or the purchasing power value, increased year by year in relation to the general increase in prices. In 1981, for example, the low-income threshold budget for a nonfarm family of four was $8410. By the time you read this book, it will have increased to correspond with changes in the consumer price index. (It varies for families of different size.)

Absolute Poverty

Since the low-income threshold is an absolute measure, if it remains the same in real terms, poverty will be reduced even if nothing is done specifically to reduce it. How can that be? The reasoning is rather straightforward. Real incomes in the United States have been growing at a compounded annual rate of about 1.6 percent per capita for the last 100 or more years, and at about 2.5 percent since World War II. If the poverty line is defined at a specified real level, more and more individuals will make incomes that exceed that poverty line. Thus, in absolute terms, eventually poverty will be eliminated (assuming continued per capita growth).

Relative Poverty

Care must be taken with the preceding analysis. Poverty has generally been defined in relative terms, that is, in terms of individual or family income levels relative to what exists in the rest of the population. As long as the distribution of income is not perfectly equal, there will always be some people who make less income than others and some people who have a relatively low income—even if that relatively low income is high by past standards. Thus, in a relative sense, the problem of poverty will always exist, although it can be reduced.

Who Are the Poor?

Individuals who are classified as poor usually fall into one or more of the following categories: (1) minority groups, (2) the elderly, (3) the young, (4) rural dwellers, and (5) households headed by women.

Minority Groups.   Minority groups—blacks, Hispanics, and so on—have a relatively high incidence of poverty. It is interesting to note that the poverty rate among black families is more than three times

384

that of white families. The statistics are even worse for native Americans and Chicanos.

The Elderly.   Family units headed by individuals over 65 years of age often have very low levels of income. One out of every five poor families is headed by an elderly person. (Note, however, that their situation is often alleviated by the fact that they own their own homes and therefore don't need income for housing. Also, they may have other wealth.)

The Young.   The young, and especially black teenagers, suffer high rates of unemployment. The minimum wage law further aggravates this situation. The younger members of society are generally not as educated or experienced as the older groups, and therefore they are not as productive. Hence, their value is often not sufficient to induce employers to pay the statutory minimum wage to hire them.

Rural Dwellers.   Poverty is far more common among families living in rural areas than among those living in the cities. Poverty rates among families living on farms are almost twice as high as among those in urban areas. (Note, however, that rural families often grow much of their own food and therefore do not require as much money income.)

Households Headed by Women.   Nearly 40 percent of all women heading a household and providing for children are defined as poor. If we look at the nonwhite population of fatherless families, this figure rises to nearly 60 percent.

Attacks on Poverty: Major Income-Maintenance Programs

Now that you have an idea as to how individuals are classified as poor, let's look at some current programs designed to help low-income families.

Social Insurance.   For the retired and unemployed, certain social insurance programs provide income payments in prescribed situations. The best known is social security, which includes old age, survivors, disability, and health insurance—or OASDHI. This is essentially a program of compulsory saving financed from compulsory payroll taxes levied on both employers and employees. Workers pay for social security while they are working and receive the benefits after they retire. The benefit payments are usually made to those reaching retirement age. When the insured worker dies, benefits accrue to the survivors, including spouse and children. There are also special benefits that provide for disabled workers.

Over 90 percent of all employed persons in the United States are covered by OASDHI.

Social security was originally designed as a social insurance program that workers would pay for themselves and from which they would receive benefits that would vary according to the size of past contributions. In reality, today, it is simply an intergenerational income transfer that, at best, is only roughly associated with past earnings. In other words, social security is a system in which income is transferred from those who work—the young—to those who do not work—older retired persons.

In 1981, there were more than 30 million people receiving OASDHI checks averaging about $365 a month. Benefit payments from OASDHI redistribute income to some degree. However, benefit payments are not based on the recipient's need. Participants' contributions give them the right to benefits even if they would be financially secure without them. In fact, social security appears to be a system whereby the relatively young subsidize the relatively old.

Social security is not really an insurance program because people are not guaranteed that the benefits they receive will be in line with the contributions they have made. It is not a personal savings account. The benefits are legislated by Congress. In the future, Congress may not be as sympathetic toward older people as it is today. It could legislate for lower real levels of benefits instead of higher ones.

Supplemental Security Income (SSI) and Aid to Families with Dependent Children (AFDC). There are a great many people who are poor and who do not qualify for social security benefits. They are assisted through other programs. In 1974, a federally financed and administered Supplemental Security Income (SSI) program was instituted. The purpose of SSI is to establish a nationwide minimum income for the aged, the blind, and the disabled.

The Aid to Families with Dependent Children (AFDC) is a state-administered program partially financed by federal grants. This program provides aid to poor families in which dependent children do not have the financial support of the father because of desertion, disability, or death.

Food Stamps. In 1964, 367,000 Americans were receiving food stamps. By 1982, there were over 17 million recipients. The annual cost jumped from $860,000 to more than $11 billion. The eligibility requirements for the program in 1982 were such that a family with a monthly gross income less than $1,008 could qualify. If after a

standard deduction ($85 per month) and utility and shelter deduc-
tions ($115 per month) the family's net income was zero or negative,
a *maximum* of $253 per month in food stamps was allotted. The
monthly food stamp allotment below this maximum depends on
individual circumstances. Also, if a family member is over 60 or
disabled, additional food stamp allotments are granted.

A congressional committee found that in 1975, one out of every
14 persons was estimated to be using food stamps. The food stamp
program has become a major part of the welfare system in the
United States. It was started in 1964 and, in retrospect, seems to
have been used mainly to shore up the nation's agricultural sector
by distributing "surplus" food through retail channels. In addition,
of course, the food stamp program was and continues to be a
method of supporting better nutrition among the poor.

Current Welfare Programs Are Inefficient

THE ARGUMENT

Poverty still exists in the United States, regardless of the definition we use. There are numerous programs to reduce poverty, and they all involve a redistribution of income – taking away from some and giving to others. Critics of these redistribution programs claim that the manner in which the poor are helped is inefficient – that is, it leads to a loss in productivity for the nation.

THE ANALYSIS

A major problem with any welfare program is its impact on the incentive for individuals to obtain gainful taxable employment. If someone is currently receiving any type of welfare benefit that will be lost or reduced if that person goes to work, there is an implied, or implicit, tax involved in going back to work. Consider the following example. A person is receiving welfare benefits equal to $400 a month, all of which is untaxed. Now assume that the individual loses $1 of welfare benefits for every $1 earned. Ignoring any taxes paid on the dollar earned, the marginal tax rate is 100 percent. The individual is no better off by working until he or she earns $401. If we take account of the fact that most earnings are taxed by the federal government and by some state governments, then the effective marginal tax rate in our example is *greater* than 100 percent.

Two economists at the University of Southern California have put together a table showing the actual effects of income and taxes on family spendable income from wages and welfare benefits. This table is reproduced as Table 19–2. The table is calculated for an inner-city family of four in Los Angeles in the year 1980. The family is assumed to be comprised of two adults, one of whom is either unemployed or disabled. The family is assumed to obtain the maximum city, county, state, and federal welfare benefits to which it is entitled. Look at the column labeled "Actual Marginal Tax Rate." That is the implicit marginal tax rate that this family of four is paying when one of the members goes to work. The lowest marginal tax rate is 58.9 percent; the highest is 121.2 percent. That means that if the family decides to earn $500 instead of $400, it is *worse off* by $21.22.

Although this example may seem exaggerated, it does drive home the point that welfare programs by their very nature must involve a high implicit marginal tax rate. And individuals may respond to these high marginal tax rates by avoiding gainful employment, by taking longer to look for a job, or by joining the cash, or underground (nonreported), economy.

The Trade-Off between Equality and Efficiency

The philosophy behind redistributing income in general and helping the poor in particular is strongly associated with the concept of egalitarianism, or equality for all. The notions

388

TABLE 19-2

The Effects of Income and Taxes on Family Spendable Income from the Total of Welfare Benefits and Wages

This table shows the effects of welfare benefits and taxes on spendable income in California for 1980. In column 1, we show monthly gross wages, which include the employment taxes paid by employers. In column 2, we show net family spendable income after all taxes and welfare benefits, both from the federal government and the state, are included. That is why we label column 2 "Net Family Spendable Income." In column 3, we show the increase in spendable income as gross monthly wages from working increase from 0 to $1000. For example, if a typical California family is making $200 a month and works enough to make $300 a month, spendable income will go up by only $30.04, even though gross monthly wages increase by $100. In column 4, the actual marginal tax rate is calculated. In the example we just discussed, since gross monthly wages increase by $100 but spendable income increases by only $30, the actual, or implicit, marginal tax rate is 70 percent.

MONTHLY GROSS WAGES (1)	NET FAMILY SPENDABLE INCOME (2)	INCREASE IN SPENDABLE INCOME (3)	ACTUAL MARGINAL TAX RATE (Percent) (4)
0	$718.33	n.a.	n.a.
100	759.43	$41.10	58.9
200	780.53	21.10	78.9
300	810.57	30.04	70.0
400	815.80	5.23	94.5
500	794.58	−21.22	121.2
600	794.58	none	100.0
700	794.58	none	100.0
800	809.92	15.34	84.7
900	832.49	22.57	77.4
1000	858.58	26.09	73.9

SOURCE: Arthur B. Laffer and Christopher R. Petruzzi, University of Southern California.

is therefore confronting policymakers. This trade-off was best described by a former member of the President's Council of Economic Advisers, the late Arthur M. Okun:

> The contrasts among American families in living standards and in material wealth reflect a system of rewards and penalties that is intended to encourage effort and to channel it into socially productive activity. To the extent that the [market] system succeeds, it generates an efficient economy. But that pursuit of efficiency necessarily creates inequalities. And hence society faces a trade-off between equality and efficiency.[4]

This trade-off will probably always confront policymakers. The more equality sought, the less productive efficiency will prevail. How much economic efficiency can the United States sacrifice to obtain more equality? That is not an easy question to answer—but it must be asked.

DISCUSSION QUESTIONS

1. What is a work disincentive effect? Are there income transfer programs that do not have a work disincentive effect?
2. Why does there have to be a trade-off between efficiency and equality?

of liberty, justice, and equality are strong sentiments in this country, and they pervade the political and social institutions. On the other hand, our economic institutions have resulted in significant income and wealth differences. To many, this is a conflict in our society. Yet, forcing more equality onto the economic system conflicts with economic efficiency. A fundamental trade-off

[4]Arthur M. Okun, *Equality and Efficiency: The Big Trade-off* (Washington, D.C.: The Brookings Institution), 1975, p. 1.

● WHAT'S AHEAD

In the next chapter, the topic of crime is discussed. We will look at crime from an economic point of view and make some predictions about the amount of crime in the United States.

● CHAPTER SUMMARY

The distribution of money income in the United States has not changed very much since World War II. The distribution of total income, including in-kind transfers, has changed dramatically, however, with the lowest 20 percent of income earners more than doubling their income share since World War II.

Income differences exist, according to the productivity theory, because of inherited abilities, education, experience, training, risk taking, job unpleasantness, and inherited wealth. Income differences can also exist because of market imperfections, such as racial and sexual discrimination.

If the definition of the number of poor in the United States is a relative one, by definition, poverty can never be eliminated. In our society, the poor generally consist of minorities, the elderly, the young, those who live in rural areas, and women who are heads of households.

In the U.S. major attacks on poverty have involved social insurance, supplemental security income, and aid to families with dependent children, as well as food stamps.

● QUESTIONS FOR REVIEW AND STUDY

1. Since World War II, pretax money income differences among families in the United States have _____ _____.

2. Since World War II, overall incomes have been _____.

3. One problem with looking at income differences is that statistics are not adjusted for _____.

4. The productivity theory of income differences states that individuals will be paid according to the _____ of their output.

5. Two factors that account for productivity differences are _____ and _____.

6. One form of productivity improvement is _____ training.

7. Two types of market imperfections that result in income differences are _____ and _____ _____.

8. If we define poverty in absolute terms, then poverty will/will not eventually be eliminated, so long as there is economic growth.

9. If we define poverty in relative terms, then poverty will/will not eventually be eliminated by economic growth.

10. Three groups in the United States that are highly represented among the poor are _____, _____, and _____.

11. Social security is a(n) voluntary/involuntary retirement system.

ANSWERS

1. remained constant   2. rising   3. age; temporary income changes   4. value
5. inherent abilities; education; training; risk taking; job unpleasantness; inherited
wealth (name two only)   6. on-the-job   7. racial; sexual discrimination   8. will
9. will not   10. minorities; the young; rural residents; families headed
by women (name three only)   11. involuntary

● ANSWERS TO CHAPTER PREVIEW QUESTIONS

1. *Why do different individuals earn different incomes?*

The major theory to account for income differences is the productivity theory. This theory states that laborers tend to be paid their productive value. Laborers who are paid less than their productive value will go to other employers who will find it profitable to pay them more. Any laborer who requires more than his or her productive value may find himself or herself without a job. Productivity differences are due to age, inherent talent, experience, and training. Of course, given the same productivity among individuals, discrimination can also lead to income differences.

2. *What do you think would be the best way to distribute income in the United States?*

Value judgments are required to determine whether one distribution of income is "better" than another. There is no objective way to decide that a more even distribution of income is preferable to a less even one. Three main theories of what the income distribution "should" be are: (1) to each according to his or her need (this is the distributive principle of communism and has obvious measurement problems; what is "need"?); (2) to each exactly the same (incentive problems obviously emerge here); and (3) to each according to what he or she produces (this theory suggests that income differences due to differences in people's value of marginal product are "fair"). Each of these theories is a normative (value) statement.

● PROBLEMS

1. It is often observed that blacks, on average, earn less than whites. What are some possible reasons for these income differences?

2. What has been happening to the distribution of income in the United States?

● SELECTED REFERENCES

Easterlin, Richard A. *Birth and Fortune: The Impact of Numbers on Personal Welfare*. New York: Basic Books, 1980.

Harrington, Michael. *The Other America: Poverty in the United States*. Rev. ed. New York: Macmillan, 1970.

Okun, Arthur M. *Equality and Efficiency: The Big Tradeoff*. Washington, D.C.: The Brookings Institution, 1975.

Thurow, Lester C. *Generating Inequality: Mechanisms of Distribution in the U.S. Economy*. New York: Basic Books, 1975.

Van Driel, G. J. *Limits to the Welfare State*. Boston: Martinus Nijhoff, 1980.

Williamson, J. G., and P. H. Lindest. *American Inequality*. New York: Academic Press, 1980.

20

Crime

Chapter Preview

1. Imagine yourself as a potential burglar. How would you determine whether a life of crime would be worthwhile?

2. What are some of the ways that crime could be reduced?

Current surveys indicate that people are worried about crime. Crime consistently ranks close to inflation and unemployment as a major concern for U.S. citizens. In the privately funded Figge Report, released in 1980, 40 percent of all Americans expressed a high fear of crime. For people in big cities, this figure was 52 percent—that's more than half the people living in large U.S. cities!

As we shall see, these fears are justified. In 1982, it was estimated that one-fourth of all U.S. households are victimized by some sort of crime at least once a year. In 1970, that annual rate was 4000 per 100,000 people; by 1979, the crime rate had risen to 5500 per 100,000 people. During the period 1971–1981, the U.S. prison population increased from about 200,000 to 350,000 inmates. It is estimated that federal and state governments plan to spend from $5 billion to $10 billion during the 1980s on prison construction alone.

At the beginning of the 1980s, the New York City police force consisted of 23,000 people; some 800 FBI agents are also located in New York. The district attorney's office in Manhattan alone—just one of the five boroughs of the city—handles about 6500 felonies per year! And the data for New York City reveal that there were over 1500 murders, over 4000 rapes, almost 78,000 robberies, nearly 160,000 burglaries, over 26,000 assaults, and many other lesser offenses. Keep in mind that these figures represent only those major crimes that have been *reported* in the early 1980s.

● A NONECONOMIC THEORY OF CRIME

Why is there so much crime in the United States? A comparison of U.S. crime data with those of Japan might give us a clue. It was estimated that in 1978, fewer than 2000 robberies were reported in *all* of Japan. Compare this with the U.S. robbery estimate of 400,000 during 1977. The U.S. population is only twice as large as Japan's, yet there were about 200 times as many robberies in the U.S. as in Japan during a one-year period! Moreover, the evidence indicates that over the past 20 years, there has been a slight reduction in Japan in the per capita incidence of reported murders, rapes, robberies, and assaults.

What difference is there between Japan and the United States that could possibly account for such a difference in the amount of serious crime? The leading explanation seems to be the close social bonds in Japanese communities and the strong *social* sanctions imposed on criminals.

Criminal prosecutors in Japan rely on family and neighborhood values to assist them in fighting crime. Nearly 99 percent of the defendants brought to trial in Japan are found guilty (since only those cases with strong evidence of guilt come to trial). But only about 4 percent of those convicted are actually sent to prison. The rest are set free with fines or suspended sentences, and they are obliged to work with a national network of 50,000 *volunteer* probation officers. The goal of Japanese prosecutors seems to be to convince the criminal to repent and return to the family and society. Public apology and confession are encouraged, as is payment to the victims by the criminal.

The contrast between crime in Japan and crime in the United States points strongly to a sociological explanation of crime. The problem in the United States may well be that neighborhood and community institutions have broken down in recent decades. There seems to be no social pressure to conform to noncriminal behavior. Whether these institutions can be revitalized and whether it is feasible for the U.S. to adopt the Japanese system are important issues. There is a strong possibility that the Japanese criminal system simply would not work in the United States. If that is the case, then something else must be done.

Enter economics.

● AN ECONOMIC THEORY OF CRIME

This text has continually stressed that individuals respond to incentives; people will compare the anticipated costs and benefits of alternative actions and select the activity that they believe maximizes their own self-interest. For the moment, assume that criminals behave in this manner also. In other words, assume that they act only in their own self-interest. Anyone considering the commission of a crime therefore will compare the anticipated *additional* costs involved in committing the crime with the anticipated *additional* benefits of committing that crime. Notice the emphasis on the word "additional." Basically, the potential criminal must look to the result of committing a crime compared with the result of not committing a crime. This is no different from a businessperson having produced a given output and then evaluating the additional cost and the additional benefit (revenue) of producing one more unit. In any event, if the potential criminal determines that the extra, or additional, benefits are greater than the extra, or additional, costs, he or she will, using this model of human behavior, commit the crime.

Although it is unlikely that potential criminals can make precise calculations as to the extra benefits and extra costs of specific crimes, they can make *intuitive* guesses about the costs and benefits of crime. And, of course, they can gain experience (or take advantage of other people's experience) in making reasonably good guesses.

It should be noted that this analysis is quite an oversimplification of human behavior. After all, it seems to imply that *everyone* is a potential criminal. Surely, many people refuse to commit crimes

395

even though the extra benefits of committing them may outweigh the extra costs of doing so. Obviously, numerous other factors that might influence the potential criminal's actions are ignored, such as emotions, religious beliefs, and the like. Still, for this theory to work, it is only required that *some* people behave in such a "rational" manner.

Even though these assumptions may sound unreasonable or unrealistic, nevertheless certain *predictions* about crime can be made based on these assumptions. And if some of these predictions are borne out in fact, then the assumptions are workable. What, then, does an economic analysis predict?

Economic Predictions About Crime

Suppose that the penalty for stealing $10 is the same as the penalty for stealing $100,000. An economic theory predicts that people who are at all inclined to steal will steal larger amounts. Why? Because the extra benefit rises with the amount stolen, but the extra, or marginal, cost (the penalty) is the same regardless of the amount stolen, assuming the risk is similar.

In general, if the benefits of criminal activities fall or if their costs rise, a decrease in the crime rate is predictable. Similarly, if the benefits of crime rise or the costs of crime fall, an increase in the crime rate is likely.

Three Phases of Law Enforcement

Three phases of law enforcement are related to the theory's predictions. The three phases are (1) detection and arrest, (2) trial and conviction, and (3) prison and/or fines.

Detection and Arrest.   According to this theory, an increase in resources allocated to the detection and arrest of criminals will reduce the crime rate. This follows because such resource allocation will increase the probability of apprehending criminals and therefore increase the expected cost of criminal activity to potential criminals.

The expected cost of criminal activity depends not only on the sentence that a person might receive if caught, but also on the probability of being caught. What's the expected cost, for example, of throwing litter out the car window, even though you've read highway signs telling you that you are subject to a fine of $500? The expected cost is close to zero because the probability of being caught is also very close to zero. The economic theory of rational criminal behavior predicts that the probability of being caught is important in the potential criminal's calculation of the expected cost of crime.

Also relevant is how the overall resources (the budget) allocated to detection and arrest are spent on specific inputs. Should commu-

396

nities purchase more labor (e.g., more officers), or more capital (more police cars, buildings, laboratory equipment, computers, and so on)? As in business, the optimal choice of inputs that can substitute for each other depends on relative prices. If the price of capital rises relative to labor, it would be efficient to substitute some labor for capital.

Moreover, given a fixed crime-fighting budget, an increase in the allocation of resources to the detection and arrest for a specific criminal activity will increase the probability of getting caught and therefore increase the extra (marginal) cost to criminals of engaging in that activity. But, given the fixed crime-fighting budget, this means that the probability of getting caught for engaging in *other* illegal activities will fall, and therefore, the anticipated cost of engaging in those other illegal activities will also fall. For example, a greater effort by authorities to crack down on illicit drug traffic will increase the cost of engaging in drug-related crimes (although not necessarily eliminate the activity if the drug is addictive). However, since resources will be taken away from *other* police activities, the chance of getting caught at other crimes will fall, and therefore, the marginal cost of these other crimes will fall! Therefore, an increased emphasis on fighting one crime may well lead to an increase in the incidence of other crimes, as the relative expected marginal costs (to criminals) of different crimes change.

Trial and Conviction.   Recent research demonstrates that the probability of conviction is of major importance in crime prevention. It is a common observation that the likelihood of conviction is quite low in the United States. First of all, the probability of getting caught is low. Then, too, the courts are so overloaded with cases that there is usually a long lapse between a criminal's capture and trial. In the meantime, the offender is out on bail—which is usually set quite low. Finally, the likelihood of being found guilty is slight; and even for those judged guilty, sentences are often light or suspended.

Potential criminals observing all this—and they certainly do—come to the conclusion that their chances of going to prison are quite slim; and if they do have to serve prison time, it won't be for long and there is always a chance of getting out for "good behavior." At the very least a long time will elapse between committing a crime and paying the "price" for it.

It has been estimated that for someone who commits a felony in New York City, the chances are less than 1 in 200 of going to jail. Not bad odds—especially if sentences are short and a convicted criminal can be released early on good behavior.

One consequence of the present law enforcement situation is that between 80 and 90 percent of those arrested are never tried in court. Instead, the defendant and the prosecutor settle out of court

—for a reduced sentence. This consideration, of course, is *also* taken into account by some potential lawbreakers.

Prison and/or Fines.   Studies about the effectiveness of prison sentences and fines in crime prevention show mixed results. The evidence seems to support the contention that stiff prison sentences do discourage crimes against property, but they may be relatively ineffective in discouraging crimes against people. In other words, long jail sentences don't seem to have much effect on the incidence of unplanned murder, rape, or assault.

● POSSIBLE SOLUTIONS TO THE CRIME PROBLEM

Consider now some of the possible solutions to the serious crime problem in the United States. In general, anything that reduces the benefits and/or increases the costs of crime can help to reduce criminal activities.

Sacrificing Political Freedoms (Trade-Offs)

The probability of detection and conviction would be increased if some constitutional rights were suspended. New technological advances in the areas of wiretapping could be used to catch criminals and provide evidence in court. Perhaps police officers could be given authority to enter and search without knocking or without search warrants. Law enforcement officials could stop giving suspects information about their "rights"—or indeed, criminals could be given fewer rights. Perhaps evidence gained illegally by police authorities could be permissible in court.

Of course, some people feel that the costs to the rest of the population in terms of loss of political freedom might outweigh any benefits derived from a decreased incidence of crime—at least in respect to some of the more radical suggestions mentioned above. What is involved here is a trade-off. Crime could be reduced at the expense of political freedom.

Compensating the Victim

Should victims be reimbursed for their medical and economic losses? Perhaps criminals should be required to pay victims for their losses. Or maybe the government should compensate the victim. Either way, the costs of crime, to the victim, at least, would fall. In the present system, a victim is injured and incurs economic damages. The criminal (if caught) is given a trial and found guilty (maybe) and sent to prison (maybe). Who ultimately pays for the trial and for the maintenance of the criminal in prison? The victim, of course, as a taxpayer.

If structured correctly, victim compensation could alter the allocation of resources in fighting crime. If the city or state were held liable for all damages sustained, the victim or his or her dependents could sue the city or state for compensation. Unlimited liability on the part of government for crimes against the populus would certainly alter the present allocation of resources between crime prevention and other public endeavors. Under present laws, the private cost of crime is borne by the individual, who has little hope of being compensated.

It should be noted, however, that a federal system of victim compensation could lead to more crime, not less. Under such a system, cities and states will have less incentive to allocate more of their own resources to crime prevention, and individuals will have less incentive to protect themselves against criminal activity. Why? Because federal crime compensation involves all taxpayers paying any victim in the United States. That means that if crime is high in a particular city or state, the residents of that city or state will pay an imperceptibly small part of the additional victim compensation that the federal government must pay for. And the potential victims will find that carelessness is compensated for by "the government"— meaning all taxpayers.

Prison Reform

As mentioned earlier, the U.S. prison population swelled from under 200,000 to about 350,000 during the 1971–1981 period. In December of 1981, U.S. Supreme Court Justice Warren Burger noted that "a person confined to a penal institution without being able to read, write, spell or do simple arithmetic and not trained with any marketable skill, will be vulnerable to returning to a life of crime." Burger then went on to suggest that prisons be used as something more than a means of separating criminals from noncriminals. In particular, he suggested that prisons educate and train prisoners in realistic situations, turning prisons into shops and factories that would produce goods and services for sale.

To put such a plan into effect, Burger added, this nation would be required to repeal laws that limit prison industrial production. Also, businesses and labor unions would be asked to change their attitudes toward the use of prison labor to produce goods.

Although not suggested by Burger, others suggest that prisoners be paid the market value of their labor—and be obligated to compensate their victims in some amount each month.

● PRIVATE CRIME PREVENTION

Clearly, the treatment of the crime problem in this country has not been effective. And because of society's failure to reduce crime, individuals and firms have increasingly sought ways to solve their crime problems *privately*. That is, they are taking on the responsibility for their own protection.

The private security business is one of the fastest growing businesses in the country. Sales of business security devices and services to protect people and property have skyrocketed. Annual sales increased from $1.9 billion in 1972 to $4.7 billion in 1978, according to Predicosts, Inc., a market research firm. Moreover, this firm predicts annual industry sales of almost $17 billion by the year 1990!

A wide range of innovative and expensive security devices has appeared on the market in recent years. The 007 Bionic Briefcase, which sold for up to $27,000 in 1981, can be used as a body shield, "bug" detector, and tracking transmitter. Armored cars were priced around $50,000 in 1982, with a $20,000 optional radar system. The going price for a pocket-sized videotape camera in 1982 was about $6000. This device could also be installed in armored cars to monitor them when unoccupied.

Other popular products include computerized fingerprint or voice verification machines, which can be used to prevent non-employees from entering buildings or offices. The cost? A mere $50,000 for a minicomputer, and another $10,000 for each access terminal. And IBM is experimenting with a handwriting verification computer that can be used to prevent forgery.

Potential kidnap victims, such as very high-placed executives in major corporations, can purchase microtransmitters that can be implanted under the skin for $25,000. Rescuers need only follow the signal.

Worried about eavesdroppers? Purchase an $18,000 Super Scout bug detector that can detect bugs even when they are not operating!

It seems that U.S. residents are long past the days of merely locking our doors to prevent crime.

Capital Punishment Can Reduce the Murder Rate

THE ARGUMENT

Many economists accept the analysis in this chapter as being valid when it is applied to crimes against property, such as theft, housebreaking, and so on. But when the analysis is extended to homicide, quite a few observers believe that the analysis breaks down. Others, however, contend that the theory still holds and that capital punishment does impact on the murder rate.

THE ANALYSIS

No economist would ever say that psychological and sociological factors don't enter into homicide decisions. Rather, economists like to use a simplified model of the world to see if they can make predictions that are at least not refuted by historical evidence. They start out with a commodity defined as the act of murder. If the act of murder is like any other commodity, then the quantity "demanded" (by perpetrators, of course, not by victims) will be negatively related to the relative price. But what is the price of murder? Ignoring for the moment all the sociological and psychological costs of murder, economists consider the cost to the murderer when he or she is caught, the probability of being caught, and then, once caught, the probability of being convicted, and then, if convicted, the possible jail term or capital punishment that might result. But here again, the probability of a particular jail sentence and the probability of going to the gas chamber or of lethal injection must be considered. Thus, it would do little good to observe the difference in murder rates between states that have capital punishment and states that do not. Rather, it would be necessary to look at the probability of a convicted murderer going to the gas chamber in those states with capital punishment compared with what happens in states where there is zero probability. In fact, there are some states with capital punishment where the probability of going to the gas chamber is effectively zero for a convicted murderer. We find, for example, that states with the death penalty for first-degree murder often change the charge to second-degree murder. But states with life maximums for first-degree murder seldom lower the charge.

Some critics of the economic model as it applies to murder contend that the murderer, either in a moment of unreasoned passion or when confronted with an unanticipated situation (as during an armed robbery), does not take into account the expected probability of going to the gas chamber at the moment the crime is being committed. That is, murderers are not acting rationally when they murder. But is this a valid criticism of the economic model of the demand for murder? No, it is not. If the model predicts poorly, then the assumptions must be changed or the model must be changed in some other way. Indeed, to contend that the expected "price" of commit-

401

ting a murder has no effect on the quantity of murders implicitly negates the law of demand or states that price has no impact. Such thinking also confuses the average murder with the marginal murder. All potential murderers do *not* have to be aware of or react to the change in the expected price of committing a murder for the theory to be useful. If there are a sufficient number of marginal murderers who act *as if* they are responding to the higher expected price of committing a murder, the demand curve for murder will be downward sloping.[1]

Actual Estimates

A few economists have actually worked through economic models of the demand for murder and other crimes. One of the variables used was the risk of being executed if caught and convicted of murder. According to one study, "an additional execution

---

[1]In fact, "rational" killers who make a living performing contract murders *do* act as we have predicted. They demand more pay in higher-risk situations. They also plan the murder with an eye on the trial rules of evidence.

per year over the period in question may have resulted, on average, in 7 or 8 fewer murders."[2] The results of this study are startling, and many economists and statisticians have challenged their validity. The point, however, is not whether the estimates are valid, but that economic analysis can be applied to a seemingly noneconomic activity.

DISCUSSION QUESTIONS

1. Apparently a large percentage of murder victims know the murderer beforehand. In other words, murders often occur between family members, friends, and lovers. Does that mean that economic analysis does not apply? Why or why not?
2. If capital punishment does have an impact on the murder rate, what is the cost to society of completely eliminating capital punishment? What is the benefit to society?

---

[2]Isaac Ehrlich, "The Deterrent Effect of Capital Punishment: A Question of Life and Death," *The American Economic Review*, vol. 65, no. 3 (June 1973), p. 414.

● WHAT'S AHEAD

In the final chapter of the book, we will examine the battle of the "isms," that is, the battle of different economic systems. Who will win that battle? The socialists, the communists, or the capitalists?

● CHAPTER SUMMARY

There are many noneconomic explanations of crime. The economic explanation involves looking at additional costs and additional benefits, assuming that criminals act in a rational manner.

The additional expected cost of crime relates to the probability of detection and arrest, the probability of going to trial and being convicted, and the potential prison sentence or fine. Anytime those probabilities increase, the expected costs of crime increase, and less crime is predicted, other things being equal.

One way to reduce crime is to reduce the amount of political freedom. By eliminating many rights, we could certainly arrest more criminals, but we would pay a price in reduced freedom. In addition, victims could be compensated, using local or state tax revenues. The more crime there was, the more taxes that would have to be paid. As a consequence there would be more incentive for local citizens to bring pressure on police authorities to reduce crime.

Because of the recent crime wave in the United States, there has been a tremendous growth in the private crime prevention industry.

● QUESTIONS FOR REVIEW AND STUDY

1. In Japan, nearly all/none of the defendants brought to trial are found guilty.

2. Looking at crime as an economic activity, potential criminals will compare the _____ _____ costs with the _____ _____ benefits of committing a crime.

3. For an economic theory of crime to predict relatively accurately, all that is required is that _____ individuals behave in a "rational" manner.

4. If the penalty is the same for both minor and major crimes, a relatively larger number of _____ crimes will be committed, given equal risk.

5. The three phases of law enforcement are _____ _____ _____, _____ _____ _____, and _____ _____ _____.

6. If more resources are devoted to the detection and arrest of criminals, this raises the _____ cost of criminal activity.

7. If the price of police personnel rises relative to the price of capital —lab equipment, computers, police cars, and so on—then more/less capital should be purchased.

8. If more resources are devoted to stamping out one particular type of crime, then more/less of other types of crime will be committed.

9. Currently, between _____ and _____ percent of those arrested are never tried in court.

10. We could always increase the probability of detection and conviction by reducing the amount of political _____.

11. If publicly provided crime prevention does not work sufficiently an increase in _____ provided crime prevention will result.

ANSWERS

1. all 2. anticipated additional; anticipated additional 3. some 4. major 5. detection and arrest; trial and conviction; prison and/or fines 6. expected 7. more 8. more 9. 80; 90 10. freedom 11. privately

● ANSWERS TO CHAPTER PREVIEW QUESTIONS

1. *Imagine yourself as a potential burglar. How would you determine whether a life of crime would be worthwhile?*

As with all potentially profitable economic activities, you would have to look at expected costs and expected benefits. You would then make a comparison of the *net* benefits expected from a life of crime compared with your net benefits from the alternatives in a life of honest work. In terms of expected benefits of criminal activity, specifically burglary, you would estimate the actual cash payment you would receive from selling the stolen goods. That cash payment would be 100 percent for you—you wouldn't have to pay any taxes. In terms of the expected costs, you would have to look at the normal cost of such an activity, such as the cost of your burglary tools. But you would also have to estimate the probability of being caught and convicted, as well as the actual fines and/or prison terms that could be assessed against you.

2. *What are some of the ways that crime could be reduced?*

Some possible ways of reducing crime involve increasing the expected costs to criminals of engaging in additional criminal activity. One way to increase such costs is to increase the probability of detection and arrest. This would require more police personnel, better equipment, and so on. Increased costs to criminals could also come about if private citizens use more sophisticated burglar alarms. Additionally, the cost to a potential criminal would go up if a larger number of those apprehended were actually brought to trial. Finally, increasing the probability of being convicted and increasing fines and jail sentences would also raise the cost to wrongdoers. Presumably, any increased cost would reduce the amount of crime. By how much, of course, is another matter.

● PROBLEMS

1. List the potential costs that face someone contemplating a life of housebreaking and robbery. Indicate how the potential criminal might estimate these potential costs.

2. List the potential benefits of a life of crime and list the potential benefits of a life of noncrime. Indicate how the potential criminal can estimate the benefits of entering a life of crime.

21

The Battle of the Isms

Chapter Preview

1. It is said that *all* economies in the world are mixed economies. What does this mean?

2. What are the characteristics of a socialist economy?

In Chapter 6, we stressed that all economies face the fundamental economic problem of scarcity. Because of scarcity, all economies must answer three basic questions: What is produced? How? And for whom? Different economies answer these questions in different ways; the way an economy answers these questions gives a clue as to how the economy should be classified.

Throughout this book, we have been concerned with how the U.S. economy works. Our economy is a mixed economy (as are all real-world economies), but it has had a strong tradition of free enterprise and is often classified as a market-oriented, capitalist economy. In this chapter, we will discuss the main characteristics of capitalism, socialism, and communism and try to classify some real-world economies according to these categories. We will end the chapter with a brief discussion about who will win the battle of the "isms."

● THE BATTLING ISMS

In this section, we will attempt to distinguish and to define capitalism, socialism, and communism in their pure forms; we discuss idealized or theoretical versions of each one. In practice, it is difficult to find any economy that fits exactly into *any* of these three economic systems; in fact, most economies have some characteristics of each of these systems. Still, economists, like other academics, like to use classification as a way of simplifying complex problems. Moreover, most economies come closer to one of these systems than to the other two.

Pure Capitalism

Pure capitalism is an idealized economic system under which capital and natural resources are owned by individuals. Individuals also own the rights to their personal labor. Thus, private property rights are an important ingredient of pure capitalism. Individuals have the right to use (or not use) their resources as they see fit—subject to minimal legal restrictions. Pure capitalism can best be described in terms of private property rights, free enterprise and free markets, self-interest (which is kept in check by competition), and a limited role for the government. Under pure capitalism, the role of government is only to provide internal and external security, enforce voluntary contracts, help maintain the natural competition of the marketplace, provide for the *very* needy—and little else.

What? How? For Whom?   Under pure capitalism, the main motivating force is the search for profit. *What* to produce (and in what quantities) is determined by profits. Only those goods that can be produced profitably will be produced; others will be driven out of

408

the marketplace. Ultimately, *consumers* determine what will be produced by their dollar votes in the marketplace—what they are willing to spend their income on.

Since resources can substitute for each other in the production process, the pure capitalist economy must decide *how* to produce a commodity once society votes for it. Producers will be forced (by the discipline of the marketplace) to combine resources in the cheapest way for a particular standard of quality. The cheapest way will depend on relative resource prices. Those firms that combine resources in the most efficient manner will earn the highest profits and force losses on their competitors. Competitors will be driven out of business or forced to combine resources in the same way as the profit makers.

What and *how* questions are concerned with production. The *for whom* question is concerned with the *distribution* of goods after they are produced. How is the pie divided? Under pure capitalism production and distribution are closely linked, because in the production of goods, incomes are automatically generated. People get paid according to their productivity; that is, a person's income reflects the value that society places on that person's resources. Since income largely determines one's share of the output "pie," under pure capitalism, what people get out of the economic system is based on what they put into it. The exception, of course, is the welfare provided to orphans, the handicapped, and others who are not capable of contributing to the productive process.

Pure Socialism

The central issues of socialism relate to who should have the property rights to capital goods, who should make decisions about the use of these goods, and how income should be distributed once it is created.

Perhaps we can best isolate the key attributes of a socialist system by seeing how it answers some basic questions. In a pure socialist system:

1. Although individuals are allowed to own many items of wealth, the government owns the major productive resources, such as land and capital goods. Individuals can own consumer goods and consumer durables, but they are not allowed to own factories, machines, and other things that are used to produce what society wants.
2. People are induced to produce by wage differentials. However, heavy taxation of large incomes to redistribute income may reduce some of the incentives to produce.
3. The forces that determine the relative rewards people get from producing are usually set by the state, not by the market. That is,

the government, rather than supply and demand, determines people's wage rates and who should be paid what in government-owned-and-operated factories.

4. Individuals are allowed to enter only certain endeavors. They cannot, for example, set up their own factories. They cannot become entrepreneurs or capitalists, for the state controls such enterprises.

This description of socialism is purely theoretical. Real-world varieties of socialist systems seem to have only one thing in common: Their governments control more factors of production than do capitalist governments.

Traditional socialism emphasized government ownership of the factors of production. Modern socialist thought appears to be heading in the direction of government *control* over industry rather than government *ownership* of the factors of production. Individuals in the private sector are permitted to own small businesses or to be shareholders in corporations that form much of a country's industry. But the government, through its agencies and lawmaking abilities, can control many aspects of these businesses, such as the wages paid, the quantity and quality of the goods produced, the working environment of the labor force, and the price that is charged for the product.

It is important to distinguish between economic control and political control. A socialist system can theoretically be as democratic as the political system in the United States. That is, government officials can be elected who will then make decisions about the use of resources and particular capital goods. On the other hand, a socialist system can also come under the political control of a dictator. The same is true for a capitalist system. It can be democratic, as it is in the United States, or there can be a dictator ruling the land, in which case there can still be a free-enterprise system.

Pure Communism

Under pure communism, all resources (including labor) are owned by "the people" *in common*. In theory, the state, or government, will eventually disappear under communism, and a new populace motivated by altruism (not self-interest) will have evolved. People will *contribute* to the economy *according to their productivity*, but will *receive according to their need*. Thus, the link between production and distribution will be totally broken. Goods will be produced for "use," not profit. Indeed, money and the price system itself will become unnecessary.

Mixed Economies

It should be noted that each of these three economic systems is idealized, and that no real-world country has ever fit perfectly into

410

any one of these categories. In reality, all economies are *mixed* economies, since private markets, self-interest, state allocation of resources, income redistribution, and altruism exist to some degree in all societies. Yet, most real-world economies can be classified, however imperfectly, into one of the three categories.

Although the pure communism model isn't even approached in the U.S.S.R. (by its own admission), all the economies under communism do share enough characteristics to permit a description of real-world "communist" countries. It is also convenient to describe another set of real-world countries as "socialist welfare state" economies. Finally, a third set of countries is classified as "capitalist, market-oriented" economies.

To some extent, these classifications are subjective, and some readers may disagree with the classifications of specific countries. We admit that we have been subjective, and we are willing to be reeducated.

● REAL-WORLD BATTLE PARTICIPANTS

We now turn to a description of real-world communist, socialist, and capitalist economies.

Communist Economies

The Countries.   Within the "communist" category, we include the U.S.S.R. and the rest of the Soviet bloc: Bulgaria, Czechoslovakia, East Germany, Hungary, Poland, and Romania. Also included are the People's Republic of China and Cuba.

What? How? For Whom?   In the communist economies, *what* and *how* are largely determined by a central plan. The rulers decide, in broad terms, what specific sectors of the economy are to be advanced. Industrial sectors and collective farms are given priority ratings and overall targets to reach. This rough plan is then turned over to the bureaucrats and technocrats, who make the plan more specific and consistent.

In these countries, economic freedom is severely limited and unions have no power to better the lot of the workers; the role of the unions is to help fulfill the economic plan! Still, a private market exists (legally and illegally) and is important to the economy. The legal private sector consists of small plots of land on which individual farmers are allowed to produce anything they want when they are not working on state collective farms. They are further allowed to sell these goods in free markets. Using less than 4 percent of total farmland in the U.S.S.R., such small plots account for nearly 30 percent of the total value of farm goods! Clearly, there is

411

more incentive to be productive on the small plots than on the giant collective farms. Professionals, such as lawyers, are also allowed to sell their services, and businesses can exist—if they are kept *very* small. In 1981, however, Hungary allowed private companies to form with a maximum of 30 people; moreover, a maximum of five such firms are free to combine. And it should be noted that Yugoslavia traditionally has been freer of Soviet domination and more market oriented. Another important part of the private sector is the U.S.S.R.'s illegal underground economy, which the Soviets tolerate because it is so productive. Also tolerated are foreign exchange black markets.

Income inequality has not been eliminated under communism, so *for whom* is not answered easily. Indeed, communist countries are (and always have been) quite elitist. Economic privileges (such as better housing and special stores with lower prices, better quality, and more variety) abound and incomes are higher for the elite. The elite consist of communist party members, the military, the police, and enterprise directors; their incomes are not necessarily related to productivity. All things considered, economic inequality among people is probably *greater* in some communist countries than in Western Europe or the United States.

"Free" services are provided to everyone, especially in the field of medicine. The Soviet Union has about twice as many doctors and hospital beds as does the United States. The average Soviet citizen sees a doctor much more often and spends many more days in the hospital than does the average American. The government, of course, pays for all medical expenses.

Unfortunately, Soviet doctors are poorly paid by the state, and their educational level is approximately equivalent to that of many U.S. registered nurses. They work short hours and give impersonal care. Hospital needles are dull and nonsterile; hospital-caused infections are commonplace. The Soviets cannot perform the "trickier" surgical operations, and "free" medication is neither abundant nor varied—there are no commercial pharmaceutical firms in the U.S.S.R. In short, medical care in the U.S.S.R. is a low priority. Mortality rates are rising in every age bracket, and infant mortality increased by more than one-third between 1970 and 1975. Recently, the life expectancy has *fallen* for Soviet citizens, and alcoholism is rampant.

The Results. What are the results of this communist economic system? Poor planning has led to occasional surpluses and perennial shortages. Shortages, as usual, have led to widespread cheating and corruption; in fact, corruption at all levels is considered a way of life in communist countries. We have already commented on the inadequate medical care provided there. And while economic growth rates during some periods in some communist countries have been

412

relatively high, in the 1980s, economic growth rates throughout the communist bloc have been disappointingly low—and in some cases cases negative.

The communist system as it exists today receives help from the West—the noncommunist countries. Western countries provide technological assistance, food imports (such as wheat to the Soviet Union), and financial support. The 1980s will be remembered as a time when numerous communist bloc countries started having difficulty paying back Western loans. Poland, a case in point, was constantly on the verge of defaulting on its loans from the West throughout 1982. The total amount of lending to communist bloc countries by the West is indeed staggering.

A study by the Austrian Institute for Economic Research concludes that in 1981, the Soviet bloc owed $47.4 billion to Western banks and another $26 billion to Western governments and corporations. In 1981, Poland alone owed $27 billion to the West. Clearly, the Soviet bloc would face economic disaster if loans were called in by Western countries.

In short, the economic miracle of communism and central planning has not come to pass.

Socialist, Welfare State Economies

The Countries.   The socialist, welfare state category includes Sweden, England, France, and Italy.

What? How? For Whom?   In Socialist economies, *what* and *how* are mostly answered by the normal market criterion—profits. The notable exceptions are "free" government services and, in some countries, the nationalization of specific industries. Despite the poor economic performance of nationalized industries in England and France, the newly elected (1981) socialist government of Mitterrand in France promised to extend industry nationalization even further. The new plan called for complete nationalization of five large industrial firms and the entire banking industry, along with partial nationalization of two other major corporations.

What is most different about the socialist, welfare state category, however, is how the *for whom* question is answered. Through a major program of taxing some and transferring to others by way of welfare, a conscious effort to reduce income inequality is made. The notion of an automatic link between production and distribution is therefore being challenged by these countries. This is a truly interesting social experiment; all the results are not in yet.

Characteristics.   Most socialist countries are characterized by a high ratio of government expenditures to gross national product (GNP)—between 40 and 60 percent—indicating the importance of the government sector. Taxes are relatively high, but expenditures

413

are even higher. As a result, public debt is ever increasing. Private debt is high too, as saving is low and consumption is high. In recent years, these countries have experienced an increasing *foreign-owned* national debt. High interest rates and inflation are evident, since pressures are strong to reduce unemployment through loose monetary policy.

The combined desire to reduce income inequality and finance large government expenditures has led to high marginal income tax rates. Indeed, most socialist welfare states have very highly progressive personal income tax structures. It is not uncommon for moderately high-income individuals to face 50, 60, and 70 percent marginal tax rates. And as you might expect, high marginal tax rates have encouraged the growth of underground economies.

Unemployment tends to be fairly high in socialist economies. Minimum wage laws exist and unions have the power to increase wages faster than productivity rises. Employers react by laying off those laborers whose productivity is less than the wage rate. Moreover, unemployed laborers have incentives to remain unemployed, since they receive untaxed unemployment compensation and many social welfare benefits. That is, the unemployed face extremely high marginal tax rates, and are therefore encouraged to remain unemployed.

If you remember the discussion of farm surpluses in Chapter 3, you will recall that for the surplus situation to continue, the government had to *buy* the surplus; otherwise, the price would have fallen. A lower price would have increased the quantity demanded and decreased the quantity supplied. Unemployment can be viewed as a surplus of labor at the going wage rate structure. Unemployment would cause wage rates to fall; then the quantity of labor demanded would rise while the quantity supplied would fall. However, minimum wage laws and unions prohibit wages from falling, resulting in a surplus of labor in the form of unemployment. This unemployed surplus remains because governments "purchase" this unemployment by providing unemployment compensation and welfare benefits to the unemployed.

Another characteristic of socialist, welfare state economies is that they are becoming increasingly protectionist in the international trade sector. They are reluctant to allow domestic firms to go bankrupt from stiff foreign competition, because unemployment would result. Consequently, businesses and labor unions demand protection from foreign competition and are supported by those concerned with the unemployment problem.

The Results. What are the results of the socialist, welfare state economic system? Unquestionably, this system has accomplished much. Lower-income groups have a fair degree of economic security and are provided services at low cost, such as health care and education, that they might not otherwise have received. Certainly, the handicapped and other disadvantaged groups have been aided. One way to judge a society is to see how the poor and disadvantaged are treated. On this score, the socialist, welfare state countries have done an excellent job.

On the other hand, economic problems have arisen in socialist countries. Inflation and progressive tax structures have generated bracket creep, or taxflation; marginal tax rates are high for many people. As a result, economic growth rates are slow and productivity is not increasing a great deal—if at all. High unemployment, combined with inflation, is causing some concern about the future of the socialist, welfare state economic system. Are inflation, high unemployment, slow economic growth, and reduced productivity the costs of a socialist welfare state? We return to this issue at the end of the chapter.

Capitalist, Market-Oriented Economies

The Countries.   The capitalist, market-oriented economic systems include Hong Kong, South Korea, Malaysia, Singapore, Taiwan, and Japan. Typically, the United States is included in the category of capitalist, market-oriented economic systems. Actually, it falls somewhere between the socialist, welfare state system and the capitalist system.

What? How? For Whom?   In capitalist economies, *what* and *how* are largely answered by market criteria, since self-interest and profit seeking are encouraged. These nations rely extensively, but not completely, on private markets to answer *what* and *how*. *For whom* is mostly determined by productivity differences. Although some transfers to the needy exist, income redistribution is slight when compared with that of the socialist, welfare state systems.

Characteristics.   As noted above, capitalist nations rely extensively on free (private) markets. As a consequence, their ratios of government expenditure to GNP are relatively small. Very few, if any, sectors of the economy are nationalized, or under public control.

Marginal tax rates are quite low in all of these capitalist countries. In Hong Kong, the highest marginal tax bracket is only 5 percent.

Japan's system of government contains built-in curbs on the growth of government bureaucracy; after five to seven years, laws and programs automatically expire unless specifically renewed by the Japanese parliament. Japan's marginal corporate tax rates are lower than those in the United States. Personal income taxes are also low—10 percent less (on average) than in the United States. Capital gains on stocks and bonds are entirely tax exempt. Japan realizes that capitalism is a profit and loss system; in 1978, there were 58 percent more bankruptcies in Japan than in the United States.

The Results.   The results of the relative degree of economic freedom in capitalist, market-oriented economies are mixed. To be sure, the nations included in this category have experienced relatively rapid rates of economic growth. Per capita incomes in these countries grew more rapidly during the 1970s than in virtually any other country in the world. But other problems have arisen and continue to exist in such places as Hong Kong, South Korea, Malaysia, Singapore, and Taiwan. The poor, the disadvantaged, and the handicapped are clearly not cared for as they are in other types of economic systems. Also, at least two of the countries mentioned— South Korea and Taiwan—have been labeled dictatorships by political analysts. In other words, even though economic freedoms exist, personal freedoms apparently do not, at least not on the same level as in socialist, welfare state economies.

● WHO WILL WIN THE BATTLE OF THE ISMS?

How will each of the three economic systems perform in the future? Who will win the battle of the isms? The prospects for each of these economic systems during the 1980s is now discussed.

Communism

The communists have long claimed that the future will prove the superiority of their economic system. With the Soviet economy currently sputtering, with economic chaos in Poland, and with economic stagnation in most of the other countries in the Soviet bloc, this result seems less than likely, at least in the near future. Nor does the future look too promising, based on recent evidence.

Central planning has proved difficult to implement in such a way that it provides not only for the basic necessities, but also for economic growth. Indeed, critics of communism believe that the area of economic growth is its greatest economic failing. Economic growth requires that entrepreneurs take advantage of opportunities when they arise. Effective entrepreneurship, therefore, requires knowledge about the appropriate time and place to take a risk. When should investment funds be risked in a new business venture? The price system makes such information available. The opportunity cost of alternative actions is readily available to all individuals immediately. In a communist system, it takes time to collect this information. And in a system where planners decide physical input and output quotas, the information about where and when to innovate is very difficult to come by. In addition, entrepreneurs require an

416

incentive to take risks. Under communism, all workers are essentially civil servants. They have little incentive to take risks because the reward may be trivial if they succeed. The incentive under a communist system is for the worker to "not rock the boat."

Socialism

The socialist, welfare state economic model seems to function reasonably well for economically advanced nations. A willingness to accept a smaller pie that is divided more evenly seems like a reasonable option for those countries that can *afford* to do so.

Proponents of socialist, welfare state economies also have an edge in the ideological trenches. Who can argue against concern for the poor? It's not easy to convince people that there are flaws in a system that wants to redistribute wealth from the rich to the poor. According to the advocates of such a system, less economic growth is not such a high price to pay for economic justice and security for the disadvantaged.

Moreover, the nations in this category have always been very successful at adapting their economies to solving problems. It may well be that during the 1980s, these nations will find a way to have an evenly divided *growing* pie. Perhaps the socialist, welfare state economies can improve incentives while retaining the best of their welfare programs. Don't bet against the resourcefulness of the likes of England and Sweden.

It must be emphasized, however, that a socialist economic system does not always work for poor, underdeveloped countries. A socialist welfare state has not proved conducive to economic development in countries starting from a very low level of per capita real GNP. India and many African nations have attempted this model (or the communist one) without much economic success.

Capitalism

The capitalist model may well be the most workable system for poorer, less-developed countries. Free markets encourage local development. Households are encouraged to save, laborers are encouraged to work, and businesses are encouraged to invest in new plants and equipment. Moreover, protection of private property rights encourages foreign investment in the domestic economy.

However, this model is not overly concerned with income inequality. Those who are not able to compete in the marketplace suffer economic hardship, while those who have marketable skills become wealthy. It may be that income inequality is the price that poor countries must pay to become economically advanced. Still, it should be noted that economic development tends to *reduce* income inequality in Third World countries. Remember, it is the lower-income classes that benefit from industrialization and mass production. For example, the more wealthy individuals, who can afford live entertainment, do not benefit as much from radio and television as do the poor. Similarly, poor people benefit the most from modern innovations in household appliances — not rich people who are able to hire servants. Indeed, *direct* evidence indicates that income inequality falls as capitalism leads to economic development.

Once a nation develops, however, it becomes more concerned with income inequality, and it seems to want more government services. In the United States and other advanced Western societies, polls indicate that people think their taxes are too high. However, the same polls also indicate that people don't want to give up any government services.

Communism and Socialism Can Be Efficient Systems

THE ARGUMENT

Critics of communism and socialism claim that these systems cannot be economically efficient. That is, under these systems, resources will not be *allocated to their highest-valued uses. Proponents of these two systems disagree.*

THE ANALYSIS

When an economic system is perfectly efficient, it is impossible to rearrange the use of resources so that a higher economic valuation of those resources results. In a system of perfect competition, a capitalist economy is completely efficient. It is useful to compare efficiency under perfect competition in capitalism with efficiency under some sort of perfect socialism. (Then it would be useful to compare efficiency under *actual* capitalism and *actual* socialism.)

One economist who attempted to demonstrate the superiority of socialism was Oskar Lange. In a series of articles entitled "On the Economic Theory of Socialism," Lange proposed a system in which socialist managers of each firm would (essentially) imitate the behavior of managers under *perfectly* competitive capitalism. There would still be central planners, but their major function would not be to issue commands; rather, they would set prices for goods, services, and factors of production. Socialist firm managers would then take these prices into account. The actual operation of the firms would be made in accordance with two rules:

1. The rate of output will be set where the marginal cost of production is equal to the assigned price of a product.
2. Factors of production will be chosen in such combinations that the cost of a given output rate will be minimized.

In other words, Lange's market socialist system does not involve planners setting physical goals or quotas for individual firms. Individual socialist firm managers would do their own planning of physical output and input.

Thus, under Oskar Lange's market socialist system—which he considered the ideal socialist system—economic efficiency could be assured. Central planners would adjust resource and output prices to market-clearing equilibrium levels, and managers would make proper adjustments in marginal product and marginal cost.

Lange also attempted to demonstrate that his perfect socialist system would do better in the real world than a capitalist system, which does not operate, to be sure, under perfectly competitive conditions in the real world. Lange pointed out that numerous monopolies exist in capitalist economies.

Thus, in many industries, price exceeds marginal cost, because monopoly managers have economic power. In the Lange system, marginal cost will always equal price, no matter if there is one firm in the market or 100. Finally, Lange pointed out that externalities could be taken account of by central planners in setting prices. That is, the appropriate penalties or incentives can be built into the prices in a market socialist system. This is not possible under most circumstances in capitalist countries today.

Market Socialism Is Not Perfect

Critics of Lange's market socialism contend that Lange's central planners would have to engage in a trial-and-error pricing system that could be unstable and that would certainly be time-consuming. Also, how does a central planner use trial-and-error methods for unique goods, such as highly complex industrial equipment made specifically for a single firm? And even if Lange's system can be shown to be more economically efficient than real-world capitalism, critics contend that efficiency is not the most important criterion for evaluating different economic systems. Critics of socialism further claim that under such a system, innovation would be less than under real-world capitalist systems.

DISCUSSION QUESTIONS

1. What incentives induce people to take risks in a capitalist system? In a socialist system?
2. If a socialist planner makes a mistake, who pays for that mistake? How?

● CHAPTER SUMMARY

Under pure capitalism, the market answers the fundamental question of what and how much to produce. The profit system dictates which goods will remain in production and how the goods will be produced. Basically, the cheapest production technique will be used for any given output and quality level. Finally, the distribution of income (for whom) is determined by the productivity of resources.

Under pure socialism, the major factors of production are owned by the government. The government, through its agencies and lawmaking abilities, also controls many aspects of private businesses.

Under pure communism, all resources, including labor, are owned by the people in common.

There is no single economy today that is a pure form of capitalism, socialism, or communism. Rather, we see mixed economies throughout the world. In the real world, the countries closest to the communist mode are currently experiencing the lowest rates of growth. The countries that are closer to the socialist and capitalist modes are experiencing higher rates of growth.

● QUESTIONS FOR REVIEW AND STUDY

1. Pure capitalism is characterized by _____ _____ rights.

2. Under pure capitalism, there is a _____ role for government. There is also free _____.

3. Under pure capitalism, self-interest is kept in check by _____.

4. Under pure capitalism, the decision about what to produce is determined by businesses concerned with _____.

5. Under pure capitalism, who gets what is determined solely upon individual _____.

6. Under pure socialism, the _____ owns the major non-human means of production.

7. Pure socialism is similar to capitalism in that household preferences determine what should be produced and relative input prices determine how it should be produced. Under socialism, however, the way both of these questions are answered is adjusted for overall _____ _____.

8. Under pure socialism, income inequality is greatly _____.

9. Under pure communism the population is motivated by _____ rather than _____.

10. In the real world, there are no pure economies. They are all _____ economies.

11. In real-world communist economies, there is a _____ role for unions.

12. In real-world communist countries, the private market is/is not important to the economy.

13. Real-world communist countries have/have not eliminated income inequality.

14. Modern-day communist countries rely heavily on Western countries for _____ _____ and _____ _____.

15. Two modern-day socialist welfare states are _____ and _____.

16. One characteristic of modern-day socialist countries is the _____ ratio of government expenditures to GNP.

17. Socialist countries have high/low marginal and personal income tax rates.

18. The normal result of a high marginal tax rate is an unreported _____ economy.

19. In socialist countries, _____ _____ _____ and _____ inhibit wages from falling to equate quantity supplied with quantity demanded in the labor market.

20. Two capitalist, market-oriented economies are _____ and _____.

21. _____ _____ answer the questions of what should be produced and how it should be produced in a capitalist economy.

22. Most income differences in capitalist economies are due to differences in _____.

ANSWERS

1. private property 2. limited; enterprise 3. competition 4. profitability 5. productivity 6. state 7. social considerations 8. reduced 9. altruism; self-interest 10. mixed 11. small 12. is 13. have not 14. technological (or financial) assistance; food supplies 15. Sweden; England; France; Italy (name two only) 16. high 17. high 18. underground 19. minimum wage laws; unions 20. South Korea; Malaysia; Taiwan; Singapore; Hong Kong; and perhaps Japan (name two only) 21. private markets 22. productivity

● ANSWERS TO CHAPTER PREVIEW QUESTIONS

1. *It is said that* all *economies in the world are mixed economies. What does this mean?*

No advanced economy in the real world is purely capitalist, communist, or socialist. As a practical matter, all advanced economies are mixed; resource allocation decisions are made by both private individuals and governments. Even in an idealized capitalist economy, important roles are played by the government; it is generally agreed that government is required for some income redistribution, national defense, maintenance of competition, protection of property rights, enforcement of contracts, and so on. On the other hand, socialist economies have found it convenient to allow for private property rights regarding labor and personal property items (clothing, housing, consumer durables, and so on).

2. *What are the characteristics of a socialist economy?*

A main characteristic of a socialist economy is government control over the large-scale means of production. As a practical matter, private ownership of *small-scale* enterprises is usually permitted. Also, socialist economies are usually characterized (at least in theory) by wide-scale redistribution of income. Workers are usually permitted freedom of choice regarding jobs and, as expected, most workers choose the higher-paying jobs; yet redistribution occurs through a system of taxing high-income earners and transferring to low-income earners.

● PROBLEMS

1. Which economic system should a Third World country adopt?

2. Suppose you are an economic planner and you have been told by your country's political leaders that they want to increase automobile production by 10 percent over the previous year. What other industries will be affected by this decision?

● SELECTED REFERENCES

Ebenstein, William, and E. Fogelman. *Today's Isms*. 8th ed. Englewood Cliffs, N.J.: Prentice-Hall, 1980, chap. 5.

Feldstein, Martin, ed. *The American Economy in Transition*. Chicago: University of Chicago Press, 1980.

Friedman, Milton. *Capitalism and Freedom*. Chicago: University of Chicago Press, 1963.

Gilder, George. *Wealth and Poverty*. New York: Basic Books, 1980.

Heilbroner, Robert L. *The Worldly Philosophers*. Rev. ed. New York: Simon & Schuster, 1972.

Lange, Oskar. *On the Economic Theory of Socialism*. New York: McGraw Hill, 1965.

McAuley, Alastair. *Economic Welfare in the Soviet Union*. Madison, Wisc.: University of Wisconsin Press, 1979.

Spulber, Nicholas. *Organizational Alternatives in Soviet-Type Economies*. New York: Cambridge University Press, 1979.

ANSWERS TO PROBLEMS

Chapter One

1. The relevant costs of going to college include only the *extra* costs of going to college—and not things like food and recreation that would have been incurred anyway. Also important are the *opportunity costs* of going to school, which are probably best measured by foregone wage earnings. Your annual estimate should look something like the following:

(1) Foregone after-tax earnings	$8,000
(2) Tuition	600
(3) Books	200
Total	$8,800

2. a. Neither
   b. Neither
   c. It doesn't matter
   d. The same as if they didn't specialize

This problem indicates that if people were identically productive, specialization would not arise. However, since it is unlikely that any two people (or nations) would be identically productive in the production of goods and services, specialization will always be possible.

Chapter Two

1. In August of 1971, President Nixon froze all prices and wages. By 1974 shortages existed for practically everything. In 1974, price-wage controls were removed on everything except crude oil and natural gas. From that period until 1979 when crude oil prices were deregulated, periodic shortages of gasoline and heating oil existed. Since shortages of these crude oil distillates did not appear in other countries, we suspect that it was the combination of OPEC oil supply restrictions *and* U.S. price controls on crude oil distillates that caused these periodic shortages.

2. As seen in the graph below, the equilibrium price is $30 and the equilibrium quantity is 10.5 million.

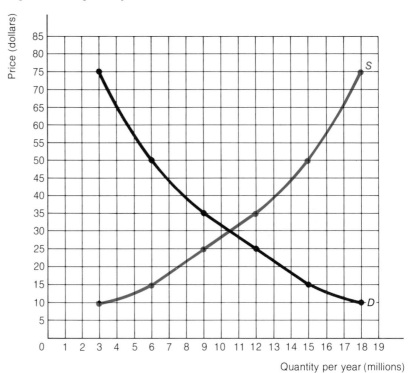

Chapter Three

1. Smaller cars, cars designed to economize on gas, electric cars, car pooling, motorcycles, bicycles, combining trips, gasohol, more frequent engine tune-ups, more air in tires, driving at slower rates, and many others.

2. **a.** 408,000
   b. With such a large number of farms, it is highly unlikely that "monopolistic" power would exist in the farm sector.

Chapter Four

1. Consumer sovereignty might not exist if (a) there is insufficient information concerning the characteristics of goods and services,

(b) widespread fraud exists, (c) monopolistic power enables businesses to produce what they want, (d) advertising influences people to buy what they don't want, and (e) governments allocate resources, directly or indirectly, to produce goods that people don't prefer. Consumer choice refers to the freedom of households to spend their incomes on goods that can be produced; consumer sovereignty exists if households ultimately determine the product mix of an economy by their dollar votes in the marketplace. It is possible that in a planned economy the product mix can be determined by the central planners, while given that constraint individual households are free to spend incomes as they choose.

2. Habits, ethics, customs, and laws are some institutions that can affect production and exchange. An evolution in the influence of religion has occurred in this country; a weakening of religious influence has led to increased work and sales on Sundays.

Chapter Five

1. **a.** The price of polluting should be set according to the marginal economic damage imposed by polluters; this means that similar quantities of pollution will cost polluters different prices in different parts of the country; pollution will be more costly in New York City than in Little Town, Mid-America.
   b. Those firms that find it cheaper to treat will do so; those firms that find it cheaper to pay to pollute will pollute; this is a sensible solution to the problem: who should treat, who should pollute?
   c. Yet, some firms will be forced to shut down due to increased costs; this is efficient, in that the true costs to society of their operations were not paid by them and their customers; they were able to remain in business only by imposing costs on third parties.
   d. This might be good because now those who are using the resources will be forced to pay for them—instead of imposing costs on others. Those who are *not* using these products were, in effect, subsidizing lower prices to those who were. This new solution seems "fair"—it certainly is efficient.

2. The problems involved are too complex for free markets (and for governments, too!); contracting costs would be prohibitive and enforcement impossible. Firms would go into the business of being paid *not* to pollute, individuals would claim all sorts of damages from pollution, and so on. Moreover, determining *marginal* costs and benefits for specific firms and individuals would be difficult indeed.

427

Chapter Six

1. **a.** Technique C, since it costs only $107 (versus $120 for A and $168 for B).
   b. $65, which equals $172 of revenues minus $107 of costs.
   c. Technique A, which will now have the lowest cost, equal to $132 (versus $182 for B, $143 for C).

This makes sense since A is the least labor intensive, and the relative price of labor has increased. Profits will fall from $65 to $40.

2. Customs, habits, ethics, and laws in a nation constitute the institutions that mold production and exchange. Virtually all institutions change over time. For example, religious customs in the U.S. have changed since colonial times. Gradually, religious sentiment grew weaker concerning work performed on the Sabbath. This has had the effect of allowing stores to remain open on Sunday.

Chapter Seven

1. **a.** The percentage of the total yearly take you account for depends largely on the charitable tendencies of your neighbors. The problem with voluntary associations like the one in Whispering Pines is that one individual may feel that the maintenance would be performed whether or not he or she contributed to its expense. Any resident may get a "free ride" off his or her neighbors, guessing that their contributions will be sufficient to support the services. In practice, such voluntary associations have gained a variety of participation rates. Fifty to 60 percent is not uncommon.
   b. Obviously, the lower the participation level, the more important the individual contribution. If nearly everybody contributes and the fund approaches $5,000, your $50 will not be very important. If membership is low—if the fund goes down to several hundred dollars, for example—then your contribution will make a difference. It is also important to know how expensive the job is that must be done.
   c. The ride may not be completely free if your failure to contribute arouses the ill will of your neighbors and this concerns you. Nor will your ride be completely free if there is a noticeable difference in the quality of maintenance because of the lack of your $50. If the service that is being provided can be varied to adjust for small changes, then you will realize the benefit of your contribution (or the cost of your refusal).

2. The "pure" public good is a theoretical concept. Most public goods are goods that have features of the pure public good—availability to one consumer implying availability to another (lumpiness)

and sometimes inability to exclude nonpayers—even though they are not 100 percent public. Providing national defense for the contiguous states probably affords some protection for Alaska and Hawaii as well. They would benefit from the home force whether or not it was committed to their protection, and there may be little additional cost to making such a commitment. To the extent that additional expenditures would have to be made to extend protection to the new states, that protection would not be entirely a public good, but it is probably more public than private; it is just not "pure." Local police protection is also a public good, although the unit of measurement of what is the public must be defined as the community buying the good. Clearly the police force of a densely populated city can serve one more or one less resident at an insignificant cost increment. Also, providing protection to some residents confers a benefit on their neighbors who live in safety, whether or not the neighbors have paid. Thus, in the limited world of the local community, police protection can satisfy the qualifications of collective provision and difficult exclusion that earmark public goods.

3. Private Goods	Public Goods
sandwich	public television
cable television	national defense
shirt	elementary education
college education	health clinic flu shots
operas	
museums	
automobile	

Note that some are difficult to place (such as college education) and the lists above may simply reflect your author's prejudices.

Chapter Eight

1. **a.** 1967
   b. increasing rapidly
   c. $(195.4 - 181.5)$ divided by $181.5 = 7.658$ percent
   d. $249.40

2. In periods of inflation fixed-income groups are obviously hurt, but since most retired people collect social security payments (which have increased more rapidly than the price level over the last ten years), this point is easily overstressed. In periods of unanticipated inflation (or when the rate of inflation is less than that anticipated) creditors are hurt, at the expense of borrowers, who gain. Also, people locked into long-term contracts to receive fixed nominal-money amounts (laborers, bondholders and other money-lenders, pensioners) are hurt if the rate of inflation is greater than

they had anticipated. People who hold money are also hurt by inflation; as prices rise, a given amount of money can buy less. Periods of inflation tend to increase the risk of signing business contracts; people who are risk averters therefore take on risk, whether they want to or not. Also, taxpayers who face progressive tax schedules will suffer.

Chapter Nine

1. Your total taxes on $100 of weekly income are $26 (7 percent plus 19 percent of $100). Your take-home pay would be $74, only $24 more than unemployment benefits. Thus the opportunity cost of staying unemployed is $24.

2. **a.** 5 percent
   b. one month
   c. 5 percent
   d. 10 percent
   e. In this example, the unemployment rate doubled, but it is not obvious that the economy has gotten "sicker," or that laborers are worse off.

Chapter Ten

1. Productive activity, nonproductive activity list:
   Productive activity: b, c, e, f, g.
   Nonproductive activity: a, d, h, i.

2. Since GNP estimates are an attempt to evaluate an economy's performance and to make statements about national well-being, one must be careful to evaluate only final goods and services—otherwise the GNP would be exaggerated. For example, since an automobile embodies plastic, steel, coke, rubber, coal, and so on, to count each of these *and* the value of an automobile would be double counting. Thus, to count coal used to make steel *and* the automobile when it is sold is to count coal twice—and hence to exaggerate the economy's performance and the group's economic well-being. Coal in this instance would not be a final good; it would be an intermediate good. Of course, coal used to heat homes would be a final good, and as such is properly counted in GNP. Briefly put, when estimating GNP, intermediate goods are ignored; GNP is an estimate of the market value of final goods and services; if intermediate goods were included, GNP would overstate the economy's performance and the group's overall level of economic well-being.

Chapter Eleven

1. **a.** Mr. Smith pays nothing on his first $1,500 of income, 14 percent on the $500 earnings between $1,500 and $2,000 ($70), and 20 percent on the $500 that he earns above $2,000 ($100). Thus, Mr. Smith has a total tax bill of $170 on an income of $2,500.

   b. His average tax rate is 6.8 percent, while his marginal tax rate is 20 percent.

2. **a.** 6.7 percent
   b. 6.7 percent
   c. 4.5 percent ($2,271.30 divided by $50,000)
   d. 2.27 percent ($2,271.30 divided by $100,000)

Since the average tax rate falls as income rises, the Social Security tax structure is regressive. Above $33,900, the marginal tax rate is zero. As a consequence, the marginal tax rate is less than the average tax rate—hence, the average tax rate is falling and approaches zero in the limit.

Chapter Twelve

1. The multiplier concept says simply that a dollar change in aggregate demand will cause the equilibrium level of national income to change by more than a dollar. In particular, a dollar increase in aggregate demand will cause the equilibrium level of national income to *rise* by more than a dollar. A dollar decrease in aggregate demand will cause the equilibrium level of national income to *fall* by more than a dollar. Let's take an example. Suppose we start from an equilibrium position and then government spending rises by one dollar. Some individuals will receive an extra dollar in income above last year's income. Thus, income already rises by one dollar in the first round. Those people who receive that dollar of government spending will spend some of their income increase and save some of it. Since one person's expenditure is another person's income, income will rise again. Let's say that everybody spends three-fourths of every extra dollar of income and saves one-fourth. That means for every dollar increase in income, there will be 75 cents spent on goods and services and 25 cents saved. The 75 cents that was spent becomes income for those who sold goods and services to the people spending the 75 cents. Note that after two rounds national income is already increased by $1.75 ($1.00 + $.75); we already have a multiplier effect. Moreover, there is no reason why this process should stop here. Those people who just received an increase in income of 75 cents will spend some and save some.

Thus, the multiplier effect exists because increases in income lead to increases in expenditures, which lead to further income increases. Since one person's expenditure is another person's income, the greater the percentage that people spend of every extra dollar they receive in income, the greater will be the change in the equilibrium level of income for a given change in government spending. In other words, the more of the increase they spend (and the less they save), the greater will be the multiplier.

2. If people saved every bit of the increase in income received from government expenditure changes and spent none of it, then the change in income would just equal the change in government expenditures. In other words, the multiplier will be one. As we change the assumption so that individuals spend a larger and larger percentage of any increase in income, the multiplier effect will become larger and larger.

Chapter Thirteen

1. **a.** The painting by Renoir might have the greatest advantage as a store of value, for works of art generally appreciate over time. As a medium of exchange or a unit of accounting, it would be deficient because of its high and sometimes variable value and the limited market for its exchange.
   b. A 90-day U.S. Treasury bill also is a good store of value; payment is guaranteed by the government and it will pay some interest. Of course, to the extent that the money to be returned for the matured bill is an imperfect store of value, so is the bill. A 90-day bill will not vary much in value over its life, because the redemption date is not far off, and there is some value as a medium of exchange and unit of accounting. But the large denominations in which these bills are issued detract from the latter functions.
   c. It is important to distinguish between the balance in a checking account and the account itself. The account is a relationship between depositor and bank. The money in the account will have the attributes of money, qualified by the solvency of the bank in Reno.
   d. There are significant transactions costs in exchanging one share of IBM stock, and its value can fluctuate in the short run, making it an imperfect medium of exchange and unit of accounting. Its qualities as a store of value depend on the health of the company and the economy in which it operates.

    e. A \$50 Federal Reserve Note is cash, and its qualities will correspond accordingly. Of course, its denomination is a multiple of the common unit of our account, which is \$1.

    f. A MasterCard, like a savings account, indicates the existence of a relationship. Its transferability is limited, and its value depends upon the terms of the credit agreement. (There probably is an illegal market for MasterCards, in which they assume an independent value for exchange, although they probably lack most of the advantages of a store of value or unit of accounting.)

    g. Assuming that the pass is for the lifetime of the Dodgers, not for an owner who could not trade the pass, the ticket would be like many other nonmoney goods. Its money qualities would depend on the market available for its exchange and the value taken on by the good in the market. The fortunes of the Dodgers, the Los Angeles consumers' taste for baseball, and other demand determinants would affect the three monetary qualities of a lifetime pass.

2. Nothing; the total money supply is unaffected. A transfer of checks from one depository institution to another does not generate any excess reserves in the banking system; hence, there will be no overall deposit (and therefore money) creation. Thus, suppose that Mr. Wong deposits a \$1,000 check in bank A, which he received for services rendered to Mr. Romano who deals with bank B. Note that bank A experiences an increase in total deposits and reserves and can increase its lending. However, just the opposite happens to bank B; it experiences a reduction in deposits and reserves and must curtail its lending. There is no *net* change in excess reserves; hence, there is no net change in deposit creation and, therefore, no net change in the money supply occurs.

Chapter Fourteen

1. Expansionary monetary policy is an attempt to eliminate a recession. In particular, the Fed can buy U.S. securities in the open market, thereby increasing bank excess reserves. Banks loan out these excess reserves by lowering interest rates. The public has more money. Lower interest rates mean that business investment will rise, also, thereby increasing, or shifting up, aggregate demand. Of course, upward shifts in aggregate demand cause a multiple increase in the equilibrium level of national income.

2.

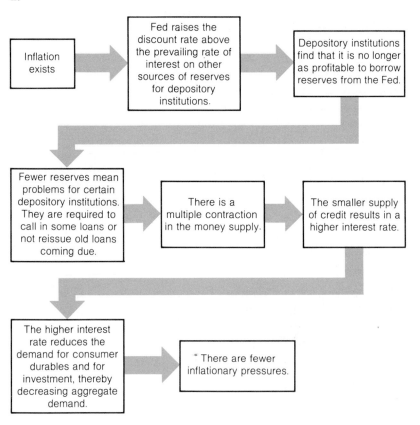

Chapter Fifteen

1. **a.** 10 percent
    b. 5.75 percent
    c. increases in welfare and unemployment compensation, higher minimum wages, more "rigidities" in the economy such as monopoly and union power, higher participation rates for the less easily employed, compositional changes in the labor force which increase the proportion of laborers less easily employed.

2. **a.** F and E; at F tax rates are so high that all income is earned in the underground economy; at E tax rates are 0; hence, tax revenues will be zero
    b. A and B
    c. they will rise
    d. fall
    e. C, that is, tax rate T_1.

434

Chapter Sixteen

1. The answer is (a). An inflation in the United States would depress the value of the dollar relative to the pound. Consequently it would require more than $2.45 to buy one pound, just as inflation raises the amount of money that must be paid for other goods and services.

2. **a.** 1 pound equals $3.50; $1 equals .2857 pounds
    b. 1 mark equals 35 cents; $1 equals 2.857 marks
    c. 1 mark equals .1 pounds; 1 pound equals 10 marks.

Chapter Seventeen

1. One obvious determinant of economic growth is the quantity and quality of a nation's natural resources—although this determinant can easily be exaggerated. Thus, many less-developed nations have bountiful natural resources while some rapidly developing areas like Holland, Denmark, South Korea, Taiwan, and Hong Kong have very little. The quality and quantity of labor and capital are also important determinants of economic growth, as is a nation's rate of technological progress. A decidedly underrated determinant of economic growth is the industriousness and willingness of people to be productive—which are surely related to personal incentives.

2. 14.4 years

Chapter Eighteen

1. **a.** Approximately 64 percent ($525,000,000 divided by $825,000,000).
    b. The ratio would rise as the industry is more narrowly defined and fall as it is more broadly defined. Since an "industry" is arbitrarily defined, concentration ratios may be misleading.

2. Oligopoly lies between the extremes of perfect competition and monopoly. Under oligopoly a small number of firms dominate the market and the firms cannot act independently. That is, an oligopolist must take into account the reactions of its rivals when it sets policy; this interdependence makes the oligopoly model unique. It also makes the price-output decision a complex one for the oligopolists—and, therefore, for economists who analyze this market structure. It is believed by many that oligopolies emerge because great economies of scale, in conjunction with a limited market demand, allow the few largest to drive out competitors. Also, oligopolies may arise due to mergers.

435

Chapter Nineteen

1. Whites may invest more in human capital; blacks might receive less, and lower-quality education and/or training; blacks in the work force may, on average, be younger; discrimination may exist; and so on.

2. Since World War II, the distribution of *money* income has not changed significantly. On the other hand, the distribution of *total* income—which includes "in-kind" government transfers—has changed significantly in recent years. Since the 1960s, *total* income inequality has been reduced significantly. The fact that more income equality has been achieved in the United States in recent years is of tremendous importance, yet few people seem to be aware of this fact.

Chapter Twenty

1. The separate categories of costs facing one contemplating a life of housebreaking and robbery include (a) detection and arrest, (b) trial and conviction, and (c) prison. Each one of these has a probability that can be assigned to it. The probability can be intuited, personally or with the help of an experienced robber. Also, conviction rates and prison time are a matter of court record; such information is easily obtained.

2. Benefits include a relatively high income, flexible hours, and excitement. Costs include possible injury or death, prison, variable income, and guilt feelings. The benefits of living a life of crime can be deduced from the experiences of known criminals and from books written about their lives. Of course, such benefits can easily be exaggerated.

Chapter Twenty-One

1. Should, of course, implies a normative economics subject, so the answer depends on subjective, not objective reasoning. If the country is concerned with economic development and growth, it would do well to initiate the capitalistic system, as did Hong Kong, Taiwan, Singapore, South Korea, and others. On the other hand, if it is interested in income distribution equality, then it might be better off adopting a socialist-welfare program.

2. To mention only a few: the steel, coal, coke, tire, rubber, plastic, railroad, air conditioner, hubcap, and radio industries. Moreover, some of these industries are interrelated. Also, labor and other resources that are affected by these industries must be considered. Planning is complex.

436

GLOSSARY

Ability-to-pay principle A principle of taxation whereby individuals are taxed according to how much they are able to pay, not how much they are willing to pay, or how much they benefit from government services.

Absolute advantage A situation in which an individual or a nation has the ability to produce a good or service at an "absolutely" lower cost, usually (but not necessarily) measured in hours of work required to produce a unit of the good in question.

Absolute price The market price given to each of the goods and services available for your purchase.

Age-earnings cycle The regular earnings profile of an individual throughout his or her lifetime. The age-earnings cycle usually starts with a low income, builds gradually to a peak at around age 45 to 50, and then gradually curves down until it approaches zero at retirement age.

Aggregate demand The total value of all planned expenditures of all buyers in the economy.

Aggregate supply The total value of all final goods and services supplied by all firms in the economy; it is equal to national product.

Annually balanced budget philosophy The belief that the federal budget should be balanced each year.

Antitrust legislation Statutes, or laws, that make it illegal for businesses to engage in anti-competitive (monopolistic) activities.

Arbitrage The simultaneous buying and selling of the same item from different people in order to make a profit.

Asset Something that has value and is owned. In other words, it is something to which a bank, business, or household has legal claim.

Automatic stabilizers Changes in government expenditures and taxes that occur naturally and do not require any action on the part of Congress or the president of the United States; they occur because of changes in economic conditions.

Autonomous consumption That part of consumption that is independent of, or does not depend on, the level of disposable income. Changes in autonomous consumption shift the consumption function.

Average tax rate The total tax bill divided by total income.

Balance of payments Refers to the annual value of all a nation's transactions in goods, services, financial assets, and military goods (and all other transactions) in the world market.

Balance-of-payments deficit The value of our transactions with other countries is such that they

437

are sending us more value than we are sending them.

Balance of payments surplus   A balance of payments surplus occurs when we are sending other nations, as a group, more value than they are sending us.

Balanced budget   Government receipts equal government outlays; that is, the government is spending exactly what it is taking in.

Barriers to entry   Barriers that prevent new firms from entering an existing industry. Some barriers include government laws against entry and patents for research discoveries.

Barter   The exchange of goods and productive services for other goods and productive services, without the use of money.

Base year   The year used to compare all other years' prices. The number 100 is arbitrarily assigned to the price index in the base year.

Benefit-received principle   A principle of taxation whereby individuals pay taxes in proportion to the benefits they receive from government.

Bilateral monopoly   A situation in the labor market where a single seller of labor confronts a single buyer (monopsonist).

Bond   An interest-bearing certificate issued by a government or a corporation. This type of security represents debt.

Bracket creep, or taxflation   The process by which inflation pushes individuals into higher and higher tax brackets.

Budget deficit   Government outlays exceed government receipts; that is, government expenditures exceed tax receipts.

Budget surplus   Government revenues (tax receipts) exceed government expenditures.

Business cycle   A general description of the ups and downs of overall economic activity; a business cycle consists of recessions, troughs, expansions, and peaks.

Business investment   Business expenditure on equipment and machinery, that is, on capital goods. Such investment yields more consumer goods in the future.

Capital   All goods made by human beings and used in the production of other goods and services. Examples are tools, equipment, buildings, and improvements to land.

Capital consumption allowance   A measure of the productive capacity of capital goods—plant and equipment—used up or destroyed during the current account period. It also includes an estimate of the natural resources depleted during that time period.

Capital deepening   A term used to refer to an increase in the stock of capital relative to the quantity of labor.

Capital gain   The positive difference between the purchase price and the sale price of an asset.

Capital goods   Durable goods used by business to produce other goods and services; examples of capital goods are machines and equipment.

Capital loss   The negative difference between the purchase price and the sale price of an asset.

Capitalism   An economic system in which individuals privately own productive resources and use them in any (legal) manner they see fit.

Cartel   An organization of the firms in an oligopoly whereby the firms formally agree on a price to charge and on the market share for each firm. In this case the firms behave very much like a monopoly.

Cease and desist order   An agreement in which the investigated party, without admitting any guilt, agrees to refrain from certain activities.

Central bank   A banker's bank, usually controlled and operated by the government.

Circular flow model   A model of the flows of resources, goods, and services, as well as money, receipts, and payments for them in the economy.

Closed shop   A business enterprise in which an employee must belong to the union before he or she can be employed. That employee must remain in the union after he or she becomes employed.

Collective bargaining   Bargaining between management of a company or of a group of companies and management of a union or a group of unions for the purpose of setting a mutually agreeable contract on wages, fringe benefits, and working conditions for *all* employees in the union(s). Different from *individual* bargaining, where each employee strikes a bargain with his or her employer individually.

Command economy   An economic system in which the allocation of resources is determined by a small centralized governmental group of individuals.

Commercial bank   A private, profit-seeking institution that was, until recently, the only financial institution that could accept demand deposits against which checks could be written. Today, many other financial institutions are legally allowed to offer checking accounts.

Common property Property owned by everyone and therefore owned by no one (e.g., air and water).

Common stock A security that indicates the real ownership in a corporation. It is not a legal obligation for the firm and does not have a maturity. It has the last claim on dividends each year and on assets in the event of firm liquidation.

Comparative advantage A situation in which an individual or a nation has the ability to produce a good or service at a lower opportunity cost than another individual or nation.

Complements Pairs of goods for which an increase in the price of one causes a decrease in the demand for the other.

Conscious parallelism Pricing behavior by oligopolists in which each presumably takes account of the other's potential reaction and therefore does not engage in vigorous price competition. No explicit collusive agreement is entered into, however.

Conservation Operationally defined as choosing the best timing in the use of resources so as to maximize the total (present) value placed on all resources.

Consumer goods and services Final goods and services purchased by households and non-profit institutions.

Consumer sovereignty The situation that exists when consumers are able to determine output by their purchasing decisions in the marketplace.

Consumers' surplus The difference between the amount consumers actually spend on a good (market price times the quantity purchased) and the amount they would be willing and able to spend for the same quantity (area under the demand curve). The latter amount could be collected only by charging a different price for each unit sold.

Consumption loans Loans taken out by households for the purpose of purchasing goods and services.

Convergence hypothesis The belief that in their struggle to solve the fundamental economic problems of *what*, *how*, and *for whom*, the capitalist and socialist economies will become progressively more alike.

Corporation A legal entity owned by stock-

holders. The stockholders are liable only for the amount of money they have invested in the company.

Cost-of-service regulation A type of regulation based on allowing prices that reflect only the actual costs of production and do not include monopoly profits.

Cost-push inflation A sustained rise in prices caused by rising input costs.

Countervailing power A term coined by John Kenneth Galbraith to refer to situations in which a large firm has to deal with other large firms, unions, or other entities, all of which have sufficient power on the other side of the market to counteract the market power of the first firm.

Craft unions Labor unions composed of workers who engage in a particular trade or skill, such as baking, carpentry, or plumbing.

Cream skimming Competing for the most profitable submarkets in a particular industry.

Credit markets Those markets through which saving passes before it goes either to governments or to business firms for investment purposes. Included are savings and loan associations, insurance companies, commercial banks, and pension plans.

Crowding out A phrase used to refer to the possibility that a reduction in private sector expenditures for capital goods may occur as a result of rising interest rates due to public borrowing.

Currency reform Situation in which the government changes the currency accounting system (e.g., 1 new franc equals 100 old francs, or—if it happened—1 new dollar equals 10 old dollars).

Cyclical unemployment Unemployment that results when total economic demand is insufficient to create full employment of labor resources.

Declining block pricing A system of price discrimination in which consumers are charged different prices per unit of electricity for each "block" of electricity that they buy. The per unit price for the first block is higher than the per unit price for the second block, which is higher than the per unit price for the third block.

Demand A relationship showing a set of intentions indicating various quantities that buyers will purchase voluntarily at each of various dif-

439

ferent prices, per unit of time, all other things held constant.

Demand curve   A graphic representation of a demand schedule that is a negatively sloped line showing the inverse relationship between price and the quantity demanded, other things held constant.

Demand-pull inflation   A sustained rise in the average of all prices caused by increases in total, or aggregate, demand—too many dollars chasing too few goods.

Demand schedule   A set of pairs of numbers showing possible prices and the quantities demanded at each price. In other words, it shows the rate of planned purchase per time period of different prices of the good.

Depreciation   The reduction in capital goods due to physical wear and tear and obsolescence.

Depression   An extremely serious recession; the moment in time when a recession becomes a depression is arbitrary.

Derived demand   Input factor demand derived from demand for the final product being produced.

Diminishing marginal utility   The increase in total utility from the consumption of a good or service becomes smaller as more is consumed.

Direct relationship   An increase in the value of one variable results in the increase in the value of another.

Discount rate   The rate of interest that the Fed charges to depository institutions to borrow reserves.

Discounting   A method by which we take account of the lower value of a dollar in the future, compared to a dollar in hand today. Discounting is necessary even after we adjust for inflation because of the trade-off between having more goods tomorrow if we consume less today.

Diseconomies of scale   The situation in which increasing output and increasing scale of operations cause unit costs, or average costs, to rise.

Distribution of income   The way income is distributed among the population. For example, a perfectly equal distribution of income would result in the lowest 20 percent of income earners receiving 20 percent of national income and the top 20 percent also receiving 20 percent of national income. The middle 60 percent of income earners would receive 60 percent of national income.

Division of labor   The segregation of a resource into different specific tasks; for example, one automobile worker puts on bumpers, another doors, and so on.

Dominant firm explanation of price leadership   This theory assumes that there is one large firm and other, smaller firms in an oligopolistic industry. The large firm sets the price, and the smaller firms accept it as a given and produce where price is equal to marginal cost—like perfectly competitive firms.

Durable goods   Goods that last for more than a specified time period, usually a year (e.g., automobiles, stereos, houses, and televisions).

Economic efficiency   The use of resources that generate the highest possible value of output as determined in the market economy by consumers.

Economic good   Any good or service for which wants exceed the available supply at a zero price.

Economic growth   Increase in a nation's standard of living; the average individual has more real goods and services to consume year after year. It can be measured by how fast available goods and services per person grow over time.

Economics   The study, or science, of how individuals in society choose to use scarce resources that have alternative uses.

Economies of scale   The situation in which unit costs fall as the scale of operations and output rise.

Embargo   A government-imposed restriction on the shipment of a particular good or goods to specified physical locations.

Entrepreneur   A person who is willing to take a risk by investing in production, choosing managers, and making sure that the business succeeds, for the profits that can be earned by the business.

Entrepreneurship   The use of human resources to raise capital, to organize, manage, and assemble other factors of production, and to make basic business policy decisions.

Equation of exchange   The number of monetary units times the number of times each unit is spent on final goods and services is identical to the prices times output (or national income).

Equilibrium   A condition that exists when there is no tendency to change. Equilibrium occurs at the price at which quantity supplied equals quantity demanded. Here there is a market-clearing price.

Excess reserves   Those reserves held by depository institutions over and above required reserves; excess reserves equal total reserves held minus required reserves.

Expansion The phase in the economy when output and employment are increasing; the date it starts is somewhat arbitrary.

Exploitation The payment to a factor of production that is less than its value of marginal product.

Exports Goods and services made domestically but sold abroad.

Externality A situation in which a private cost or benefit diverges from a social cost or benefit. The costs or benefits of an action are not fully borne by two parties engaging in an exchange, or by an individual engaging in a scarce resource-using activity.

Fallacy of composition The error in logic that is made when it is assumed that what is true for one person or for part of an economic entity is also necessarily true for society as a whole or for the economic entity as a whole.

Fiduciary monetary standard A monetary standard in which the value of the currency rests upon the public's confidence that the currency can be exchanged for goods and services. The word *fiduciary* comes from the Latin *fiducia*, which means "trust" or "confidence."

Financial intermediaries Firms that take funds received from depositors or other sources and lend them to third parties. Banks and savings and loans are two examples.

Firm An organization that brings together different factors of production, such as labor, land, and capital, to produce a product or service that can be sold for a profit. A firm is usually made up of an entrepreneur, managers, and workers.

Fiscal policy The changing of government expenditures and/or taxes to affect national income and output.

Five-year plans Economic plans set up by the central government in a country that plots the future course of its economic development. The first five-year plan was devised in Russia by Stalin after Lenin's death.

Fixed investment Purchases, made by businesses, of newly produced producer durables, or capital goods, such as production machinery and office equipment.

Fixed, or pegged, exchange rate system A system in which a unit of each nation's domestic currency can be exchanged for a unit of every other nation's domestic currency at a fixed price.

Flow Something that is defined per unit time period. Income is a flow that occurs per week, per month, or per year. Consumption is a flow. So is saving.

Foreign exchange market A market in which foreign currencies are bought and sold.

Foreign exchange rate The price of foreign currency in terms of domestic currency, or vice versa.

Fractional reserve banking system A banking system in which banks keep only a fraction of their deposits on reserve in the form of cash or deposits with the central bank.

Free enterprise A system in which private business firms are able to obtain resources, to organize those resources, and to sell the finished product in any way they choose.

Free goods Any goods or services that are available in quantities larger than are desired at a zero price.

Free rider A person who pays nothing for the services of a public good but does indeed derive utility, or satisfaction, from those services nonetheless.

Freely floating, or flexible, exchange rate system A system in which exchange rates are allowed to fluctuate in response to changes in the supply and demand.

Frictional unemployment The continuous flow of individuals from job to job and in and out of employment; it is due to a lack of perfect information in the job market about all opportunities.

Full employment The situation occurring when the nation's resources are being fully utilized, or being worked to capacity.

Full-employment government budget An indication of what the federal government budget deficit or surplus would be if the economy were operating at full employment throughout the year.

Functional finance philosophy The belief that a balanced budget is of secondary importance to keeping the economy at a full employment but noninflationary level of income through appropriate spending and taxing policies on the part of the federal government.

General equilibrium analysis Economic

analysis that takes account of the interrelationships among markets; to be contrasted with partial equilibrium analysis, which does not.

Goods   Those things that human beings desire.

Gross national product (GNP)   The total money value of the nation's final goods and services, or output, produced each year. It is the total market value of all final goods and services produced over a one-year period.

Gross return to capital   The amount left over after the costs of raw materials, intermediate goods, depreciation, the opportunity cost of owner-managers' contributed talents, and taxes are deducted from total revenues. The gross return to capital represents the total amount available for payments to owners of capital and includes a pure, or opportunity cost, return to capital, as well as economic profits.

Import quota   A limit on the quantity of a particular commodity that can be imported.

Imports   Goods and services purchased from abroad.

Incentives   Those things that stimulate, cause, or encourage people's actions.

Income elasticity of demand   The percentage change in the quantity demanded divided by the percentage change in money income; the responsiveness of the quantity demanded to changes in income.

Income velocity of money   The average number of times per year a dollar is spent on final goods and services. It is equal to NNP divided by the money supply.

Index number   A *weighted* average of a compilation of other numbers. The CPI, for example, represents an index number of the prices of a representative sample of goods and services.

Indirect business taxes   The excise taxes, sales taxes, and property taxes. Such taxes do not include taxes on corporate profits.

Industrial unions   Labor unions that consist of workers from a particular industry, such as automobile manufacturing or steel manufacturing.

Industry   A group of firms producing similar commodities.

Industry concentration ratio   The percentage of total industry sales accounted for by either the top four or the top eight firms in the industry.

Infant industry argument   The argument that tariffs should be imposed to protect a domestic industry while it is trying to develop.

Inferior goods   Goods for which demand decreases as income increases.

Inflation   A year-in and year-out rise in the average of all prices in the economy.

Inflationary expectations   Those predictions that individuals make about the future rate of inflation based on available information and "gut" feelings about future price increases.

Inflationary premium   A premium that is tacked on to the real interest rate on a loan to take into account expected inflation in the future. The higher the expected rate of inflation, the greater the inflationary premium will be.

Innovation   The *adaptation* of an invention to an actual production technique.

Input-output analysis   The empirical study of the interdependence among the various sectors in the economy.

Inside information   Inside information is any kind of information that is available only to a few people, such as the officers of a company.

Institutions   The laws of the nation as well as the habits, ethics, mores, folkways, and customs of the citizens of that nation.

Interlocking directorate   A situation where one person serves on the boards of directors of two companies.

Intermediate goods   Goods used in the production of other goods and services (either final or intermediate).

Inventories   The finished goods that firms keep on hand from which they fill orders.

Inventory investment   Changes in the stocks of finished goods, goods in process, and raw materials.

Inverse relationship   An increase in the value of one variable results in a decrease in the value of the other.

Investment   Expenditures by businesses on new plant and equipment purchases (capital goods) for the purpose of increasing future production.

Investment loans   Loans taken out by businesses for the purpose of investing in physical capital.

Invisible hand   Term used by Adam Smith to denote the fact that in a market economy the price system influences the actions of individual economic units so that it appears that an invisible hand is guiding economic activity in a way that the welfare of society is promoted while individuals are acting in their own self-interest.

Joint costs   Costs that are common to several of a firm's products. The post office, for example, could be using the same building to service first-, second-, third-, and fourth-class mail. It is difficult to allocate joint costs to the various separate services or products that use them.

Labor   The human productive resource that includes not only human beings per se, but their abilities and talents, however obtained.

Laffer curve   A representation of the relationship between tax rates and tax revenues, showing that after a certain high tax rate, an even higher tax rate will yield smaller tax revenues. Alternatively, in certain situations, a reduction in tax rates can lead to higher tax revenues.

Land   A factor of production that includes all naturally formed resources that exist without the help of humans. Land includes water, minerals, ores, earth, climate, and so on.

Law of demand   Price and quantity demanded are *inversely* related. A change in price, other things held constant, leads to an opposite change in the quantity demanded per unit of time.

Law of diminishing returns   As additional units of a variable factor of production are added to all fixed factors, after some point the additional output from each additional unit of the variable factor decreases.

Law of increasing relative cost   An economic principle stating that the opportunity cost of additional units of a commodity generally increases as society attempts to produce more and more of that commodity.

Law of supply   There is a direct relationship between price and quantity supplied, other things being equal.

Linear curve   A straight line over the whole range of the relationship between two variables. A relationship in which the trade-off between two variables remains constant will be linear.

Liquid assets   Assets that can be transformed into money quite readily without significant loss of value. The most liquid of assets is, of course, money itself. However, short-term government bonds and savings and loan shares are nearly as liquid.

Liquidity   The degree to which an asset can be acquired or disposed of without danger of intervening loss in nominal value. Money is the most liquid asset, by definition. A liquid asset can be used easily as a means of payment without risk of loss in nominal value.

Marginal cost pricing   A system of pricing in which the price charged is equal to the opportunity cost to society of producing one more unit of the good or service in question. The opportunity cost is the marginal cost to society.

Marginal costs   The change in total costs due to a change of one unit of production.

Marginal factor cost (MFC)   The change in total costs due to a one-unit increase in the variable input. The cost of using more of a factor of production.

Marginal tax rate   The change in the tax bill divided by the change in income.

Marginal utility   The change in total utility due to a one-unit change in the quantity of a good consumed.

Market   An institutional arrangement wherein buyers and sellers voluntarily make exchanges.

Market economy   An economic system in which decisions about what is produced, how it is produced, and how it is distributed are determined by the interaction of the various markets for goods and services.

Market failure   A situation in which the signals in the marketplace are unable to fully reflect the value of resources, and the actors in the marketplace are unable to direct the flow of these resources to the best possible use.

Merger   The joining together of two separate firms.

Minimum wage rate   The wage rate below which employees in most industries cannot be paid. It is imposed by federal, state, and certain local governments.

Mixed system   An economic system in which the *what, how,* and *for whom* questions are answered partly by the private sector and partly by the public, or government, sector.

Models, or theories   Simplified representations of the real world used to make predictions or to better understand the real world.

Monetary policy   All those actions that the Fed engages in to change the supply of money in circulation.

Monopsonist   A single buyer.

Multiplier effect The impact of changes in aggregate demand on the equilibrium level of national income; a $1 change in aggregate demand may cause the level of national income to change by *more* than $1.

Mutual interdependence A term used to refer to a situation where the market share of one firm is significantly affected by the actions of one or more of its rival firms.

National income The yearly amount earned by the nation's resources, which includes wages, rent, interest, and profit.

National, or public, debt The total value of all outstanding federal government securities (bonds). It is the sum of past budget deficits that have not yet been repaid.

Negative income tax A system of transferring income to the relatively poor by taxing them negatively—that is, giving them an income subsidy that varies depending upon how far below a "target" income their earned income lies.

Net exports The difference between total exports and total imports over a one-year period.

Net investment Gross investment minus depreciation.

Net national product (NNP) The sum of total consumer and government expenditures on final consumption goods plus *net* investment, in a simplified economy.

Nominal interest rate The apparent or *market* rate charged for borrowing funds.

Nominal, or absolute, prices The actual market prices at which goods are sold.

Nominal values The values of variables such as GNP and investment expressed in current dollars. Also called money values. Otherwise stated, measurement in terms of actual market prices at which goods are sold.

Normal goods Goods for which demand increases as income increases.

Normal profits Profits that are just high enough to encourage a firm to stay in business in a particular industry. When profits are any lower, the firm will leave.

Normative economics Analysis involving value judgments about economic policies; relates to whether things are good or bad. A statement of *what ought to be.*

Oligopoly A market structure in which a small number of firms dominate an industry's output and sales; under oligopoly, each firm must take into account its rival's reactions to its pricing, advertising, and quality variation policies.

Open market operations Refers to the Fed's buying and selling of U.S. government securities in the open market.

Opportunity cost The *highest-valued alternative* that must be foregone in order to obtain the optional selection.

Opportunity cost of capital The normal rate of return or the amount that must be paid to an investor to induce her or him to invest in a business. Economists consider this a cost of production and it is included in our cost examples.

Parity A term used to refer to the situation where farm prices are high enough that crops have the same purchasing power in terms of other commodities as they did in 1910–1914. The period 1910–1914 is often called the "golden age" of agriculture.

Partial equilibrium analysis A way of analyzing a market in isolation without taking account of the interrelationships among markets.

Participation rate A group's percentage of the noninstitutionalized population in the labor force. We talk about labor force participation rates for females or for teenagers or for married males, for example.

Partnership A business entity involving two or more individuals who join together for business purchases, but who have not incorporated. In most instances, each partner is liable for the debts of the business to such an extent that he or she can lose his or her personal wealth if the business incurs debt.

Permanent-income hypothesis A theory of the consumption function that states that people's desire to spend is a function of their permanent or long-run expected income rather than of their current disposable income.

Per se violation An activity that is specifically spelled out as a violation of the law. In antitrust law, whether or not competition is lessened does not have to be proven. A violation based on the facts only and not on the effects, which are taken as given.

Phillips curve An inverse relationship between

the percentage change in prices (rate of inflation) and the rate of unemployment.

Planning horizon   Another name for long-run cost curves. All inputs are variable during the planning period.

Plant   The physical establishment that manufactures or distributes a commodity.

Positive economics   Analysis that is strictly limited to making either purely descriptive statements or scientific predictions; for example, *If A, then B*. A statement of *what is*.

Preferred stock   A security that indicates financing obtained from investors by a corporation. It is not a legal obligation for the firm and does not have a maturity, but pays a fixed dividend each year. It has preferred position over common stock, both for dividends and for assets in the event of firm liquidation.

Price-discriminating monopolist   A monopolist that discriminates among groups of demanders with different elasticities of demand. This firm will charge a higher price to those with relatively less elastic demand than to those with relatively more elastic demand.

Price elastic demand and supply   Demand and supply exhibiting strong responses to price changes.

Price elasticity   A measurement of the responsiveness of quantity demanded or supplied to a change in price.

Price inelasticity   A relatively weak responsiveness to a price change.

Price searcher   A firm that must seek the price that benefits it most. The firm has some control over the price it charges.

Price supports   Minimum prices set by the government for agricultural commodities.

Price taker   A buyer or seller whose influence in the market is too small to affect price by his or her purchases or sales. Under pure competition, everyone is a price taker by definition.

Principle of equal marginal utilities per dollar   Each commodity is demanded up to the point where the marginal utility per dollar spent equals the marginal utility per dollar spent on all other goods and services.

Principle of exclusion   The principle whereby one person's use of a good excludes the possibility of anyone else using it simultaneously.

Private costs   Those costs incurred by individuals when they use scarce resources. For example,

the private cost of running an automobile is equal to the gas, oil, insurance, maintenance, and depreciation costs. Private costs are also called *explicit costs*.

Private goods   Goods that are subject to the principle of exclusion; that is, when one person consumes a private good, that person can prevent others from consuming it.

Production function   The relationship between inputs and output. A production function is a technological, not an economic, relationship.

Production possibilities curve   A curve showing the maximum output rates of one good, given specific levels of another.

Productivity principle   A principle of taxation whereby individuals are taxed according to their productivity, so that each individual's after-tax income exactly reflects the relative productivity in society.

Productivity theory   The assumption that individuals are paid only according to their productivity; those with high productivities will be paid more than those with low productivities.

Profit   The income earned by entrepreneurs. It is the difference between total revenues and the total cost of the goods and services sold.

Progressive tax system   A tax system in which the average tax rate rises as income rises. The marginal tax rate is above the average tax rate. Higher-income groups pay a higher percentage of their income to a particular tax than do lower-income groups.

Proportional tax system   A tax system in which the percentage of income paid to taxes is the same for all taxpayers; the average tax rate remains constant as income rises.

Public goods   Goods for which the principle of exclusion does not hold. These goods must be, or usually are, consumed collectively.

Public information   Public information is any kind of information that is widely available to the public.

Purchasing power   The ability to consume real goods and services, generally measured by how much you can buy in real things with your money income.

Pure competition   A market structure in which there are many buyers and many sellers, such that no one individual can influence the price.

Pure economic rent   The payment to any resource that is in completely inelastic supply. The

445

payment to any resource over and above what is necessary to keep the resource in supply at its current level.

Pure market economy   An economy without government intervention. Owners of resources buy and sell those resources freely without constraints and use them any way they wish.

Pure monopoly   A market structure in which there is a single seller of a good or service for which there are no close substitutes.

Pure return to capital   The opportunity cost of capital, or what capital could earn in an alternative investment.

Quantity demanded   A specific numerical quantity demanded per unit time period, at a specific price.

Quantity theory of money and prices   The theory that changes in the price level are directly related to changes in the money supply. The quantity theory is based on the equation of exchange.

Racial discrimination   In regard to income, refers to the practice whereby members of different races with similar jobs and similar productivities receive significantly different incomes.

Random walk   The term *random walk* refers to the situation in which future behavior cannot be predicted from past behavior. Stock prices follow a random walk.

Rate-of-return regulation   Regulation that seeks to keep the rate of return in the industry at a competitive level by not allowing excessive prices to be charged.

Rational expectations   A hypothesis or theory stating that individuals combine the effects of past policy changes on important economic variables with their own judgment about the future effects of current and future policy changes.

Rationing   The term that relates to the government using some imposed method of deciding who gets what. Typical government rationing schemes use ration coupons.

Real income   A measure of the real purchasing power of nominal income; real income is nominal income adjusted for changes in the general price level, or income corrected for inflation or deflation.

Real income effect   When the price of one commodity falls, other things held constant, people experience an increase in their purchasing power. As a result, they may purchase more of

the good whose price has fallen. Conversely, if the price of a good rises, other things held constant, people will feel poorer and they may purchase less of that good.

Real interest rate   The inflation-adjusted rate charged for borrowing funds.

Real values   Measurement of economic values after adjustments have been made for changes in prices between years.

Real wages   Money wages divided by a price index. Real wages are different from money or nominal wages because they represent the true purchasing power of the dollars paid to workers.

Recession   The phase in the economy when output and employment are decreasing; the date when it starts is somewhat arbitrary.

Regressive tax system   A tax system in which higher-income groups pay a smaller percentage of their income to taxes than do lower-income groups; that is, the marginal rate is below the average rate. The average rate falls as income increases.

Relative price   The price of a good expressed in terms of the price of another good, or in the average price of all other goods.

Rent control   A form of price control in which rents in designated apartments are not permitted to be raised at all, or can be raised only by some specified amount each year.

Required reserves   The minimum amount of reserves that must be held, as required by the Fed; the Fed requires banks and other financial institutions that accept deposits to hold specified minimum reserves in the form of vault cash or deposits with the nearest Federal Reserve District Bank.

Reserve army of unemployed   In Marxian terminology, the mass of unemployed workers, the size of which will grow as workers become more and more exploited by the capitalists.

Resource allocation   The assignment of resources to specific uses. More specifically, it means determining what will be produced, how it will be produced, who will produce it, and for whom it will be produced.

Resources   Scarce inputs necessary for the production of desired goods and services.

Retained earnings   Those earnings that a corporation saves for use in investment These earnings are not distributed to the stockholders of the corporation.

Right-to-work laws Laws that make it illegal to require union membership as a condition of continuing employment in a particular firm.

Roundabout method of production A method of production involving the use of capital (machinery, plant). Such a method is called roundabout because the equipment is made before consumer goods are produced.

Rule of 72 A method to approximate doubling time; divide the number 72 by the coefficient of the annual percentage rate of growth.

Scarcity Wants exceed the ability to satisfy those wants; individuals and societies can never be capable of satisfying, or producing enough to satisfy, all their wants at exactly the same time.

Seasonal unemployment Unemployment caused by the seasonal nature of certain types of jobs, such as construction and resort work.

Security The tangible evidence of an investment by individuals and institutions in the affairs of business firms and governments.

Services Things purchased by consumers that do not have physical characteristics. Examples of services are those purchased from doctors, lawyers, dentists, repair personnel, housecleaners, educators, retailers, and wholesalers.

Sexual discrimination In regard to income, refers to the practice where women are paid less than men even though they have similar productivities and are doing similar jobs.

Shortage A situation that exists when at some specific price the quantity demanded exceeds the quantity supplied.

Social costs The full costs that society bears when a resource-using action occurs. For example, the social cost of driving a car is equal to all of the private costs plus any additional cost that society bears, including air pollution and traffic congestion.

Sole proprietorship A business owned by only one person. Also called an individual proprietorship.

Specialization The condition occurring when resources used in production are concentrated in the production of a limited variety of goods or services.

Spillover A situation in which a benefit or cost associated with an economic activity spills over to third parties.

Stable equilibrium An equilibrium situation in which a movement away from the equilibrium price or quantity will put into play forces that push price and/or quantity back toward the equilibrium level or rate.

Stagflation The simultaneous existence of both recession (economic stagnation) and inflation.

Stock The quantity of something at a point in time. An inventory of goods is a stock. A bank account at a point in time is a stock. Stocks are defined independently of time although they are assessed at a point in time; different from a flow. Savings are a stock.

Structural unemployment Unemployment that results when there is a shift in the demand for a particular product or service such that certain skills and jobs are no longer needed or desired.

Substitutes Pairs of goods for which an increase in the price of one causes an increase in the demand for the other.

Substitution effect A situation in which a reduction in the price of one good, holding all other prices constant, leads to an increase in the quantity demanded for the good whose price has fallen. This occurs because people will substitute the relatively cheaper good for the relatively more expensive good.

Supply A set of intentions indicating each quantity that sellers will offer voluntarily at each different price per unit of time, all other things held constant.

Supply curve A graphic representation of a supply schedule that is a positively sloped line showing the direct relationship between price and quantity supplied.

Supply schedule A set of numbers showing various prices and the quantity supplied at each of those prices. It shows the rate of planned production at each price per specified time period.

Supply-side economics The theory that a reduction in marginal tax rates will lead to more productivity and, hence, higher economic growth. Supply-side economics utilizes the proposition that individuals respond to incentives or, more specifically, to changes in the after-tax rate of return to working, saving, and investing.

Surplus A situation that exists when the quantity supplied exceeds the quantity demanded at a specific price. This is also called an *excess quantity supplied.*

Surtax Any tax that is levied in addition to some "normal" tax rate.

Tariff   A tax levied on imports.

Tax bracket   A specified interval of income to which a specific and unique marginal tax rate is applied.

Tax loophole   A legal method of reducing tax liabilities, properly called tax avoidance. Tax avoidance should not be confused with tax evasion, which is illegal and punishable by penalties, fines, and/or imprisonment.

Taxflation, or bracket creep   The process by which inflation pushes income earners into higher marginal tax brackets.

Technical efficiency   The utilization of the cheapest production technique for any given output rate. No inputs are willfully wasted.

Terms of exchange   The terms under which the trading takes place. Usually the terms of exchange are given by the price at which a good is traded.

Third parties   Those external to negotiations between buyers and sellers.

Trade balance   The value of exports equals the value of imports.

Trade deficit   The value of imports exceeds the value of exports.

Trade-off   A sacrifice that must be made in order to obtain a good or service. Trade-offs are related to opportunity costs, for scarcity demands that one desired item must be foregone in order to obtain another.

Trade surplus   The value of exports exceeds the value of imports.

Traditional economic system   An economic system in which people simply follow in the footsteps of their ancestors and do not attempt to alter the way in which goods are produced, who produces them, and who consumes them.

Transactions costs   All the costs associated with exchanging, including information costs, such as finding out about the price, quality, service record, and durability of a product, plus the cost of contracting and enforcing that contract.

Transfer payments   Money payments made by governments to individuals for which no services are concurrently rendered (e.g., welfare and unemployment insurance benefits).

Transfers in kind   Payments made in the form of actual goods and services to individuals for which no goods or services are rendered concurrently.

Tying agreement   An agreement whereby a firm agrees that the goods sold or leased by another firm will be used only with other goods of the seller or lessor.

Underground, or subterranean, economy   The cash economy in which no taxes are paid and no official government statistics are kept.

Union shop   A business enterprise that allows nonunion members to become employed, conditional upon their joining the union by some specified date after employment begins.

Unions   Organizations of workers that usually seek to secure economic improvements for their members.

Unitary elasticity of demand   A property of the demand curve, where the quantity demanded changes exactly in proportion to the change in price. Total revenue is invariant to price changes in the unit elastic portion of the demand curve.

Unstable equilibrium   An equilibrium situation in which, if there is a movement away from equilibrium, there are forces that push price and/or quantity further away from equilibrium, or at least do not push them toward the equilibrium level or rate.

Util   An artificial unit by which utility is measured.

Utility   The want-satisfying power that a good or service possesses.

Value-added tax (VAT)   A tax assessed on the value added by each producing unit. The value added is simply the sum of all wages, interest, rent, and profits. Otherwise stated, it is the total sale price of output minus the cost of raw materials and intermediate goods purchased from other firms.

Wage and price controls   A system of government-mandated maximum prices that can be charged for different goods and services, and maximum wages that can be paid to different workers in different jobs.

INDEX